D1525619

EMISSARIES
TO A
REVOLUTION

EMISSARIES
TO A
REVOLUTION
Woodrow Wilson's Executive Agents

in Mexico

LARRY D. HILL

LOUISIANA STATE UNIVERSITY PRESS

BATON ROUGE

ISBN 0-8071-0055-2
Library of Congress Catalog Card Number 73-81848
Copyright © 1973 by Louisiana State University Press
All rights reserved
Manufactured in the United States of America
Printed by The Colonial Press Inc., Clinton, Massachusetts
Designed by Albert R. Crochet

E
183. 8
· M 6
H 5 +
1974

For Doris and Lea

Contents

Preface

From the earliest days of the Republic, presidents of the United States have utilized the services of special executive agents in the conduct of diplomatic relations. George Washington set the precedent in designating Gouverneur Morris as his "private agent" to carry on secret negotiations with agents of the king of Great Britain. Subsequent administrations found the services of such agents invaluable, especially in the conduct of clandestine diplomacy.

His use of executive agents allows the president to conduct foreign relations without consulting the Senate in any way. Their salaries and expenses are usually drawn from the president's secret contingent fund, for the expenditure of which he is not required to make an accounting. They are not, strictly speaking, public ministers or foreign service officers, but they are usually accorded the same privileges and immunities by foreign governments as are officially accredited representatives of the United States government.

Today it is commonplace for the president to employ executive agents at the highest levels of diplomacy. But few, if any, presidents have utilized executive agents as extensively as did Woodrow Wilson. For example, he sent Colonel Edward M. House on missions to England and Europe during World War I; he approved Elihu Root's goodwill mission to Russia following the revolution of March, 1917; and he named a board of experts, called the Inquiry, to advise him on postwar problems; many of these men accompanied him to the Versailles Conference. But his very implementation of this policy occurred even before World War I, when, beginning in 1913, he sent executive agents scurrying all over Mexico. Wilson sent some of his agents to Mexico on fact-finding missions, and, although their reports were often routed through the Department of State, they were directly responsible to the president. This group included William Bayard Hale, Reginaldo Del Valle, and Duval West. Others were sent to carry on diplomatic relations with the government in Mexico City or with leaders of the revolutionary factions. John Lind and Paul Fuller were diplomatic agents. Both of them also served as fact finders. Another, David Lawrence, went of his own volition but with the president's blessing, and had only the most tenuous ties to the White House. Others, including George C. Carothers, John R. Silliman, Leon J. Canova, and John W. Belt, were State Department agents. Carothers and Silliman served simultaneously as consuls, Belt as a consular secretary, and their salaries were paid by the Consular Service. H. L. Hall was sent to Mexico with only his expenses being paid by the State Department, but his services were terminated before they really began.

This book is a narrative of the activities and the diplomacy of these eleven men and the influence they exerted on Wilson's foreign policy and on the course of the Mexican revolution. For all practical purposes their efforts terminated when, on October 19, 1915, Wilson accorded *de facto* recognition to the regime of Venustiano Carranza; hence, that is the terminal date of this account. Despite the fact that much scholarly effort has been devoted to the study of Wilson's relations with Mexico, no treatment has concentrated specifically on the special agents. My effort has been to fill that void.

Any scholar who researches in the area of United States–Mexican relations in the period 1910–1920 is indebted to Berta Ulloa of the Colegio de México for her *Revolución*

Mexicana, 1910–1920, a guide to the Archivo de la Secretaría de Relaciones Exteriores which, if used carefully, can save many precious hours of research time. I particularly owe Ms. Ulloa a debt of gratitude, because it was largely through her intercession, and after considerable delay, that I gained access to Archivo de la Secretaría de Relaciones Exteriores in the summer of 1968. Another research tool deserves special mention—*Fuentes de la historia contemporánea de México,* compiled by Stanley R. Ross, eased my efforts greatly in utilizing the newspaper collections of the Hemeroteca Nacional in Mexico City, the Latin American Collection of the University of Texas, and the Library of Congress.

I shall always be grateful to Professor Burl Noggle of Louisiana State University for his wise counsel in directing my graduate studies on the topic of this book. Jane Orr Noggle has my thanks for her editorial help and stylistic criticisms. This project could not have been completed without the aid so cheerfully rendered by Hunge-Chih Yu and Freda Rucker of the Texas A & M University Library's interlibrary loan department. I also thank both Texas A & M University, which provided the funds to defray the cost of typing this manuscript, and Gloria A. Johnson, who did the typing. Finally, I owe a debt of gratitude to my wife Doris and my daughter Lea for their patience and understanding.

L.D.H.

Texas A & M University
College Station, Texas

EMISSARIES
TO A
REVOLUTION

CHAPTER I

A Need for Information

Mexico provided Woodrow Wilson with the first stern test of his skill as a diplomatist. When he began his presidency, he had no experience or training in the conduct of foreign relations. During his notable academic career as a professor of political science and history and as president of Princeton University, Wilson devoted himself mainly to the study of domestic politics and legislative processes. He scarcely mentioned foreign affairs in the presidential campaign of 1912, and his inaugural address dealt exclusively with domestic problems.[1]

Wilson did not consider himself handicapped by these apparent deficiencies in his training. The orthodox tenets of foreign policy, such as expediency, protection of material interests, and national self-interest, were relatively unimportant to him. He insisted that morality should be the principal consideration in international conduct, and he envisioned a new era in which the foreign policy of the United States would be determined by moral purposes and guided by idealism. Wilson's own idealism grew out of the beliefs and values of Christianity, more particularly the Presbyterian theology inculcated in him by his father.[2]

1. Ray Stannard Baker, *Woodrow Wilson: Life and Letters* (Garden City, N.Y., 1931), IV, 55–56; Arthur S. Link, *Wilson the Diplomatist* (Baltimore, 1957), 3–11.

2. Link, *Wilson the Diplomatist*, 16–18; Harley Notter, *The Origins of the Foreign Policy of Woodrow Wilson* (Baltimore, 1937), 269; Arthur S. Link,

In selecting William Jennings Bryan as his first secretary of state, Wilson chose a man equally ignorant of foreign affairs, but one who shared his president's Presbyterian background and faith in Christian ethics as the proper guidepost in relations between men and nations. Incorporated in Wilson's and Bryan's idealism was a missionary zeal to do good works and a concept in America's unique mission in world affairs. Because democratic institutions, which to them were the most Christian and ideal, had flourished in the United States, they believed that their country was divinely commissioned to promote the establishment of such institutions in nations that did not possess them. This often led them to believe that they knew, better than did the leaders of those countries themselves, what was best for countries that seemed less fortunate than the United States. Their determination to render service caused Wilson and Bryan to interfere in the internal affairs of other nations on a scale greater than any previous administration had contemplated.[3]

Wilson never bore criticism well, and, more often than not, he believed those who attacked his policies were inadequately informed. More likely to follow his own intuition than to accept expert advice, he particularly suspected any adverse opinions that might come from State Department staff members and Foreign Service officers, most of whom were Republican holdovers. Despite the fact that most of those men had received their appointments on a merit basis, Wilson and Bryan looked upon them as pseudo experts, representa-

---

Wilson: The New Freedom (Princeton, N.J., 1956), 277–78; John Morton Blum, *Woodrow Wilson and the Politics of Morality* (Boston and Toronto, 1956), 84–85.

3. Link, *New Freedom,* 278; Arthur S. Link, *Woodrow Wilson and the Progressive Era* (New York, 1954), 81–82; Paolo E. Coletta, *William Jennings Bryan: Progressive Politician and Moral Statesman, 1909–1915,* (Lincoln, Neb., 1969), 92–95, 182–83, hereinafter cited as Coletta, *Progressive Politician;* Richard Challener, "William Jennings Bryan," in Norman A. Graebner (ed.), *An Uncertain Tradition: American Secretaries of State in the Twentieth Century* (New York, 1961), 81–84.

tives of an aristocratic clique, who would be more inclined to promote the material interests of Americans abroad than to pursue altruistic goals.[4]

Desiring a housecleaning, Bryan argued that the merit system should be scrapped; Republican incumbents should be removed and replaced by "deserving Democrats." Wilson rejected this appeal for an outright return to the spoils system; but when foreign affairs grew critical he continued to show his distaste for the professionals of the State Department by taking personal command of the situation and relying upon special executive agents to carry out his diplomatic missions.[5] His reliance upon special agents rather than professionals to help solve a particular diplomatic problem, along with his frequent simultaneous employment of men who sometimes held conflicting opinions, partly explains why his conduct of foreign affairs seemed erratic, even impulsive, at times. Perhaps there is no better example of this than his relations with Mexico.

4. Link, *New Freedom*, 67–70; Link, *Wilson the Diplomatist*, 24–25. Beginning with the Theodore Roosevelt administration, the State Department increasingly made appointments on a merit basis. By executive order, Roosevelt placed all diplomatic and consular posts, except for the rank of ambassador and minister, on a civil-service system requiring competitive examinations. In 1906 Congress gave legislative sanction to his moves in regard to the consular service. William Howard Taft continued this policy and, during his administration, created a Bureau of Appointments to review applications and administer examinations for diplomatic and consular posts. See Graham H. Stuart, *The Department of State: A History of its Organization, Procedure and Personnel* (New York, 1949), 205–206, 219.

5. Baker, *Woodrow Wilson*, IV, 217–18; Link, *New Freedom*, 105–107; Link, *Wilson the Diplomatist*, 22–25; Coletta, *Progressive Politician*, 100–102; Stuart, *Department of State*, 225–30. Because of the civil-service system established by Roosevelt and Taft, Bryan was able to make relatively few changes in the personnel of the consular service. Since there were no such restrictions preventing him from making changes in the diplomatic corps, Bryan, whenever Wilson permitted it, replaced Republicans with Democratic office-seekers. He was particularly prone to reward political confederates who had remained loyal to him since 1896. See Seward W. Livermore, "'Deserving Democrats': The Foreign Service Under Woodrow Wilson," *South Atlantic Quarterly*, LXIX (Winter, 1970), 144–56.

On February 18, 1913, just weeks before Wilson's inauguration, Mexican president Francisco I. Madero was toppled from power by a military *coup d'état*. Madero himself had been elevated to power by leading a revolution which overthrew the thirty-five-year-old dictatorship of Porfirio Díaz. Madero, however, was no radical, but a nineteenth-century liberal, and he failed to gauge accurately the urgency of the revolutionary demands of many who had rallied to his side in fighting the dictator. He placed too much faith in the ability of free elections and democratic institutions to right the social and economic inequities that plagued his nation. Once elected president, he proved incapable of leading what proved to be one of the great social revolutions of the twentieth century.[6]

Whatever the limits of his own reformism, even Madero's modest efforts to challenge the status quo were hampered by a hostile Senate held over from the Díaz regime and a Chamber of Deputies which was hopelessly split by factional disputes. The influential Catholic party and the conservative press vociferously opposed liberal reform. To add to his woes, Madero faced several armed rebellions, two of them by former comrades against Díaz. In the state of Morelos, Emiliano Zapata declared against the government, calling for immediate and extensive agrarian reform. Citing the need for reform but accepting conservative support, Pascual Orozco initiated a rebellion in Chihuahua. Former *Porforistas* Bernardo Reyes and Felix Díaz (a nephew of Porfirio) launched revolts in Nuevo León and Vera Cruz respectively. Although the uprisings were abortive and both Reyes and

6. Anita Brenner and George R. Leighton, *The Wind That Swept Mexico* (New York, 1943), 25–29; Charles Curtis Cumberland, *The Mexican Revolution: Genesis Under Madero* (Austin, Tex., 1952), 30, 208–28, 256–58; Stanley R. Ross, *Francisco I. Madero* (New York, 1955), 218–49; Manuel González Ramírez, *La Revolución Social de México: Las Ideas—La Violencia* (México, D.F., 1960), 175–80, 312–18, 325–34, hereinafter cited as González Ramírez, *Las Ideas—La Violencia*.

Díaz were captured and imprisoned, such movements made Madero's government increasingly dependent upon the federal army, the Achilles heel of many a Latin American constitutional regime.[7]

Compounding Madero's difficulties was the hostile attitude of the ambassador from the United States, Henry Lane Wilson. Because he was the only ambassador accredited to Mexico City (the other diplomatic representatives held the rank of minister), Wilson assumed the role of dean of the diplomatic corps. In this capacity, and as the official representative of what he considered to be a superior people, Ambassador Wilson assumed that President Madero would seek his advice. Wilson's personal attitudes, however, made this impossible. An admirer of former dictator Porfirio Díaz, the ambassador did not think the Mexican people capable of self-government. Such an attitude made his counsels incompatible with Madero's expressed desires to promote political democracy in his country. His advice spurned, Wilson grew increasingly antagonistic toward the new government and vocally critical of President Madero.

Madero's refusal to be guided by the American diplomat was not the only source of antagonism between the two. An appointee of the William Howard Taft administration, Henry Lane Wilson naturally believed that his major responsibility in Mexico was to promote American business interests and ensure the protection of Americans and their property. The rebellions in Mexico—which took a toll in American lives and property—and Madero's inability to quell them, were a constant source of irritation to the ambassador. It was no

7. Cumberland, *Mexican Revolution*, 185–207; Ross, *Francisco I. Madero*, 226–32, 254–56, 268–75; González Ramírez, *Las Ideas—La Violencia*, 304–306; Michael C. Meyer, *Mexican Rebel: Pascual Lrozco and the Mexican Revolution, 1910–1915* (Lincoln, Neb., 1967), 55–62; John Womack, Jr., *Zapata and the Mexican Revolution* (New York, 1969), 124–28; Victor Niemeyer, "Frustrated Invasion: The Revolutionary Attempt of General Bernardo Reyes from San Antonio in 1911," *Southwestern Historical Quarterly*, LXVII (October, 1963), 213–25.

secret that he yearned for a more authoritarian regime in Mexico and repeatedly prophesied that Madero's ineffective government could not last. Knowing well that the Democratic party in the United States had adopted an anti-imperialist stance since 1898, Madero looked forward to the inauguration of Woodrow Wilson, anticipating the recall of the Republican ambassador.[8]

Madero's wish was ultimately fulfilled, but not soon enough to do him any good. On February 9, 1913, Felix Díaz, having been released from prison by fellow conspirators, led several army units in revolt against the government in Mexico City. The commandant of Madero's loyal garrison was wounded in the initial exchange of gunfire and the president reluctantly designated General Victoriano Huerta to command the government forces. Huerta had a good military record, but his handling of the campaign against Orozco had displeased Madero. Relieved of command, the general went into voluntary retirement in December, 1912, ostensibly for medical reasons. Yet when Felix Díaz initiated his *coup*, Huerta offered his services to the president. Madero's decision to rely on Huerta was doubtless an act of desperation.[9]

At fifty-nine, Huerta was bald, stocky in build, and had an oval, high cheekboned face that revealed his Indian ancestry. A consumer of legendary quantities of cognac, he was plagued by cataracts and usually wore smoked glasses. When he appeared without the glasses he squinted, which gave him a sinister appearance. He had little faith in the workability of

8. Ross, *Francisco I. Madero*, 236–40; Howard F. Cline, *The United States and Mexico* (Cambridge, Mass., 1953), 128–30; Lowell L. Blaisdell, "Henry Lane Wilson and the Overthrow of Madero," *Southwestern Social Science Quarterly*, XVIII (September, 1962), 128–29; Eugene F. Massingill, "The Diplomatic Career of Henry Lane Wilson in Latin America," (Ph.D. dissertation, Louisiana State University, 1957), 87–93.

9. The military career as well as the sources of conflict between Madero and Huerta may be traced in George J. Rausch, Jr., "The Early Career of Victoriano Huerta," *The Americas* (October, 1964), 136–45; Michael C. Meyer, *Huerta: A Political Portrait* (Lincoln, Neb., 1972), 1–50.

democratic institutions in Mexico. As an army officer, he was a stern exponent of order and was distressed by the recurrent disorders that had followed the downfall of Porfirio Díaz. Although he was not a party to the original Felix Díaz revolt, Huerta did not make a serious attempt to put it down. Instead, while his troops mounted feeble attacks on the rebel stronghold, he negotiated with the insurrectionists and ultimately conspired with Díaz to oust Madero. On February 18 Huerta ordered the arrest of Madero and Vice-President José M. Pino Suárez and assumed control of executive power.[10]

During the ten days of mock battle (February 9–18, known as the *Decena Trágica*), Ambassador Henry Lane Wilson took an active part in efforts to terminate the military action. Instead of blaming the insurrectionists, he insisted that Madero's faltering leadership was responsible for the protracted violence which threatened the lives and property of innocent people, including foreigners. He had long since concluded that the little president's ineffectual regime would be toppled sooner or later; therefore, he believed, his responsibility was to hasten its fall in order to put an end to the carnage and destruction. Through government officials and members of the diplomatic corps, he sought Madero's resignation, but the beleaguered president refused to capitulate. The ambassador then approached General Huerta, who reported that the conflict would soon be terminated. Although he was not a party to the Díaz-Huerta conspiracy before the arrest of Madero, Ambassador Wilson was made aware that the president's ouster was imminent. Indeed, Wilson was informed of the success of the *coup* well before it became a matter of public knowledge.

With Madero removed from power, Ambassador Wilson set about ensuring that the successor would be strong enough

10. Cumberland, *Mexican Revolution*, 233–38; Ross, *Francisco I. Madero*, 191–202, 263–67, 284–309; Meyer, *Huerta*, 50–56; William L. Sherman and Richard E. Greenleaf, *Victoriano Huerta: A Reappraisal* (México, D.F., 1960), 63–71.

to maintain order. On the day of Madero's arrest, Wilson arranged a conference at the American embassy between Díaz and Huerta. Under the aegis of the American ambassador, an agreement known as the Pact of the Embassy was worked out whereby Huerta was to become provisional president. Huerta, in turn, agreed to operate with a cabinet which suited Díaz. Since the constitution precluded a provisional president's succeeding himself as elective president, Huerta agreed to support Díaz in the next election. At the ambassador's urging, both Huerta and Díaz promised to do all in their power to restore order in Mexico. Confident that he had played a key role in saving a prostrate nation from further chaos, Wilson then triumphantly presented Huerta and Díaz to a gathering of the diplomatic corps, heralding them as the guarantors of stability in Mexico.[11]

The next day President Madero and Vice-President Pino Suárez were forced to resign, making Foreign Minister Pedro S. Lascuráin the constitutional successor. As soon as the Chamber of Deputies ratified these changes, Lascuráin appointed General Huerta minister of government, thus making Huerta the legal heir to the presidency. Within minutes, Lascuráin, too, resigned, and the chamber ratified Huerta's succession to the provisional presidency. At least technically, therefore, Huerta's accession to power was carried out in accordance with constitutional processes.

The manner in which the cynical old general had usurped the power of state was entirely in keeping with the precedents of Mexican history. The one incident in the whole episode that shocked the world was the murder of Madero

11. Cumberland, *Mexican Revolution*, 238; Ross, *Francisco I. Madero*, 297–311; Cline, *United States and Mexico*, 131–32; Massingill, "Henry Lane Wilson in Latin America," 137–71; Blaisdell, "Wilson and the Overthrow of Madero," 130–33; Meyer, *Huerta*, 60–61; Alberto M. Carreño, *La Diplomacia Extraordinaria entre México y Estados Unidos* (México, D.F., 1951), II, 265–66; Isidro Fabela, *Historia Diplomática de la Revolución Mexicana* (México, D.F., 1958–59), I, 69–118; Kenneth J. Grieb, *The United States and Huerta* (Lincoln, Neb., 1969), 15–21.

and Pino Suárez on February 22. Although the government's report of the incident indicated that they had been shot during an attempt to prevent them from being incarcerated in the federal penitentiary, few accepted this official explanation. It is difficult to assess absolute responsibility for the murders. Both the *Huertistas* and the *Felicistas* (the Felix Díaz faction) had discussed the advisability of their being eliminated; whether it was Huerta, Díaz, or one or more of their subalterns who ordered the assassinations, the records do not reveal. Neither faction can be absolved of partial blame, since neither made adequate precautions for the safety of the murdered men.[12]

Nor was Henry Lane Wilson innocent of responsibility. Because of his involvement in the events of the *Decena Trágica*, the American embassy naturally became the focal point of those who wished to save the deposed president's life. Secretary of State Philander C. Knox, members of the diplomatic corps, and friends and relatives of Madero all beseeched Wilson to use his obvious influence with the new government to ensure the safety of Madero and Pino Suárez. Wilson did reluctantly accompany the German minister to ask Huerta for such guarantees, and the old general responded favorably. On another occasion, however, Huerta asked the ambassador's advice on the advisability of exiling Madero or confining him to a lunatic asylum. Wilson revealed his indifference to Madero's welfare by replying that the general should do what was "best for the peace of Mexico." To others who approached him concerning the safety of the fallen president, the ambassador responded that he could not interfere in the internal affairs of Mexico.[13]

12. Cumberland, *Mexican Revolution*, 240–41; Ross, *Francisco I. Madero*, 326–31; Meyer, *Huerta*, 69–82; Sherman and Greenleaf, *Victoriano Huerta*, 79–84; Ramón Prida, *From Despotism to Anarchy* (El Paso, Tex., 1914), 196–201.

13. Cumberland, *Mexican Revolution*, 239–40; Ross, *Francisco I. Madero*, 321–26; Massingill, "Henry Lane Wilson in Latin America," 180–90; Fabela, *Historia Diplomática*, I, 154–58; Grieb, *United States and Huerta*, 24–28.

By Huerta's own admission, the most critical problem
facing his provisional government was that of securing
diplomatic recognition from the world powers, particularly
from the United States. Recognition meant a renewal of old
loans and possibly new ones that would be needed to make his
regime a stable one.[14] At a meeting of the diplomatic corps on
February 21, Henry Lane Wilson urged the envoys of the
foreign powers to impress upon their governments, as a
means of promoting stable conditions in Mexico, the necessity
of according diplomatic recognition to the new government.
Thus he implied without justification that the United States
would soon extend recognition. All of the European powers
and most of the Latin American governments accorded
Huerta's regime diplomatic recognition in March and April.
Despite Wilson's urging, the Taft administration refused to
follow suit. The ambassador emphasized that Huerta was
pro-American and would give prompt attention to his requests, but Secretary of State Knox wanted several matters,
including damage claims, the Chamizal controversy, and the
distribution of Colorado River waters, settled before extending recognition. These disputes had not been settled when
Woodrow Wilson became president on March 4, and the
matter of recognition passed into his hands.[15]

President Wilson had little knowledge of Latin American
history and politics, and he looked at the Mexican situation
from a frame of reference based on Anglo-American history
and theory. He seemed unaware that the succession of Latin
American governments was more likely to result from
violence than from fair and free elections. Because Madero

14. Victoriano Huerta, *Memorias de Victoriano Huerta* (México, D.F.,
1957), 93.
15. Cline, *United States and Mexico*, 133–34; Massingill, "Henry Lane
Wilson in Latin America," 202–209; Grieb, *United States and Huerta*, 36–37.
The "Chamizal" is a 600-acre tract of land near El Paso which was claimed by
both the United States and Mexico because of a change in the course of the
Rio Grande. For an account of this dispute, including its settlement in 1963,
see *Department of State Bulletin*, XLIX (August 5, 1963), 199–203.

had championed political democracy while being elected president in the freest elections ever held in Mexico, Wilson assumed that the maintenance of democratic institutions was as important to Mexicans as to Anglo-Americans. Failing to perceive that, among Mexican reformers, social and economic adjustments were considered vastly more important than political democracy, Wilson believed that a government established by force must be oppressive. He remained blind to the fact that most of the cabinet members designated by the Pact of the Embassy were enlightened, talented administrators and that the provisional government did attempt to initiate reforms. Instead, he fixed his eyes on Huerta's conservative sources of support and judged the regime thoroughly reactionary.[16]

On the other hand, Ambassador Henry Lane Wilson still sought for himself and his nation favorable relations with the Huerta government. He wasted no time in bombarding the new Democratic administration with recommendations for recognition of the Mexico City regime. He pointed out that it was the *de facto* government of the republic and had been established "in accordance with constitutional precedents." [17]

16. Grieb, *United States and Huerta*, 42–43; Meyer, *Huerta*, 140–41, 157–77; Samuel Flagg Bemis, "Woodrow Wilson and Latin America," in Edward H. Búehrig (ed.), *Wilson's Foreign Policy in Perspective* (Bloomington, 1957), 113–16; Jorge Vera Estañol, *La Revolución Mexicana: Orígenes y resultados* (México, D.F., 1957), 277–84. Although not an unbiased source, Jorge Vera Estañol, who was Huerta's first minister of public instruction, describes the background of each cabinet member and suggests that only the minister of war, General Manuel Mondragón, was not a reformer. Vera Estañol argues that revolutionary propaganda, which branded the group as reactionary throwbacks to the Porfirian regime, gave a false and unjustified impression of the cabinet. Revisionist Michael Meyer reveals that the Huerta government attempted to inaugurate reforms in education and agriculture and that it adopted an enlightened attitude toward organized labor. Because of financial difficulties and a stubborn Congress, little permanent reform was achieved. Meyer also points out that neither the Madero nor Carranza governments achieved more reform, but they still have not been judged reactionary.

17. Wilson to Department of State, March 8, 12, April 9, 1913, Depart-

President Wilson, however, arrived at his own conclusion: the constitutional government of Mexico had been usurped, and he could not recognize a government of murderers. In order to make his position clear to the world and to discourage future military *coups* in Latin America, on March 11, just a week after taking office, the president issued a statement of foreign policy making himself the judge of the constitutional legitimacy of Latin American governments: "We hold . . . that just government rests always upon the consent of the governed . . . . We can have no sympathy with those who seek to seize the power of government to advance their own personal interests or ambitions . . . . As friends, therefore, we shall prefer those who act in the interests of peace and honor, who protect private rights and respect the restraints of constitutional provision." [18] Thus Wilson announced his intention of breaking the tradition of recognizing *de facto* regimes if they did not meet his standards of constitutional legitimacy.

If Wilson had needed a more practical reason for denying Huerta *de facto* recognition, it was readily available. There was serious doubt that the old general would be able to control his country. Although all but four state governors had acknowledged allegiance to the new regime, and the federal army was devotedly loyal to Huerta, the dissidents were growing in number. Emiliano Zapata refused to come to terms with the new government, and his bands controlled the mountains that ringed Mexico City to the south and west. At this stage in his long revolutionary career, the agrarian reformer from Morelos had already surrounded himself with ardent revolutionaries who made his faction the most radical in Mexico. Just thirty-four, Zapata, a small man with darting black eyes and an enormous drooping mustache, was suspi-

ment of State, *Papers Relating to the Foreign Relations of the United States, 1913* (Washington, D.C., 1920), 760, 772, 776.
18. New York *Times*, March 12, 1913, p. 1.

cious of any government that established itself in the capital city. Each one that he had confronted had attempted to persuade him to compromise his reform program outlined in the Plan of Ayala, a document that amounted to a holy writ to the rebels who rallied to his side. In accordance with the plan, Zapata fully intended to return lands that had been despoiled from the peasants during the Porfirian regime and to expropriate and redistribute one third of the *hacienda* (large plantation or ranch) lands of his district. Not concerned with reforming all of Mexico, he waged a local peasant revolution and was prepared to fight until his demands were unconditionally accepted.[19]

In the northeastern state of Coahuila, Venustiano Carranza, the constitutionally elected governor, refused allegiance to the Huerta regime. Tall and taciturn, with a flowing white beard, Carranza, at age fifty-five, was a patriarchal figure. He was no radical, but rather, as Madero had been, the heir to Mexico's nineteenth-century liberal tradition; as a lawyer, he represented the urban middle class. He surrounded himself with lawyers and other middle-class professionals and was approachable only through these intermediaries. He was too insufferably certain of his own rectitude to be popular and lacked the charisma to be a beloved leader of the masses. Yet he was to dominate the Mexican revolution until 1919.

Carranza followed the hallowed Mexican practice of stating at the outset the purposes of a revolt. On March 26, 1913, he promulgated his Plan of Guadalupe. Claiming that Huerta had assumed power by unconstitutional means, Carranza dedicated his revolution to restoring constitutional govern-

19. Womack, *Zapata*, 159–77; González Ramírez, *Las Ideas—La Violencia*, 259, 278–83; Manuel González Ramírez, *La Revolución Social de México: El Problema Agrario* (México, D.F., 1966), 202–205, hereinafter cited as González Ramírez, *El Problema Agrario*; Robert P. Dillon, *Zapata: The Ideology of a Peasant Revolutionary* (New York, 1969), 39–41; "Plan de Ayala," Manuel González Ramírez (ed.), *Fuentes para la Historia de la Revolución Mexicana: Planes políticos y otros documentos* (México, D.F., 1954), 73–85, hereinafter cited as González Ramírez, *Planes políticos*.

ment; hence, the name of his followers became the "Constitutionalists." Refusing to take the title of "provisional president," since by doing so he would be ineligible to become elective president, Carranza assumed the title of "First Chief of the Constitutionalist Army in Charge of Executive Power." Before initiating his rebellion, Carranza sent agents to Mexico City to discuss the possible recognition of the provisional government. As conditions he demanded a high degree of state sovereignty for Coahuila and extensive power for himself. These negotiations may also have been Carranza's ruse to gain time for gauging the strength of the anti-Huerta sentiment in northern Mexico. At any rate, Huerta refused Carranza's terms. The murders of Madero and Pino Suárez certainly gave the First Chief a more righteous cause, and the Coahuila legislature responded willingly to his plea for a resolution condemning Huerta as a usurper. Carranza's rebellion, therefore, was prompted as much by personal ambition as by idealistic considerations. Forced temporarily to flee from the federal armies, the First Chief and his "cabinet" established their headquarters at Piedras Negras, across the Rio Grande from Eagle Pass, Texas.[20]

20. González Ramírez, *Las Ideas—La Violencia*, 375–81; "Decreto de la Legislatura del Estado de Coahuila por el que se desconoce Victoriano Huerta, 19 de Febrero 1913," and "Plan de Guadalupe, 26 de Marzo 1913," in González Ramírez, *Planes políticos*, 134, 137–40; Juan Barragán Rodríguez, *Historia del Ejército y de la Revolución Constitucionalista* (México, D.F., 1946), I, 63–100; Robert E. Quirk, *The Mexican Revolution, 1914–1915* (Bloomington, Ind., 1960), 8–11; Kenneth J. Grieb, "The Causes of the Carranza Rebellion: A Reinterpretation," *The Americas*, XXV (July, 1968), 28–32. The main object of contention between Huerta and Carranza was the disposition of irregular state troops. These troops, the remnants of Madero's revolutionary armies, were kept under control of the state governor, but Carranza wanted the federal government to pay their expenses. Huerta refused unless they were brought under direct control of the government in Mexico City. Carranza had also quarreled over this matter with President Madero before he was deposed. See Miguel Alessio Robles, *Historia política de la Revolución* (México, D.F., 1946), 24–25.

In the northwestern state of Sonora, Governor José M. Maytorena also refused to recognize the Huerta government. As in the case of Coahuila, the paramount issue was state sovereignty, and, again, Huerta refused to make concessions. Maytorena, however, was reluctant to declare himself in open rebellion, and, when he hedged, the state legislature pressured him into taking a leave of absence. On March 5, after he had crossed the border into Arizona in temporary exile, the Sonoran legislature named Ignacio L. Pesquiera governor and declared the state to be in rebellion against the Huerta regime. The Sonorans then linked their fortunes to the Constitutionalist cause and acknowledged Carranza as their First Chief.

The Sonoran revolt, however, was soon dominated by Alvaro Obregón, the commander of the state's military forces. In 1913 Obregón was still a relatively obscure figure, but he was to become the ablest military leader of the revolution and one of the dominant political figures of the 1920s. At age thirty-three, he was a slender, strikingly handsome man. Like Pesquiera and the other leaders of the Sonoran revolt, Obregón came from a *ranchero* (middle-class farmer) background. More than any other revolutionary leader, he was a pragmatist. Although he was no radical, when circumstances dictated he did not shrink from using the language of a radical demagogue in enticing the lower classes into the revolutionary armies. Within weeks of the outset of the Sonoran revolt, his forces controlled the border towns and the capital, Hermosillo.[21]

21. González Ramírez, *Las Ideas—La Violencia*, 247, 381–87; Barragán Rodríguez, *Historia . . . de la Revolución Constitucionalista*, I, 131–51; "Decreto del Congreso del Estado de Sonora por el que se desconoce a Victoriano Huerta," and "Acta de la Conferencia, 18 de Abril 1913," in González Ramírez, *Planes políticos*, 135–36, 145–57; Alberto Morales Jiménez, "Alvaro Obregón," *Hombres de la Revolución Mexicana* (México, D.F., 1960), 183–84; Ernest Gruening, *Mexico and Its Heritage* (New York and London, 1928), 97; Lesley Byrd Simpson, *Many Mexicos* (Berkeley, 1964), 271–72; John W. F. Dulles, *Yesterday in Mexico: A Chronicle of the Revolution, 1919–1936* (Austin, Tex., 1961), 4–6.

In the north-central state of Chihuahua, the revolution coalesced around Francisco (Pancho) Villa. Possibly the most colorful and controversial of all the revolutionary leaders, he had been born Doroteo Arango and adopted the name Pancho Villa after becoming an outlaw. The origin of his outlawry is uncertain; the most popular legend of the day claimed that he had slain the son of an *hacendado* (owner of a large plantation or ranch) who had raped his sister. Joining the *Maderistas* in 1910, he had proved his worth in battle and been commissioned a colonel in the revolutionary army. Villa had been given an opportunity to live a respectable life by Madero, and he was probably the only revolutionary leader who truly revered the memory of the fallen president. To Villa everything was personal and concrete; therefore his revolt was prompted by hatred of Huerta and a desire to avenge the death of Madero. No ideologue, he reveled in the camaraderie of the army camp and in leading men in battle. He was stocky in build, an earthy, passionate, and robust man—Mexican *machismo* incarnate. He inspired fear and loyalty among his followers, to whom he was fiercely loyal in return. He also declared his allegiance to Carranza but, for all practical purposes, remained an independent force.[22]

22. González Ramírez, *Las Ideas—La Violencia*, 387–88; Barragán Rodríguez, *Historia . . . de la Revolución Constitucionalista*, I, 229–40; Haldeen Braddy, *Cock of the Walk: The Legend of Pancho Villa* (Albuquerque, N.M., 1955), 1–31, 90–101; Martín Luis Guzmán, *Memoirs of Pancho Villa*, (Austin, Tex., 1965), 3–4, 90–103; Francisco R. Alamada, *La Revolución en el Estado de Chihuahua* (México, D.F., 1965), II, 25–32. Pancho Villa had a personal reason to dislike Huerta. In April and May, 1912, Villa and his irregulars served under the general in a campaign designed to crush the Orozco rebellion. When the two quarreled over the ownership of an expropriated horse, Huerta charged Villa with insubordination and ordered his execution. Villa was already standing before the firing squad when his life was spared by order of President Madero, and he was transferred to Mexico City for trial. He escaped from prison and made his way to El Paso, Texas. Although an exile, he remained grateful to Madero for having saved his life, while he harbored a personal hatred for Huerta. See Ross, *Francisco I. Madero*, 266–67.

Victoriano Huerta had to contend with all of these revolutionary forces, and, ultimately, so did Woodrow Wilson, whose nonrecognition policy drew him into the Mexican imbroglio. Ambassador Henry Lane Wilson, meanwhile, continued to push for recognition, insisting that Huerta was the only man who could pacify Mexico. He also pointed up the possible consequences of a delay in recognition: the rebels would be encouraged, the civil war prolonged, and the toll of American lives and property damage much greater.[23] Such arguments were hardly well calculated to impress the president. As he told one of his advisors: "I am President of the whole United States and not merely of a few property holders in the Republic of Mexico." [24]

The administration could ignore the pleadings of Ambassador Wilson but not the charges leveled against him by Robert H. Murray, Mexico City correspondent for the New York *World*. Beginning on March 7, the *World* printed a series of Murray's articles, presenting a somewhat distorted exposé of Ambassador Wilson's role in the *Decena Trágica*. President Wilson already disagreed fundamentally with the views of his official representative in Mexico; now Murray charged that the ambassador had helped instigate the Huerta *coup* and was largely responsible for the downfall of Madero.[25]

For weeks thereafter, President Wilson pondered the situation, his inexperience in foreign affairs denying him satisfactory answers. He discussed the problem with his

23. Wilson to State Department, April 9, 25, and May 15, 1913, in General Records of the Department of State, National Archives, Record Group 59, File 812.00/7066, 7273, 7652. All Department of State Records cited herein, unless designated otherwise, are from Record Group 59; hereinafter, such materials will be cited NA, plus file and document numbers.

24. Gary T. Grayson, *Woodrow Wilson: An Intimate Memoir* (New York, 1960), 30.

25. New York *World*, March 7–13, 1913. Later Murray expanded his original exposé into a series of magazine articles. See Robert H. Murray, "Huerta and the Two Wilsons," *Harper's Weekly*, LXII (March 25–April 29, 1916), 301–303, 341–42, 364–65, 402–404, 434–36, 466–69.

cabinet and came to the conclusion that they all lacked trustworthy information upon which to base a policy. During the course of the cabinet meeting of April 18, the advisability of sending "a confidential man" to Mexico to "study the situation and get at the exact facts" was one of the topics of discussion.[26] Having previously utilized the services of a special agent to gather information in the Philippine Islands, Wilson decided to follow the same course in Mexico.[27] On April 19, the day after the cabinet discussed the matter, the president pecked out a letter on his portable typewriter, requesting the services of his first special agent to Mexico.

26. E. David Cronon (ed.), *The Cabinet Diaries of Josephus Daniels, 1913–1921* (Lincoln, Neb., 1963), 43.

27. Baker, *Woodrow Wilson*, IV, 455; Roy Watson Curry, "Woodrow Wilson and Philippine Policy," *Mississippi Valley Historical Review*, XLI (December, 1954), 436. Even before taking office, Wilson dispatched Professor Henry J. Ford, a former Princeton colleague, on a fact-finding mission to the Philippines. Ford began reporting his findings in April, 1913.

CHAPTER II

Suspicions Confirmed

Wilson chose a friend, journalist William Bayard Hale, to be his first fact-finding agent to Mexico. Forty-four years old in 1913, Hale was slender and dark, with thick black eyebrows that met above the bridge of his nose and gave him a devilish appearance. A native of Indiana, he had been educated for the ministry at Episcopal Theological Seminary in Cambridge, Massachusetts, after first studying at Boston University and Harvard. Upon his ordination in 1893, he became rector of a church in Middleboro, Massachusetts, but his influence soon extended beyond his parish. Urging all Christians to be as revolutionary as Christ, he reflected the outlook of the Social Gospel movement in his articles in *Arena* magazine and in his book, *The New Obedience*.[1]

After building a new church for his congregation, Hale left the parish to engage in university extension work in Europe and, in 1895, lectured at Oxford University. Upon his return to the United States, he took a parish in Ardmore, Pennsylvania. Dissatisfied with the confinements of parish preaching, he again took to the road in 1900 and stumped the West for Democratic presidential hopeful William Jennings Bryan.

1. *Dictionary of American Biography, s.v.* "Hale, William Bayard." *National Cyclopedia of American Biography s.v.* "Hale, William Bayard." New York *Times*, August 25, 1895; March 22, 1897. Hale's reform ideas resembled those of Henry George. He believed that the landholding system of the United States promoted an inequitable distribution of wealth and should be revised.

Although he retained his clerical orders for another eight years, Hale abandoned the active ministry in 1901 for a career in journalism.

During the first few years in his new profession, Hale served on the editorial staffs of *Cosmopolitan* and *Current Literature*, then as special correspondent for the New York *World*, before becoming managing editor of the Philadelphia *Public Ledger*. Moving to the New York *Times* in 1907, he took an assignment that gained him national recognition—he spent a week in the White House with Theodore Roosevelt and wrote a series of articles depicting the everyday life of the chief executive. The articles were assembled in book form in 1908 under the title, *A Week in the White House With Theodore Roosevelt*. Even before the book was published, Hale went abroad for a second time as the *Times*'s Paris correspondent. Returning to the United States after a year's service in Europe, he took a position as associate editor and feature writer for *The World's Work*.[2]

The World's Work, which owner-editor Walter Hines Page had dedicated to promoting democratic ideals,[3] gave Hale an opportunity to champion social and political reform. Between 1910 and 1913, he contributed thirty-four articles to the journal, making him one of the most prolific journalists of the Progressive era.[4] Muckraker Ray Stannard Baker character-

2. *Dictionary of American Biography*, s.v. "Hale, William Bayard." *National Cyclopedia of American Biography*, s.v. "Hale, William Bayard." *Who's Who in America, 1916–1917*, s.v. "Hale, William Bayard."

3. Burton J. Hendricks, *The Life and Letters of Walter Hines Page* (Garden City, N.Y., 1922–25), I, 69–72.

4. Notable among Hale's articles were "The Speaker or the People," *The World's Work*, XIX (April, 1910), 12805–12, in which he defended the House "insurgents" in their attempt to check the power of conservative Speaker Joseph G. (Uncle Joe) Cannon; "A Dramatic Decade of History," *ibid.*, XXI (January, 1911), 3855–68, in which he catalogued the Progressive reforms of the first decade of the twentieth century; and his favorable characterizations of Progressive governors Robert M. La Follette of Wisconsin, Woodrow Wilson of New Jersey, and Judson Harmon of Ohio in successive issues, XXII (May, June, July, 1911), 14339–52, 14446–59, 14591–99.

ized Hale as a "brilliant journalist." [5] Through his association with Page, who was championing Woodrow Wilson for the presidency, Hale was called upon to write a biography of the New Jersey governor. The flattering account, which ran serially for six issues beginning in October, 1911, was so well received by Wilson that it was adopted in book form as the official campaign biography in the 1912 presidential race.[6] After the election victory, moreover, Hale edited some of Wilson's speeches which were published and widely read under the title *The New Freedom*.[7]

Having given ample evidence that his views were in tune with Wilson's New Freedom, Hale was a logical choice to serve the administration in some capacity. Adding to his otherwise meager qualifications for a mission to Mexico—he did not even speak Spanish—was the fact that he had seen much of Latin America firsthand. In the summer of 1912, as a member of the journalist entourage, Hale accompanied Secretary of State Philander C. Knox on a tour of the Caribbean and Central America. On the eve of the opening of the Panama Canal, Knox had undertaken the tour as a means of reestablishing good relations with all the Caribbean and Central American republics and to offer them assistance in putting their fiscal affairs in order.

A deep sense of Anglo-Saxon superiority and responsibility pervaded Hale's accounts of the tour. He found particularly

5. Baker, *Woodrow Wilson*, IV, 243. Baker also indicated that he thought Hale "temperamentally unfitted" for the mission to Mexico.

6. William Bayard Hale, "Woodrow Wilson: A Biography," XXII, 14940–53; XXIII, 64–76, 229–34, 297–310, 466–71, 522–23. The campaign biography was published under the title, *Woodrow Wilson: The Story of His Life* (Garden City, N.Y., 1912). Thereafter, Hale often referred to himself as Wilson's biographer.

7. In the introduction to the book, which is accepted as an epitome of Wilson's political philosophy, Wilson stated: "I did not write this book at all. It is the result of the editorial literary skill of Mr. William Bayard Hale, who put together here in their right sequences the more suggestive portions of my campaign speeches." See Woodrow Wilson, *The New Freedom* (Garden City, N.Y., 1913), vii.

pervaded Hale's accounts of the tour. He found particularly repulsive the culture of the Negro population in Haiti, and thought the racially mixed population of Central America incapable of maintaining stable political conditions without outside assistance. He suggested that nations outside the Western Hemisphere, especially Germany, would be willing to perform the service, but the Monroe Doctrine restrained them. The United States, therefore, should take the responsibility. Never explicit about how his country should pursue the task, he did, however, laud the results of the American customs receivership in Santo Domingo; on the other hand, he suggested that mere loans would only encourage revolutions by perpetuating unpopular governments.[8]

Such attitudes were clearly in keeping with the goals of Wilsonian diplomacy and must have been a source of comfort to the president as he typed the letter requesting Hale to undertake a tour of Central and South America, "ostensibly on your own hook," in order "to find out just what is going on down there."[9] With possible military *coups* brewing in other Central American republics, Wilson obviously meant for Hale's inspection to cover several nations. As it turned out, Hale visited only Mexico. He apparently was given no written instructions, but an examination of his reports from Mexico reveals the purpose of his mission: to investigate fully the activities and attitudes of Ambassador Henry Lane Wilson—especially to determine the validity of the rumors that the ambassador had been involved in the overthrow of Madero—and to judge the legality and stability of Huerta's provisional government and its ability to restore peace in Mexico. Accepting the mission, Hale put his personal affairs in order,

8. William Bayard Hale, "With the Knox Mission to Central America," *The World's Work*, XXIV (June, July, 1912), 179–93, 323–36; "Our Danger in Central America," *ibid.*, XXIV (August, 1912), 443–51.
9. Wilson to Hale, April 19, 1913, in Papers of Woodrow Wilson, Division of Manuscripts, Library of Congress, Ser. 3, Letterbook 2.

drew $2,500 from the president's secret contingent fund, and sailed for Mexico by steamer on May 15.[10]

That Hale's mission was meant to be confidential was evident from the manner in which he reported his findings to the president. The special agent sent telegrams and letters to one F. A. Muschenheim, a resident (whether real or fictitious the records do not reveal) of the Hotel Astor in New York City. The messages were forwarded to the Washington residence of Ben G. Davis, chief clerk of the State Department. Notes to Hale were also routed through the New York intermediary.[11] As a cover, the State Department issued a press release, coincident with Hale's departure for Mexico, to the effect that the president did not take seriously the charges being leveled at Ambassador Wilson and that no investigation of his activities was necessary.[12]

Despite these precautions, the persistent rumors of an investigation of Ambassador Wilson's activities, plus the arrival in the Mexican capital of a known friend of President Wilson, caused considerable speculation concerning the purpose of Hale's visit. Being a distinguished journalist, he was called to speak at a dinner honoring him at the exclusive Jockey Club. In the course of his address, he attempted to squelch the rumors, assuring the gathering that he was merely collecting data for a series of magazine articles. But the special agent fanned the flames of rumor when he called upon Francisco de la Barra, the minister of foreign relations. De la Barra eased the speculation by announcing that he and

10. Hale to Wilson, May 3, 1913, in Wilson Papers, Ser. 2, Box 93; William Bayard Hale's expense account and itinerary, *ibid.*, Box 101.

11. The Hotel Astor was Hale's residence before he left for Mexico. He probably sent ciphered messages to the Astor. Neither the Wilson Papers nor the State Department records contains a receipt indicating that Hale definitely had a copy of the State Department code book. Other agents signed receipts upon receiving a copy, but Henry Lane Wilson later insisted that Hale did possess one. See New York *World*, July 27, 1913.

12. New York *Times*, May 18, 1913, p. 1; *Mexican Herald* (Mexico City), May 19, 1913.

Hale were just renewing an old friendship. Although de la Barra did not say so, it is quite possible that the two had met earlier in Washington while de la Barra served there as ambassador from Mexico.[13]

As Hale went about gathering information, the nature of his inquiries was bound to stimulate curiosity. Robert H. Murray, Ambassador Wilson's nemesis, noted in his column in the New York *World* "that everyone, especially the Government officials and the friends of the American Ambassador, are deeply interested in finding out what brought Hale to Mexico." Commenting on the secrecy that shrouded Hale's activities, the reporter added that "compared to the discreet three-ply silence he [Hale] has maintained . . . the proverbial reticence of the clam is verbal fireworks." [14] Because of his reticence, Hale was able to come and go from his residence in the Hotel Iturbide with minimum attention to his actions.

In carrying out his confidential inquiries, Hale established numerous contacts in Mexico City. Speaking no Spanish, he naturally sought out Americans who were willing to provide him with information. E. N. Brown, president of the Mexican National Railway, who maintained intimate relations with the Huerta government, provided Hale with details of the government's fiscal transactions and the activities of foreign concessionaires. The special agent also found a confidant in the American consul general Arnold Shanklin, who for some time had been at odds with Ambassador Wilson. From the embassy staff itself, Hale enlisted a willing informer in Louis D'Antin, a clerk-interpreter. Reporter Robert H. Murray also provided information. From among American business interests, Hale befriended J. N. Galbraith, the agent of oilman

13. *Mexican Herald*, June 3, 6, 1913; "The Week: Mexico," *Independent*, LXXIV (June 5, 1913), 1310. One historian suggests that Hale revealed his presence in Mexico City, and hence the nature of his mission, by speaking at the Jockey Club. See George J. Rausch, Jr., "Poison-pen Diplomacy: Mexico, 1913," *The Americas*, XXIV (January, 1968), 274. To the contrary, his speech at the club was designed to cover his real purpose for being in Mexico.

14. New York *World*, June 23, 1913.

Henry Clay Pierce, and C. A. Hamilton, a mine operator. His dispatches also reveal that he made acquaintances of numerous middle-class Americans, who operated small businesses in Mexico City.[15]

The fact that so many of Hale's informants were known enemies of Ambassador Wilson ultimately caused Boaz Long, the chief of the State Department's Division of Latin American Affairs, to question the reliability of the agent's information.[16] Bryan and Wilson, however, had complete confidence in their agent and ignored Long. They were not entirely unjustified, because Hale did solicit a variety of viewpoints. He maintained confidential relations with Foreign Minister de la Barra and, although he never mentioned them by name, he indicated that he communicated with other members of Huerta's cabinet. Two notable politicians, conservative Manuel Calero and liberal Jesús Flores Magón, who collaborated with the provisional government, provided information. Hale also interviewed Felix Díaz's private secretary. Last but not least, he conferred with Henry Lane Wilson who, despite his veiled suspicion of Hale, discussed candidly his relations with both the Madero and Huerta governments.[17]

15. Hale did not reveal the sources of information for each report, but in scattered passages of his numerous dispatches he identified the above informants. See Hale to State Department, June 3, 18, July 12, 24, August 5, 1913, in NA 812.00/7798½, 23616, 23626, 23632, 23639; Hale to State Department, June 12, 1913, in Wilson Papers, Ser. 2, Box 94; Memorandum (by Hale), September 28, 1913, ibid., Box 97. Except for document no. 7798½, Hale's dispatches were withheld from the regular State Department files. They were kept in the private possession of Secretary of State Bryan. They were not delivered to the Index Bureau until March, 1920. Therefore, they do not appear in the proper chronological sequence with other documents that arrived at the State Department at the same time, but may be found mixed with documents dated March, 1920.

16. Long to Bryan, August 22, 1913, in NA 812.00/17669.

17. Hale to State Department, June 3, July 12, 24, August 5, 1913, ibid./23616, 23626, 23632, 23639; Hale to State Department, June 12, 1913, in Wilson Papers, Ser. 2, Box 94; Alberto Noél to Felix Díaz, June 30, 1913, enclosed in Henry Lane Wilson to Woodrow Wilson, July 1, 1913, ibid.; Memorandum (by Hale), September 28, 1913, ibid., Box 97; Henry Lane

On June 3, after nine days of investigation, Hale began reporting his findings to the president.[18] He noted that the prevailing opinion in Mexico City was that Huerta's government was stable and that his triumph over the rebels was inevitable. The American colony, he added, was virtually unanimous in its recommendations for recognition of the provisional government. Hale did not think the confidence in the Huerta regime was justified. He noted that the Associated Press reports and the government's "official" versions of the campaigns against the rebels differed considerably. A

Wilson, *Diplomatic Episodes in Mexico, Belgium, and Chile* (Garden City, N.Y., 1927), 305–306. Alberto Noél, Felix Díaz's private secretary, reported his interview with Hale to his employer, who passed the letter on to Ambassador Wilson. Noél's letter contained a highly critical characterization of Hale, which the ambassador sought to use to discredit the special agent.

For the nature of the political affiliations of Manuel Calero and Jesús Flores Magón, see Cumberland, *Mexican Revolution*, 10–11, 153–54, 196–217; James D. Cockroft, *Intellectual Precursors of the Mexican Revolution, 1910–1913* (Austin, Tex., 1968), 91–98, 179, 185, 212, 220. Calero had served as Madero's minister of foreign relations and Flores Magón had served as minister of government. Both supported the Huerta regime.

18. Grieb charges that Hale went to Mexico determined to find Huerta and Henry Lane Wilson guilty of the charges that had been brought against them, and that he "commenced reporting immediately after his arrival indicating that he failed to conduct an investigation before formulating his recommendations." See Kenneth J. Grieb, "Reginald Del Valle: A California Diplomat's Sojourn in Mexico," *California Historical Society Quarterly*, XLVII (December, 1968), 321. An itinerary of Hale's movements (which the above author did not cite) located in the Wilson Papers, Ser. 2, Box 101, reveals that Hale reached Mexico City on May 24 and did not file his first report until June 3, nine days after his arrival. See Hale to State Department, June 3, 1913, in NA 812.00/23616. Although this report does not reveal the sources of Hale's information (the only informant mentioned was Foreign Minister de la Barra), Hale had ample time to conduct an investigation before filing his report. The note itself was not a definitive statement of his findings but merely a brief telegraphic message relating his first impressions. Hale had been briefed by Wilson and Bryan, and he doubtless had some preconceived notions about the Mexican situation, but there is little reason to suppose that he went to Mexico with his mind already made up. In his book, *The United States and Huerta*, 80, Grieb also charges that Hale "avoided diplomats and government officials, seeking only individuals who could provide information that corroborated his own convictions." As pointed out above, there seems to be little basis for this charge.

study of the map and wire-service reports convinced Hale that Huerta's grip on the nation was slipping. By July 9 he had investigated fully enough to report on the condition of the country, state by state. He concluded that Huerta controlled and was able to maintain order in no more than one third of the national territory.[19]

More importantly, Hale also reported that Huerta's dominance of his own government and control of the capital city were rather tenuous. He cited numerous turnovers in Huerta's cabinet as evidence of dissension in the government. Influential men, he discovered, were openly discussing the propriety of asking Huerta to resign.[20]

The most impressive evidence the American agent marshaled against the usurper concerned the financial condition of the provisional government. Huerta had inherited a near-empty treasury and a tremendous national debt. Because the nation was in turmoil and the means of securing revenue were intermittently interrupted, Huerta needed large foreign loans to sustain the government until the nation was pacified. In the early days of June, the government announced the negotiation of a substantial loan from an international banking syndicate, and it was widely assumed that this loan would enable Huerta to mount a decisive military campaign against the rebels.[21] Hale, however, pointed out the fact that less than half of the loan had been subscribed immediately, the syndicate merely taking an option to supply the remainder six months later. Most of

19. Hale to State Department, June 3, 6, 16, 25, 1913, in NA 812.00/23616, 23618, 23621; Memorandum on Affairs in Mexico (by Hale), July 9, 1913, *ibid.*/8203; Hale to State Department, June 12, 1913, in Wilson Papers, Ser. 2, Box 94. Hale's estimates of Huerta's control of the national territory were essentially correct. See Vera Estañol, *La Revolución Mexicana*, 326–27; González Ramírez, *Las Ideas—La Violencia*, 403–405.

20. Hale to State Department, June 14, 22, 25, July 8, 1913, in NA 812.00/23617, 23620, 23621, 23625; Memorandum on Affairs in Mexico (by Hale), July 9, 1913, *ibid.*/8203.

21. New York *Times*, June 2, 3, 1913, p. 1.

what Huerta did receive, Hale explained, went to pay off already-matured bonds, while only a fraction remained for government operating expenses. Hale added, moreover, that E. N. Brown of the Mexican National Railway had confided that the remaining options would never be filled. Within six months, Brown feared, the Huerta government would be bankrupt. The crowd of politicians around Huerta, the American railroad man told Hale, had not yet abandoned the government only because they were intent upon looting it of as much as possible before it fell.[22]

Hale was alarmed by the anti-American sentiment in Mexico City. Particularly ominous, he believed, was the attempt of government officials to blame the United States for Mexico's declining economic fortunes. Wilson's refusal to grant diplomatic recognition to the provisional government, the charges ran, encouraged the revolutionaries and discouraged foreign investors from coming to Mexico's aid. While there was much truth in the allegations, Hale also noted that the *Huertistas* falsely charged that the ultimate design of American foreign policy was to reduce Mexico to anarchy in order to justify military intervention and possible annexation. This anti-American propaganda, the special agent believed, was designed to divert the public's attention from the government's poorly managed military effort against the rebels.[23]

22. Hale to State Department, June 22, 1913, in NA 812.00/23620; Memorandum on Affairs in Mexico (by Hale), July 9, 1913, *ibid.*/8203. Hale's estimates on the true nature of the loan were essentially correct. He did not state exact figures, but the total amount of the loan was twenty million pounds of which only six million was contracted immediately, with options being given to supply the remainder later. See Meyer, *Huerta*, 186–87; Edgar Turlingon, *Mexico and Her Foreign Creditors* (New York, 1930), 248–51; Jan Bazánt, *Historia de la deuda exterior de México, 1823–1946* (México, D.F., 1968), 175.

23. Hale to State Department, July 12, 17, 1913, in NA 812.00/23626, 23629. Anti-Americanism did indeed run high in Mexico City. The Huerta press was full of charges such as the ones Hale had reported. See *Mexican Herald*, July 7–11, 1913. A champion of American business interests in

From Hale's point of view, the most disturbing aspect of this anti-American propaganda was its effect on the approximately three thousand American middle-class businessmen who lived in Mexico City. This element of the American colony, which, according to Hale, constituted "a strong force making for order and decency," had stayed with their businesses through the bad times of the revolution of 1910 and the *Decena Trágica*, but now felt that their livelihoods were threatened by the wave of anti-Americanism. The special agent pointed out that these people were not great capitalists "of the Standard Oil or Guggenheim type, with employees who could readily leave the country," but were "Americans of our own type with our own sentiments and ideals. They live in American houses; they practice and hold American standards of morality and rectitude. . . . To ask these people to withdraw from Mexico," Hale concluded, "would be to push civilization backwards." [24] It was just such people that Wilson's New Freedom was designed to protect and aid at home. Reading Hale's dispatches, the president must have wondered if he could do less for such Americans abroad, especially when they were apparently being intimidated by the likes of Victoriano Huerta.

Hale characterized Huerta himself as "an ape-like old man, of almost pure Indian blood. He may almost be said to subsist on alcohol. Drunk or only half-drunk (he is never sober), he never loses a certain shrewdness." [25] The shrewdness that Hale described was the cunning of a Machiavelli. The American agent painted a sinister picture of Huerta coming to President Madero on the first day of the *Decena Trágica* and offering his services in the defense of legal authority.

Mexico and a supporter of the Huerta regime, the *Herald*, an English-language newspaper, almost daily printed translations of *Huertista* editorials condemning the Wilson administration.

24. Hale to State Department, July 2, 1913, in NA 812.00/23623; Memorandum on Affairs in Mexico (by Hale), July 9, 1913, *ibid.*/8203.

25. Memorandum on Affairs in Mexico (by Hale), July 9, 1913, *ibid.*/8203.

Once he had gained the president's trust, the old general had cynically allowed Felix Díaz and the other leaders of the *cuartelado* (military revolt) to make overtures. After extracting favorable terms, including the office of provisional president for himself, Huerta joined the conspirators in overthrowing the constitutional government and murdering Madero.[26]

Just as fond of moralizing as his president, Hale concluded that extending diplomatic recognition to a government thus established would, in effect, be an endorsement of "treason and assassination" and an "abandonment of all the principles by which social order is maintained in a civilized country. European powers, with their own clouded histories," he added, "can afford perhaps to connive at the overthrowing [of] lawful authority by murder, but surely the United States, especially if it would wield any moral influence in Latin America, can afford anything sooner than give its countenance to savage contempt for constitutional government." [27]

Although Wilson himself had articulated similar sentiments earlier, Hale's dispatches, arriving in Washington when they did, served to bolster the president at a time when his resolve not to recognize Huerta was wavering. He was under pressure from several sources to at least grant conditional recognition. Several members of his cabinet, along with his close personal friend Colonel Edward House and the eminent counselor of the State Department, John Bassett Moore, insisted that *de facto* recognition would carry with it no moral acceptance of Huerta and his methods.[28]

26. Hale to State Department, June 18, 1913, *ibid.*/7798½.

27. Hale to State Department, June 3, 1913, *ibid.*/23616 (author's punctuation).

28. House to Wilson, May 6, 1913, in Wilson Papers, Ser. 2, Box 93; John Bassett Moore (enclosing memorandum for the president) to Bryan, May 14, 1913, in NA 812.00/8378; Cronon (ed.), *Cabinet Diaries of Josephus Daniels*, 42–44; David F. Houston, *Eight Years With Wilson's Cabinet* (Garden City, N.Y., 1926), I, 69.

Businessmen, such as James Speyer of the Wall Street banking firm Speyer and Company, which held ten million dollars in Mexican bonds, beseeched the president to clarify his Mexican policy. Wilson gave one proposal from the business world close scrutiny, mainly because it was endorsed by an old friend, former Princeton classmate Cleveland H. Dodge. Early in May, Julius Kruttschnitt, chairman of the board of directors of the Southern Pacific Railroad, approached Wilson through Colonel House with a plan of conditional recognition. The plan had already been approved by several other large firms with interests in Mexico, including Phelps Dodge and Company, the Greene Cananea Copper Company, and Edward L. Doheny's Mexican Petroleum Company. The brainchild of Judge D. J. Haff of Kansas City, the plan called for Wilson to accord Huerta diplomatic recognition, with the provisos that the old general should call free and impartial elections as soon as possible in the states he controlled and that the Constitutionalists should suspend hostilities and hold impartial elections in the states they controlled. Both sides would then support the president thus elected. That Wilson gave this proposal serious consideration is evidenced by the fact that he drafted instructions to Ambassador Wilson embodying the Haff plan.[29]

These plans, as they matured in May, gave promise of a more positive Mexican policy. Apparently awaiting news from his special agent in Mexico City, Wilson hesitated before sending the instructions to his ambassador. Then in early June, when Hale's dispatches painting such a dismal future for Huerta's government began pouring in, Wilson dropped the plan of conditional recognition. Instead, he adopted an alternate proposal, also presented by Julius Kruttschnitt, which omitted conditional recognition and asked only that the administration use its good offices to arrange elections in Mexico and mediate the differences between the provisional

29. Baker, *Woodrow Wilson*, IV, 245–53; Link, *New Freedom*, 351–52.

government and the Constitutionalists. President Wilson, in fact, sent a note embodying this proposal to Mexico City to serve as a guide for Henry Lane Wilson in his relations with the Huerta government.[30]

Wilson and Bryan never doubted the accuracy of Hale's reports. Such unqualified acceptance was not justified. Hale was a man of unquestionable integrity, and he was diligent in his efforts to make a full investigation. But his superficial knowledge of Mexican politics and his sense of Anglo-Saxon superiority betrayed him into making some false assumptions. True enough, there was considerable conflict within the provisional government, but this was hardly evidence of weakness on Huerta's part. The numerous changes in the cabinet resulted from Huerta's determination to eliminate the *Felicistas*, whom he had been forced by the Pact of the Embassy to include in his original government. In fact, Huerta was strengthening his hand by replacing the deposed *Felicistas* with his own loyal followers. His campaigns against the rebels were, indeed, languishing, and he did not control most of the national territory; but Huerta did hold the important rail centers—the keys to military dominance of the nation—as well as most of the centers of dense population. Nor was the old general entirely unhappy over the course of the civil war. Prolonging the war for the time being provided him with a pretext for remaining in power. Although the international loan had netted the government very little, it had relieved the immediate financial crisis. Thus, at the time when Hale was prophesying doom for the provisional government, Huerta's strength was on the rise.[31]

Maintenance of this strength, even Huerta realized, de-

30. *Ibid.*; State Department to H. L. Wilson, June 15, 1913, in NA 812.00/7743. President Wilson went further than the Kruttschnitt proposal, insisting that Huerta pledge himself not to be a candidate for president in the arranged elections.

31. Meyer, *Huerta*, 92–96, 140–43, 185–87; Sherman and Greenleaf, *Huerta*, 105–106; Vera Estañol, *La Revolución Mexicana*, 318–29.

pended upon the stabilizing influence that diplomatic recognition from the United States would provide.[32] The importance of Hale's early dispatches, regardless of how accurate, was that they reinforced Wilson's original image of Huerta, hardened his puritanical will, and eliminated any possibility of diplomatic recognition for the usurper. This, in turn, prolonged Huerta's difficulties.

Hale's revelations about the activities of Ambassador Henry Lane Wilson were equally influential. Hale wasted no time in confirming President Wilson's worst fears concerning his official representative in the Mexican capital. In his first dispatch to Washington, Hale revealed that the ambassador was a "vain busybody [of] highly nervous temperament increased by indulgence . . . which [his] slight frame is not equal to." Even more revealing, the special agent insisted that "it is no secret that [the] fall [of] Madero was hastened by Ambassador Wilson." [33]

Two weeks later, the president received Hale's elaborately detailed thirty-three-page account of the *Decena Trágica*. For the most part, his narrative of the facts was accurate, but he overemphasized Ambassador Wilson's involvement. He pointed out correctly that Wilson looked upon Madero with open contempt and had been discourteous to the Mexican president on more than one occasion. Hale was accurate in his charges that the ambassador harried Madero throughout the *Decena*, blaming him for the violence and trying to force his resignation. The agent also noted correctly that, on more than one occasion, Wilson claimed to be speaking for the entire diplomatic corps when only two or three ministers agreed with him.[34]

32. Huerta, *Memorias de Victoriano Huerta*, 93–94.
33. Hale to State Department, June 3, 1913, in NA 812.00/23616.
34. Hale to State Department, June 18, 1913, *ibid.*/7798½; John P. Harrison, "Henry Lane Wilson, El Trágico de la Decena," *Historia Mexicana*, VI (January–March, 1957), 374–405. The latter citation is a Spanish translation of the first, with notes and editorial comments. Harrison suggests that

In reporting Wilson's involvement, however, Hale often allowed his own righteous indignation and loathing for the ambassador to cloud his judgment. Without justification he concluded that "without the countenance of the American Ambassador given to Huerta's proposal to betray the President, the revolt would have failed." [35] Such a supposition did not do justice to the conspiratorial talents of Felix Díaz and Victoriano Huerta. Although Wilson was forewarned, the two generals carried off their *coup* without the active involvement of the ambassador. Even had Wilson disapproved of their plans, there is no reason to suppose that they would have scrapped them or would have failed to oust Madero.

Hale also contended that "the plan for the immediate settling of a military dictatorship would never have been formed except in the American Embassy." [36] Again, he assumed too much. The provisional government was not as yet a full dictatorship,[37] nor was Wilson responsible for creating the Huerta regime. Huerta and Díaz agreed upon the bare bones of the provisional government before they

this document, which was as much an indictment of Huerta as an exposé of Henry Lane Wilson's activities, was the decisive factor in preventing the recognition of the Huerta regime. Mexican historian Isidro Fabela, who served as Carranza's minister of foreign relations, accepted Hale's report as *prima facie* evidence of Ambassador Wilson's guilt. See "La Participación de Henry Lane Wilson: Fragmento del informe confidencial Enviado al Presidente Woodrow Wilson por su Emisario William Bayard Hale, 18 de Junio 1913," Isidro Fabela y Josefina E. de Fabela (eds.), *Documentos históricos de la Revolución Mexicana* (México, D.F., 1965), IX, 187–205.

35. Hale to State Department, June 18, 1913, in NA 812.00/7798½.

36. *Ibid.*

37. Huerta had used the veiled threat of force to keep some of the state governments in line and placed military men in power wherever possible, but the national congress, which had been elected with Madero in 1911, was still functioning and was by no means amenable to all of the provisional president's proposals. His pretensions were also challenged by the *Felicistas* who remained in the cabinet. Huerta was unable to consolidate his power into a dictatorship until October, 1913. See Meyer, *Huerta*, 83–87, 127–55; Sherman and Greenleaf, *Victoriano Huerta*, 101–102, 105–106, 116–19; Vera Estañol, *La Revolución Mexicana*, 321–33.

consulted the ambassador. Wilson's involvement in the *coup* took place after the arrest of Madero and was confined to the negotiation of the Pact of the Embassy, which merely designated the individuals who would serve in the cabinet and provided for a permanent government to be elected in the future.

Finally, Hale charged that Ambassador Wilson was responsible for the assassinations of Madero and Pino Suárez. By his refusal to accept responsibility for their safety, Hale reasoned, the ambassador "might be said to have delivered the men to death." [38] At best Wilson had looked upon Madero's safety with calculated indifference, but to accuse the ambassador of total responsibility for the deposed president's death was a grossly irresponsible statement on the part of Hale.

The special agent admitted that Ambassador Wilson talked freely and candidly of his role in the drama and gave "evidence in every sentence that he believed it to have been the only part humanity and patriotism (alike from the standpoint of Mexico and the United States) allowed him to play." Hale also conceded—and in doing so, largely contradicted his earlier characterization—that it would be "absurd to picture Mr. Wilson as a malicious plotter." Despite such admissions, Hale could not close his report without driving his point home. Again, he exaggerated: "It cannot but be a course of grief that what is probably the most dramatic story in which an American diplomatic officer has ever been involved, should be a story of sympathy with treason, perfidy and assassination in an assault on constitutional government." Then, in language calculated to have the greatest effect upon President Wilson, he added:

> It is particularly unfortunate that this should have taken place in a leading country of Latin America, where, if we have moral work to do, it is to discourage violence and uphold law.

38. Hale to State Department, June 18, 1913, in NA 812.00/7798½.

Trifling, perhaps, in the sum of miseries that have flowed from it, yet not without importance in a way, is the fact that thousands of Mexicans believe that the Ambassador acted on instructions from Washington and look upon his retention under the new President as a mark of approval and blame the United States for the chaos into which the country has fallen.[39]

Clearly this was a call for the president to clarify his Mexican policy, at least by recalling Henry Lane Wilson. President Wilson was indeed moved by the report. Just before departing for a short holiday in New Hampshire, he sent a short note to Bryan: "The document from Hale is indeed extraordinary. I should like, upon my return from my little outing, to discuss with you very seriously the necessity of recalling Henry Lane Wilson in one way or another, perhaps merely 'for consultation' until we can talk with the man himself." The secretary of state fully agreed.[40] Actually, they had been moving toward this decision for days. On June 25, approximately a week before Bryan and Wilson received Hale's lengthy letter condemning Ambassador Wilson, Bryan had received a telegram from the special agent revealing that the ambassador had invited Huerta to dine at the embassy. In transmitting a copy to the White House, Bryan scrawled a pencil message across the bottom of the telegram: "What do you think of Huerta dining with Wilson?" The president replied, adding his own pencil note beneath Bryan's: "Think it most seriously unwise. Probably make it worse to interfere." Then, as if in anger and as an afterthought, he scribbled a second note on another part of the page: "I think Wilson should be recalled."[41]

39. *Ibid.*

40. Wilson to Bryan, July 1, 1913, in Correspondence of Secretary of State Bryan with President Wilson, General Records of the Department of State, National Archives, Record Group 59, hereinafter cited as Bryan-Wilson Correspondence; Bryan to Wilson, July 3, 1913, *ibid.*; copies of both in Wilson Papers, Ser. 4, Box 275.

41. Hale to State Department, June 25, 1913, in NA 812.00/23621. The pencil notes were scribbled on the White House copy. See Hale to State Department [n.d.], in Wilson Papers, Ser. 2, Box 94.

Wilson and Bryan's response to Hale's revelations indicated that their indignation had mounted sufficiently to cause them to take more positive steps against Ambassador Wilson and the Huerta government. But on July 4, exhausted from his efforts to influence Congress on the tariff and currency questions, President Wilson departed on a ten-day vacation.[42] During his absence no new moves were made. The administration still did not have a clear-cut Mexican policy. Wilson's temporary reluctance to move more forcefully in Mexican affairs was due to his lack of information concerning the nature of the Constitutionalist revolution in northern Mexico. Hale's trusted opinions had given him ample reason to believe that Huerta would never establish a regime that he could accept. But could he expect any better from the rebels? Already another special agent was in the field, attempting to provide the answer to this question.

42. New York *Times*, July 4, 1913, p. 1.

CHAPTER III

No One Worthy of
Consideration

Reginaldo (often anglicized as Reginald) F. Del Valle of Los
Angeles was Wilson's second fact-finding agent to Mexico. A
longtime political confederate of Bryan, Del Valle was a
member of a prestigious old southern California family, his
grandfather having come to the area in 1819 as an officer in
the Spanish army. Remaining in California after Mexico won
her independence from Spain, the Del Valle family secured
land grants and became substantial ranchers and vintners.
Reginaldo, therefore, was reared in comfortable circumstances. He was graduated from Santa Clara University in
1873 and was admitted to the bar four years later. Using his
legal career as a stepping-stone to politics, in 1880, at age
twenty-five, he was elected to the lower house of the state
legislature; two years later, he ran a successful race for the
state senate. A lifetime Democrat, he was later unsuccessful
in election bids for congressman and lieutenant governor. In
1893, Grover Cleveland offered Del Valle the post of ambassador to Chile, but he declined the honor. He supported Bryan
in all his presidential bids and backed Wilson's nomination in
1912. At the time Wilson called him to serve in Mexico, he
was a member of the Los Angeles Public Service Commission
and one of the few remaining *Californios* (Californians of
Spanish-Mexican descent) of political prominence.[1]

1. New York *Times*, July 19, 27, 1913, II, 2; Los Angeles *Times*,
September 22, 23, 25, 1938; Leonard Pitt, *The Decline of the Californios*
(Berkeley and Los Angeles, 1966), 272–74.

In 1913 Del Valle was fifty-eight, gray-haired, and mustached. Short and portly, he spoke fluent Spanish and, by appearance and cultural background, was hardly distinguishable from the Mexican leaders he was being sent to observe. But other than his Spanish-Mexican heritage and his old acquaintance with Bryan, he had no particular qualifications to commend him for the mission. He was not an acknowledged expert on Mexican affairs and, unlike most of the other agents Wilson and Bryan sent to Mexico, Del Valle did not share their view of the situation south of the border. He had a Spanish patrician's disdain for lower-class Mexicans, particularly those of Indian blood, and his dispatches revealed that he had little faith in the workability of democracy among the Mexican people. Wilson and Bryan obviously did not know this at the outset. Only as Del Valle's mission drew to a close did it become apparent that his sympathies were at variance with those of the president and the secretary of state.

The purpose of Del Valle's mission was supposed to be a secret. The State Department supplied him with a code book for enciphering his telegraphic messages. As in the case of Hale, he was to send his reports to a private address—in this case, to the home of the chief clerk of the State Department. A memorandum jotted down by Bryan provided Del Valle with guidelines to follow in making his inquiries:

1. It is desirable to know the character, standing and popularity of those who have influence in any community?
2. Where is the dissatisfaction with the Government, it is important to know the cause of dissatisfaction, and to what extent there is a concentration of opinion as to cause and agreement as to remedy?
3. Are conditions improving or growing worse? This can be determined somewhat by the spirit of hopefulness or feeling of depression.
4. What was the real cause of the first revolution, and does the sentiment upon which it was founded still exist?
5. What is the situation in respect to land ownership and tenure? Are the conditions satisfactory, and what changes, if any, are contemplated?

Del Valle drew three thousand dollars from the president's contingent fund, and the secretary of state provided him with a letter identifying him only as a personal friend traveling in Mexico on professional business and instructing all American diplomatic and consular officials to accord him every courtesy.[2]

Del Valle's itinerary called for him to go first to the Constitutionalist stronghold in the northwestern state of Sonora, then to make his way eastward across northern Mexico. In order to gather information from the antirevolutionary elements, as well as from the revolutionaries, he went first to Tucson, Arizona, where a sizable community of refugees from northern Mexico had gathered. Accompanied by his wife and daughter, he arrived in Tucson on June 7.[3] Thus he started his investigations at about the same time that Hale began reporting his impressions from Mexico City.

From the outset, Del Valle's mission had a carnival atmosphere. He apparently revealed either to reporters from Los Angeles or to members of the refugee colony the fact that he represented President Wilson, because little secrecy shrouded his activities. The Los Angeles *Times* anticipated his movements, reporting his presence in Tucson on the very day of his arrival.[4] Refugees, pouring out their tales of suffering and privation and beseeching the aid of the Wilson administration, swarmed around him as soon as he debarked from the train. The border newspapers, moreover, identified him without qualification as the special agent of President Wilson.[5]

2. Memorandum, [n.d.]; receipts for code book and three thousand dollars; letter, to the diplomatic and consular officers of the United States of America, May 31, 1913, enclosed in Bryan to Del Valle, May 31, 1913, in NA 812.00/20446.
3. Los Angeles *Times*, June 7, 1913; Tucson *Daily Citizen*, June 10, 1913.
4. Los Angeles *Times*, June 7, 1913.
5. Tucson *Daily Citizen*, June 10, 1913; Tucson *Daily Star*, June 10, 1913; *Border Vedette* (Nogales, Ariz.), June 14, 1913; El Paso (Tex.) *Morning Times*, June 10, 1913.

Garbled versions of Del Valle's purposes began to circulate immediately upon his arrival on the border. The two major Los Angeles dailies, the *Times* and the *Examiner*, first created—and the border papers spread—the impression that the Californian had been sent to arrange a truce between the Constitutionalists and the Huerta government.[6] The Los Angeles *Times*, in particular, presented Del Valle as a prospective peacemaker. The front page of the June 17 issue bore his photograph encircled by elaborate artwork. Embossed in the lower right corner of the picture was a toga-draped female figure—apparently symbolizing liberty—holding a Mexican flag and an olive branch in one hand, while the other hand released a dove of peace which flew upward toward Del Valle's photograph. The obvious implication to be drawn from the picture was that Mexico implored his aid in restoring peace.[7]

Both Los Angeles newspapers were also responsible for originating a rumor that Del Valle would succeed Henry Lane Wilson as ambassador to Mexico.[8] There may have been a measure of validity in this report. In the early weeks of the Wilson administration, Del Valle had gone to Washington seeking the ambassadorship.[9] That Bryan may have considered the Californian for the post is evidenced by his remarks to Huerta's chargé d'affaires in Washington. When the chargé discovered that an American was in northern Mexico interviewing revolutionary leaders, he naturally questioned Bryan concerning the nature of the intruder's activities. Although Bryan denied that Del Valle had any official status

6. Los Angeles *Times*, June 10, 1913; Los Angeles *Examiner*, June 10, 1913; Tucson *Daily Citizen*, June 11, 1913; *Border Vedette*, June 14, 1913; El Paso *Morning Times*, June 20, 1913.

7. Los Angeles *Times*, June 17, 1913.

8. *Ibid.*, June 7, 1913; Los Angeles *Examiner*, June 7, 1913.

9. Upon his return from Mexico in late July, Del Valle revealed to eastern reporters that he had earlier come to Washington seeking the post of ambassador to Mexico. See New York *Times*, July 27, 1913, II, 2.

at the time, he did reveal that the Californian was "one of the probable candidates for Ambassador to Mexico." [10] Whatever Bryan's intentions, the border press picked up and spread the story until it ultimately made news in Mexico City.[11]

Del Valle was not as discreet in his public comments as one would expect from a "secret agent." When queried concerning the nature of his visit to northern Mexico, he did not deny outright that he was an agent of the president, but gave equivocal answers that only served to increase the speculation. For example, to the reporter of the Los Angeles *Times*, he commented: "While I am acting in a personal capacity, the fact is that I am simply an instrument of President Wilson and Secretary Bryan." [12] The El Paso *Times* reported him as saying: "I am not representing the United States government as an official, but as an envoy for the purpose of submitting reports of conditions in Mexico to President Wilson and Secretary Bryan." [13] By involving his wife and daughter—who were invited to a round of parties by the ladies of Tucson and Nogales—in his interviews, Del Valle allowed his mission to take on the air of a social outing.[14]

However indiscreet he may have been, Del Valle took his mission quite seriously and, in his own fashion, was a diligent investigator. Between June 7 and 13, he divided his time between Tucson and Nogales, interviewing refugees. Most notable among them were José M. Maytorena, self-exiled

10. Encargado de Negocios ad-ínterin a Secretario de Relaciones Exteriores, June 12, 1913, Archivo General de la Secretaría de Relaciones Exteriores, Ramo de la Revolución (hereinafter cited as AGRE), L–E–786, Leg. 28.
11. Tucson *Daily Citizen*, June 10, 11, 1913; *Border Vedette*, June 14, 1913; El Paso *Morning Times*, June 20, 1913; *El Imparcial* (Mexico City), June 18, 1913.
12. Los Angeles *Times*, June 10, 1913.
13. El Paso *Morning Times*, June 20, 1913.
14. Los Angeles *Times*, June 14, 1913. The society page of the *Times* lauded the conduct of the Del Valle women, indicating that their activities had been a smashing social success.

governor of the state of Sonora; Felipe Rivera, deposed
governor of the state of Sinaloa; and Martín Espinoza, who
was still governor of the district of Tepic. All three professed
sympathy for the Constitutionalist cause. Most of the other
exiles were middle- to upper-class property owners, professionals, and merchants. Del Valle referred to them as the
"reputable citizens" of Sonora. This group immediately won
the Californian's sympathy. They had endured great suffering, Del Valle revealed, and longed for peace, even under
Huerta's rule, if that was the surest way to end the chaos in
northern Mexico. They charged that the Constitutionalist
armies were composed of the "worst elements" in their state.
The refugees grieved that in their absence the rebels were
systematically despoiling their property. Should they return
to protect their interests, their lives would be endangered.
The sale of their confiscated cattle and other movable
property, they further lamented, was providing the revenue
to finance the revolutionary war effort.[15]

To judge these matters firsthand, Del Valle entered
Mexico on June 13, bound for the Sonoran capital, Hermosillo. The Constitutionalist leaders eagerly anticipated his
arrival and attempted to make a good impression. Well aware
that he represented President Wilson, the rebel leaders had
the Californian investigated before he entered their bailiwick. The revolutionaries' Hermosillo newspaper, *La Voz de
Sonora*, sent a reporter to interview Del Valle in Nogales.
Overly impressed by the fact that the special agent was of
Mexican descent and spoke Spanish fluently, the newspaper-

15. Del Valle to State Department, June 8, 9, 12, 1913, in NA
812.00/23641, 23642, 23643; Tucson *Daily Citizen*, June 10, 11, 1913; *Border
Vedette*, June 14, 1913. Governor Rivera revealed that Huerta had used
police-state terrorism in an attempt to extract a profession of loyalty to the
provisional government. When he refused to submit, Rivera claimed, he was
arrested, but escaped and made his way to Tucson. Governor Espinoza
apparently came to the border in order to be beyond Huerta's reach while he
made up his mind about his loyalties.

man pronounced Del Valle completely sympathetic to the rebel cause.[16] Not surprisingly, Del Valle was cordially received in Hermosillo. The rebel leaders granted him interviews and allowed him to wander about the city, observing conditions and conversing with the local inhabitants. Encountering no obstacles, he completed his investigation in two days and returned to Tucson on June 16.[17]

After resting a day in Tucson, Del Valle sent his wife and daughter home to Los Angeles, while he proceeded to El Paso, Texas. Arriving there on June 18, he spent two days in conferences with Constitutionalist agents and sympathizers and civic leaders in El Paso and with Huerta's officials across the Rio Grande in government-held Ciudad Juárez. Since the Constitutionalists had destroyed a length of the railroad tracks south of Juárez, Del Valle was unable to travel into the state of Chihuahua.[18]

Denied access to the interior of north-central Mexico, the special envoy continued his journey along the border until he reached perhaps his most important destination, Venustiano Carranza's headquarters in Piedras Negras, Coahuila. Arriving across the border in Eagle Pass, Texas, on June 21, Del Valle crossed the Rio Grande the next day and, armed with a letter of introduction from Maytorena, arranged to interview Carranza and his staff. Apprehensive about his future relations with the Wilson administration, Carranza was truculent and uncooperative in his meeting with Del Valle. Extremely nationalistic, the First Chief was hypersensitive to any encroachment upon his independence in directing the course of the revolution. From the press reports that preceded Del

16. *La Voz de Sonora* (Hermosillo, Sonora), June 14, 1913, enclosed in Del Valle to State Department, June 17, 1913, in NA 812.00/23644.

17. Louis Hostetter (American consul, Hermosillo) to State Department, June 17, 1913, in NA 812.00/7862; Del Valle to State Department, June 17, 1913, *ibid.*/23644.

18. Del Valle to State Department, June 27, 1913, *ibid.*/23648; El Paso *Morning Times*, June 20, 1913.

Valle's arrival in Piedras Negras, Carranza could have inferred that the agent's purpose was to infringe upon that independence by attempting to arrange a truce between the Constitutionalists and Huerta's provisional government. So as to accentuate his own official character, the First Chief refused even to speak to the special agent except in the presence of an official of the United States government—in this case, Consul Luther T. Ellsworth. The bearded revolutionary leader absolutely refused to discuss the Mexican political situation and terminated the interview abruptly, with little more than social amenities having been exchanged.[19]

In his report of the incident, Del Valle was at a loss to explain why Carranza was so suspicious. Ignoring the obvious impression the press reports and his own misguided comments might have made, the Californian could not understand how the First Chief got the misinformation that the United States was trying to bind the rebels to a conciliatory arrangement with the provisional government in Mexico City. The special agent conjectured that Carranza was so cautious because he had recently received a representative of General Felix Díaz who had attempted to bind him to an unsatisfactory peace arrangement.[20] Actually, Del Valle was just beginning to be haunted by his own indiscreet behavior.

Del Valle had intended to make his way to Mexico City by railway, observing conditions as he went; again, rebel destruction of the rail lines denied him access to the interior. With this route closed, he journeyed to New Orleans in order to take a steamer to Vera Cruz. At this juncture, Secretary

19. Ellsworth to State Department, June 21, 23, 1913, *ibid.*/7845 (no document number for June 23); Del Valle to State Department, June 23, 27, 1913, *ibid.*/23646, 23648; R. S. Bravo, Consul, Mexico (Eagle Pass) a Secretario de Relaciones Exteriores, June 24, 1913, AGRE, L–E–846, Leg. 1; Maytorena a Carranza, June 18, 1913, in Isidro Fabela (ed.), *Documentos históricos de la Revolución Mexicana* (México, D.F., 1960), I, 88–89.
20. Del Valle to State Department, June 27, 1913, in NA 812.00/23648.

Bryan, apparently unaware of the publicity his agent had received on the border, was pleased with the progress of the mission and decided that Del Valle should continue his investigations beyond Mexico City. President Wilson fully agreed, and Del Valle found new instructions awaiting him in Havana when he arrived there on June 28. He was directed to visit Zapata's stronghold, then to investigate conditions in all the states surrounding the Mexican capital. The note also informed Del Valle of the presence of William Bayard Hale in Mexico City and directed the Californian to confer confidentially with the president's other agent.[21]

Meanwhile, enough of Del Valle's dispatches had reached Washington to give Wilson and Bryan an evaluation of the Constitutionalists. Of all the Mexican leaders who professed sympathy for the Revolution, Del Valle, strangely enough, seemed most favorably impressed with José M. Maytorena, who had gone into self-imposed exile rather than declare himself in rebellion against Huerta. The Californian, however, accepted the former Sonoran governor's excuse for his absence from his state—Maytorena claimed that illness had forced him into exile—and believed that the refugee was sincere in his devotion to the Constitutionalist cause. The special agent was, however, skeptical of the revolutionary ardor of the other two refugee governors he interviewed in Tucson.[22]

Del Valle was also favorably impressed with Sonora's interim governor, Ignacio L. Pesqueira, picturing him as being "greatly liked and respected," a man of "deep convictions," but of only "fair ability." Despite the fact that he interviewed Alvaro Obregón, who was currently winning important military victories over Huerta's armies, the special

21. Bryan to Wilson, June 25, 1913, in Bryan-Wilson Correspondence; Wilson to Bryan, June 27, 1913, in Wilson Papers, Ser. 4, Box 125; Bryan to AmLegation (Havana), June 28, 1913, in NA 812.00/23649a.
22. Del Valle to State Department, June 8, 9, 1913, in NA 812.00/23641, 23642.

agent gave the Sonoran military chieftain only scant notice.[23] Nor did the other rebel leaders in northern Mexico fare very well under Del Valle's critical eye. He characterized Pancho Villa, who controlled most of the Chihuahua countryside, as "a man of very bad repute." [24] But more important, he pictured Venustiano Carranza, the titular leader of the Constitutionalists, as having "personally a good appearance, little ability, narrow, inordinate stubbornness," and as being "inclined to severity, not liked." He added, furthermore, that Carranza was "a detriment to his cause on account of his injudicious leadership." [25] Secretary of State Bryan took special notice of Del Valle's unfavorable impression of the First Chief and, in reporting it to the president, asked if the rebel leader's belligerent attitude might not have resulted from the refusal of the United States to allow the revolutionaries to purchase arms across the border.[26]

If, according to Del Valle, the rebel leaders were not of the highest quality, he did, nevertheless, acknowledge that they held common principles. All professed a filial devotion to the memory of the martyred Madero and a determination never to acknowledge the legality of the Huerta government. Accepting these professions at face value, the special agent also noted that the rebels insisted that Huerta had gained power by fraud and murder and, for that reason, they had revolted in an attempt to restore constitutional government. Only the resignation of the usurper and his cabinet and the

23. Del Valle to State Department, June 17, 19, 1913, *ibid.*/23644, 23645.
24. Del Valle to State Department, June 27, 1913, *ibid.*/23648.
25. *Ibid.;* Del Valle to State Department, June 23, 1913, *ibid.*/23646.
26. Bryan to Wilson, June 25, 1913, in Wilson Papers, Ser. 4, Box 125; copy in William Jennings Bryan Papers, Division of Manuscripts, Library of Congress, Box 43. Since March 14, 1912, the export of arms and munitions from the United States to Mexico had been forbidden by executive order of President Taft and continued by President Wilson. See "Proclamation prohibiting the exportation of arms and munitions of war to Mexico," March 14, 1912, U.S. Department of State, *Papers Relating to the Foreign Relations of the United States, 1912* (Washington, D.C., 1919), 745.

naming of a Constitutionalist as president ad interim would satisfy the rebels, he added. When he asked if they would agree to an armistice, during which time impartial elections could be held, the Constitutionalist leaders all responded that they would never agree to such an arrangement unless Huerta first resigned. To the American agent, moreover, they asserted their determination to fight to the last man and, if necessary, to sacrifice all their worldly possessions for the cause.[27]

Although Del Valle endorsed unhesitatingly the Constitutionalist leaders' sincerity of purpose, he had reservations about the designs of the rank and file of the revolutionary armies. Many of the secondary officials, particularly the guerrilla chieftains, he insisted, were more eager to despoil the substantial property-holders than defeat Huerta. They seemed to take great pleasure in levying forced loans and confiscating private property. Even worse from Del Valle's middle-class point of view, the propertyless were being swayed into joining the revolutionary armies by promises of a general confiscation and redistribution of property. Such promises, plus numerous "incindiary [sic] and socialist publications" which circulated in northern Mexico, had incited many who had little understanding of the Constitutionalist cause to form roving guerrilla bands. Equally distressing, the special agent added, Constitutionalist leaders, including Pesquiera and Carranza, justified the depredations as the only means of financing the rebel war effort. Del Valle lamented that the end result would be the economic desolation of Mexico. In Sonora, Chihuahua, and Coahuila, where the rebels were most active, he had already found that most

27. Del Valle to State Department, June 9, 17, 27, 1913, in NA 812.00/23642, 23644, 23648. Exiled Governor Maytorena was the first to state the purposes of the Constitutionalist revolt, and Del Valle, instead of repeating those principles as they were enunciated by each rebel leader, referred to the statement of Maytorena as being representative of the sentiments of all of the Constitutionalist leaders.

of the banks and commercial houses were closed. Industry was at a standstill, and even the land was not being cultivated. He found conditions in Nuevo León and Tamaulipas slightly better, mainly because the revolutionaries were relatively inactive in those states. The agent also acknowledged thankfully that, for the most part, American-owned property had been spared.[28] Overall it was a grim picture that the special agent painted.

Del Valle's impressions of Zapata and the other revolutionaries in Central Mexico would doubtless have added to the gloomy view of the revolution, but he never got the opportunity to form them firsthand. By the time he reached Mexico City, his mission had become a fiasco. Despite the supposedly secret nature of his activities, the Huerta government and representatives of the press anticipated his arrival. Huerta's chargé d'affaires in Washington, after speaking to Bryan, had reported the nature of the Californian's activities along the border, and the Mexican consul in Eagle Pass, Texas, had reported the agent's conference with Carranza. The context, if not the details, of his conferences in Hermosillo, El Paso, and Piedras Negras were reported in the Mexico City newspapers, along with the agent's itinerary and all the rumors that accompanied his movements. Even before his arrival in the capital city, officials of the provisional government branded the activities of the special agent as "not only officious but injurious to the interests of peace." Since the Constitutionalists were interpreting his visit as a practical recognition of their belligerency, Huerta prophesied that the end result of Del Valle's mission would be the prolonging of the civil war.[29]

28. *Ibid.;* Del Valle to State Department, June 12, 19, 1913, in NA 812.00/23643, 23646.
29. Encargado de Negocios ad-ínterin a Secretario de Relaciones Exteriores, June 12, 1913, AGRE, L–E–786, Leg. 28; R. S. Bravo a Secretario de Relaciones Exteriores, June 24, 1913, *ibid.,* L–E–846, Leg. 1; *El Imparcial,* June 18, July 7, 1913; *Mexican Herald,* June 20, 1913.

Having been preceded by so much publicity, Del Valle was a natural target for reporters when he arrived in Mexico City on July 6. He then compounded his earlier indiscretions by submitting to more interviews, in the course of which he revealed the full nature of his mission. To the reporter of Mexico City's pro-Huerta English-language newspaper, the *Mexican Herald*, for example, Del Valle stated that his purpose was "to obtain all the information possible bearing upon the actual political conditions of the country to lay before President Wilson and Secretary of State Bryan." [30] Other papers repeated this or similar statements, along with the persistent rumor that Del Valle would replace Henry Lane Wilson as ambassador. Not surprisingly, then, the special agent was hounded constantly by newspapermen during his stay in the Mexican capital.[31]

Fearing that the publicity might impair his own mission, William Bayard Hale was annoyed by the excitement that surrounded Del Valle's arrival in Mexico City. The "atmosphere is electric," he wrote to Bryan, and "the possibility of grave indiscretion is distressing." [32] In fact, Bryan himself learned of Del Valle's arrival in Mexico City from the sensational press reports and was angered by his agent's bungling behavior. In an attempt to muzzle the Californian, Bryan wired Del Valle on July 8 "to avoid newspapers and take care not to permit yourself to be considered an official." Closing with stern words of caution, Bryan added that "the success of your mission depends upon this." Even more concerned the next day when he received no reply, Bryan wired Hale to direct Del Valle to call at the telegraph office for a message. A week passed before the Californian replied.

30. *Mexican Herald*, June 8, 1913.
31. *El Diario* (Mexico City), July 7, 1913, enclosed in Henry Lane Wilson to State Department, July 15, 1913 in NA 812.00/8165; *El Imparcial*, July 8, 1913; *Diario del Hogar* (Mexico City), July 9, 1913; *Mexican Herald*, July 9, 10, 1913.
32. Hale to State Department, July 8, 1913, in NA 812.00/23624.

Even then he insisted that he had "emphatically assured" all the Mexicans he had interviewed that he was doing so in a "private capacity." He also suggested that the news releases were purely speculative, probably originating from the provisional government for propaganda purposes.[33]

The arrival of a second special agent in Mexico City drove Ambassador Henry Lane Wilson to adopt extreme measures for his personal defense. Earlier he had attempted to discredit Hale. Bypassing normal State Department channels, he penned a letter directly to the president: "I have assumed that Dr. Hale has no official mission in Mexico and that he is not charged with the making of any report to you concerning conditions in Mexico, but in the event that information should be offered you from this source I deem it my duty, as your personal representative here, to say that this person is by temperament and habit entirely unfit to form a just and clear idea of the situation here." Hale, the ambassador continued, failed completely "to grasp the underlying causes of the unrest in Mexico." In closing, Wilson added that he felt it his duty to make sure that the president was not misled by "the reports of sentimental idealists." [34]

After the arrival of Del Valle, the ambassador's official dispatches grew increasingly caustic. He claimed that he could not protect the interests of Americans because "the presence in Mexico of persons claiming to be representatives of the President are [sic] lowering the dignity of the Embassy and detracting from the respect the Mexican people have been taught to regard it [with] during the last three years." [35] The belligerent ambassador did get to the heart of the matter, however, when he wrote that "the President should

33. State Department to Del Valle, July 8, 1913, *ibid.*/23650a; State Department to Hale, July 9, 1913, *ibid.*/23625; Del Valle to State Department, July 16, 1913, *ibid.*/23651.
34. Ambassador Wilson to President Wilson, July 1, 1913, in Wilson Papers, Ser. 2, Box 94.
35. Wilson to State Department, July 9, 1913, in NA 812.00/7999.

understand that . . . he is now face to face with grave responsibilities which cannot be avoided by a halting or uncertain policy." [36] Such was the tone of the messages that President Wilson found on his desk when he returned to Washington from his holiday in New Hampshire on July 14.

He also found fresh dispatches from Hale, adding new justification for Ambassador Wilson's recall. The special agent reported that Wilson, in collusion with Huerta, was rounding up all possible support in Mexico City in favor of diplomatic recognition of the provisional government. At the same time, Hale insisted, the ambassador was ingratiating himself and blackening the reputation of the Wilson administration in the eyes of American businessmen. Rumor had it, the agent added, that, in speaking to members of the American colony, Ambassador Wilson had referred to the administration in Washington as a "vicious pack of fools." In defending himself, the ambassador had even released to the press a letter of commendation from former President William Howard Taft.[37] Clearly the time for a change had come.

By this time, however, Hale was pleading for more than the mere recall of Henry Lane Wilson. Like the ambassador himself, Hale wanted the administration to adopt a more positive Mexican policy. "We [Americans] are, in spite of ourselves, the guardians of order and justice and decency on this Continent," he wrote to the president: ". . . we are providentially, naturally and inescapably, charged with the maintenance of humanity's interests here. Civilization and humanity look to us, and have a right to look to us, for protection on this Continent." To ensure that he was not misunderstood, Hale added: "This is no argument for intervention in Mexico. Intervention is not necessary. Firm

36. Wilson to State Department, July 11, 1913, *ibid.*/8027.
37. Hale to Davis, July 12, 17, 1913, *ibid.*/23626, 23692; Hale to State Department, July 15, 1913, in Wilson Papers, Ser. 2, Box 94.

representation, politely made, as by a perfectly friendly, yet fully determined and powerful neighbor, would, I believe, save Mexico. To frame the exact plan, to hit upon just the fashion and manner in which the necessary influence can be brought to bear, without involving us too deeply, may take long and hard thought. Then, let the Government of the United States give it that thought. But let it not abandon Mexico." [38]

Indeed, the president had been giving a great deal of thought to the situations in Mexico. Acting quickly upon his return to Washington, President Wilson recalled Ambassador Wilson to Washington for "consultation." Making a clean sweep of his worrisome diplomats, he also recalled Special Agent Del Valle. The Californian was ordered to cease his interviews, slip out of Mexico City quietly, and inform no one of his destination.[39]

Ironically, Wilson and Del Valle returned to the United States aboard the same steamer. Even before their departure, Del Valle called upon the ambassador for an interview. At that time or during the cruise home, the special agent revealed to Ambassador Wilson that he held both the defunct Madero regime and the Constitutionalists in low esteem. Finding themselves in basic agreement, the two deposed diplomats developed a cordial relationship by the time they arrived in New York. Del Valle, Wilson wrote in his memoirs, had "refused to be used by any particular faction" in Mexico and had made a serious effort "to ascertain the truth." [40] Such

38. Hale, Memorandum of Affairs in Mexico, July 9, 1913, in NA 812.00/8203.

39. State Department to Wilson, July 15, 1913, *ibid.*/7743; State Department to Del Valle, July 15, 1913, *ibid.*/23650b.

40. *Mexican Herald*, July 18, 1913; New York *Times*, July 19, 1913, p. 2; Wilson, *Diplomatic Episodes*, 307–308. Upon their return to the United States, rumor also leaked from the State Department that Wilson and Del Valle were in basic agreement on conditions in Mexico and what policy the United States should follow. See New York *Times*, July 27, 1913, II, 2; New York *World*, July 27, 1913. On April 16, 1920, in testimony given before

comments were a far cry from the ambassador's response to Del Valle's arrival in Mexico. His attitude toward Hale, with whom he disagreed, remained implacably hostile.

On July 26 Del Valle called at the Department of State and, after a personal conference with Secretary Bryan, dictated his final report. His summation of conditions in northern Mexico was substantially the same as he had reported earlier. He again acknowledged that the rebel leaders of Sonora and perhaps a thousand men surrounding Carranza were sincere revolutionaries. They were attempting to overthrow a government which they considered to have been established by unconstitutional means. The other rebels in the field, he added, followed "dangerous leaders" who were "pursuing neither the justification of ideals nor . . . any honest motives." Having made only a brief study of conditions in the center of Mexico, Del Valle noted that this type of irresponsible guerrilla activity was present in virtually every state. He acknowledged that the most formidable uprising in the center was that of Emiliano Zapata in the states of Morelos, Guerrero, and Puebla. But Del Valle made the mistake, as other special agents in the future would, of associating Zapata with rebel leaders who had no legitimate aims in view.

Senator Albert B. Fall's subcommittee of the Committee on Foreign Relations, Henry Lane Wilson again praised Del Valle as an unbiased investigator whose opinions resembled his own. See "Investigation of Mexican Affairs," *Senate Documents*, 66th Cong., 2nd Sess., No. 285, pp. 2289–91. In the course of his testimony, Wilson also charged that Secretary of State Bryan had not trusted the reports of William Bayard Hale and had sent Del Valle to Mexico City for the purpose of keeping an eye on Hale. The available evidence indicates that his charge is false, but at least one historical account has perpetuated this view by citing Wilson's testimony. See James Morton Callahan, *American Foreign Policy in Mexican Relations* (New York, 1932), 535. The scholar must use considerable caution in utilizing the testimony contained in the Fall Committee report. The subcommittee conducted its investigations in 1919 and 1920 with the intention of embarrassing President Wilson during his fight for the ratification of the Treaty of Versailles. Most of the witnesses were hostile to the Wilson administration, and the committee's final report condemned the president for his handling of Mexican affairs.

Del Valle also noted that while Huerta was unable to put an end to the guerrilla activities in the countryside, wherever possible he was entrenching himself in power by installing generals as state governors. Huerta and other officials of the provisional government justified their arbitrary rule, Del Valle noted, on the ground that the populace was illiterate and without understanding of the responsibilities of citizenship. What was needed, the officials insisted, was a man like Huerta, who possessed "the iron hand to bring into submission the people who cannot be controlled by any other methods." Then Del Valle allowed his own bourgeois prejudices to creep in, concluding that forceful methods were partially justified, because Mexico did not possess "that powerful middle class which is the backbone of free government."

Although Del Valle obviously had little sympathy for the Mexican revolutionaries, he noted with considerable insight what he considered to be the two basic causes of the current upheaval in Mexico. One was the personal ambitions of politicians, stultified by thirty-five years of Porfirio Díaz's despotic rule, but given free reign by his ouster. More important, once elevated to power, these politicians, especially Madero, found they had made more promises than they could immediately redeem. As a result, they were unable to control the passions they had helped to arouse.[41]

The purpose of Del Valle's mission had been to present the administration with accurate information on conditions in Mexico. Wilson and Bryan solicited no policy recommendations from their agent, nor did he offer any outright. Implied recommendations inevitably crept into his reports. The member of a substantial Spanish-Mexican-American family, Del Valle's sympathies went out to those in Mexico whose status paralleled his own. Thus the impression emerged that the

41. New York *Times*, July 27, 1913, II, 2; Del Valle to Bryan, July [n.d.], 1913, in Wilson Papers, Ser. 2, Box 95.

rebels, with their uncertain leadership and confiscatory methods, were not worthy of support from the United States. If Del Valle's reports implied that the rebels were unworthy of support, they also hinted at the advisability of supporting the Huerta government as a means of promoting order in Mexico. Such tacit recommendations, plus the opinion offered by Hale to the effect that Del Valle should not "be taken seriously as a reporter," [42] placed the Californian in an increasingly unfavorable light with the administration. Del Valle, moreover, continued to exhibit a complete lack of judgment in meeting the press. Even after his return to Washington, Wilson and Bryan repeatedly denied that Del Valle had been serving the administration in any official capacity. When reporters cornered him as he was leaving the State Department building and questioned him personally on this matter, he blurted out the following comment, correcting himself in midstatement: "I cannot talk at this time about my mission to Mexico—that is, as to the purpose of my going there." [43]

His patience worn thin by Del Valle's repeated errors of judgment, the president received even more distressing news concerning his special agent from another Californian, progressive Republican congressman William Kent. Kent revealed that Del Valle was considered a reactionary by progressives in Los Angeles and was said to be a political associate of newspapermen William Randolph Hearst and Harrison Gray Otis, both of whom had extensive property interests in Mexico.[44] Their Los Angeles newspapers—Hearst's *Examiner* and Otis' *Times*—had, of course, been

42. Hale, Memorandum on Affairs in Mexico, July 9, 1913, in NA 812.00/8203.
43. New York *Times*, July 27, 1913, II, 2; New York *World*, June 27, 1913.
44. Edwin T. Earl to William Kent, August 1, 1913, in Wilson Papers, Ser. 4, Box 123. Kent, gravely concerned over American economic exploitation of Latin America, from time to time passed on to Wilson correspondence from his constituents and friends that touched upon the subject, especially when one of the president's agents was involved. He remained one of the few congressional Republicans who sympathized with Wilson's Mexican policy.

booming Del Valle for the position of ambassador to Mexico from the outset of his special mission, and they continued to do so upon his return to the United States.[45]

If Bryan had ever seriously entertained thoughts of appointing Del Valle to the ambassadorship, those notions were now completely dashed. In view of his apparent relationship with Hearst and Otis, the outcome of such an appointment could have proved as disastrous as that of James M. Sullivan—another deserving Democrat with big-business connections—whom Bryan rewarded with an appointment as minister to the Dominican Republic.[46] Whatever Del Valle's affiliations may have been, Wilson and Bryan now suspected him and terminated his services shortly after his return to the United States. By August 4 he was back in Los Angeles singing the praises of the Wilson administration's Mexican policy. He resumed his position on the Los Angeles Public Service Commission and was elected its president, but no longer did the local press hint at ambassadorial possibilities, nor is there any evidence that Wilson or Bryan ever again solicited his advice.[47]

What was the effect of Del Valle's impressions? President Wilson assuredly ignored the agent's implied approval of the Huerta regime. Still, despite the Californian's blundering behavior, the president may not have ignored his negative expressions concerning the revolutionaries. One thing is certain: for three months, while the administration applied

45. Los Angeles *Examiner*, June 10, 11, July 31, 1913; Los Angeles *Times*, June 7, 10, 11, 1913, July 27, 1913. Both Hearst and Otis owned more than a million acres of Mexican agricultural property, while Hearst was also involved in oil and railroad enterprises. For the nature of their holdings, see John Kenneth Turner, *Barbarous Mexico* (Austin, Tex., 1969), 216–17.

46. For the nature of the Sullivan episode in the Dominican Republic, see Link, *New Freedom*, 107–10; Coletta, *Progressive Politician*, 116–19, 196–99; Wilfrid Hardy Callcott, *The Caribbean Policy of the United States, 1890–1920* (Baltimore, 1942), 397–98.

47. New York *Times*, August 5, 1913, p. 3; Los Angeles *Times*, August 6, 1913.

moral pressure on the Huerta regime in an attempt to
promote a change of government that would affect all
Mexicans, it ignored the *Zapatistas* and Constitutionalists.
Wilson made no attempt to secure either their approval of his
policy or their cooperation in carrying it out. Temporarily he
failed to see the revolutionaries as a positive force in Mexican
national affairs.

Meanwhile, both Del Valle and Ambassador Wilson had
been summoned to testify before the Senate Committee on
Foreign Relations. Del Valle was sent packing off to California and did not appear before the committee; Wilson did, and
he used the opportunity to defend his diplomacy and at the
same time to lash out at the president's use of special agents,
who, he insisted, provided misleading information. This
inference that the executive was relying upon the advice of
diplomats who had not been sanctioned by senatorial confir-
mation led members of the Foreign Relations Committee,
ever sensitive to encroachments upon their foreign policy-
making prerogatives, to insist that the agent's reports be
made available for their perusal. Determined to save himself
further embarrassment at the hands of the recalcitrant
ambassador, the president asked for his resignation, which
was duly delivered to the State Department on August 4.[48]

While President Wilson was dispensing with the services of
two of his representatives to Mexico, the one remaining in
Mexico City, William Bayard Hale, continued his barrage of
pessimistic reports. Economic conditions continued to deterio-
rate, he reported. France had announced that she would
provide no more loans, the minister of finance had been
dismissed, and the president of the Mexican National Railway
had resigned in despair. The complete financial collapse of the
Huerta government, Hale believed, was inevitable. Huerta,
nonetheless, was determined to remain in power and threat-

48. New York *Times*, July 31, August 5, 1913, p. 1; New York *World*, July
31, 1913.

ened anyone who hinted at the advisability of his resigning.[49] The time, Hale insisted, was "auspicious for the inauguration of a positive policy in Mexico." "Would you," he inquired of the president, "consider a suggestion?" [50] When no reply was forthcoming from Washington, the special agent proceeded with his own unsolicited recommendations. The responsible American in Mexico, he believed, no longer desired recognition for the Huerta government. The rebels, he added, had done nothing to justify special consideration from the United States. Therefore, the plans for immediate recognition, conditional or otherwise, should be scrapped. Instead, he suggested that the administration state categorically what conditions Mexico must meet for future recognition. These should include free elections and Huerta's self-elimination as a candidate for president. Hale was aware that Henry Lane Wilson had earlier been directed to make such conditions the basis of his negotiations with the provisional government, but he was certain that the ambassador had offered them to Huerta rather "apologetically." Hale then insisted that the administration must make it clear to Huerta that it was prepared to compel such a settlement, but added that he was "inclined to the opinion that only moral determined compulsion would be necessary to carry these points." [51]

A week passed with no response to his suggestions. Meanwhile, Huerta took the initiative to secure an accommodation with the Wilson administration. Certain that Hale was secretly reporting to President Wilson, Huerta sent Hale's friend and recently resigned minister of foreign relations, Francisco de la Barra, to the special agent with a proposition. De la Barra was being sent on a mission to Europe and, en route, was to stop in the United States. Huerta was hopeful of arranging a personal conference for de la Barra with

49. Hale to State Department, July 15, 17, 18, 28, August 5, 1913, in NA 812.00/23627, 23628, 23629, 23633, 23639.
50. Hale to State Department, July 15, 1913, *ibid.*/23627.
51. Hale to State Department, July 17, 1913, *ibid.*/23629.

President Wilson, at which the Mexican diplomat could hopefully present a persuasive case for recognition. Hale earnestly recommended that the president meet with de la Barra, but not for the reasons Huerta envisioned. Hale believed that the conference would afford Wilson an excellent opportunity to personally apply his moral suasion and impress upon the usurper's representative the necessity of accepting the previously recommended prerequisites for future recognition. Wilson declined to meet with de la Barra, because he had already decided to send another special agent to Mexico City to carry out Hale's recommendations.[52]

52. Hale to State Department, July 24, 29, 1913, *ibid.*/23632, 23634; State Department to Hale, August 1, 1913, *ibid.*/23634.

CHAPTER IV

The First Rebuff

By the end of July, 1913, President Wilson had decided to follow William Bayard Hale's advice to eliminate Huerta and to aid in establishing a new government in Mexico City by applying "moral determined compulsion." The procedure that he had decided upon, one which was endorsed by several business firms with interests in Mexico, was based on a plan proposed earlier by Judge J. D. Haff of Kansas City.[1] Wilson must have been aware that adoption of the Haff plan might place him in a compromising position. Months before, on March 11, he had declared that his administration would not support special interests in Latin America.[2] There was, moreover, a growing conviction among his advisors that economic support by industrial concessionaires, especially British oil interests, was all that sustained Huerta's power.[3] Adoption of the Haff plan, therefore, might later be construed as a move by the president to support one group of special interests against another.

1. Judge Haff's plan, which was endorsed by the Southern Pacific Railroad, Phelps Dodge and Company, the Greene Cananea Copper Company, and the Mexican Petroleum Company, is outlined above in Chapter II, pp. 33–34.

2. New York *Times*, March 12, 1913, p. 1; Baker, *Woodrow Wilson*, IV, 64–67.

3. Houston, *Eight Years With Wilson's Cabinet*, 69, 73–74; Cronon (ed.), *Cabinet Diaries of Josephus Daniels*, 43–44; Haff to Wilson, May 12, 1913, in NA 812.00/7576. Judge Haff, in submitting his plan to the president, had insisted that British oil interests were primarily responsible for propping up the Huerta regime.

Determined that his policy should not perpetuate "dollar diplomacy," Wilson resolved that his plan be carried out in a disinterested manner by a special agent who sympathized with New Freedom ideals and had absolutely no connection with business concessionaires. John Lind of Minnesota was such a man. In fact, Lind insisted that he was chosen for the mission for no other reason than the fact that he had never been associated with concessionaires or any other kind of interest in Mexico. Other than this, he had no obvious qualifications as an emissary to the republic south of the border. He did not speak Spanish, he knew nothing of Mexican affairs, and he had no previous diplomatic experience. He did offer what Wilson and Bryan considered a most important qualification: he was a loyal progressive Democrat.[4]

A politician most of his adult life, Lind shared many of the beliefs, anxieties, and other characteristics common to reformers of the Progressive era. Only the fact that he was a Swedish immigrant prevented him from completely fitting the urban, middle-class, Anglo-Saxon, Protestant, Progressive stereotype. Arriving in the United States in 1868, Lind was reared on a Minnesota farm. But like so many other midwestern Progressives, he spent much of his adult life in the city, practicing law and engaging in public affairs. Seeking to emulate his childhood hero, Abraham Lincoln, Lind began his political career as a Republican. He served

4. Testimony of William F. Buckley, December 6, 1919, and John Lind, April 27, 1920, *Senate Documents*, 66th Cong., 2nd Sess., No. 285, pp. 767–814, 2318; Interview with Lind, November 12, 1919, in William F. Buckley Manuscripts, Latin American Collection, University of Texas; "John Lind as a Strong Personality," *American Review of Reviews*, XLVIII (September, 1913), 281. Buckley, a lawyer and speculator in Mexican real estate and oil leases, served as counsel for the Huerta delegation at the Niagara Falls Conference, arranged by Argentina, Brazil, and Chile to settle disputes growing out of the American military intervention at Vera Cruz in April, 1914. He was openly hostile to Wilson's Mexican policy, and he acknowledged that Lind was chosen as the president's agent because of his complete lack of association with any interests in Mexico.

three successive terms in Congress between 1887 and 1893. During that time he became increasingly dissatisfied with his party's failure to check the domineering and corruptive tendencies of big business, and before he retired from Congress he had earned the reputation of a reformer of unimpeachable honesty. Supporting such measures as pure food laws, forfeiture of unused lands by the railroads, a more effective Interstate Commerce Commission, and the Sherman Antitrust Act, he won repeated endorsements from Minnesota's Farmers' Alliance and was wooed by the People's party. Although he was alienated by the Populists' jeremiads and by their reliance on panaceas, he nonetheless endorsed William Jennings Bryan for president in 1896 and became an undying supporter of the Great Commoner for the remainder of his political life.[5]

Having bolted the Republican party, Lind accepted support of reform Democrats and Populists while contesting unsuccessfully for the Minnesota governorship in 1896. But in 1898 he embellished his domestic reform appeal with ardent support for America's righteous war against Spain and with his equally outspoken criticism of the Republicans' postwar imperialism. With fusion support, and now calling himself a Democrat, he was elected governor. At the beginning of his term, he called for a thoroughgoing reform program, including: tax reform; expansion of the activities of the state correctional and charitable institutions; stricter antitrust laws; reservation for the state of mineral rights on lands disposed of in the future; and direct democracy devices, such as the direct primary, initiative, and referendum. The noted reformer-economist Richard T. Ely was moved to characterize Lind's proposed program as "the epitome of the drift of opinion of those who truly had the public welfare at heart."

5. George M. Stephenson, *John Lind of Minnesota* (Minneapolis, 1935), 3–117; John D. Hicks, "The People's Party in Minnesota," *Minnesota History*, V (November, 1924), 555–59; Carl H. Chrislock, "A Cycle of the History of Minnesota Republicanism," *Minnesota History*, XXXIX (Fall, 1964), 102–103.

Like Wilson's later New Freedom, Lind dedicated his program to freeing politics and business from the grip of special interests; but he faced an obstructionist legislature throughout his term and secured few reforms. His administration, nonetheless, served as a harbinger of progressivism in Minnesota.[6]

Swept out of office by the Republican landslide of 1900, Lind remained a powerful force in Minnesota politics. He was again elected to Congress in 1902 but retired voluntarily after one term. Thereafter he served actively in Minneapolis civic affairs and as a member of the board of regents of the University of Minnesota. He campaigned actively for Bryan in all his presidential bids. Although he was wooed by the Bull Moose party in 1912, he remained a loyal Democrat and was instrumental in securing a Minnesota delegation that supported Woodrow Wilson at the Democratic National Convention. Following the election, he was called to Washington to discuss policy and patronage with his old friend, secretary of state–designate Bryan, and with Wilson's personal advisor, Colonel Edward House.[7]

Lind himself was an obvious candidate for appointment. Indeed, he declined the ambassadorship to Sweden because he did not think it ethical for a Swedish immigrant to serve in that post. Being the most popular Democrat in Minnesota, he also declined to serve as assistant secretary of the interior, because neither he nor his friends thought the position adequate for one of his political status.[8] Thus politics and personal scruples combined to make the Minnesota Progressive available for the more publicly noteworthy mission to Mexico.

6. Stephenson, *John Lind*, 133–78; Russel B. Nye, *Midwestern Progressive Politics* (East Lansing, Mich., 1959), 214–15.
7. Stephenson, *John Lind*, 180–206, 348–50.
8. Wilson to Lind, June 11, 1913, and Lind to Wilson, June 12, 1913, in Wilson Papers, Ser. 4, Box 285; Congressman W. S. Hammond (Minnesota) to Lind, June 23, 1913, in John Lind Papers, Minnesota Historical Society, St. Paul, Minnesota.

Lind's Scandinavian ancestry was reflected in his blue eyes
and gray-flecked sandy hair. Tall and slender, with a tousled,
unkempt appearance and gaunt features, he was described by
the wife of the American chargé d'affaires in Mexico City as
"Lincolnesque." [9] His earlier reputation for unimpeachable
honesty persisted in 1913, and he was considered an impatient
man of action. Although he had a nervous habit of tapping on
the stump of his left wrist to emphasize a point—his hand had
been amputated after a boyhood hunting accident—he was
noted for his cool, forthright manner of meeting problems
under pressure. As President Wilson noted in a letter to his
wife: "Lind . . . is just the well balanced sort not to be
disquieted by what goes on about him." [10]

With no warning, on July 28 Lind received a telegram
from Bryan asking him to come to Washington for "consultation" on a confidential matter of great importance. Bryan
revealed only that Lind should come prepared to remain for
several weeks. Thus Lind was completely unaware of the
purpose of his call to service until he arrived in Washington
on August 1. He received only two days of briefing before
setting out for Mexico.[11]

Future events revealed that Lind shared his president's
belief that the United States had a tutelary role to perform in
Latin America. Otherwise he would not likely have undertaken the mission that Wilson had laid out for him. Wilson
assumed that Huerta and the Mexican people would sub-

9. Edith O'Shaughnessy, *A Diplomat's Wife in Mexico* (New York, 1916),
3.
10. "John Lind as a Strong Personality," *American Review of Reviews*,
XLVIII, 281; "The Week: Mexico," *The Nation*, XCVII (August 7, 1913), 112;
"Mexico: What Does Mediation Mean?" *Outlook*, CIV (August 16, 1913), 833;
New York *Times*, August 5, 1913, p. 3; Eleanor Wilson McAdoo (ed.), *The
Priceless Gift: The Love Letters of Woodrow Wilson and Ellen Axson Wilson*
(New York, 1962), 295.
11. Bryan to Lind, July 28, 29, 1913, in Lind Papers; Bryan to Wilson,
July 31, 1913, in Bryan-Wilson Correspondence; Testimony of Lind, *Senate
Documents*, 66th Cong., 2nd Sess., No. 285, pp. 2317–18.

merge their nationalism temporarily and accept a change of government dictated by the United States, because that is precisely what Wilson's personally prepared instructions to Lind called for. The special agent was to inform Huerta that: "The Government of the United States does not feel at liberty any longer to stand inactively by while it becomes daily more and more evident that no real progress is being made towards the establishment of a government at the City of Mexico which the country will obey and respect." He was then to dictate terms which Mexico should follow in establishing an acceptable government:

> (a) An immediate cessation of fighting throughout Mexico—a definite armistice solemnly entered into and scrupulously observed;
> (b) Security given for an early and free election in which all will agree to take part;
> (c) The consent of General Huerta to bind himself not to be a candidate for election as President of the Republic at this election;
> (d) The agreement of all parties to abide by the results of the election and cooperate in the most loyal way in organizing and supporting the new administration.

Lind was then to offer American aid in arranging such a settlement and to promise diplomatic recognition for the regime thus established. Perhaps Wilson's naivete was most evident in the last paragraph of Lind's instructions (a closing statement that Huerta would later use in order to ignore Wilson's tacit ultimatum and offer a countersolution): "If Mexico can suggest any better way in which to show our friendship, serve the people of Mexico, and meet our international obligations, we are more than willing to consider the suggestion." [12]

John Lind was an ambassador in every respect except name. He was invested with full power to negotiate with the

12. Instructions (Mexico), in Lind Papers; draft of instructions prepared on President Wilson's portable typewriter, in Wilson Papers, Ser. 3, Box 95.

head of state in Mexico City and was granted an ambassador's salary, but he could not be given the title since that would constitute diplomatic recognition of the Huerta government.[13] Instead, he bore a letter designating him as the "personal representative" of the president and "advisor to the Embassy." [14] In dispatching their third agent, Wilson and Bryan consulted no one—neither Huerta, the Constitutionalists, nor the Senate of the United States. On the day of Lind's departure from Washington, Bryan informed the embassy in Mexico City simultaneously of Ambassador Wilson's resignation and of the special agent's impending arrival. Everyone else, Huerta included, was informed by a State Department press release issued the same day.[15]

Neither the State Department's message to Mexico City nor its press release offered the slightest hint of the mission's purpose, but a security leak from within the administration resulted in the publication of garbled versions of Lind's instructions. From these press comments, the impression invariably emerged that Lind had been sent to force the immediate resignation of Huerta and that he would then direct the formation of a new provisional government in which the Constitutionalists would participate.[16]

Sensing that to defy the United States would add stature to his faltering regime, Huerta quickly exploited the rumor-clouded situation by launching a series of verbal blasts at the policy of the Wilson administration. He whipped the people of

13. Bryan to Lind, August 5, 1913, in Lind Papers. In this note, Bryan informed Lind that he would receive an ambassador's salary—$17,500—while serving in Mexico.

14. Letter, To Whom It May Concern, August 4, 1913, in Lind Papers.

15. State Department to American chargé d'affaires, Mexico City, August 4, 1913, in *Foreign Relations, 1913*, 817–18; New York *Times*, August 4, 1913, p. 1.

16. New York *Times*, August 5, 10, 1913, p. 1; New York *World*, August 5, 1913. Similar versions of Lind's instructions also appeared in the Mexico City press. See *Mexican Herald*, August 6, 1913; *El Imparcial*, August 6, 1913.

the capital city into a patriotic frenzy by announcing that he would refuse any mediation offers by the United States, declaring that "national dignity and decorum will not brook interference by outside parties." [17] Besieged by reporters, and knowing no more than they about the true nature of Lind's mission, American chargé d'affaires Nelson O'Shaughnessy frantically cabled Washington for authority to deny the rumors. Denial was necessary, he reported, since the populace of the capital city was so aroused by Huerta's comments that the governor of the federal district had come to the embassy, warning that Lind might be mobbed at the railway station when he arrived. The only explanation Bryan allowed O'Shaughnessy to give was that Lind came on a "mission of peace" and that the "misrepresentations of sensational newspapers" should be ignored.[18] With this reply, the chargé could not quell the excitement that Huerta had provoked.

His prestige on the rise, Huerta ignored the conciliatory tone of Bryan's note and directed his foreign minister to reply that if "Mr. Lind . . . does not properly establish his official character or if he is not the bearer of recognition of this government by yours, his sojourn in this Republic will not be pleasing." When the text of this note was splashed across the headlines in Mexico City, anti-Americanism intensified. In their exuberance to support Huerta's nationalism, representatives of the press condemned the sending of a special agent instead of an ambassador, insisting that this action was designed by Wilson to make the Mexican nation appear inferior. The most vehement columnists insisted that Lind be expelled as *persona non grata*. Special agent Hale, who was still in Mexico City, noted that informed Mexicans were comparing the Lind Mission to the indignities suffered by the

17. *Mexican Herald*, August 6, 1913; *El Imparcial*, August 6, 1913.
18. O'Shaughnessy to State Department, August 5, 1913, and State Department to O'Shaughnessy, August 6, 1913, in *Foreign Affairs, 1913*, 818.

United States in the Citizen Genét and Sackville-West incidents.[19]

Retaining his righteous plane, Wilson retorted that he was fully within his rights in sending an "advisor to the Embassy" and was certain that the provisional government would not regard the nature of Lind's mission as unfriendly.[20] Huerta, having defended the dignity of the nation, could now magnanimously offer guarantees for Lind's safety. His minister of government issued a directive outlawing violent demonstrations, while the minister of foreign affairs issued a statement to the effect that Lind, like any other foreigner, could travel freely in Mexico, but that he would be treated as a private citizen and accorded no special consideration.[21]

Lind's arrival in Vera Cruz on August 9 served to heighten the tension. The fact that he had journeyed to Mexico aboard a battleship lent credence to rumors that ascribed a punitive character to his mission. The crowd that gathered when Lind debarked demonstrated no outward signs of hostility; nevertheless, a troop of policemen was on hand to guard the envoy.[22] After spending the night in the port city, the Linds journeyed to Mexico City. Concurrent with their arrival, the

19. O'Shaughnessy to State Department, August 7, 1913, in NA 812.00/10637; Hale to State Department, August 7, 1913, *ibid.*/23636; *Mexican Herald*, August 7, 1913; *El Imparcial*, August 7, 1913; *El Independiente* (Mexico City), August 7, 1913.

20. State Department to O'Shaughnessy, August 8, 1913, in NA 812.00/10637.

21. O'Shaughnessy to State Department, August 8, 9, 1913, *ibid.*/8274, 8276; *El Imparcial*, August 10, 1913.

22. *El Imparcial*, August 10, 1913; *El País* (Mexico City), August 10, 1913; Washington *Times*, August 11, 1913, in Wilson Papers, Ser. 2, Box 95; William W. Canada (American consul, Vera Cruz) to State Department, August 14, 1913, in NA 812.00/8536. Wilson had intended for his agent to catch a commercial steamer from New Orleans. When the Linds arrived at that city, no ship was scheduled to sail. Wishing to avoid delay, Wilson wired Lind to proceed to Galveston, Texas, where the battleship *New Hampshire* waited to take him to Vera Cruz. See Bryan to Lind, August 5, 1913, in Lind Papers; Lind to State Department, August 6, 7, 1913, in NA 812.00/8250, 8251.

government staged a pro-Huerta demonstration in another
part of the city. Evidencing a lack of concern, Lind, in
addressing reporters at the railway station, revealed a talent
for diplomacy that would characterize the early phase of his
mission. He assured them that he had in no way been
menaced and was gracious in his praise of Mexican hospital-
ity. "All the Mexican authorities [with whom] I have come in
touch," he announced, "have treated me with the courtesy
which is characteristic of Latins." [23]
    Actually, Lind had been well coached. Bryan had ordered
Hale to greet the new agent at Vera Cruz. The two met
aboard ship and conferred for some time before going ashore.
Since neither spoke Spanish, Bryan directed the American
consul at Vera Cruz, William W. Canada, to accompany the
two agents to Mexico City and offer his advice. Thus, when
Lind arrived in the capital, he was fully abreast of the
situation and knew what behavior might have the best effect.
He and Hale agreed that conditions in the Mexican capital
were potentially explosive and that if Wilson's demands were
presented immediately, aroused public opinion might force a
negative reply. Lind, therefore, requested that the nature of
his instructions be kept a secret temporarily. Meanwhile, Lind
remained close to Hale, residing at the latter's hotel, the
Lascuráin, before moving to the embassy on August 13. Not
surprisingly, the two agents, finding that they held many
views in common, became fast friends and confidants, and
each praised the efforts of the other to Washington.[24]
    Wilson accepted the advice of his agents and directed Lind

23. *Mexican Herald*, August 11, 1913; Canada to State Department,
August 14, 1913, in NA 812.00/8536.
24. State Department to O'Shaughnessy, August 8, 1913, and State
Department to Lind, August 8, 1913, in NA 812.00/10637; State Department
to Canada, August 8, 1913, *ibid.*/8265a; Canada to State Department, August
14, 1914, *ibid.*/8536; Lind to State Department, August 28, 1913, *ibid.*/10487;
Bryan to Tumulty, August 8, 1913, in Wilson Papers, Ser. 4, Box 48; Hale to
State Department, August 20, 1913, *ibid.*, Ser. 2, Box 96; Lind to Bryan,
[n.d.], in Lind Papers; *El Imparcial*, August 10, 1913; *El País*, August 10,
1913.

to withhold the proposals until he received further instructions. Meanwhile, Lind was to report on conditions as he found them.[25] The president had reason to pause. He had not anticipated the intensity of the criticism provoked by the Lind mission. Not only had the agent's coming caused a furor in Mexico, but most of the governments which had recognized Huerta also expressed dismay. Their diplomats regarded the mission with "merriment," prophesied failure, and were not the least inhibited from saying so publicly.[26] Republicans in the Senate also seized the opportunity to embarrass the president. Condemning this most recent use of an "unofficial" emissary, Clarence D. Clark of Wyoming introduced a resolution calling for a Senate investigation of the administration's Mexican policy. With Albert B. Fall of New Mexico and Boies Penrose of Pennsylvania supporting the resolution, Democrat Augustus Bacon of Georgia, chairman of the Committee on Foreign Relations, succeeded only through parliamentary maneuvering in placing it at the bottom of the calendar.[27]

While President Wilson collected his thoughts, Lind busied himself by touring the city and meeting various members of the foreign colony and diplomatic corps. He had several callers at the Hotel Lascuráin and received numerous telegrams, letters, and petitions from members of the diplomatic corps, well-wishers, and cranks, as well as from friends and enemies of Huerta. A model of discretion throughout these early days of his mission, he remained placid and cordial but refused to discuss the nature of his instructions with anyone except Hale. He would reveal only that President Wilson's policy was designed to restore peace to Mexico and that it was animated by an honest and sincere desire to render assistance.[28]

25. State Department to Lind, August 10, 1913, in NA 812.00/8247a.
26. New York *Times*, August 5, 1913, p. 2.
27. *Congressional Record*, 63rd Cong., 1st Sess., 3133, 3171–76; New York *Times*, August 7, 1913, p. 3; *ibid.*, August 8, 9, 1913, p. 2.
28. *Mexican Herald*, August 10–13, 1913; New York *Times*, August 10–13, 1913, p. 1; New York *World*, August 13, 1913.

Huerta, despite his earlier bombastic statements, was anxious to reach some accord with the United States and therefore looked forward to seeing Lind reveal the purpose of his mission. The old general now felt that in any negotiations he would be able to deal from a strong position. No doubt he had strengthened his hand in the national capital as a result of his nationalistic pronouncements against outside interference in Mexican internal affairs. Although the financial condition of his government was rapidly deteriorating, his armies were victorious in the field. In early August they captured Zapata's headquarters at Cuautla, and the campaign in the South seemed to be gaining momentum. The federal armies controlled the Northeast and had repulsed Carranza's army at Torreón in the center and Obregón's at Guaymas in the West. Despite Huerta's lack of religious fervor, the Church and the powerful Catholic party supported him because his regime seemed to promise law and order.[29] Lind, therefore, met no resistance when he sought unofficial talks.

Although Lind later had an interview with Huerta, the agent carried on actual negotiations with Foreign Minister Federico Gamboa. Gamboa had just been recalled from his post as minister to Belgium and had arrived in Mexico almost simultaneously with Lind. The career diplomat's new appointment resulted primarily from Huerta's latest move to eliminate the *Felicistas* from his cabinet; it may have also been conditioned by the fact that Gamboa was the scion of the Catholic party, with which the old usurper wished to solidify his relationship.[30] At any rate, the choice was fortunate for the provisional government. Gamboa proved a stubborn but skillful negotiator.

29. Barragán Rodríguez, *Historia . . . de la Revolución Constitucionalista*, I, 150, 196–209; González Ramírez, *Las Ideas—La Violencia*, 404; Womack, *Zapata*, 173–76; Meyer, *Huerta*, 169.

30. *Mexican Herald*, August 7, 1913; Peter Calvert, *The Mexican Revolution, 1910–1914: The Diplomacy of Anglo-American Conflict* (Cambridge, England, 1968), 41–42, 204–205.

Accompanied by O'Shaughnessy, Lind called at the foreign ministry for preliminary talks on August 12. Gamboa was conciliatory. He assured the American agent that the provisional government would give "earnest consideration" to President Wilson's suggestions and urged Lind to reveal the exact nature of his mission as soon as possible, preferably the next day. But he also intimated that no suggestions would be considered that did not include provisions for recognition. Lind, in reply, explained the "spirit" of his instructions, adding that he was certain that President Wilson "did not contemplate recognition under existing circumstances." [31]

The fact that Lind and Gamboa were able to conduct cordial conversations eased much of the tension surrounding the Minnesotan's mission. Encouraged by this meeting, the next day President Wilson personally drafted new instructions for Lind, directing him to present the proposals to Gamboa. At the same time, he was to emphasize that the United States, having "canvassed" the world powers, was certain that she had "the sympathy and moral support of the governments of Europe." Lind was also to point up to Gamboa that the United States was "offering Mexico the only possible plan by which she may find a way out of her difficulties and avoid worse ones." Failure to comply fully, Wilson added, would be interpreted as a refusal by Huerta to abide by the agreements he made upon assuming power, especially the one calling for early elections.[32]

Wilson persisted in interpreting the terms of the Pact of the Embassy as he saw fit. He assumed that the portion calling for early elections meant that they should have been held in a matter of weeks after the signing of the pact. On

31. Lind to State Department, August 12, 1913, in NA 812.00/8314; New York *World*, August 13, 1913; *Mexican Herald*, August 13, 1913; New York *Times*, August 13, 1913, p. 1.

32. State Department to Lind, August 13, 1913, in NA 812.00/15335a. The note, which was drafted by Wilson on his personal typewriter, was sent under Bryan's signature.

May 13, 1913, the Mexican Congress had, indeed, passed a law calling for elections on October 26 that same year. Huerta, assuming that he would reach the peak of his power in July, had wanted the elections to be held at that time, but his opponents in the Congress succeeded in postponing them. Wilson seemed ignorant of the fact that elections had been called.[33]

Wilson was bluffing when he claimed European support for his demands. On August 8 the Department of State had sent a circular note to the foreign representatives in Washington, urging their governments' cooperation in obtaining a favorable hearing for the president's proposals. Without knowing what Wilson's exact intentions were, all they could have done was what Great Britain did. Foreign Secretary Edward Grey directed his minister in Mexico City, Francis William Stronge, to "unofficially" indicate to the Mexican government that a refusal to at least hear the proposals of Washington would be a "grave mistake." No nation exerted pressure for the acceptance of Wilson's demands.[34]

Lind was struck by the international implications of his latest instructions. Unaware that Bryan had made representations to the foreign powers, the special agent was reluctant to present Wilson's demands as representing the will of other nations. From what information he had gathered, he reported to Washington that it appeared to him that his mission was "considered an unwarranted attempt to dictate in the conduct of Mexican domestic affairs." Gravely concerned over the impression that would result from an outright refusal of his demands, Lind inquired of the secretary of state what

33. Vera Estañol, *La Revolución Mexicana,* 325–26; George Jay Rausch, Jr., "Victoriano Huerta: A Political Biography," (Ph.D. dissertation, University of Illinois, 1960), 110–11; copy of election law in O'Shaughnessy to State Department, September 3, 1913, in NA 812.00/8779.

34. State Department to the representatives of certain foreign powers, August 8, 1913, in NA 812.00/8284a; Calvert, *Diplomacy of Anglo-American Conflict,* 204; Grieb, *United States and Huerta,* 97–98.

course he should pursue if this occurred. Paradoxically, Lind, with his doubts, suggested also that if he was to present the president's proposals they should be delivered as an ultimatum, with a four-day time limit set for the Mexican minister's final reply. Mistakenly assuming that delay would give other nations time to exert pressure for acceptance, Wilson and Bryan refused to fix a time limit for the answer and offered Lind no advice on future moves until they received Huerta's response.[35]

Without knowing how much, if any, foreign support Wilson's proposals would receive, Lind delivered them to Gamboa on August 15, and waited while the minister read the memorandum. His attention drawn to the last paragraph, Gamboa quickly informed Lind that this passage offered Mexico justification for submitting a counterproposal. He also pointed out that nothing in the document justified the American agent's earlier insistence that recognition was out of the question. He then questioned the good will professed in the document, insisting that the United States encouraged strife in Mexico by sympathizing with the revolutionaries and by not strictly enforcing the arms embargo. Noting the recent debate in the United States Senate, Gamboa also suggested that the proposals did not represent the will of the American people.

In reply, Lind evidenced none of the doubts he had earlier expressed to Washington. He dodged the matter of a counterproposal, but he emphasized that the president's memorandum "implied the impossibility of recognition." He insisted, moreover, that the United States had not sympathized knowingly with the rebels and that the patrol of the border exceeded international requirements. But he was most determined in warning that Mexico should never interpret one Senate debate as evidence of division among the people of the

35. Lind to State Department, August 13, 1913, and State Department to Lind, August 14, 1913, in NA 812.00/8334.

United States. The American people would support their
president, he asserted, even to the extent of armed intervention. Veiling his threat somewhat, Lind went on to explain
that this frightening prospect had prompted his president to
offer his proposed peace settlement. Both diplomats then
agreed that the content of the memorandum should remain
an absolute secret, and Gamboa promised to reply the next
day. Wilson was heartened by Lind's report of the conversation and congratulated his emissary for his conduct, especially
for emphasizing the unity of the American people.[36]

Wilson's optimism was short-lived. On August 16, through
Chargé O'Shaughnessy, Gamboa delivered a lengthy formal
reply in which he refused to accede to any of the president's
conditions. The note was so polished—"suave," as Lind put
it—and polite that the minister's veiled sarcasm was seldom
offensive. Gamboa reiterated to Lind, whom he referred to as
"Mr. Confidential Agent," all the earlier points he had made
concerning recognition and, at the same time, declared as
"unfounded" Wilson's charge that no progress was being
made toward the establishment of a government in Mexico
City which enjoyed the Mexican people's "respect and obedience." In answer he proclaimed with some exaggeration that
twenty-two of twenty-seven states, all three territories, and
the Federal District were under the "absolute control of the
present government." Wilson, he continued, "is laboring
under a serious delusion when he declares that the present
situation of Mexico is incompatible with the compliance with
her international obligations." Other nations, he counseled,
had seen fit to extend diplomatic recognition, tender loans,
and even continue investing in Mexican industry.

After defending the legality and stability of the provisional government, Gamboa explained why none of Wilson's
proposals could be accepted. As if counseling on a point of

<hr/>

36. Lind to State Department, [n.d. (received August 15, 1913)], and State
Department to Lind, August 15, 1913, in NA 812.00/10639.

international law, he emphasized that "Bandits [the revolu-
tionaries], Mr. Confidential Agent, are not admitted into
armistice . . . Were we to agree with them to the armistice
suggested this would, *ipso facto*, recognize their belligerency."
The request that General Huerta should agree not to appear
as a candidate for the presidency, he insisted, "cannot be
taken into consideration . . . This point can be decided only
by Mexican public opinion." The pledge that all parties agree
beforehand to the results of the election and support the
government thus established, he acknowledged, was something to be desired. But his government could not speak for
the rebels. Having refused Wilson's propositions, Gamboa,
referring to the last paragraph of Wilson's memorandum,
offered Huerta's counterproposal: "One, that our Ambassador
be received in Washington; two, that the United States of
America send us a new ambassador without previous conditions." [37] No compromise was suggested.

Rejection apparently had never seriously entered Wilson's
thoughts. His administration was totally unprepared for that
eventuality. Lind was given no new instructions or guidance
for his future relations with the provisional government. In
the face of Washington's silence, Lind seized the initiative.
On August 18, two days after Gamboa delivered his reply, the
American agent again confronted the foreign minister. He
warned Gamboa that the rejection "was a grave and perilous
step." For Mexico to "hope for a division among the American people along partisan lines . . . was utterly futile." When
President Wilson, he continued, is "compelled to communicate
to the Congress and to the American people . . . all the
incidents accompanying the change of government, no American in or out of public life would dare to publicly defend the
character of the present government." Rejection of the

37. Gamboa to Lind, August 16, 1913, in *Foreign Relations, 1913*, 823–27;
Spanish original in Estados Unidos Mexicanos, Poder Ejecutivo, Secretario
de Relaciones Exteriores, *Diario Official*, CXXVII (August 27, 1913), 2–4;
Lind to Wilson, August 17, 1913, in Wilson Papers, Ser. 2, Box 95.

president's proposal, he further warned, left the United
States with three options: one, to alter the neutrality laws to
allow Mexicans to purchase arms in the United States; two,
to recognize the belligerency of the revolutionaries; and
three, armed intervention by the United States. Gamboa
would only reply that he thought President Wilson would
modify his views after he had an opportunity to read the full
text of his rejection note.[38]

Still having received no new directions from Washington,
on August 19 Lind, aided by Minister Stronge of Great
Britain, arranged a meeting with Huerta. The interview did
nothing more than give the general an opportunity to boast
of the imminent pacification of the country and to outline his
plans for future reforms. Huerta also indicated that he was
anxious for the negotiations to continue. Of more signif-
icance, the day following the interview Minister Stronge,
having just come from Huerta, called on Lind to relate the
general's impressions of the previous night's meeting. For
days Stronge had been impressing upon Lind that, in the
interests of peace and stability in Mexico, the United States
should extend diplomatic recognition to the Huerta regime.
This day, in the course of their conversation, Stronge stated
unofficially that he believed that a "working agreement"
could be arranged with Huerta if the State Department
would urge American bankers to extend the provisional

---

38. Lind to State Department, August 18, 1913, in NA 812.00/24649; Lind
to State Department, [n.d.], in Lind Papers. The latter citation is a draft of a
telegraphic message sent between August 16 and 19. The original is not to be
found in the State Department files. Several of the messages Lind sent
between August 16 and 29 are missing. They apparently were received in
Washington, because the department's Index Bureau assigned them document numbers; but they are absent from the files. In cases where there is a
draft in the Lind Papers and corresponding original in the department files,
they are identical in their wording. The drafts for which there is no
department copy, therefore, appear to be accurate and are invaluable in
recreating what otherwise seems to be an inexplicable series of events.

government a loan. Lind thought the proposal worthy of consideration and reported it to Washington.[39]

Bryan was intrigued by the loan proposal. Ignoring the inconsistency of having denied State Department support for bankers' loans to China,[40] the secretary of state had recently come to the conclusion that such loans, by promoting economic stability in Latin America, might further political stability. American loans were certainly preferable to loans from other foreign sources. He urged Wilson, therefore, to consider seriously Lind's suggestion. Only a loan "sufficient to meet the temporary requirements of the *de facto* government" would be necessary. After all, he pointed out, "some government is necessary—without it elections could not be held." In conclusion he suggested that the offer should be conditioned on acceptance of the president's original proposals.[41]

While Wilson and Bryan pondered their next step, Gamboa attempted to seize the initiative. On August 21, he called upon Lind and informed the special agent that he desired to travel to Washington in order to meet personally with President Wilson. He was positive that he could alter the president's attitude. Lind's first impulse was to believe that

39. Lind to State Department, [n.d.], in Lind Papers; Lind to State Department, August 20, 1913, in Wilson Papers, Ser. 2, Box 95.

40. Wilson and Bryan reversed a policy adopted by the Taft administration whereby the State Department supported American participation in an international banking consortium loan to China. They took the position that the terms of the loan seemed to be an impingement on China's administrative independence. See Link, *New Freedom,* 283–86; Roy Watson Curry, *Woodrow Wilson and Far Eastern Policy, 1913–1921* (New York, 1957), 18–27.

41. Bryan to Wilson, [n.d.], in Wilson Papers, Ser. 2, Box 96. Actually, Bryan would have preferred a policy of having the United States government extend loans to Latin American nations at $4\frac{1}{2}$ percent interest, the money to be secured by selling 3-percent bonds. Wilson did not believe the Congress or the American people would condone such a "novel and radical proposal" and rejected the scheme. As an alternative, Bryan looked to bankers' loans. See Link, *New Freedom,* 330–31; Paolo Coletta, "Bryan, Anti-Imperialism and Missionary Diplomacy," *Nebraska History,* XLIV (September, 1968), 179.

Gamboa was sincere, but he counseled that Huerta might be stalling for time.[42] Although Lind only suspected it, stalling was precisely what Huerta had in mind. He was near to consummating a loan with Mexican bankers. The funds, he hoped, would enable him to crush the revolutionaries and leave Wilson no alternative but to extend diplomatic recognition of his regime.[43]

The ruse did not work. Wilson refused to budge an inch. In his first positive move in days, he instructed Lind to inform Gamboa that he would be received unofficially in the United States only if his reply to the initial proposals was withdrawn and if he came with the understanding that the attitude of the United States with regard to recognition was unchanged. Wilson also revealed that he was accepting Lind's earlier advice. He notified his agent that he was preparing an address for Congress relating to his Mexican policy and that he intended to include a statement on the recent negotiations. He also noted that, since Gamboa's latest move seemed to indicate that Huerta was softening, he would delay his message several days in order to give Gamboa an opportunity to make concessions.[44]

When on August 24 Gamboa had made no further advances, Bryan directed Lind to proceed with the loan proposal. He also revealed that the president would, indeed, address Congress in two days unless there was a change of attitude in Mexico City.[45] Lind had lost his patience for negotiating; he was ready for a final showdown. Hoping to cow Huerta into submission, he decided to offer the proposals and, if a satisfactory reply was not forthcoming in one day, to depart for Vera Cruz. "I suggest this course," he explained to Bryan, "because I believe it dignified and also because I have

42. Lind to State Department, August 21, 1913, in NA 812.00/10642.
43. Calvert, *Diplomacy of Anglo-American Conflict*, 213; Rausch, "Huerta," 146.
44. State Department to Lind, August 22, 1913, in NA 812.00/10642.
45. State Department to Lind, August 24, 1913, *ibid.*/8526; pencil draft in Wilson Papers, Ser. 2, Box 95.

become satisfied that silence and action at the opportune time are the most effective arguments. Let the ultimatum be action. They discount words." [46] Lind had hoped to use the British minister as an intermediary in broaching the matter of a loan. When by August 25 Minister Stronge had not received permission from his government, Lind submitted a new set of proposals that bore his own mark. He insisted that the elections be held as scheduled and that Huerta should not be a candidate for president. Somewhat more realistically, he also suggested that the other propositions in his original instructions—an immediate armistice and all parties to support a newly elected government—should "be taken up later, but speedily and resolved as circumstances permit." Then he promised that if Huerta would accede to this program, President Wilson would "express to American bankers and their associates assurances that the Government of the United States will look with favor upon the extension of an immediate loan sufficient in amount to meet the temporary requirements of the *de facto* government of Mexico." At the same time, Lind also informed Gamboa that he would depart for Vera Cruz the next day. Early the next morning, as promised, the special agent boarded the morning train to the coast. [47]

Huerta was not the least intimidated by Lind's departure nor by the fact that Wilson planned to address Congress. He felt particularly secure because negotiations for an eighteen-million-peso domestic loan were drawing to a close, and the old general expected these funds to sustain him until late November. [48] Gamboa's formal reply was sent to Vera Cruz aboard the night train on August 26, the same day as Lind's departure from Mexico City. Fairly bristling with sarcasm

46. Lind to State Department, [n.d.], in Lind Papers.

47. Lind to State Department, August 25, 1913, in NA 812.00/24650; *Mexican Herald*, August 26, 1913.

48. Rausch, "Huerta," 146; Turlington, *Mexico and Her Foreign Creditors*, 253–54; Bazánt, *La deuda exterior de México*, 179.

and innuendo, the reply revealed the confidence of the
provisional government. After refusing to accede to any one
of the demands, Gamboa noted the inconsistency of the
Wilson administration: it insisted that as a sovereign nation
the United States had the right to withhold diplomatic
recognition from certain nations, yet would deny Mexico her
sovereignty by interfering in her internal affairs. "If once we
were to admit the counsels and advice (let us call them thus)
of the United States of America," he remonstrated, "not only
would we . . . forego our sovereignty, but we would as well
compromise for an indefinite future our destinies as a
sovereign entity and all the future elections for President
would be submitted to the veto of any President of the
United States. And such an enormity, Mr. Confidential
Agent, no government will ever attempt to perpetuate. . . ."

Gamboa suggested that the "disproportionate interest"
President Wilson had evidenced in Mexican internal affairs
would lead one to believe that he "would know perfectly well
the provisions of our Constitution in the matter of elections."
Were this the case, chided Gamboa, the current impasse could
have been avoided, since the Constitution prevented "an ad
interim President of the Republic from being a candidate at
the forthcoming elections." Nor had Huerta done anything,
he added, to indicate that he was seeking the elective
presidency. In conclusion the foreign minister intimated that
the loan proposal constituted an attempted bribe. "When the
dignity of the nation is at stake," he insisted, "I believe that
there are not loans enough to induce those charged by law to
maintain it to permit it to be lessened." [49]

At 1:00 P.M. on August 27, well before Gamboa's note was
completely translated and relayed to Washington, and with
only scant knowledge of its contents, Wilson went before
Congress and revealed the facts—as he saw them—of the

49. Gamboa to Lind, August 26, 1913, in *Foreign Relations, 1913*, 832–35;
also in *Diario Official*, CXXVII, 6–8.

Lind mission. Acknowledging that Huerta had spurned his proposals, he lamented that the United States could do no more than adopt a waiting policy—"watchful waiting," as the press dubbed it. "We can not thrust our good offices upon them," he concluded. "The steady pressure of moral force will before many days break the barriers of pride and prejudice down, and we shall triumph as Mexico's friends sooner than we could triumph as her enemies." Since the violent civil war was bound to intensify south of the border, he urged all Americans to leave Mexico at once. At the same time, he promised to enforce strictly the arms embargo against both sides of the conflict.[50]

While Wilson was addressing Congress, Lind, Consul Canada, and embassy interpreter, Louis D'Antin, who had come to Vera Cruz, pored over Gamboa's note. Not until 11:00 P.M. on August 27 had D'Antin completed the translation, and only then did Lind grasp the importance of the Mexican foreign minister's comments relating to Huerta's eligibility for the presidential election. "Every point contended for in the last note is accepted in fact, though not in form," he triumphantly, if inaccurately, proclaimed in a telegram to Bryan. In Washington, Bryan and Wilson had also grasped the implications of Gamboa's note. Two days before, in fact, David Lawrence of the Associated Press, a reporter close to Wilson, had presented the president with a memorandum in which he revealed that the Mexican Constitution forbade an ad interim president from succeeding himself as elective president. Lawrence's memorandum and the translation of Gamboa's note, plus Lind's euphoric dispatch, struck the president and the secretary of state with the force of revelation. "Accept my hearty congratulations," Bryan wired his agent.[51] Wilson must also have congratulated himself. By

50. New York *Times*, August 28, 1913, p. 1.
51. Lind to State Department, August 27, 1913, in Wilson Papers, Ser. 2, Box 96; Lawrence to Wilson, August 25, 1913, *ibid.*; State Department to Lind, August 27, 1913, in NA 812.00/8593.

prompting Gamboa to admit this constitutional technicality publicly, the main object of the Lind Mission had seemingly been accomplished. Even the policy of "watchful waiting" which he had outlined to Congress seemed the most reasonable course to follow. The success of his Mexican policy now seemed to hinge only on Huerta's good faith in allowing the elections to proceed as scheduled.

Mexico's impression of Gamboa's note was quite different. On August 28 the provisional government released the complete texts of the Lind-Gamboa exchange, and the press again indulged in an orgy of patriotism. Huerta's popularity was definitely enhanced, but the main hero of the press commentaries was Federico Gamboa. An editorial in *El Diario* proclaimed that "John Lind thought to come, to see and to conquer, but Federico Gamboa was able to counter and dominate him." *El Independiente* insisted that the foreign minister had met the "Colossus of the North" in battle and had driven him from the field. As for Huerta, a writer for *El País*, ignoring constitutional technicalities, touched the truth when he commented that "President Wilson has not only launched the candidacy of Huerta, but has advanced it, since should he be proposed, he could find no better argument in his favor than the odium of a Yankee President." [52] Certainly his supporters did not think that Huerta had made any concessions to the United States.

Lind remained confident that Wilson's stand had been a proper one, but he was gravely concerned for the safety of Americans in Mexico City. Press attacks on the United States, plus Wilson's plea for all Americans to leave Mexico, had indeed caused a near panic in the American colony. The railway station was crowded with would-be refugees seeking passage to Vera Cruz. The American consul general was

52. *Mexican Herald*, August 28–31, September 1, 1913; *El Imparcial*, August 29–31, September 1, 1913; New York *World*, August 28–31, 1913; *El Diario*, *El Independiente*, and *El País* quoted in New York *Times*, August 30, 1913, p. 2.

inundated with requests for financial assistance from those who could not pay their own passage.[53]

Lind was particularly fearful for the safety of William Bayard Hale. Beginning as early as August 12, the Mexico City press had launched a series of attacks on Hale. His advice, it was said, had prejudiced President Wilson against the provisional government and, hence, he was responsible for the strained relations between his country and Mexico. In the United States, Senator Penrose, claiming that he knew Hale personally and considered him a dishonorable character, seized upon the Mexican press comments and attempted to embarrass the administration. When news of Penrose's remarks reached Mexico City, the press called for Huerta to enforce against Hale Article 33 of the constitution, which allowed the president to deport "pernicious aliens." Hale and Lind were certain that former ambassador Wilson was behind the attacks, and O'Shaughnessy acknowledged that Wilson had earlier attempted to have Hale arrested by Mexican authorities. Although Bryan directed O'Shaughnessy to appeal to the provisional government for guarantees for this agent's safety, and Gamboa responded favorably, Hale's usefulness as an informant was clearly at an end. On August 26, he was directed to go to Vera Cruz, then to return to the United States with Lind.[54]

Lind, in the meantime, had expected his precipitous departure from Mexico City to pose enough of a threat to

53. New York *World*, August 29, 30, 1913; *Mexican Herald*, August 29, 30, 1913.

54. *Congressional Record*, 63rd Cong., 1st Sess., 3385–86; Hale to State Department, August 15, 1913, in NA 812.00/20447; State Department to O'Shaughnessy, August 16, 1913, *ibid.*/20447; Lind to State Department, August 16, 1913, *ibid.*/8379; Lind to State Department, August 26, 1913, in Lind Papers; O'Shaughnessy to State Department, August 18, 1913, in Wilson Papers, Ser. 2, Box 96; State Department to Hale, August 26, 1913, in NA 812.00/10643b; Bryan to Wilson, August 26, 1913, in Wilson Papers, Ser. 2, Box 96; New York *Times*, August 12, 1913, p. 5; *ibid.*, August 14, 1913, p. 4; *ibid.*, August 16, 1913, p. 3; *ibid.*, August 17, 1913, II, p. 1; *ibid.*, August 18, 1913, p. 5; New York *World*, August 16, 17, 18, September 1, 1913.

induce Huerta to seek new parleys. When no overtures came from Mexico City, the special agent, on his own initiative, wired O'Shaughnessy to approach Gamboa and assure the foreign minister that he was prepared to return to the capital and reopen the talks. In a disheartening reply, O'Shaughnessy reported that Gamboa could think of no reason for the special agent to come to Mexico City. By this time, also, Bryan and Wilson were concerned that further advances by the United States might be construed as a willingness to make concessions. But they were not willing to give up hope that Lind might ultimately be summoned by Huerta. Instead of calling him home, therefore, Lind was ordered to remain in Vera Cruz and assume the role of an observer, to be available for negotiations only if they were requested by the Mexicans.[55]

Hale was now expendable. At Lind's behest, he agreed to return immediately to Washington, partly because of the antagonism that had developed toward him in Mexico City and partly because both men felt that their impressions of the Mexican situation could best be expressed verbally in a conference with the president and the secretary of state. Certainly Lind trusted Hale to convey his impressions accurately. Indeed, no two agents whom Wilson sent to Mexico were more like-minded and compatible than these two. Expressing a need for another agent with whom to confide and consult, Lind urged that Hale be returned to Vera Cruz as soon as possible.[56] Wilson, instead, sent Hale on a diplomatic mission to another part of Mexico. It is a paradox that Lind, the man of action, became a passive observer, while Hale, the more contemplative of the two, became an active diplomat. Thus the diplomatic phase of Lind's mission was

55. State Department to Lind, August 26, 27, 1913, in NA 812.00/10634a, 8593; Lind to O'Shaughnessy, August 28, 1913, and O'Shaughnessy to Lind, August 28, 1913, in Lind Papers.
56. Lind to State Department, August 28, 1913, in NA 812.00/10487; New York *World*, August 30, 1913.

temporarily ended. Now he was left to swelter in the tropical heat of Vera Cruz and serve as Wilson's eyes and ears in Mexico, a task he did not relish but one that he performed with characteristic conscientiousness.

CHAPTER V

More Encounters
More Rebuffs

John Lind's residence in Vera Cruz lengthened from an expected few weeks into almost eight months. During that time "El Manco," the one-handed one, as the natives called him, became a familiar figure throughout the city and was received cordially everywhere. Walking about the city, along the docks, or through the railroad yards, his appearance—he wore dark gray suits and a felt hat—contrasted sharply with that of the shorter, brown-skinned, cotton-clad, straw-sombreroed Mexicans. Lind was regarded with some affection by the *Veracruzanos*, particularly after he and Mrs. Lind danced in the streets during the *Fiesta de Covadonga*, the city's biggest annual celebration. At first the Linds lived at the Hotel Terminal, but after Mrs. Lind returned to Minnesota in late October, Lind made a starkly furnished room in the American consulate his headquarters. Probably to afford himself easier access to his sources of information, he declined an opportunity to live more comfortably aboard Admiral F. F. Fletcher's flagship which was anchored in the harbor.[1]

Mexico's largest and busiest port, Vera Cruz was an advantageous location for gathering information. In the course of his daily afternoon walks, Lind often stopped to drink coffee or beer or smoke a cigar with a group of the local

1. Stephenson, *John Lind*, 224–25; *La Opinión* (Vera Cruz), September 9, 1913; San Antonio (Texas) *Express*, January 18, 1914.

inhabitants. From such informal contacts, the agent drew many of the impressions that he forwarded to Washington. He solicited information from a wide variety of people—Mexicans, as well as Europeans and Americans; diplomats and officials, as well as interested private citizens; landowners and businessmen, as well as propertyless laborers and peasants; conservatives as well as radicals. On occasion others sought him out. He received dozens of letters, petitions, and memorandums from anonymous or insignificant persons from all over Mexico. He had numerous visitors at the consulate.[2]

Some of his many conferences with well-known visitors drew considerable publicity. For example, in November the ministers of Germany, Norway, and Russia, disturbed by degenerating economic conditions in the Mexican capital, came to Lind and hinted at the advisability of American intervention as a means of restoring order in Mexico. Although they were ostensibly on a hunting trip, the Mexico City press reported the true purpose of their visit to Vera Cruz.[3] Many were particularly intrigued by Lind's well-publicized conversations with Jesús Flores Magón, whose revolutionary reputation predated the Madero upheaval of 1910–1911. Actually, Flores Magón came to Vera Cruz to plead for the recognition of Huerta as a means of ending Mexico's fratricidal strife.[4]

Lind also harbored numerous fugitives from Huerta's persecution, including several members of the Madero family, and helped some of them escape the country aboard U.S. Navy warships. In fact, Mrs. Lind, upon sailing for the United States, hid two refugees in her stateroom aboard the

2. Lind's contacts and interviews were too numerous to cite individually, but the Lind Papers and the State Department's 812.00 file reveal that Lind drew his information from numerous sources.

3. Lind to State Department, November 3, 1913, in NA 812.00/9513; *Mexican Herald*, November 1–3, 1913; *El Imparcial*, November 1–3, 1913.

4. Lind to State Department, January 19, 1914, in NA 812.00/10600; *Mexican Herald*, January 20, 27, 1914; *El País*, January 20, 24, 1914.

steamer *Morro Castle*, while she remained on deck all night during the voyage to Cuba.[5] By mid-December Lind had established confidential relations with Constitutionalist sympathizers in the Vera Cruz region and he brazenly allowed them to frequent the consulate. In March, 1914, he began communicating with agents of Emiliano Zapata.[6] In maintaining such contacts, Lind became a constant source of irritation to officials of the provisional government, and, not surprisingly, the very mention of Lind's name sent Huerta flying into a rage.[7]

Lind also had his regular confidants, men who were perfectly acceptable to Huerta. Chargé O'Shaughnessy was a regular correspondent and Consul Canada was a constant companion while Lind was in Vera Cruz. Both were mildly pro-Huerta but were loyal to the administration. Two pro-Huerta businessmen also offered their views regularly: an American, J. J. Slade, and an Englishman, Fred Adams. Adams and Lind became close friends despite the fact that the former was a local agent for British oilman Weetman Pearson, First Viscount Cowdray, whom Lind suspected of providing financial support for the Huerta regime. Embassy counselor-interpreter Louis D'Antin, who was anti-Huerta,

5. Lind to State Department, November 20, 1913, January 23, 27, 1914, in NA 812.00/9841, 9850, 10652, 10703; Admiral F. F. Fletcher to Navy Department, November 21, 1913, January 31, 1914,*ibid.*/9889, 10907; Mrs. Lind to Lind, [n.d.], Lind Papers; New York *Times*, October 28, 1913, p. 1; Raúl Dehesa y Núñez, "Yo Conocí a Mr. Lind," *Excélsior* (Mexico City), February 20, 1954, p. 6.

6. Lind to State Department, December 12, 13, 1913, in NA 812.00/10152, 10170; Testimony of Lind and William W. Canada, April 30, 1920, *Senate Documents*, 66th Cong., 2nd Sess., No. 285, pp. 2350–55, 2435–39; Louis M. Teitelbaum, *Wilson and the Mexican Revolution, 1913–1916* (New York, 1967), 143–47; Womack, *Zapata*, 184. Because of Lind's clandestine activities, Mexican historian Alberto María Carreño has suggested that Huerta would have been justified in having him executed as a spy. See Carreño, *La Diplomacia extraordinaria entre México y Estados Unidos*, II, 276.

7. Huerta, *Memorias*, 95; O'Shaughnessy, *A Diplomat's Wife in Mexico*, 54.

provided much information. For antigovernment advice, however, Lind relied most heavily upon Loring Olmstead, an American who managed the exclusive British Club in Mexico City.[8] Thus Lind suffered from no dearth of informants and received the widest range of opinion.

Lind's own advice to Washington was endless. He had proven himself a trustworthy servant, and his impressions were received eagerly by the president and the secretary of state. To a remarkable degree, Lind, Bryan, and Wilson responded to changing situations in Mexico in the same way, except that Lind's responses were usually more vehement. His voluminous dispatches exuded an air of Teutonic superiority—being Scandinavian, he preferred the term Teuton to Anglo-Saxon. Possessing a midwestern progressive's yearning for honest men and fair play in politics and business, he was naturally outraged by the circumstances which elevated Huerta to power and sustained him there. Yet his first inclination was to accept conditions as they were. On August 28, shortly after settling in Vera Cruz, he advised Bryan: "I have learned enough of the Latin character to realize that we cannot expect to make them [Mexicans] conform in any very great degree to our standards in the matter of government . . . The sense of cooperation in government and in business, which is a strong characteristic of the Teutonic race, is utterly wanting in them." Referring to the upcoming elections of October 26, in which, supposedly, Huerta's successor would be chosen, Lind counseled that "we simply cannot expect elections to be held in the sense they are conducted in the United States . . . Judged by our standards the elections here are a farce." Closing with a note of opprobrium, but recommending no remedial action by the United States, Lind added that "anyone who has had the misfortune to deal with

8. Again, Lind's correspondence with his informants is too voluminous to cite individually. It is contained in the Lind Papers and the State Department's 812.00 file. See also Stephenson, *Lind*, 230–33.

the Irish of our cities . . . has his mind prepared in slight degree to appreciate conditions in Mexico." [9] Lind, nonetheless, began his vigil in Vera Cruz with an almost euphoric outlook.

Throughout the month of September, the Wilson administration remained optimistic about conditions in Mexico. Huerta, for a change, made an advance to promote better relations. He proposed to send Manuel Zamacona, a retired diplomat who had served earlier as ambassador to the United States, to Washington to serve in a capacity similar to Lind's. Forwarding the proposal to Washington, O'Shaughnessy reported his conviction that Huerta was "desirous of coming to an understanding with our government" and that the general was "convinced of the impossibility of recognition by the United States." [10] Assuming that Huerta had made an ironclad commitment to step down after the October elections, Wilson did not think further negotiations with the provisional government were necessary. He therefore refused to receive Zamacona. Lind, Wilson, and Bryan were further heartened when, on September 16, Huerta addressed the Mexican Congress and assured the legislators that he would not be a candidate for office and that the greatest triumph of his interim government would occur when he relinquished his power to an elected successor. A few days later, in a press interview, the usurper also promised to remain neutral and refrain from endorsing any candidate.[11]

By mid-September several parties had nominated presi-

9. Lind to Bryan, August 28, 1913, in Wilson Papers, Ser. 4, Box 120.
10. O'Shaughnessy to State Department, September 1, 1913, in NA 812.00/8648.
11. O'Shaughnessy to State Department, September 7, 1913, *ibid.*/8735; Lind to State Department, September 4, 5, 1913, *ibid.*/8671, 10500; State Department to Lind, September 8, 1913, *ibid.*/24260a; New York *Times*, September 6, 1913, p. 2; *ibid.*, September 11, 1913, p. 3; *ibid.*, September 12, 1913, p. 8. Wilson remained undecided about receiving Zamacona until the Mexican diplomat arrived in New York, but then informed him that it would be useless for him to come to Washington.

dential candidates, including the *Felicistas*, who put forward Felix Díaz. Wilson and Bryan were particularly encouraged when the Catholic party nominated Federico Gamboa. Despite the harsh words the nationalistic diplomat had leveled at them, the president and the secretary of state had been impressed by Lind's favorable characterization of Gamboa and announced that they would recognize him if he was elected.[12] So comforted was Bryan that he wrote to Wilson: "It seems to me that things are going quite well at present and we have only to sit tight and await the election." Again the secretary of state congratulated Lind on the success of his mission, suggesting that the whole turn of events was the result of the agent's diplomacy.[13]

In the last days of September, this euphoria began to evaporate. Hale, who had returned to Washington and was serving as a resident counselor on Mexican affairs, noted that even if the elections were held as scheduled, the results might prove unsatisfactory for the United States. The liberals in the Mexican Congress, he insisted, would oppose Gamboa, because he represented the conservative Catholic party. Hale also pointed out that the revolutionaries had announced their refusal to either participate in the election or abide by the results. "It seems to me," he warned, "that to eliminate Huerta and yet leave Mexico in disorder is a small practical gain." There was no assurance, moreover, that the usurper would be eliminated by the elections. Among the options available to the national Chamber of Deputies, should no

12. F. D. Roosevelt (assistant secretary of the navy) to Bryan, forwarding radiogram from Lind, September 15, 1913, in NA 812.00/10502; Lind to State Department, September 16, 1913, *ibid.*/8880; O'Shaughnessy to State Department, September 16, 1913, *ibid.*/8867; State Department to Lind, September 18, 22, 26, 1913, *ibid.*/8880, 10645a, 10645b; Bryan to Wilson, September 17, 1913, in Bryan-Wilson Correspondence; *Mexican Herald*, September 17, 22, 1913; *El Diario*, September 26, 1913; New York *Times*, September 17, 1913, p. 3; Meyer, *Huerta*, 149–51.

13. Bryan to Wilson, September 25, 1913, in Bryan-Wilson Correspondence; State Department to Lind, September 26, 1913, in NA 812.00/10645b.

candidate receive a majority, was nullification of the election results. If the elections were voided, Hale revealed, Huerta would remain in power. Hale suggested that one possible way to avoid these eventualities was to secure Constitutionalist participation in the elections. The liberals in the Chamber of Deputies, he assured Wilson, desired Constitutionalist participation and would likely support their candidate. "So far as I know," he told the president, "our government has made no approach to the Revolutionaries. Ought we not do so?" [14]

Hale's revelations stirred the president into immediate action. Having ignored the Constitutionalists since June, he suddenly recognized their disruptive potential. On October 1 Wilson personally drafted a telegram, which Bryan relayed to Lind, directing the special agent to contact leaders in the Mexican Congress and urge them to make an "earnest and sincere effort" to induce the rebels to participate in the coming elections. Within three days, Lind was able to report that certain legislators were, indeed, encouraging the revolutionaries to vote. Not satisfied with this indirect approach, Lind also suggested that the administration appeal directly to the rebel leaders.[15]

Wilson was already moving in that direction. At the same time he instructed Lind to contact the Mexican legislators, the president apparently directed Hale to establish communications with Constitutionalist agents in Washington. The records reveal no written instructions by Wilson, but the report of the conversations between Hale and the Constitutionalist agent, M. Pérez Romero, which Romero sent to Carranza, reveals that the American agent was directed to take a hard line. President Wilson favored Gamboa to win the upcoming presidential election, Hale informed the Constitutionalists, and, if he won and the elections appeared to be

14. Hale to Wilson, [n.d.], in Wilson Papers, Ser. 2, Box 97.
15. Wilson to Bryan, October 1, 1913, in NA 812.00/9583; State Department to Lind, October 1, 1913, *ibid.*/10645c; Lind to State Department, October 2, 4, 1913, in NA 812.00/10646, 9563.

conducted legally, he would receive the moral support of the United States. Hale then indicated that Wilson believed that the Constitutionalists had been justified in revolting against the Huerta regime, but he also insisted that the elections of October 26 should eliminate any justification for continued revolution. In conclusion Hale counseled that his president wanted Mexicans to learn to use votes instead of bullets to win their political battles.[16]

The implications of Hale's comments were clear. Wilson had thrown down the gauntlet to the Constitutionalists: participate in the elections and accept the results, even if a conservative such as Gamboa was elected president, or suffer the odium of having their cause repudiated by the United States. But Wilson had misgauged Venustiano Carranza's nationalism and pertinacity of purpose. The First Chief was incensed by the American president's latest attempt to dictate the course of Mexican politics. Without once mentioning the elections, but obviously declining to participate in them, he instructed his agent to inform Hale that, as the leader of the Constitutionalist revolution, he alone would decide what was best for his country and that his "line of conduct" would not change.[17]

Having mistakenly ignored the Constitutionalists for months, Wilson should now have known that the rebels were not only unwilling to compromise with their political enemies but were determined to continue fighting until they were all eliminated. His future relations with the revolutionaries, however, revealed that he had not learned this lesson. As yet he did not fully understand their lack of faith in the electoral process. Instead, he looked to those who seemingly respected

16. S. Gil Herrera a Carranza [n.d.], AGRE, L–E–861, Leg. 5; M. Pérez Romero a Carranza, September 30, October 3, 1914, *ibid.;* Fabela, *Historia Diplomática,* I, 243–44. S. Gil Herrera was an alias for Sherbourne G. Hopkins, an Anglo-American, who served as Constitutionalist commercial agent and legal counsel.

17. Carranza a Romero, October 6, 1913, AGRE, L–E–861, Leg. 5.

democratic processes and hoped that they would elect a government which he could recognize.

Events in Mexico City during the month of October proved most disillusioning for Wilson. Constitutionalist sympathizers in the national Chamber of Deputies—mostly holdovers from the Madero regime—became increasingly defiant of Huerta. Having recently blocked several of the usurper's appointments, they grew more brazen after Senator Belisario Domínguez, who had openly called for Huerta's removal, mysteriously disappeared. When he was found murdered several days later, the Chamber of Deputies called for an investigation. Already pressed by unrest in the national capital, the *Huertistas* were further stunned when, on October 8, the rebel armies under General Villa overran Torreón, the key to the federals' northern defenses. It was by far the most impressive rebel victory to date, and it encouraged the Constitutionalist sympathizers in the chamber to circulate petitions calling for Huerta's ouster. They even threatened to completely disrupt the government by endorsing a resolution to disband the chamber and reconvene elsewhere, presumably in rebel-held territory.[18]

After lengthy discussions, Huerta and his cabinet agreed that only ruthless action could forestall an insurrection in the capital city. On October 10, therefore, Huerta packed the galleries of the chamber with secret police and surrounded the hall with soldiers. When the deputies refused even to reconsider their recent actions, 110 of the legislators were arrested on the grounds that they were attempting to usurp executive power and were acting in collusion with the revolutionaries. The next day Huerta assumed dictatorial

18. O'Shaughnessy to State Department, October 8, 10, 11, 1913, in *Foreign Relations, 1913*, 835–36; Meyer, *Huerta*, 145–47; Vera Estañol, *La Revolución Mexicana*, 337–39; Barragán Rodríguez, *Historia . . . de la Revolución Constitucionalista*, I, 263–67.

powers and announced that a new Congress would be chosen in the upcoming elections.[19]

By unfortunate coincidence, the day Huerta assumed dictatorial powers, Sir Lionel Carden, the new British minister, arrived in Mexico City and presented his credentials. Lind did not think it a coincidence. He saw the makings of a monstrous conspiracy. The American agent had been on hand to greet the new minister when he arrived in Vera Cruz. In the course of their conversations, Carden had revealed great admiration for Huerta and had even suggested that the general was the only man strong enough to restore order in Mexico. He had also been critical of Wilson's nonrecognition policy, claiming that it encouraged revolution and was largely responsible for the heavy losses suffered by British investors in Mexico. Lind was aroused by the crass materialism implied in Carden's remarks. But even more incriminating in Lind's eyes was the fact that the minister had been greeted at Vera Cruz not by a legation official but by Fred Adams, the local agent for Lord Cowdray's El Aguila Oil Company.[20] This was incriminating because weeks before Carden's arrival Lind had reported his conviction that British oil interests were angling for favorable treatment from Huerta and were urging him to be a candidate for president.[21] Lind assumed,

19. O'Shaughnessy to State Department, October 10, 1913, in NA 812.00/9166, 9167, 9168; O'Shaughnessy to State Department, October 11, 1913, in *Foreign Relations, 1913*, 836–37; *Mexican Herald*, October 11, 1913; Vera Estañol, *La Revolución Mexicana*, 339–41; Meyer, *Huerta*, 147–48; José Mancisidor, *Historia de la Revolución Mexicana* (México, D.F., 1958), 198–200.

20. *Mexican Herald*, October 12, 1913; Lind to State Department, October 8, 1913, in NA 812.00/9127; Calvert, *Diplomacy of Anglo-American Conflict*, 225–26, 233. Actually the British chargé d'affaires had gone to Vera Cruz to meet the new minister, but Carden disembarked aboard the pilot boat. Before the chargé could locate him, Carden had been greeted by Cowdray's agent and had conferred with Lind.

21. F. D. Roosevelt to Bryan, transmitting radiogram from Lind, September 15, 1913, in NA 812.00/10502. In this dispatch, Lind refers to the "largest interest in Mexico not American," which was British.

moreover, that Carden, by presenting his credentials when he did, signified England's moral approval of the dictatorship.[22]

Lind quickly became obsessed by the specter of British duplicity. The arrival of Carden at the same time Huerta assumed dictatorial power, he wrote to Bryan, "was no accident. I believe the whole was carefully planned." [23] Almost two weeks elapsed before Lind unraveled the threads of what he thought to be an evil plot. But the day after his conversations with Carden, he reported the bare bones of his hypothesis: "Lord Cowday [sic] through Adams controls Huerta Administration absolutely." [24] Basing his assumptions on rumors and reports from American oilmen, including J. N. Galbraith, a representative of Standard Oil, Lind came to the conclusion that Lord Cowdray's money kept Huerta in power. In return for his support, Cowdray was demanding new concessions which would enable him to deliver oil to the Royal Navy under fifty- to one-hundred-year contracts. Having recently converted to oil-burning ships, and being dependent upon Mexican oil, the British cabinet, Lind believed, had readily acceded to Cowdray's demand that their ineffective minister in Mexico City, Francis Stronge, be replaced with the oilman's handpicked tool, Sir Lionel Carden. Fearing the disruptive potential of the rebel sympathizers in the Mexican legislature, Cowdray and Carden had insisted upon the establishment of a dictatorship. The ultimate end of the conspiracy, the American agent insisted, was the complete control and monopoly of the Mexican oil fields and oil business by the British. To insure the success of this scheme, Carden would find some means of maintaining Huerta in power despite the upcoming elections.[25]

The results of those elections served to confirm Lind's suspicions. As election day approached, Huerta's own inten-

22. Lind to State Department, October 15, 1913, *ibid.*/9218.
23. *Ibid.*
24. Lind to State Department, October 8, 1913, *ibid.*/9127.
25. Lind to State Department, October 15, 16, 23, 25, 1913, *ibid.*/9218, 9355, 9401, 10647.

tions, at least, did become apparent. Instructions were sent to state governors and local *jefes políticos*, directing them to insure that the polling places were manned by loyal *Huertistas*. Although he was not an official candidate, leaflets urging the electorate to vote for Huerta appeared everywhere. Felix Díaz, who returned to Vera Cruz on October 23 in order to stand for election, passed this information on to Lind and, in counseling the agent, prophesied that the elections would be so well managed that Huerta would receive an overwhelming majority.[26] Apathy on the part of the electorate and *Huertista* intimidation in some areas did result in an exceedingly small voter turnout on election day. Although Huerta received a majority of the votes cast, the total did not meet constitutional minimums and it was generally conceded that the election results would be nullified.[27]

Ignoring his earlier counsels to Wilson and Bryan that they should not expect Mexican elections to conform to Anglo-American standards, Lind condemned the fraud and intimidation. More important, he insisted that the election results were part of a conspiracy in which the British were deeply implicated.[28] His analysis had little basis in fact. To be sure, Huerta had managed the elections and was determined to remain in power, but the supposed British determination to sustain him there, in defiance of Wilson's wishes, and to

26. Lind to State Department, October 23, 26, 27, 28, 1913, *ibid.*/9355, 9406, 9441; Meyer, *Huerta*, 151–52; Sherman and Greenleaf, *Victoriano Huerta*, 108–109. Díaz was watched closely by Huerta's police and was a virtual prisoner in his hotel. When the results of the election went against him, Díaz and an aide crawled across the hotel roof and gained asylum in the American consulate, which was located immediately next door. Lind and Canada then escorted Díaz to an American warship, from which the general transferred to a commercial steamer and went into exile. See Canada to State Department, October 27, 1913, in NA 812.00/9418; *Mexican Herald*, October 29, 30, November 2, 1913.

27. *Mexican Herald*, October 27, 1913; New York *Times*, October 27, 1913, p. 1.

28. Lind to State Department, October 26, 27, 1913, in NA 812.00/9392, 9406, 9415.

monopolize the Mexican oil industry, was a fiction derived from rumors and false information provided by American competitors. Lord Cowdray did have influence in the majority Liberal party in England, but he did not exert pressure on the cabinet in behalf of Carden's appointment. Minister Stronge's failing health, plus the need for a diplomat with abundant experience in Latin America, were the primary considerations behind the choice of Carden, who had served at various consular and diplomatic posts in Latin America since 1877. Nor was there valid evidence that Cowdray took advantage of Huerta's diplomatic difficulties with the United States to press for larger concessions. The opposite seems to have been the case. More likely, Huerta was exerting pressure on the British oilman by using his interests in Mexico as a hostage to secure monetary support. Only in one respect was Lind correct. The British cabinet, Cowdray, and Carden were concerned primarily with the protection of English material interests in Mexico and believed Huerta the most capable of guaranteeing their safety.[29]

However faulty Lind's notions might have been, the important point is that Wilson and Bryan believed him, primarily because his suppositions were supported by others. As early as April, 1913, the possible connection between England's recognition of the Huerta government and her oil interests had been discussed at one of Wilson's cabinet meetings. In August, Boaz Long, chief of the Latin American Division of the State Department, after a secret conference with Henry Clay Pierce, had reported the American oilman's conviction that England had recognized Huerta at Cowdray's insistence. At almost the same time Lind began his tirades against the British, the New York *World* published an exposé which charged that Cowdray had dictated the appointment of

29. Calvert, *Diplomacy of Anglo-American Conflict*, 216–84. Calvert utilizes recently available British Foreign Office records in revealing the true intentions of Cowdray and the Foreign Office.

Carden as the man best qualified to protect and expand British oil interests.[30] The upshot of all these faulty suppositions was that Wilson launched campaigns of diplomatic pressure designed to force the British cabinet to give up its alleged Mexican policy and to unseat Huerta immediately.

In exerting pressure directly on Huerta, Wilson inexplicably bypassed Lind and, on November 1, sent an ultimatum to Huerta through the embassy in Mexico City, demanding that the dictator retire immediately or face possible intervention.[31] Only three days before, O'Shaughnessy had conferred with Foreign Minister Querido Moheno, who revealed that, because of faltering finances, the provisional government's position was becoming increasingly untenable. O'Shaughnessy also received the impression that the Mexican cabinet thought the retirement of Huerta might serve the best interests of Mexico. "I am of the opinion," he wrote to Bryan, "that if you make suggestions to the administration in Mexico City in such a manner as to save their *amour-propre* (for any man who listens to the direction of the United States is ruined politically) such suggestions will be listened to and substantially followed." That same day he also spoke with Huerta's private secretary and received the same impression.[32] Wilson's ultimatum of November 1 was hardly suited to allow the dictator to bow out with dignity; the chargé, therefore, withheld the full impact of Wilson's new demands and began secret parleys with the minister of foreign relations.[33]

With O'Shaughnessy making repeated visits to the foreign

30. Cronon (ed.), *Cabinet Diaries of Josephus Daniels*, 43–44; Long to Bryan, August 26, 1913, in NA 812.00/8693-1/2; New York *World*, October 21, 23, 24, 25, 1913.

31. State Department to American embassy, November 1, 1913, in NA 812.00/11443a.

32. O'Shaughnessy to State Department, October 30, 1913, *ibid.*/9469, 9474.

33. O'Shaughnessy to State Department, November 3, 1913, *ibid.*/9510; O'Shaughnessy, *A Diplomat's Wife in Mexico*, 32.

ministry, the rumor inevitably emerged that Wilson's Mexican policy had taken a new turn. Wishing to maintain the secrecy of his efforts, O'Shaughnessy staunchly denied the rumors. Bryan, approving of the chargé's course of action, also issued a denial. But when Lind heard the rumors, he wired immediately for permission to participate in the Mexico City negotiations. The secretary of state acceded unwisely to his agent's wishes. The mere fact that Lind was returning to Mexico City hinted strongly that the Wilson administration was increasing its diplomatic pressure on Huerta. Then Lind completely sabotaged O'Shaughnessy's efforts by revealing to a reporter of the *Mexican Herald* that the United States had, indeed, made new advances to the provisional government. With secret parleys no longer possible, Foreign Minister Moheno notified the chargé that, since it would appear to be a surrender to Yankee pressure and thus a blow to Mexican sovereignty, no agreement could be made at that time. Although Bryan was as much at fault, the dejected American chargé blamed Lind for the failure to secure Huerta's resignation.[34]

Lind, still hopeful of a confrontation with Huerta, went to Mexico City anyway, arriving there on November 7. His conduct in November was decidedly different from what it had been at the outset of his mission in August. Then he had conducted himself as a man of peace and goodwill. In November, however, he was brusque with everyone and no longer cared if his actions were considered an unwarranted breach of Mexican sovereignty. Noting that members of the diplomatic corps and foreign colony feared above all else the destructive possibilities of a revolutionary victory, he delighted in taunting them with threats of a possible lifting of

34. State Department to O'Shaughnessy, November 2, 1913, in NA 812.00/9564e; Lind to State Department, November 2, 1913, *ibid.*/9507; O'Shaughnessy to State Department, November 6, 1913, *ibid.*/9598; *Mexican Herald*, November 4–6, 1913; New York *Times*, November 6, 1913, p. 1; O'Shaughnessy, *A Diplomat's Wife in Mexico*, 33–34, 39.

the twenty-month-old embargo on American arms sales to Mexico. With access to American weapons, Lind threatened, the Constitutionalists would make short work of Huerta and all his supporters, natives and foreigners alike.[35]

Of course Lind's hostility for the British was boundless. The day of his arrival in Mexico City he conferred with Carden, and the minister told the American agent that it did not seem reasonable to expect Huerta to "efface himself" by resigning under pressure. The next day Huerta addressed a circular note to all the powers, in which he denounced the latest American attempt to unseat him. Taking his cue from Carden's comment, Lind reported his conviction that the usurper's renewed defiance was British-inspired. He insisted, also, that Carden's newest scheme was to have Huerta install the congress chosen in the inconclusive October elections and allow it to validate British and other European concessions. These validations, supposedly, would guarantee Huerta increased revenue and European support.[36]

Lind's long-sought direct confrontation with Huerta never took place. Harried by Wilson's new demands, rumblings in his own cabinet, and deteriorating national finances, Huerta, as he often did, escaped his miseries by taking to the bottle. With the old general hiding among the many cafés and bars of Mexico City, Lind had to be content to confer with Huerta's private secretary, Jesús M. Rábago. At a meeting arranged by the German minister, the special agent insisted that both Huerta and the recently elected congress must resign. Rábago replied that Huerta's resignation could be accomplished only in a manner that would allow him to bow out with dignity and that it would be impractical to disband

35. New York *Times*, November 9–11, 1913, p. 1; *ibid.*, November 12, 1913, p. 2; Testimony of Nelson O'Shaughnessy, May 3, 1920, *Senate Documents*, 66th Cong., 2nd Sess., No. 285, p. 2710; O'Shaughnessy, *A Diplomat's Wife in Mexico*, 40–46.

36. Lind to State Department, October 30, November 5, 7, 8, 9, 1913, in NA 812.00/9491, 9565, 9619, 9523, 11440.

the new congress and leave the nation without a legislature. Both the Belgian and German ministers, who were present, agreed with Rábago, but Lind remained immovable. His judgment affected increasingly by his personal hatred for Huerta, the special agent complained to Washington, "Were it not for the fact that we are dealing with a man who is little less than a madman much of the time an adjustment could be arrived at." [37]

Attempting once again to badger the provisional government into making concessions, on November 12 Lind delivered his own ultimatum. Huerta, he demanded, was to guarantee that the recently elected congress would not convene, then he was to resign. Exceeding his instructions, Lind further demanded that the dictator agree to these terms by 6:00 P.M. that same day and carry them out completely by midnight or face a complete rupture in diplomatic relations with the United States. When no reply was forthcoming, Lind packed his bags and returned to Vera Cruz. O'Shaughnessy, on the other hand, refused to give up hope and continued to negotiate with members of Huerta's cabinet. President Wilson, moreover, showed no inclination to completely sever relations with the Huerta regime.[38]

Wilson enjoyed more positive results in his campaign against the British. He began on an almost belligerent note. In an address delivered on October 27 to the Southern Commercial Congress at Mobile, Alabama, he attacked foreign concessionaires as the instigators of most of the strife in Latin America. Obviously directing his comments at the British, he suggested that the United States would aid the people of Latin America in freeing themselves from the yoke of commercial oppression by foreign business interests.

37. Lind to State Department, November 12, 1913, *ibid.*/9677.
38. Lind to State Department, November 11, 12, 1913, *ibid.*/9675, 9677; O'Shaughnessy to State Department, November 12, 1913, *ibid.*/9680; New York *Times*, November 13, 1913, p. 2; *El País*, November 15, 1913; O'Shaughnessy, *A Diplomat's Wife in Mexico*, 47–48.

Through the press and official diplomatic channels, he let the British know in no uncertain terms that he believed them to be taking undue advantage of the chaos in Mexico to gain preeminence in the oil business. Alarmed by these angry outbursts, the British cabinet moved quickly to mollify the American president. Foreign Secretary Sir Edward Grey helped clear the air by dispatching his private secretary, Sir William Tyrell, to Washington for conferences with Wilson and Bryan. At the same time, Grey and Lord Cowdray made representations to the American ambassador, Walter Hines Page. The foreign secretary even instructed Carden to attempt to mediate between the United States and Huerta; but the usurper refused the good offices of the British. At any rate, Huerta now knew he would receive no support from Great Britain in his conflict with President Wilson.[39]

The British government never withdrew diplomatic recognition of the Huerta regime, but by early December, 1913, the foreign office had made it abundantly clear to Wilson that Lord Cowdray had little influence in formulating British foreign policy or in choosing His Majesty's diplomatic representatives, that British policy with regard to Mexico had never been designed to thwart his purposes, and that Great Britain would never support Huerta against the United States.[40] Lind, nonetheless, persisted in seeing a British plot to maintain Huerta in power and enhance their material interests. When Lind continued to report that Carden was hatching plots in Mexico City, Bryan asked for concrete evidence of British wrongdoing. The agent could only reply: "My evidence against Carden is not of a character cognizable in a court of justice." He based his charges, he revealed, on

39. Link, *New Freedom*, 369–77; Calvert, *Diplomacy of Anglo-American Conflict*, 254–84; Walter V. Scholes and Marie V. Scholes, "Wilson, Grey and Huerta," *Pacific Historical Review*, XXXVII (May, 1968), 151–58; William S. Coker, "Mediación Britanica en el conflicto Wilson-Huerta," *Historia Mexicana*, XVIII (October–December, 1968), 249–50.
40. Lind, *New Freedom*, 377.

"the general sentiment that pervades the atmosphere so to speak and little incidents that occur from day to day." Falling back upon his reputation for personal integrity, the Minnesotan pleaded for understanding: "While I am not in a position to prove my assertions, I am morally certain that I have in no instance overstated the facts." [41] Certainly Wilson and Bryan did not doubt their agent's sincerity, but since he could not prove his assertions, his anti-British tirades were thereafter ignored.

Other European nations soon followed England's example, especially after Wilson sent notes to the powers revealing that he was determined to deny Huerta all foreign sympathy, material aid, and credit. Although none of them withdrew its recognition of the provisional government or evidenced any sympathy for Wilson's moralistic policy, they were careful to determine the attitude of the United States in formulating their own policies toward Mexico. The result was the virtual diplomatic isolation of the Huerta regime.[42]

Wilson, however, was no longer willing to rely entirely upon diplomatic pressure as a means of ousting the dictator. Even while O'Shaughnessy and Lind were seeking Huerta's resignation, Wilson renewed his efforts to secure cooperation from the Constitutionalists. In September, Carranza had moved his headquarters from the state of Coahuila to a safer location at Hermosillo, Sonora. There he established his own provisional government. Late in October, therefore, Wilson sent Hale to Tucson, Arizona, to secretly locate himself near the Constitutionalist headquarters. Should Huerta have resigned, the special agent would have conferred directly with Carranza and attempted to persuade the rebels to participate in creating a new provisional government in Mexico City.[43]

41. State Department to Lind, December 16, 1913, in NA 812.00/10185; Lind to State Department, December 17, 1913, *ibid.*/10239.
42. Link, *New Freedom*, 377, 386–87; Grieb, *United States and Huerta*, 113–17; Cline, *United States and Mexico*, 148–53.
43. Bryan to Wilson and Wilson to Bryan, October 24, 1913, in Wilson Papers, Ser. 2, Box 98; Bryan to Wilson, [n.d.], *ibid.*; Hale's itinerary, *ibid.*,

Adopting a fictitious name, Hale spent several days quietly inquiring about the strength and character of the Constitutionalist movement. He added these impressions to those he had received from inquiries in El Paso, Texas, and reported his conviction that the revolutionaries were much stronger and more unified than was generally believed in Washington. Support from the United States, he noted in his first dispatch to Wilson, might provide them with an added incentive to step up their military effort. On November 5 his investigations were interrupted when he was recognized by a newspaper reporter. In order to maintain the secrecy of his mission, he fled Tucson for the seclusion of a nearby ranch owned by the father-in-law of William Jennings Bryan, Jr. But once it became apparent in Washington that Huerta would not accede to Wilson's latest demands, and since Hale had been discovered on the border, the secretary of state abandoned any pretense of secrecy and ordered the agent to await new instructions in Tucson.[44]

When the new instructions came, they marked a definite change of attitude on Wilson's part. The recent events in Mexico City made him more determined than ever to eliminate Huerta. After the usurper's latest rebuff, he considered, for a time, armed intervention, at least to the extent of blockading Mexican ports. Secretary of War Lindley M. Garrison supported intervention, but Secretary of the Treasury William G. McAdoo and Attorney General James C. McReynolds were reluctant to use military force. They

Box 101; William Jennings Bryan, Jr., to State Department, October 30, 1913, in NA 812.00/9745. The son of the secretary of state, who lived near Tucson, served as Hale's intermediary while the special agent temporarily hid his identity.

44. Bryan to Wilson, [n.d.], in Wilson Papers, Ser. 2, Box 98; Hale to State Department, November 5, 9, 1913, in NA 812.00/9637, 10195; Wilson to Bryan, November 7, 1913, in Wilson-Bryan Correspondence; Bryan to William Jennings Bryan, Jr., November 8, 1913, in NA 812.00/10648c; Tucson *Daily Citizen*, November 7, 11, 1913; New York *Times*, November 7, 1913, p. 1.

suggested, as an alternative, recognition of the belligerency of the Constitutionalists and a lifting of the arms embargo.[45] From Vera Cruz, Lind spelled out graphically the advantages of such a policy. He insisted that only a military victory by the rebels would completely eliminate all the elements supporting the Huerta regime. The military forces of the United States, he concluded, "could defeat but . . . could neither humble nor humiliate them. This can only be done by their own people, their own blood, the people of the North. They can do it to perfection if given a fair chance. To make a dog feel that he really is a cur he must be whipped by another dog preferably by a cur. Consequently let this housecleaning be done by home talent." [46]

Even before Lind submitted his colorful comments, Wilson had decided to offer aid to the Constitutionalists. On about November 11, he directed Bryan to instruct Hale, who was still in Tucson, to inform the Constitutionalist leaders that the administration in Washington was contemplating lifting the embargo on the sale of arms to Mexico. But at the same time, Hale was to issue this stern warning: "We desire above all else to avoid intervention. If the lives and interests of Americans and all other foreigners are safeguarded we believe intervention may be avoided. If not we anticipate that we will be obliged to intervene. We are confident that the leaders of the North will give us no motive to intervene in their territory." [47] By issuing this warning, Wilson doubtless

45. Link, *New Freedom*, 380; Cronon (ed.), *Cabinet Diaries of Josephus Daniels*, 83.

46. Lind to State Department, November 15, 1913, in NA 812.00/9760.

47. El Secretario del Estado a William Bayard Hale, [n.d.], AGRE, L–E–861, Leg. 5 (English translation by author); pencil draft in Wilson Papers, Ser. 2, Box 99.

Bryan wanted former Democratic governor of Missouri, Joseph W. Folk, who was currently solicitor of the State Department, to join Hale for the negotiations with the Constitutionalists, but Wilson vetoed this move. The president did not want anyone officially connected with the State Department to be involved. See Bryan to Wilson [n.d.], in Wilson Papers, Ser. 2, Box 98; Wilson to Bryan, November 7, 1913, in Bryan-Wilson Correspondence.

was attempting to forestall the growth of interventionist
sentiment among foreigners with investments in Mexico. But
he may also have wanted the Constitutionalists to make some
limited commitment to abide by his wishes.

With rumors of a possible lifting of the embargo circulat-
ing in Washington and on the border, Carranza's earlier
demonstrated reluctance to treat with the Wilson administration diminished. The road toward more cordial relations had
also been paved by Dr. Henry Allen Tupper, director of the
International Peace Forum. An old friend of Bryan, Tupper,
in early November, was completing his third junket into
northern Mexico. Although his avowed purpose was to
mediate between the revolutionaries and the provisional
government, he established a very close relationship with
Carranza—indeed, in time, he became completely enamored
of the Constitutionalist cause. Before entering Mexico the
second time in June, he had asked Bryan for a letter of
introduction. There is no record of such a letter being issued;
nonetheless, the self-styled peace commissioner reported his
findings to the secretary of state by periodically issuing an
open letter to the press. On November 1 he wired Bryan from
Nogales that the Constitutionalists had authorized him to
offer a proposition in their name. In reply Bryan refused to
receive the offer as being official, but stated that he would be
pleased to have any information that the peace commissioner
cared to report. On November 2, therefore, Tupper directed
one of his statements to the press, proclaiming Carranza's
eagerness to buy arms in the United States, along with the
rebels' promise to respect the lives and property of foreigners. This declaration clearly anticipated the purpose of Hale's
instructions.[48] Carranza, meanwhile, had been informed by

48. Bryan to Wilson, June 16, 1913, in Bryan Papers, Box 43; Tupper to
Bryan, November 1, 1913, and Bryan to Tupper, November 2, 1913, in NA
812.00/9499; William Jennings Bryan, Jr., to State Department, November 2,
1913, *ibid.*/9506; El Paso *Morning Times*, November 1, 1913; Tucson *Daily
Citizen*, November 4, 1913; New York *Times*, November 3, 1913, p. 3. In

his agents in the United States that Hale sought to parley. Underlining his own willingness to negotiate, the First Chief moved his headquarters to the border at Nogales, Sonora.[49]

After holding preliminary conferences with Constitutionalist agents in Tucson, Hale motored to Nogales on November 11, where he was cordially greeted by Carranza's *official mayor* of *fomento* (public works), Ignacio Bonillas, a graduate of Massachusetts Institute of Technology, who served as an intermediary between Hale and Carranza. Later that same day, the American agent crossed the border in the company of the American consul, Frederick R. Simpich, and held a preliminary conference with Carranza and Bonillas. As if to clear the air before entering into official parleys, the ever-cautious First Chief reiterated his earlier stated determination never to accept Huerta or any remnant of his regime. He then acknowledged that the next day he and the members of his cabinet would be willing to discuss other matters.[50]

The conference of November 12 was held in a sparsely decorated, drab little room in the Mexican border customs house. Sensing that the future conduct of the Constitutionalist revolution was the matter at issue, crowds of curious observers gathered on both sides of the border, hoping to

August, 1914, after Huerta had been eliminated, Bryan suggested to Wilson that Tupper make official representations to Carranza in behalf of the State Department. At that time, however, the president was reluctant to engage any more special agents and declined the secretary's proposition. As Wilson put it, Tupper was likely to go to Mexico "on his own hook" anyway and, despite his lack of official character, would probably report his findings to Washington. See Bryan to Wilson, August 22, 1914, and Wilson to Bryan, August 26, 1914, in Bryan-Wilson Correspondence. For the nature of his visits to Mexico, see testimony of Henry Allen Tupper, September 19, 1919, *Senate Documents*, 66th Cong., 2nd Sess., No. 285, pp. 497–528.

49. El Paso *Morning Times*, November 8, 1913; Tucson *Daily Citizen*, November 9, 1913; Isidro Fabela, "Carranza," *Excélsior* (Mexico City), December 27, 1957, A–6.

50. Hale to State Department, November 11, 12, 14, 1913, in NA 812.00/9668, 9674, 9735; El Paso *Morning Times*, November 12, 1913; Tucson *Daily Citizen*, November 12, 1913.

hear, or at least see, the proceedings. A cordon of Constitutionalist troops kept the spectators out of hearing range, but through the open windows they could see the patriarchal figure of Carranza as he expounded, gesturing with his hands for emphasis, while Simpich and Bonillas huddled near Hale, quietly interpreting the First Chief's comments. The impression that reporters received from their observations was that the meeting proceeded quite amicably.[51]

Certainly Hale felt that Wilson's proposals had been cordially received. Carranza and his lieutenants immediately expressed their eagerness to receive arms from the United States and seemed most sincere in promising to protect foreign lives and property. They were temporarily disconcerted by Wilson's threat of intervention, but after they had fully digested the prospects offered by the special agent they seemed quite gratified and Carranza personally expressed his satisfaction. Careful to accurately represent the Constitutionalists' attitude, Hale agreed to submit his report of the meeting to Carranza for editing before forwarding it to Washington.[52]

While awaiting the First Chief's revisions, the special envoy began reporting his impressions of the revolutionary leaders. His characterizations were more favorable than those offered a few months before by Reginald Del Valle. Hale was struck by what he called their "moral enthusiasm." "With few exceptions," he revealed, "the leaders are plain men, their speech is remarkable for Quaker-like conscientiousness and precision . . . There is no mistaking the settled determination of these men and their complete confidence in ultimate complete success." Noting that they were determined to

51. El Paso *Morning Times*, November 12, 1913; Tucson *Daily Citizen*, November 13, 15, 1913; New York *Times*, November 13, 1913, p. 1. Isidro Fabela locates this first meeting at the Hotel Escobosa in Hermosillo. See Fabela, *Historia Diplomática*, I, 246. State Department records and newspapers locate the meeting at Nogales.

52. Hale to State Department, November 12, 1913, in NA 812.00/9685.

make the current upheaval Mexico's last, Hale concluded, "These men are plainly bent on complete political and social revolution." The special agent offered the following characterization of the First Chief: "Carranza is positive character, huge slow-moving body and mind. He is deferred to absolutely. Carranza might be somewhat more refined Oom Paul. His capacity for silent deliberation is remarkable, though when he speaks it is with fluency and appositeness . . . The Government is, so to speak, in Carranza's hat."[53] Hale's vignette was quite accurate. At this stage of the Constitutionalist revolution, the First Chief had surrounded himself with a group of advisers—he called them his cabinet—who were entirely subservient. He made almost all the decisions and, as a result, the movement enjoyed a greater unity than at any other time.[54]

After waiting two days for the rebel chieftain's formal reply to Wilson's arms proposal, Hale reported some disturbing news: "Urgent. I have just learned that Carranza believes Washington is not sincere in its declared intention of allowing importation of arms."[55] When, later that same day, Carranza delivered his formal response, it reflected the rebels' suspicions. The special agent reported that the formal reply differed greatly from the verbal response Carranza had given at the conference two days before. Now the First Chief dwelt at length on Wilson's threat of intervention. Acknowledging that he still wished to receive arms from the United States, he also warned that any foreign interference in Mexico's

53. Hale to State Department, November 14, 1913, *ibid.*/9733, 9737. In comparing Carranza to Oom Paul, Hale was probably referring to Paul Kruger, the intensely nationalistic late-nineteenth-century leader of the South African Boers.

54. Barragán Rodríguez, *Historia . . . de la Revolución Constitucionalista*, I, 219–20; Martín Luis Guzmán, *The Eagle and the Serpent*, (Garden City, N.Y., 1965), 51–57. Although the latter citation is a historical novel, in many ways it is a memoir, because Guzmán was a revolutionary who served in the camps of both Carranza and Villa.

55. Hale to State Department, November 14, 1913, in NA 812.00/9736.

domestic affairs was "inadmissible upon any grounds or upon any pretext." [56] Presumably he extended this exclusion to the arranging of a peaceful transfer of power to a new provisional government in Mexico City.

Carranza must have been struck by the incongruity of Wilson's actions: while negotiating through Lind and O'Shaughnessy for the peaceful ouster of Huerta, the president was also offering the Constitutionalists weapons so that they could eliminate the dictator by force. Hale suspected that this prompted the First Chief's change of attitude. The rebel leaders, he reported, feared that Washington was "using the threat of lifting the arms embargo merely to unseat Huerta and to set up another President in Mexico City." "This," he insisted, "they would never forgive." [57] But Carranza's suspicions probably went deeper. He wished to avoid making any commitment to Wilson for fear that the American president would use it as a means of attempting to influence the course of the Constitutionalist revolution.

After contemplating the First Chief's response, Hale himself made a plea for a change of attitude in Washington. "The Constitutionalists," he again emphasized, "are totally irreconcilable towards the capitalistic and military elements, which they hold would still be in power in the capital even with Huerta out of the Presidency." The rebel leaders had told him that Madero, by allowing these elements representation in the interim regime that preceded his election to the presidency, had subverted his own chances of success. Hale noted that the Constitutionalists were determined that the same situation should not be allowed to happen again. They "know their own minds perfectly," he insisted, "their programme is definite, their pertinacity is intense and their prospects bright." Then he inquired: "Do they not thus constitute the most powerful, single factor in the whole

56. Hale to State Department, November 14, 15, 1913, *ibid.*/9738, 9759.
57. *Ibid.*

problem and is not any attempted solution which ignores [this] factor certain to fail to give Mexico peace?" [58] What he was suggesting as subtly yet forcefully as possible was that President Wilson should forget about his efforts to negotiate a peaceful change of governments in Mexico City, because the Constitutionalists would neither acknowledge it nor lay down their arms until they were completely triumphant.

Wilson was perplexed by Carranza's attitude. He seemed transfixed by the very name Constitutionalists, a name that carried with it a pledge to restore constitutional government to Mexico. It seemed incomprehensible to him that those who made this pledge should use other than constitutional means to purge those who had traditionally subverted constitutional processes. Not surprisingly, he sought clarification of several matters before making any more proposals to the rebels. Hale was to make the following inquiries:

> Are the Constitutionalists willing to have Constitutional Government restored by peaceable means or do they prefer force? If assured of free and fair elections would they submit their cause to the ballot or do they still insist on the sword as the only weapon? Are there any men outside of their army in whose wisdom and patriotism they have confidence[? If] so secure as many names as possible[.] If the Constitutionalists succeed in setting up a government by force do they intend to give the people an early opportunity to elect a president and congress at a free and fair election? If so would they be willing to surrender the government into the hands of those selected by the people at such an election even though the persons selected were not the ones preferred by those in power?

In providing the special agent with new instructions, Bryan

---

58. Hale to State Department, November 15, 16, 1913, *ibid.*/9759, 9769. One of the provisions of the Treaty of Ciudad Juárez, by which Porfirio Díaz capitulated to Madero's triumphant revolutionary armies, was that an interim government, headed by Francisco de la Barra, Díaz's minister of foreign relations, should serve until elections could be held. The de la Barra government did much to disillusion many of the revolutionaries and helped produce the chaos that Madero inherited. See Cumberland, *Mexican Revolution*, 150–71.

revealed the extent of Wilson's distress: "He is deeply disturbed by the impression he gets from your last telegram that the leaders of the Constitutionalists would trust no one but themselves. He would not be willing, even indirectly, to assist them if they took so narrow and selfish a view. It would show that they do not understand Constitutional processes." [59]

Hale must have been disappointed that his previous explanations had gone for naught; nonetheless, he sought another conference with Carranza and attempted to present his president's point of view. As forcefully as possible he argued for the acceptance of a constitutional transfer of power, but the rebel leaders were just as stubborn as Wilson. They did not even honor Wilson's inquiries with specific answers to his questions, but once again stated their determination never to compromise on their revolutionary goals. Carranza, moreover, continued to issue public statements to the effect that he would brook no foreign interference in Mexico's internal affairs and that all he wanted from the United States was the right to purchase arms.[60]

Hale soon grew impatient with the First Chief's outbursts. The American agent felt that the public statements were meant for domestic consumption, an attempt on Carranza's part to pose as a supernationalist and to counter Huerta's patriotic pronouncements. The rebel chieftain further chagrined Hale on November 17 by launching a war of nerves. Claiming that he had more pressing problems to occupy his time, Carranza refused to meet again with the American agent and insisted that all communications should be submitted in writing to Francisco Escudero, the minister of foreign affairs. When Escudero, and later the previously congenial

59. State Department to Hale, November 16, 1913, in NA 812.00/9759.

60. Hale to State Department, November 17, 1913, *ibid.*/9812; Tucson *Daily Citizen*, November 15–18, 1913; El Paso *Morning Times*, November 15–18, 1913; New York *Times*, November 15, 1913, p. 1; *ibid.*, November 16, 1913, p. 2.

Bonillas, refused to comment on Wilson's recent inquiries, Hale insisted upon a personal meeting with Carranza. Again the First Chief excused himself, whereupon Escudero demanded that Hale present formal credentials before the Constitutionalists would agree to any more conferences.[61]

Faced with such evasive tactics, Hale's attitude toward the rebels began to change. He came to the opinion that they were too enamored with their own power because of their recent military victories: Obregón's at Culiacán, the capital of the state of Sinaloa, on November 14, and Villa's at Ciudad Juárez, across the Rio Grande from El Paso, Texas, two days later. No doubt both victories bolstered the confidence of the Constitutionalist leaders, some of whom intimated that they did not need arms from the United States. Hale also believed, and he was probably correct, that Escudero's demand for formal credentials was a ploy to secure diplomatic recognition of the Constitutionalists' belligerency. The special agent was further annoyed when the minister of foreign relations told reporters that he had asked for Hale's credentials as a preliminary step to starting formal negotiations. All previous talks, he insisted, had been held out of friendship for Hale and had been "extra-official." When queried on the matter by correspondents, the American agent clearly evidenced his pique, charging that Escudero's comments were a "complete misrepresentation." [62]

Feigning indifference to American support, Carranza announced on November 19 that he would return to Hermosillo. Later that same day, he departed by rail. By this time, also, Wilson was tiring of the Constitutionalists' evasiveness, and he ordered Hale to return to Tucson.[63] Before departing from

61. Fabela, "Carranza," *Excélsior*, December 27, 1957, A–6; Hale to State Department, November 17, 18, 1913, in NA 812.00/9768, 9807, 9814.

62. *Ibid.*; Tucson *Daily Citizen*, November 19, 20, 1913; El Paso *Morning Times*, November 19, 20, 1913; New York *Times*, November 19, 1913, p. 2.

63. Hale to State Department, November 19, 1913, in NA 812.00/9819, 9820; State Department to Hale, November 19, 1913, *ibid.*/9825.

Nogales, the harried special agent, his words loaded with sarcasm, revealed to reporters his unhappiness over the rebels' attitude: "You know, the world is full of all kinds of people. Some are not only impossible, but highly improbable. Please understand that I am not speaking of the gentlemen across the border who are with such admirable skill preventing their friends from helping them." [64]

If by evasions and harassing tactics Carranza hoped to induce Wilson into offering arms without attached strings, he overplayed his hand. That he did, indeed, want American arms was evidenced by the fact that he left Escudero and Bonillas behind in Nogales to arrange another conference with Hale, while he paused at Magdalena, a short distance from Nogales, to await the outcome. When Consul Simpich notified Escudero and Bonillas that Hale had left Nogales, rebel agents were sent to Tucson to invite him to continue the negotiations at Hermosillo. Wilson, however, believed that further contacts with the Constitutionalists would be fruitless. On November 24 he recalled Hale to Washington.[65]

Although Hale probably understood the reasons for Carranza's obstinacy better than did Wilson, both were disappointed at their inability to promote a rapprochement with the Constitutionalists. To make matters worse, the failure of Hale's negotiations had the effect of bolstering Huerta's confidence. The old general was definitely shaken by the news of Hale's visit to Nogales and the prospect of American aid to the revolutionaries. For a time he seemed on the verge of succumbing to Wilson's pressure. On November 15 his minister of government, Manuel Garza Aldape, promised to provide O'Shaughnessy with a list of names from which Huerta's successor might be chosen. But when news of Carranza's response to Wilson's propositions reached Mexico City, the

64. New York *Times*, November 20, 1913, p. 2.
65. Hale to State Department, [n.d.], in NA 812.00/9902; Simpich to State Department, November 20, 1913, *ibid.*/9843; State Department to Hale, November 24, 1913, *ibid.*/9825; Tucson *Daily Citizen*, November 22, 1913.

usurper again became defiant. He absolutely refused to step down. Not wanting to seem less nationalistic than the rebel chieftain, he renewed his pronouncements against foreign interference in Mexican internal affairs.[66] If, as Carranza suspected, Wilson was using the conferences with the Constitutionalists as a double-edged sword, the results did more to hinder than help his efforts to unseat Huerta.

The Constitutionalists themselves were anything but pleased with the results of the conference at Nogales. Disappointed at not securing a lifting of the arms embargo, they also feared that Hale had returned to Washington with the wrong image of the revolutionaries and that he would prejudice the Wilson administration against them. Throughout the month of December, therefore, the Constitutionalist agents in Washington maintained contact with Hale and sought to cultivate a more favorable impression. To their surprise, they found that the American agent held the Constitutionalist leaders in high regard and that he was sympathetic to their cause. Yet he warned them that their attitude prevented a formal lifting of the arms embargo. He did suggest, probably without the knowledge of President Wilson, that it would be easy for the rebels to smuggle arms across the border at carefully selected isolated spots.[67]

Although there is no evidence that Hale attempted to influence the president in favor of the Constitutionalists, the rebel agents temporarily lost their liaison with the administration when, in January, Hale fell ill and was indisposed for months. Because of his illness, he asked to be relieved of his

66. O'Shaughnessy to State Department, November 13, 15, 1913, in NA 812.00/9705, 9720, 9755, 9756, 9757; New York *Times*, November 15, 1913, p. 2.

67. Hale to Wilson, December 31, 1913, in Wilson Papers, Ser. 2, Box 101; Francisco Urquidi (Constitutionalist agent, New York) a Antonio J. Villarreal, November 24, 1913, Buckley Papers, File No. 233; Robert V. Pesqueira (Constitutionalist agent, Washington) a Carranza, December 24, 30, 1913, in Fabela (ed.), *Documentos históricos de la Revolución Mexicana*, I, 180–81, 184–85.

duties. Wilson was saddened by the loss of so loyal and sympathetic a servant and, in acceding to the resignation, noted that he and Bryan would "be at a loss where to turn for similar service in the time ahead of us." [68] His services as an executive agent at an end, Hale ratified his faith in Wilson by publishing an article, "Our Moral Empire in America," in the May, 1914, issue of *The World's Work*. As the title suggests, the article was a defense of the president's righteous stand against the Huerta style of politics in Latin America.[69]

The mutual admiration and common political philosophies which had marked the relationship between Wilson and Hale did not survive World War I. As the war in Europe progressed in 1914–1915, the former special agent, a thorough Germanophile, became convinced that America's neutrality policies favored the Allies. Wilson's attitude especially disturbed him. He believed that the president's mind was "warped by the fact that he had never studied anything but British history." [70] Hale's dissatisfaction, plus the offer of a fifteen-thousand-dollar annual salary, led him, early in 1915, to accept a position with the German Information Service, a cover agency for Germany's propaganda effort in the United States. Although he later professed that the sinking of the *Lusitania* sickened him and that his enthusiasm for his work thereafter waned, he was a member of the propagandists' "Inner Council" for almost a year and a half. In May, 1916, he quit the German Information Service to accept the post of Berlin correspondent for the Hearst newspapers.[71]

Within months after American entry into the war, dis-

68. Hale to Wilson, December 31, 1913, January 13, 1914, in Wilson Papers, Ser. 2, Box 101; Wilson to Hale, January 14, 1914, *ibid.*, Ser. 3, Vol. 9, pp. 327–28.
69. William Bayard Hale, "Our Moral Empire in America," *The World's Work*, XXVIII (May, 1914), 52–58.
70. New York *Times*, July 27, 1918, p. 1.
71. *Ibid.*, December 7, 1918, p. 1; *ibid.*, April 11, 1924, p. 21; George Sylvester Viereck, *Spreading Germs of Hate* (New York, 1930), 53–54, 58, 113–14; *Dictionary of American Biography, s.v.* "Hale, William Bayard."

torted versions of Hale's role in the German propaganda effort were revealed to the public. Although his service to Germany had occurred before the United States became a belligerent, he was harried by the press, the Justice Department, and army intelligence throughout the remainder of the war.[72] Branded a traitor to his country, Hale denied any wrongdoing, and the fact that he was never prosecuted would seem to indicate that the government had no case against him.[73] During his travails, neither the president nor anyone else in the administration came to his defense. Rejected by his friends and journalist colleagues, Hale, an embittered man, retreated to Europe after the war. In the more friendly environs of Munich, he died on April 10, 1924, a relatively obscure figure.[74]

For almost seven months, from June to December, 1913, Hale was Wilson's most trusted adviser on Mexican affairs. He had forcefully, if not with complete accuracy, brought to the president's attention the sordid details of Huerta's rise to power. He was the first to impress upon Wilson and Bryan the strength of the revolutionaries. The recall of Henry Lane Wilson, the sending of John Lind, and the first attempts to promote cooperation with the Constitutionalists all resulted, in part, from his counsels. He left Wilson's service with a

72. New York *Times*, October 11, 1917, p. 1; *ibid.*, October 12, 1917, p. 3; *ibid.*, January 11, 1918, p. 5; *ibid.*, July 16, 1918, p. 1; *ibid.*, July 26, 1918, p. 20; *ibid.*, July 27, 1918, p. 1; *ibid.*, August 2, 1918, p. 10; *ibid.*, August 9, 1918, p. 1; *ibid.*, August 12, 1918, p. 9; *ibid.*, December 7, 1918, p. 1; *ibid.*, December 8, 1918, p. 4; *ibid.*, December 14, 1918, p. 3; *ibid.*, December 15, 1918, p. 10.

73. *Ibid.*, July 18, 1918, p. 10; *ibid.*, August 1, 1918, p. 11; *ibid.*, August 25, 1918, I, 2; *ibid.*, December 8, 1918, p. 4.

74. *Ibid.*, April 11, 1924, p. 21; *Dictionary of American Biography, s.v.* "Hale, William Bayard." Hale was the subject of numerous persecutions. He was expelled from social clubs and literary societies. His name was expunged from biographical directories. For example, the last edition of *Who's Who in America* to contain a biography of Hale was the 1916–1917 edition. Striking back at Wilson for his lack of support, Hale produced one more book, *The Story of a Style* (1920), in which he ridiculed his former master's rhetoric, literary ability, and idealism.

better understanding of what motivated the revolutionaries than any other member of the administration. But other agents would soon go beyond mere understanding and develop an emotional attachment to the rebels. It was their pleadings that would have the greatest effect on Wilson's attitude toward the Mexican revolution.

CHAPTER VI

A Budding
Friendship

All of Wilson's diplomatic efforts in Mexico in the fall of 1913 had met with failure. Having been rebuffed by both Huerta and Carranza, uncertain that either would ever establish a government in Mexico City that he could recognize, and fearful that military intervention would provoke war with both, Wilson announced on November 20 that he would again revert to a policy of "watchful waiting." [1] In what was perhaps the clearest statement of his Mexican policy to date, the president directed a circular note to the world powers announcing his determination "to isolate General Huerta entirely; to cut him off from foreign sympathy and aid and from domestic credit, whether moral or material, and so to force him out." He insisted, moreover, that he was willing to "await the results without irritation or impatience." [2] Presumably, he meant that he was willing to allow the civil war in Mexico to remain a war of attrition until the revolutionaries, whom he assumed had the best interests of the masses of Mexican people at heart, were victorious.

The siege-like operation implicit in the administration's Mexican policy was not to John Lind's liking. He believed that the Constitutionalists deserved the active support of the United States. Lind's sympathy for the rebels resulted from

1. New York *Times*, November 21, 1913, p. 1.
2. State Department to all embassies except Turkey and Mexico, and to European legations, Belgium, Netherlands, Norway, Sweden, Denmark, and Portugal, November 24, 1913, in NA 812.00/11443b.

his personal hatred of Huerta and, more important, from his growing awareness of what he considered to be the true causes of the Mexican revolution. As early as September 19, he wrote to Bryan that a purely political settlement, a mere transition in government, would solve none of Mexico's problems permanently. "There can be no lasting peace," he insisted, "without judicious and substantial social and economic reforms." [3]

Lind drew this conclusion from the information he gathered in his many interviews and voluminous correspondence. The initial spark likely came from William Bayard Hale, who had described the revolution as a struggle "between surviving medievalism, with its ideas of aristocracy, exploit [and] peonage, and modern civilization." [4] It was in such terms that Lind attempted to describe the conflict. But it was his own personal observations of the *hacienda* system and peasant life that made the greatest impact on Lind's thinking. Early in September he and Admiral Fletcher visited a *hacienda* near Vera Cruz which was managed by a fellow Minnesotan, R. M. Emery. Lind was appalled by the squalor in which the peons lived. He was outraged by the spectacle of peasants being worked mercilessly under the supervision of armed overseers. What astounded him most was that Mr. Emery, a well-educated man who was a former member of the University of Minnesota's board of regents, defended the system. "When Americans and 'Democrats' at that, in the course of a few

3. Lind to Bryan, September 19, 1913, in Bryan-Wilson Correspondence; John P. Harrison, "Un análisis norteamericano de la Revolución Mexicana," *Historia Mexicana*, V (April–June, 1956), 598–618. The latter citation is a Spanish translation of the first, with an introduction and notes. Harrison contends that, despite being an amateur diplomatist, Lind understood Mexico's needs better than did the professionals in the State Department. President Wilson was greatly impressed by the letter. In returning it to Bryan he noted: "It is a splendid letter and most instructive from every point of view. It will furnish us much food for thought and conference." See Wilson to Bryan, October 6, 1913, in Bryan Papers, Box 43.
4. Hale to State Department, June 3, 1913, in NA 812.00/12616.

years become so entranced with this method of appropriating the toil and blood of human beings that they wantonly repudiate the noblest accomplishments of our people," he wrote indignantly to Bryan, it was no wonder that revolution was ravaging Mexico. He intimated, moreover, that virtually every native and foreign-owned *hacienda* was guilty of exploiting the Mexican people.[5]

In reporting his analyses of the problems that beset Mexican society, Lind was often naïve, his information faulty. For example, he blamed Spanish colonial policy entirely for Mexico's contemporary agrarian problems, including the inequitable distribution of land. He seemed completely ignorant of the fact that many of the great aggregations of agricultural property had been secured within the past fifty years, during the Juárez and Díaz regimes of the late nineteenth century.[6] A man of definite anti-Catholic bias, Lind ignored any positive role the Church played in Mexican society and insisted that the clergy, from the bishops to the curates, were little more than agents of repression. If a Mexican was to succeed in business or politics, Lind intimated to Washington, he must cooperate with the Church. "Saint Peter holds the keys [to success]," he wrote to Bryan; "the Padre has some 'pull' with him; appease the Padre, make him well disposed, and the chances of enjoying the goodwill of Saint Peter are fair." [7] He suggested, also,

5. Lind to Bryan, September 19, 1913, in Bryan-Wilson Correspondence; *La Opinión* (Vera Cruz), September 5, 1913; New York *World*, September 2, 1913.

6. Lind to Bryan, September 19, 1913, in Bryan-Wilson Correspondence; John Lind, "The Mexican People," *The Bellman*, XVII (December 5, 12, 1914), 715–18, 749–54. This article, published after Lind's return to the United States, represents his comprehensive view of Mexico's problems. The article was originally delivered as an address to the Chicago Traffic Club in the fall of 1914.

For scholarly accounts of land acquisition and exploitation in the late nineteenth and early twentieth centuries, see George M. McBride, *The Land Systems of Mexico* (New York, 1923), 71–81; González Ramírez, *El Problema agrario*, 116–240.

7. Lind to State Department, August 28, 1913, NA 812.00/10487; Lind, "The Mexican People," XVII, 815–18, 749–54. This article was immediately

that the revolution resulted largely because the Church had lost its control over the common people. That Lind believed they were losing their reverence for the Church was demonstrated in a remarkable dispatch in which the agent suggested that the United States should secure an option on the National Cathedral as a likely site for building a new embassy.[8]

Lind mistakenly ignored all local influences and divided the Mexican people into two geographical groupings: northerners and southerners. Although he had never been in the northern part of the republic, he developed the notion that, with the possible exception of the wealthy propertied and professional classes of the South, the northern Mexicans were decidedly superior to their southern counterparts in intellectual and economic potential. He suggested that the backwardness of the southern Indians was comparable to that of the Negroes in the southern United States, except he believed that the potential of the Indians was greater than that of the black man. In fact, he had greater faith in the Indians than in the *mestizos* (mixed Indian and European). The single most stultifying influence in southern Mexico, he insisted, was "the mongrel progeny of the early Moorish Spaniards."[9] "It is absolutely futile to hope for orderly government at the hands of the Mexicans of the South," he wrote to Bryan, shortly after Huerta assumed dictatorial powers. Having concluded that a revolutionary settlement was necessary, Lind placed

branded as being anti-Catholic by Father Francis G. Kelley, an outspoken critic of the Wilson administration's Mexican policy. Claiming that Lind encouraged the revolutionaries, hence the persecution of the Catholic Church, Father Kelley used the article as anti-Wilson propaganda. Father Kelley also charged that Lind plagiarized most of his historical data from the *Encyclopaedia Britannica*, which may explain Lind's superficial knowledge of Mexican history. See testimony of Buckley, Lind, and Father Kelley, *Senate Documents*, 66th Cong., 2nd Sess., No. 285, pp. 774–79, 2336, 2682; Stephenson, *Lind*, 279–80.

8. Lind to State Department, December 18, 1913, in NA 812.00/10256; Lind to Wilson, January 10, 1914, in Wilson Papers, Ser. 2, Box 101.

9. Lind to Bryan, September 19, 1913, in Bryan-Wilson Correspondence.

his faith in the rebels of the North and dismissed those of the South, the followers of Emiliano Zapata, as little more than brigands.[10]

But Lind believed that more than the racial composition of the populations of the two sections was responsible for the North's advancement. He contended that northern Mexico's proximity to the United States was the single most important determinant. Northern Mexicans were afforded a greater opportunity to come into contact with Anglo-American ideas and institutions. The most fortunate among them, Lind noted, had even lived in the United States. They had labored for American businessmen, and they or their children had been educated in American schools. The total result was that the northerners had appropriated "progressive ideas" from the United States.[11] Lind naturally assumed, therefore, that the Constitutionalists of the North drew their revolutionary fervor from their association with American ideas and institutions. Their revolution, he wrote to President Wilson, was an attempt "to keep step with the march of our people." [12]

By the end of September, Lind felt that the United States had a definite responsibility to give moral support to the Constitutionalists; after his mid-November failure to pressure Huerta into resigning, he advocated outright assistance to the revolutionaries.[13] A revolutionary settlement "will be a little rough," he noted: "We must see to it that the walls are left intact, but I should not worry if some of the verandas and French windows are demolished . . . As a good friend and as

10. Lind to State Department, October 11, 1913, in NA 812.00/14966; Testimony of Lind, *Senate Documents*, 66th Cong., 2nd Sess., No. 285, pp. 2327–30; Lind, "The Mexican People," XVII, 718–19, 749, 752.

11. Lind to Bryan, September 19, 1913, in Bryan-Wilson Correspondence; Lind to Bryan, December 5, 1913, in Wilson Papers, Ser. 2, Box 42; Testimony of Lind, *Senate Documents*, 66th Cong., 2nd Sess., No. 285, pp. 2327–30.

12. Lind to Wilson, January 10, 1914, in Wilson Papers, Ser. 2, Box 101.

13. Lind to Bryan, September 19, 1913, in Bryan-Wilson Correspondence; Lind to State Department, November 13, 15, 1913, in NA 812.00/9704, 9760.

a true and unselfish one, only desirous of Mexico's good, we should be near enough to prevent a neighborhood scandal, and as a good neighbor we shall be glad also when the house is ready for permanent repairs to lent [sic] a helping hand and see to it that the work is done fairly and that the required material is not wasted." [14] In these comments Lind revealed his true thoughts concerning the Mexican revolution. Despite his sincere sympathies for the Constitutionalists, he had an early-twentieth-century American Progressive's middle-class fear of social upheaval. In this note and those that followed, in which he discussed the advisability of a rebel victory, Lind insisted that the Wilson administration be prepared to mitigate the extreme inclinations of the revolutionaries. The president read Lind's opinions with great interest. His own actions and statements ultimately revealed that he agreed with his agent's point of view. But for the time being Carranza's refusal to cooperate offered him no means by which to influence the revolution.

Lind even offered a solution to his problem. He suggested that aid be extended, instead, to General Pancho Villa. By late November, Lind had come to the opinion that Villa was a "true, virulent type of the most promising element of the Mexican population." He admitted that the general had faults, that he was "avaricious" and "cruel," but insisted, nonetheless, that he had attained the highest degree of "physical, moral and mental efficiency . . . [the Mexican] environment could reasonably expect to produce." But again Lind counseled that if aid was extended to Villa, the administration should attempt to restrain his extreme violent tendencies.[15]

Restraining the Constitutionalists, especially when their campaigns threatened the lives and property of foreigners, was a matter of grave concern to Wilson in December, 1913.

14. Lind to State Department, November 15, 1913, *ibid.*/9760.
15. Lind to State Department, December 5, 1913, *ibid.*/10077.

Having pressured the European powers into following his lead in formulating Mexican policy, Wilson, in turn, was being pressured by those nations to accept the responsibility for protecting the interests of all foreigners in Mexico. Accordingly, the president, in his annual address to Congress on December 2, promised that all efforts would be made to provide such protection.[16] Even as Wilson made this commitment, his resolve to stand by it was being tested by none other than Pancho Villa.

While Carranza was establishing his provisional government in the northwestern state of Sonora, General Villa was carving out a bailiwick of his own in north-central Mexico. After his smashing victory at Torreón, Coahuila, on October 8, he moved northward, captured Ciudad Juárez on November 16, then established dominion over the entire state of Chihuahua with the exception of the capital, Chihuahua. On December 3 this federal garrison fell, making Villa the strongest military force among the Constitutionalists.[17] Along with the news of Villa's military triumphs, State Department officials in Washington also received an increasing number of reports of *Villista* depredations upon foreign property.[18] These reports had begun to trickle in following the rebel victory at Torreón, but at that time it was hard for Wilson to be too concerned about the maltreatment of foreigners in northern Mexico, when at the same time Huerta was rigging elections, arresting legislators, and establishing himself as dictator. But when Villa captured

16. Cline, *United States and Mexico*, 152–53; New York *Times*, December 3, 1913, pp. 1–2.
17. Quirk, *Mexican Revolution*, 17; Barragán Rodríguez, *Historia . . . de la Revolución Constitutionalista*, I, 263–87.
18. All American counsuls in Mexico had standing instructions from the State Department to make representations in behalf of the lives and interests of all foreigners in their territory of jurisdiction. The instructions and representative complaints from American, French, Spanish, German, Japanese, and Chinese nationals concerning depredations by the revolutionaries may be found in *Foreign Relations, 1913*, 898–956.

Chihuahua, the crisis in Mexico City had passed and Wilson had made his commitment to protect foreign interests. He could no longer ignore the depredations, especially after Villa ordered every Spaniard to leave Mexico within ten days or face a firing squad.[19]

Out of this new problem that confronted Wilson came one ray of hope. Villa obviously favored Americans over other foreigners and, because Wilson had not recognized Huerta, gave them preferential treatment. He clearly demonstrated this attitude at Torreón. Immediately after the capture of that city, the *Villistas* began an indiscriminate looting of the business establishments. The American consular agent, George C. Carothers, quickly sent a note of protest to General Villa's headquarters, demanding the protection of American lives and property. Within an hour, an officer and a squad of soldiers were placed at Carothers' disposal. Taking orders from him, the soldiers were posted before American-owned businesses. At the same time, Villa ordered the cessation of all looting and punished some of the perpetrators. Thereafter Carothers reported the *Villistas* were orderly.[20]

What was also encouraging about the Torreón episode was that Consul Carothers was able to persuade Villa to mitigate his harsh attitude toward other foreigners. Calling upon the general to thank him personally for protecting American interests, Carothers also protested the persecution of the Spaniards in Torreón.[21] Most of the Spaniards in question were not remnants of the colonial regime, but had immigrated to Mexico during the presidency of Porfirio Díaz and

19. Marion Letcher (American consul, Chihuahua) to State Department, December 11, 1913, and State Department to Letcher, December 12, 1913, in *Foreign Relations, 1913*, 903–904.

20. Theodore C. Hamm (American consul, Durango, forwarding Carothers' report of conditions in Torreón, September 25–October 11, 1913) to State Department, October 15, 1913, in NA 812.00/9658; copy in Wilson Papers, Ser. 2, Box 97; Testimony of George C. Carothers, February 28, 1920, *Senate Documents*, 66th Cong., 2nd Sess., No. 285, p. 1766.

21. *Ibid.*

had become some of his staunchest supporters. Most of the Spaniards were proprietors of small businesses, and their credit policies had always been unpopular with the lower classes;[22] now Villa charged that they were all *Huertistas* and had aided the federals in the defense of Torreón. Carothers argued that the general's charges were unfounded and, whether a result of the consul's persuasion or some other influence, Villa temporarily halted his persecution of the Spaniards.[23]

Before Villa left Torreón to begin his campaigns in Chihuahua, he called upon Carothers, wished him well, and promised to cooperate with other American officials in the future. But when Villa captured Chihuahua and renewed his persecution of the Spaniards, the American consul there, Marion Letcher, was unable to change the general's attitude.[24] By this time the State Department had decided that a special agent was needed in Constitutionalist-controlled territory to reinforce the efforts of the consuls. Not surprisingly, the man chosen for the delicate mission was George C. Carothers, the consular agent at Torreón.

Carothers was a longtime resident of Mexico. In 1889, aged fourteen, he had emigrated with his parents from San Antonio, Texas, to Saltillo, Coahuila. In 1902 he was made the consular agent at Torreón. Since consular agents did not receive a regular salary, but merely a percentage of the fees

22. The economic activities of the Spaniards were aptly described by Edith O'Shaughnessy: "The Spaniards are the traders of Mexico. They keep countless pawn-shops (*empegnos*); they are usurers and money-lenders of all kinds; they are the overseers on the *haciendas* and, incidentally, they keep all the grocery-shops; in fact, they control the sale of nearly everything in Mexico." See O'Shaughnessy, *A Diplomat's Wife in Mexico*, 94.

23. Hamm to State Department, October 15, 1913, in NA 812.00/9658; Testimony of Carothers, *Senate Documents*, 66th Cong., 2nd Sess., No. 285, p. 1766.

24. Hamm to State Department, October 15, 1913, in NA 812.00/9658; Letcher to State Department, December 18, 1913, in *Foreign Relations, 1913*, 909.

collected for official services, Carothers occupied himself mainly as a commission merchant, grocer, and real estate speculator. Never a large operator, he estimated in 1914 that his holdings were worth no more than 25,000 pesos.[25] Because of his penchant for gambling, he was perpetually in debt. Indeed, in February, 1912, State Department officials, after a special investigation, had ordered Carothers dismissed from the consular service because of his inability to meet his financial obligations. Before the dismissal order was put into effect, Torreón was swept up in the Orozco rebellion against the Madero government. During those troubled days, Carothers worked tirelessly to protect American lives and property and won the admiration of his superiors and the citizens of Torreón, including his creditors. The director of the Consular Service, Wilbur J. Carr, decided therefore that Carothers deserved another chance.[26]

In his late thirties, George Carothers was a portly figure of a man; his belly hung over his belt, forming what his Mexican friends called the "curve of felicity." He wore small-apertured, metal-rimmed eyeglasses that accentuated the full-moon shape of his face. Despite his bulk, he was fastidious in his dress and presented a pleasing appearance.[27] His dispatches reveal that he was not excitable and that he was almost always in good spirits. From his childhood days in San Antonio, he seemed to prefer the companionship of Mexicans

25. *Register of the Department of State, 1917* (Washington, D.C., 1918), 81; Raymond G. Carroll, "United States Special Agents Powerful in Mexico," New York *Sun*, August 15, 1915; copy in Buckley Papers, File No. 233; National Archives, Record Group 59, File No. 111.70C22/59; Carothers to State Department, October 8, 1914, *ibid.*, 125.36582/111. For the nature of the office of consular agent, see Graham H. Stuart, *American Diplomatic and Consular Practice* (New York, 1952), 343–44.

26. George H. Murphy (consul general at large) to State Department, January 20, 1912, in NA 125.36582/40; State Department to Hamm, February 5, 1912, *ibid.*/40a; Hamm to State Department, March 30, 1912, *ibid.*/42; State Department to Hamm, April 10, 1912, *ibid.*

27. Edward Larocque Tinker, *Corridas and Calaveras* (Austin, Tex., 1961), 6.

to that of Anglo-Americans. In Torreón his business interests brought him into contact with all strata of Mexican society. He knew their problems and understood their moods.[28] As a journalist who watched Carothers in action put it, "he knew latino psychology as a cow knows its calf." [29]In the vernacular of the border, he was *simpático*.

In the beginning, the nature of Carothers' service was different from that of previous agents. He was directly responsible to the secretary of state rather than to the president. His communications went through formal department channels. At first his observations and opinions were not solicited. He was instructed to perform specific tasks and report the results. Only after months of service was he encouraged to operate on his own initiative.

At the time of his appointment to the post of special agent, Carothers was on a leave of absence attending to some personal affairs in the United States. On November 17 he stopped in Washington long enough to have an interview with Boaz Long, chief of the State Department's Division of Latin American Affairs. He again described his relations with Villa, picturing the general as not only capable, well-meaning, and just, but as willing to cooperate with American officials.[30] Coincidentally, Carothers gave a verbal account of his cordial relations with Villa at the same time that the department was receiving William Bayard Hale's reports of his own troubled relations with Carranza at the Nogales Conferences. The friendly attitude of the Chihuahua strong man contrasted dramatically with the bellicose pronouncements of the First Chief and offered tantalizing possibilities for influencing the course of the Mexican revolution that

28. Carroll, "United States Special Agents," New York *Sun*, August 15, 1915.

29. Tinker, *Corridas and Calaveras*, 6.

30. Hamm to State Department, October 27, 1913, in NA 125.36582/50; Long, Memorandum of conversation with G. C. Carothers, November 26, 1913, in NA 812.00/9836½.

Wilson could not ignore. Carothers' impressions, moreover, were strongly reinforced by those of Lind. The decision to send a State Department agent to northern Mexico, therefore, was prompted as much by a desire to establish cordial relations with at least one Constitutionalist leader as by a desire to protect foreign lives and property.

The probability of a new assignment must have been mentioned to Carothers while he was in Washington, because he sent Bryan an itinerary of his movements for the month of December. The department's initial instructions, dated December 9, found Carothers aboard ship en route from New York to Galveston, Texas. He was "to make a trip into the State of Chihuahua with the view of conferring with General Villa and other leaders, for the purpose of insuring, in so far as may be possible, lives and property of Americans and other foreigners." [31] More urgent instructions awaited his arrival in Texas City, Texas. He was informed that Villa had ordered some four hundred Spaniards at Chihuahua to abandon their property and leave Mexico or be shot and that Consul Marion Letcher was unable to persuade the rebel general to reverse his decree. Carothers was instructed to "proceed directly to Chihuahua" and "renew and reinforce Letcher's representations." These instructions, as did the ones that followed, also hinted that Carothers' mission would entail more than merely looking to the protection of foreigners' lives and property. He was directed to "represent to him [Villa] . . . in the most impressive manner . . . the horror that would be felt throughout the civilized world by the infliction of such a penalty." [32] If Wilson was ever to openly support the revolutionaries, he wanted them to be more respectable than Huerta.

31. Carothers to State Department, December 2, 1913, *ibid.*, 125.36582/134; Carothers to State Department, December 5, 1913, *ibid.*, 312.52/79; State Department to Carothers, December 9, 1913, in *Foreign Relations, 1913*, 902.

32. State Department to Carothers, December 13, 1913, in *Foreign Relations, 1913*, 906.

Pausing briefly in San Antonio and El Paso to confer with Constitutionalist agents, Carothers arrived in Chihuahua on December 22, where he met with a hostile reception at the American consulate. Letcher viewed the special agent's presence as evidence of Bryan's displeasure with the consulate's efforts. His pride obviously wounded, Letcher told Carothers that he could accomplish nothing in Chihuahua and stalked haughtily from the room. Bewildered, the special agent set out on his own to find Villa. The enmity that developed in this first encounter between Letcher and Carothers was to plague their relationship throughout Carothers' tenure as special agent.[33]

The special agent found Villa indisposed on the evening of December 22, but the next morning they breakfasted together. During the course of their meal, Carothers confronted Villa about the mistreatment of the Spaniards. In response, the rebel general poured out his bitter hatred for the Spaniards, reviewing all of his earlier charges against them. He also claimed that during the battle for Chihuahua he had found arms and ammunition in the hands of the Spaniards and had positive knowledge that they had aided the federals in the defense of the city. Carothers then insisted that no one should be executed without a fair trial, and Villa agreed that none would be molested unless a court proved them guilty of aiding the *Huertistas.* He also promised that all who could establish their innocence could return to their property.[34]

33. Carothers to State Department, December 31, 1913, in NA 312.52/104; El Paso *Morning Times,* December 16, 1913; San Antonio *Express,* December 19, 1913. By February, 1914, the antagonism between Carothers and Letcher intensified to such a degree that Carothers asked Secretary Bryan to intercede and order Letcher to cooperate. Shortly thereafter Bryan ordered the consul to afford the special agent "all assistance in your power." See Carothers to State Department, February 10, 1914, and State Department to Letcher, February 18, 1914, in NA 812.00/10903.

34. Carothers to State Department, December 26, 31, 1913, in NA 312.52/94, 104; El Paso *Morning Times,* December 24, 1913.

Having acceded to Carothers' requests, Villa in turn urged that President Wilson lift the arms embargo. He insisted that with access to arms from the United States, he would be in Mexico City within sixty days. Having no authority to discuss this matter, Carothers could offer no encouragement. After the interview, the special agent left Chihuahua, fully confident that in the future Villa would be cooperative. Congratulating himself on the success of his efforts, Carothers paused in El Paso long enough to file a brief telegraphic report to Washington before hastening to Fort Worth, Texas, to join his family for Christmas.[35] In his initial effort, Carothers seemingly had met with more success than any of the previous agents.

Meanwhile, John Lind was experiencing nothing but frustration as he grew increasingly impatient with the Constitutionalists' slow advance toward Mexico City. Having accompanied Admiral Fletcher on a voyage to Tuxpan and Tampico in late November and early December, Lind returned to Vera Cruz convinced that the rebels could easily capture those cities with the encouragement of the United States. They were inhibited from doing so, the special agent insisted, because they feared intervention by United States Marines if any American oil properties were threatened. In a patently absurd reply, Bryan offered no encouragement for the rebels, but advised Lind to suggest to Admiral Fletcher and British naval authorities that they urge the federals to surrender the cities without a fight and thus prevent the destruction of the oil production facilities.[36]

Throughout the month of December, Lind reported repeatedly that economic conditions in Mexico City were deteriorating, that Huerta and his henchmen were hanging on only to

35. El Paso *Morning Times*, December 24, 1913; Carothers to State Department, December 24, 1913, in NA 312.52/88.

36. Lind to State Department, November 24, 27, 29, December 3, 1913, in NA 812.00/9900, 9931, 9975, 10045, 10046; State Department to Lind, November 24, 30, 1913, *ibid.*/9954a, 9975.

plunder the treasury and enrich themselves. If the rebels were not speeded to victory, he warned, conditions in Mexico might become so critical that the outcry of European and American interests for protection would become so intense that the United States might be forced to intervene militarily.[37] When by mid-month the administration offered the rebels no encouragement, Lind asked for a personal conference with the president.[38] Pressured by Bryan and the counselor of the State Department, John Bassett Moore, Wilson agreed to meet Lind while on Christmas vacation at Pass Christian, Mississippi.[39]

On December 30 Admiral Fletcher placed the cruiser U.S.S. *Chester* at Lind's disposal, and Lind sailed for the Mississippi coast. Since his instructions did not specify that his departure be secret, the special agent, unable to contain his jubilation, told reporters that he welcomed the opportunity to speak directly with the president and hoped that the meeting would herald a change in the administration's policy. Wilson was visibly annoyed when reporters descended upon his holiday retreat and gave the conference the fullest publicity. Lind's views being well known, rumors spread that Constitutionalist officials were aboard the *Chester* and that more active support of the revolutionaries would follow the meeting. Another widely circulated rumor had it that Lind was accompanied by officers of Huerta's government, who were prepared to lead an American-backed *coup* to oust the dictator.[40]

37. Lind to State Department, December 5, 8, 14, 15, 19, 22, 1913, *ibid.*/10077, 10098, 10185, 10196, 10269, 10291.

38. State Department to Lind, December 13, 1913, *ibid.*/10152; Lind to State Department, December 19, 1913, *ibid.*/10269.

39. Bryan to Wilson, December 25, 1913, in Wilson Papers, Ser. 2, Box 100; Moore to Wilson, December 29, 1913, *ibid.*, Ser. 4, Box 285; Wilson to Moore, December 29, 1913, in NA 812.00/10454.

40. Josephus Daniels, secretary of the navy, to Admiral Fletcher, December 29, 1913, in Josephus Daniels Papers, Division of Manuscripts, Library of Congress, Box 39; Canada to State Department, December 30,

Wilson, now fearful of his agent's discretion in meeting the press, did not even allow him ashore. Instead, the president steamed several miles into the Gulf of Mexico aboard a revenue cutter to meet Lind aboard the *Chester*. Although reporters chartered a tug and shadowed the president, they were not allowed aboard ship to witness the conference. The secrecy of the meeting, plus Wilson's refusal afterwards even to discuss it with the press, only served to multiply and amplify the rumors.[41] Aboard ship Lind applied every argument in his repertoire to try to persuade Wilson of the necessity of giving outright support to the Constitutionalists.[42] But as Wilson indicated in reporting the character of the meeting to Secretary Bryan, Lind offered "nothing new" to persuade the president to change his policy. Lind, nonetheless, returned to Vera Cruz confident that he had been persuasive and certain that a lifting of the arms embargo and more active support of the rebels would soon follow.[43]

A month passed without Wilson taking action on his agent's suggestions. For one thing, Bryan opposed lifting the arms embargo. To him it seemed inconsistent to make representations to the rebels for the protection of foreign lives and property, then to intensify the violence in Mexico by

1913, in NA 812.00/10377; New York *Times*, December 30, 1913, January 1, 2, 1914, p. 1; *Daily Picayune* (New Orleans), January 1, 2, 1914.

41. New York *Times*, January 2, 1914, p. 1; *ibid.*, January 4, 1914, p. 2; *Daily Picayune*, January 3–5, 1914.

42. A transcript of Wilson's shorthand notes taken at the Pass Christian conference gives only hints of the topics of discussion but suggest that Lind urged vigorous action. See notes from conversation with Lind (transcript made under direction of Ray Stannard Baker), [n.d.], in Wilson Papers, Ser. 2, Box 101.

43. Wilson to Bryan, January 6, 1913, in Bryan Papers, Box 29; Lind to Wilson, January 10, 1914, in Wilson Papers, Ser. 2, Box 101; Lind to Mrs. Lind, January 22, 1914, in Lind Papers; Lind to Bryan, January 15, 1914, in NA 812.00/10652½. Lind left no record of his comments to the president at the Pass Christian conference, but from his correspondence to Wilson, Bryan, and Mrs. Lind, it is apparent that he believed Wilson was in complete agreement with his views.

giving them easier access to weapons.[44] His apprehension was eased somewhat by Luis Cabrera, Carranza's new agent in Washington. Late in January Cabrera held several secret conferences with Third Assistant Secretary of State William Phillips. He offered assurances that the Constitutionalists would respect foreign-owned property. In a move that seemed to signal a greater willingness by Carranza to cooperate with the Wilson administration, Cabrera also assured Phillips that the revolutionaries intended to accomplish their program of social and economic reform by constitutional methods.[45]

Wilson still had reservations about openly supporting the rebels. Phillips noted that even after receiving Cabrera's assurances, the president was determined to "do what he believed right and not to be overinfluenced by the Mexicans." [46] Yet a policy change which favored the Constitutionalists did follow soon after the Phillips-Cabrera meetings. If the Mexican agent's reassuring words sparked this policy change, then, even more certainly, Lind's advice had earlier paved the way. In a letter to Ambassador Page on January 29, Wilson revealed a greater understanding of the Constitutionalists than ever before. Excluding the *Zapatistas*, as Lind would have, Wilson concluded that the "men in the North" are "not mere rebels . . . They are conducting a revolution with a programme which goes to the very root of the causes which have made constitutional government in Mexico impossible." [47]

By this time another factor may have influenced the president as much as or more than the advice of his agent. For months administration officials had been aware that the Constitutionalists were smuggling arms across the border.

44. Bryan to Wilson, [n.d.], in Bryan Papers, Box 41.
45. Link, *New Freedom*, 388–89; William Phillips, *Ventures in Diplomacy* (Boston, 1952), 60–62.
46. Phillips, *Ventures in Diplomacy*, 61.
47. Link, *New Freedom*, 389.

But in the early weeks of 1914, the Justice Department gained positive evidence that Huerta's agents were purchasing large quantities of weapons and ammunition from American firms. Most of these arms reached his hands by way of Havana, although some were smuggled out of New Orleans aboard private yachts.[48] Since Huerta was apparently receiving more illicit arms than the Constitutionalists, maybe even benefiting from the embargo, Wilson finally decided that Lind's advice was sound. On January 31 he sent a circular note to his diplomatic corps directing them to inform the powers that he no longer felt "justified in maintaining an irregular position as regards the contending parties in the matter of neutrality" and that he intended to "remove the inhibition on the exportation of arms and ammunition from the United States into Mexico." Three days later he took the fateful step.[49]

Lind, meanwhile, had chafed at Wilson's delay in lifting the embargo. When the president finally made the move, the special agent interpreted it as an unqualified endorsement of the policies he had been advocating. Not satisfied with this triumph, he now demanded even more active support for the Constitutionalists. "The cause of the revolutionists is now our cause," he proclaimed in a note to Bryan, "we must see to it that they make the best of their opportunity and we must help them to do so." [50] Even before the lifting of the embargo, he urged that the United States somehow take over the commissary operations of the revolutionary armies. He insisted that the rebels "should not be permitted to fritter away

48. Michael C. Meyer, "The Arms of the *Ypiranga*," *Hispanic American Historical Review*, L (August, 1970), 544–50.

49. State Department to all diplomatic missions of the United States, January 31, 1914, and proclamation revoking the proclamation of March 14, 1912, prohibiting the exportation of arms or munitions of war to Mexico, February 3, 1914, Department of State, in *Papers Relating to the Foreign Relations of the United States, 1914* (Washington, D.C., 1922), 446–48.

50. Lind to State Department, January 30, 1914, in NA 812.00/10737.

their time foraging in a country that must be well nigh exhausted." [51] Later he suggested that the United States provide advisors to organize the Constitutionalists' transportation, communications, and intelligence systems. "We must see to it that they get brains as well as bullets," he counseled. Urging rapid victory at any cost, he offered a plan by which the revolutionaries might capture Mexico City without losing a man. He suggested means by which the city could be denied its fuel, food, and power supplies. The population of the capital would be so alarmed, he insisted, that, for their own self-interest, the people would rise up and drive Huerta from office.[52]

Perhaps his most ambitious scheme for aiding the rebels called for the capture of Huerta's gunboats, which guarded the Gulf Coast. Trained by the U.S. Navy and commanded by a U.S. Marine officer—who would temporarily assume civilian status—a small band of Mexican guerrillas, Lind insisted, could easily capture the gunboats and use them to invade Tampico and Vera Cruz. With the gunboats in rebel hands, the agent believed that the revolution would be over in thirty days. When the gunboat *Zaragoza* sailed for New Orleans for repairs early in February, Lind wired Washington that a naval officer friend at Vera Cruz had suggested that one Armin Hartrath, a graduate of the Annapolis class of '88 and currently a resident of New York City, might be willing to lead a group of Mexican guerrillas in an attempt to capture the gunboat as it left the mouth of the Mississippi River on its return to Tampico. Although the president vetoed this wild scheme, he congratulated Lind on the detailed information he had compiled.[53]

The pace of the revolutionaries' offensive was never fast

51. Lind to State Department, January 12, 1914, *ibid.*/10517.

52. Lind to State Department, January 30, 1914, *ibid.*/10737.

53. Lind to Wilson, January 10, 1914, Ser. 2, Box 101; Lind to State Department, February 5, 6, 1914, in NA 812.00/10792, 10818, 10819; State Department to Lind, February 8, 1914, *ibid.*/10818.

enough for Lind, and the three-month period of January through March, 1914, was a time of great anguish for him. After victories—Villa's at Chihuahua and Ojinaga, Obregón's at Culiacán, and General Pablo González' at Ciudad Victoria —in December and January, the rebel advance halted.[54] Huerta's regime, having been at a low point both militarily and financially in November and December, showed signs of rejuvenation in January and February. Even in December, Huerta enjoyed a glimmer of success; while his armies were losing in some sectors, other federal forces recaptured the all-important rail center of Torreón. Shortly thereafter the Church hierarchy, *hacendados,* and bankers closed ranks behind the usurper as their best hope for survival.[55] Lind viewed this reactionary tendency with increasing alarm; instead of seeing the turn of events as evidence of Huerta's growing strength, he insisted that the old general's stepped-up programs of military conscription, forced loans, and taxation were signs of impending anarchy. In the face of such conditions, on February 24 he suggested a new course of action, one that obviously had been on his mind for weeks: "I believe, and I say this after serious reflection, that if the revolutionists fail to take active and efficient action by the middle of March it will be incumbent on the United States to put an end to Huerta's saturnalia of crime and oppression." [56] Thereafter he never relented in his demands for military intervention.

Even though Bryan insisted that intervention was out of the question, Lind proceeded, on his own initiative, to plan a campaign for the capture of Mexico City. First he sent a

54. Quirk, *Mexican Revolution,* 17–19; Barragán Rodriguez, *Historia . . . de la Revolución Constitucionalista,* I, 113, 271, 289–93; González Ramírez, *Las Ideas—La Violencia,* 406–409.

55. Meyer, *Huerta,* 169; Vera Estañol, *La Revolución Mexicana,* 350–57; Edwin Walter Kemmerer, *Inflation and Revolution: Mexico's Experience of 1912–1917* (Princeton, N.J., 1940), 11–26.

56. Lind to State Department, January 7, 14, 24, 26, February 18, 24, 1914, in NA 812.00/10462, 10539, 10677, 10688, 10924, 10965.

marine officer to the capital to make a reconnaissance of Huerta's military installations. Then he arranged with the American manager of the Mexican National Railway to transport secretly several hundred marines to Mexico City by night. At dawn the marines would seize strategic locations, arrest Huerta, and establish a military government which would serve until the Constitutionalists could occupy the city. Huerta was to be given political asylum in the United States.[57] Lind acknowledged that Carranza should be informed of the operation in advance but did not think the Constitutionalist leader would raise objections. "The taking of Mexico City," he euphorically assured the secretary of state, "if limited to the purpose of putting a stop to Huerta's anarchical career and to afford the Mexican people an opportunity to resume orderly government should not be regarded as intervention in the offensive sense it seems to me." [58] Significantly, Bryan replied that "the President has received your recent reports and has them under consideration." [59] Was this a hint that Wilson's patience was also wearing thin and that he considered intervention a likely prospect?

Sharing Lind's frustrations over Huerta's tenacity and the Constitutionalists' inability to rapidly unseat the usurper, Wilson also had to cope with the problems resulting from the predatory actions of the revolutionaries. Even after Carothers' apparently successful trip into Chihuahua in December,

57. State Department to Lind, March 3, 1914, *ibid.*/11000; Lind to State Department, February 24, March 8, 12, 23, 1914, *ibid.*/10965, 11098, 11227, 27482; Captain W. A. Burnside (U.S.M.C.) to Lind (conveying summary of military strength and action, February 26–March 4, 1914), [n.d.], *ibid.*/16251; Stephenson, *John Lind*, 259–60. Stephenson, using only the Lind Papers, and not having access to complete State Department files, suggested that the "most charitable" conclusion to be drawn from this scheme is that it was pressed upon Lind by marine and navy officers who were "itching for a scrap with the greasers." State Department records indicate that Lind was the instigator of the plan.
58. Lind to State Department, March 12, 1914, in NA 812.00/11227.
59. State Department to Lind, March 25, 1914, *ibid.*/11265.

A Budding Friendship   145

the State Department continued to receive news of depredations against the Spaniards. In addition to these complaints
came reports that Villa was confiscating coal from American-
owned mining companies and making threatening gestures
toward German and Japanese firms. Special agent Carothers
had no sooner arrived in Fort Worth, Texas, for a Christmas
holiday when dispatches from Washington directed him to
find Villa and investigate the reports.[60]

On January 1 Carothers rendezvoused with Villa on the
border at Ciudad Juárez. This time the general became
annoyed that the American should repeatedly involve himself
in affairs that did not directly concern the United States.
When Carothers refused to back down, explaining that he
was acting on orders from President Wilson, Villa's attitude
softened. The next day he provided the agent with a written
explanation of his actions, which Carothers forwarded to
Washington. In emotion-packed phrases (since Villa could
barely write, he must have dictated the note to a stenographer or had one of his advisors prepare it), the rebel general
again poured out his bitter hatred for the Spaniards. He
claimed that he had intended to keep his earlier promises but
found it necessary to continue the deportations as a means of
protecting the Spaniards from the wrath of his soldiers. Any
of them who could vindicate themselves, he promised, could
return to their homes and property without fear of reprisals.
Again Carothers was satisfied that Villa was acting in good
faith.[61]

It took Carothers longer to settle a dispute between Villa
and the Guggenheim-owned American Smelting and Refining
Company. The rebel general had demanded that the company
purchase some $500,000 worth of confiscated ores, much of

60. State Department to Carothers, December 27, 1913, in *Foreign
Relations, 1913*, 909–10.
61. Carothers to State Department, December 30, 31, 1913, in NA
312.11/3073, 312.52/104; Villa to Carothers, January 1, 1914, *ibid.* 312.52/104;
New York *Times*, February 22, 1914, II, p. 1.

which had been taken from the company itself or from its preferred customers. On January 20 Carothers reported that Villa had agreed to return the ores he had confiscated from the company and promised that it would not be required to purchase any ores confiscated from other foreign-owned mines.[62] Thereafter Villa's relations with American Smelting and Refining were cordial. He protected its shipments to the border and it provided him with coal for his railroads.[63]

Carothers was far less successful in securing protection for *El Desengaño* Mine of Guanacevi, Durango, which was owned jointly by Spanish, Mexican, and American citizens. Since the order to confiscate the mine allegedly came from Villa, Carothers brought the matter to the general's attention. Villa denied having issued the decree. While Carothers was attempting to determine the source of the order, the State Department directed Consul Frederick Simpich at Nogales to take up the matter with Carranza. In response the First Chief issued a directive that gave local rebel leaders a temporary respite from American diplomatic pressure. Asserting his prerogative as leader of the revolutionary forces, Carranza demanded that all complaints of foreigners be directed to his minister of foreign affairs, Isidro Fabela, only by diplomatic representatives of the country directly concerned.[64] At approximately the same time, Cabrera, in Washington, was giving assurances that the Constitutionalists would respect foreign-owned property. Theoretically there was no contradiction between Carranza's directive and Cabrera's promises, since each nation was given an opportunity to make represen-

62. State Department to Carothers, January 19, 1914, in NA 312.115an3/84; Carothers to State Department, January 20, 1914, *ibid./*85.
    63. Clarence C. Clendenen, *The United States and Pancho Villa* (Ithaca, N.Y., 1961), 73–74.
    64. Spanish ambassador to State Department, January 7, 1914, in *Foreign Relations, 1914*, 786; State Department to Carothers, January 10, 1914, *ibid.*, 787–88; Simpich to State Department, February 19, 1914, *ibid.*, 793; Carothers to State Department, January 11, 12, 1914, in NA 312.52/114, 118.

tations in behalf of its own citizens. At any rate, Wilson and Bryan paid no heed to the First Chief's newest demand and continued to direct their appeals in behalf of all foreigners directly to Villa and other subordinate rebel leaders.

Further complicating Carothers' efforts, Bryan also involved him in matters that concerned only Mexican citizens. For example, the agent was instructed to intercede in behalf of Luis Terrazas, Jr., a wealthy Chihuahua *hacendado* and son of a former governor of the state, whom the *Villistas* were holding under arrest and daily threatening to execute.[65] The plight of the entire Terrazas family, whose multi-million-acre *haciendas* had been confiscated by the revolutionaries, had become a cause célèbre in the United States. The New York *Times* condemned Villa's actions as "brigandage," numerous Americans urged the State Department to intercede, and Senator Albert B. Fall of New Mexico, an old friend of the family, even went to the border to apply pressure on Villa's agents in El Paso.[66] But Villa remained impervious even to Carothers' appeals. He promised that Luis, Jr., would not be harmed but insisted that he be held hostage to guarantee that his father would not finance a counterrevolution in Chihuahua as he had against Madero.[67] As Villa put it to Carothers:

65. Secretary of war to secretary of state (forwarding letter from General Hugh L. Scott, El Paso), December 13, 1913, in *Foreign Relations, 1913*, 905; State Department to Carothers, December 15, 1913, *ibid.*, 907; New York *Times*, December 12, 1913, p. 1; El Paso *Morning Times*, December 12, 17, 1913; Alamada, *La Revolución en el Estado de Chihuahua*, II, 68–70.

66. New York *Times*, December 12, 1913, p. 1; Fall to State Department, December 16, 1913, in NA 812.00/10223; Carothers to State Department, December 31, 1913, *ibid.* 312.52/104. The State Department 812.00 and 312.12 files contain numerous appeals in the Terrazas' behalf from Americans and Mexicans.

67. Carothers to State Department, January 28, February 3, 1914, in NA 812.00/10706, 10780, 10820; Ronald Atkin, *Revolution! Mexico, 1910–1920* (New York, 1970), 164–65. Villa never released Terrazas. He remained a hostage for months. Ultimately he escaped and made his way to safety in El Paso. Villa's reasons for holding young Terrazas hostage were not entirely unjustified. In 1912 Luis, Sr., helped finance the Orozco rebellion against Madero. See Meyer, *Pascual Orozco*, 108–109.

"Cuando se amara el becerro la vaca no anda muy lejos." [68]

Despite only mixed success in his early relations with General Villa, Carothers immediately formed a high opinion of this bandit-turned-revolutionary. The special agent was especially impressed by the quick, simple justice which the *caudillo* (chieftain) meted out to his followers and how they adored him. Carothers acknowledged that Villa often committed unspeakable atrocities against the *Huertistas*; but since the Federals murdered, even hanged, prisoners, Villa contended that he was only fighting fire with fire.[69] The agent continued to be encouraged by the general's pro-American attitude. Overjoyed by the lifting of the arms embargo, Villa had proclaimed openly that President Wilson was "the most just man in the World. All Mexicans will love him." Hereafter, he announced, "We [the *Villistas*] will look upon the United States as our friend." [70] In the enthusiasm of the moment, he promised Carothers that, even if his actions seemed "arbitrary and contrary to custom," he would reveal "the real truth about everything" to President Wilson and would "take the consequences of his acts." [71]

Events soon proved that Villa would not always be truthful in his relations with the United States. On February 19 the Associated Press carried a story that Villa had arrested Gustave Bauch, an American, and William S. Benton, a Scotsman, on a charge of filibustering against the revolution. Although Bauch's whereabouts was never determined, and the diplomatic wrangling over his case lasted for months, the Benton case caused the greatest notoriety.[72] The British

68. Carothers to State Department, February 10, 1914, in NA 812.00/10903.

69. Carothers to State Department, February 3, 1914, *ibid.*/10820.

70. "Letting the Guns into Mexico," *Literary Digest,* XLVIII (February 14, 1914), 303–304.

71. Carothers to State Department, February 3, 1914, in NA 812.00/10820.

72. New York *Times,* February 19, 1914, p. 1; Fabela, *Historia Diplomática,* I, 298–308. Although Villa revealed through Carranza's foreign minister, Isidro Fabela, that Bauch was released hours after his arrest, his exact fate has never been determined.

embassy in Washington, having received an urgent appeal for help from the Scotsman's Mexican wife, requested the State Department to investigate. Both Carothers and Thomas Edwards, the American consul at Juárez, were thereupon directed to see Villa and determine Benton's fate.[73] Before Carothers received the dispatch, he was contacted by friends and relatives of Benton. At their request, he went to Villa and asked what had happened to the Scotsman. Uncharacteristically, the general asked Carothers if he was there in an official capacity. When the agent replied that he was only representing friends, Villa would offer nothing more than assurances that Benton was safe. Although puzzled by Villa's attitude, Carothers returned to El Paso where he found the dispatch from the State Department awaiting him. He immediately wired Washington his belief that Benton was merely being held until Villa left Juárez the following day. Carothers was confident that Benton was unharmed.[74]

Carothers next decided that Consul Edwards should make an official inquiry to insure Benton's safety. Confronted by the consul, Villa confessed that Benton was dead. He claimed that the Scotsman had come to his headquarters armed with a pistol and had attempted to kill him. Villa would give no details of Benton's death but agreed that his wife might claim his property. Before Edwards could report his findings to Washington, the department, on the strength of Carothers' telegram, issued a press release giving assurances of Benton's safety. When the news in Consul Edwards' report was released, it caused an international crisis.[75]

73. State Department to Carothers and Edwards, February 19, 1914, in *Foreign Relations, 1914*, 842–43. This and other documents relating to the Villa-Benton incident cited hereinafter from *Foreign Relations, 1914*, may also be found in "Documentos secretos del Departamento de Estado de Washington sobre el incidente provacado por el escandaloso caso Benton-Villa," *El Universal* (Mexico City), July 24, 25, 27, 30, 1923.

74. Carothers to State Department, February 19, 1914, *ibid.*, 843; Testimony of Carothers, *Senate Documents*, 66th Cong., 2nd Sess., No. 285, p. 1784; El Paso *Morning Times*, February 21, 1914.

75. Edwards to State Department, February 19, 1914, in *Foreign Relations, 1914*, 843; New York *Times*, February 21, 1914, p. 1.

The revolutionaries had killed foreigners before and Washington had not been held responsible. But in this case, the State Department, by issuing a statement which it was quickly forced to repudiate, made it appear that the Wilson administration had attempted to cover up Villa's transgressions. The impression had been growing at home and abroad for weeks that Wilson was on the verge of giving the rebels active support. The lifting of the arms embargo had been viewed as the first step in that direction. If the administration was going to persist in this policy, European critics demanded that it also make an even greater effort to protect foreign lives and property. This opinion was expressed most vehemently in the British press. Always critical of Wilson's anti-Huerta and nonrecognition policies, the British newspapers now placed the blame for Benton's death squarely on the American president's shoulders.[76] Villa had given the British lion's tail a nasty twist; Carothers spent the next few days trying to bandage it.

The Benton killing, like the persecution of the Spaniards, grew out of Villa's deep-seated hatred of the privileged classes. Benton was a wealthy Chihuahua *hacendado*. Antagonism between the two dated back to the Madero revolution; it had intensified in the few months preceding Benton's death.[77] Claiming that Benton was a *Huertista*, Villa had confiscated many of the Scotsman's cattle. Benton apparently went to Juárez on February 18 to protest and seek the release of the remainder of his stock. The Associated Press reported that the rancher's friends and relatives insisted that he had been unarmed when he crossed the Rio Grande. These same people revealed to Carothers that they had warned Benton not to go to Juárez and that he had gone anyway, looking for trouble.[78]

76. "Letting the Guns into Mexico," *Literary Digest*, XLVIII, 303–304; "The British Press on Benton's Fate," *ibid.* (March 7, 1914), 481.
77. Clendenen, *United States and Pancho Villa*, 66.
78. New York *Times*, February 21, 1914, pp. 1–2; Carothers to State

In order to answer the critics, Bryan directed Carothers to see Villa immediately and determine exactly how Benton had met his fate. When the special agent returned to Juárez, Villa was gone. He reportedly had departed for Chihuahua in order to begin preparations for his next campaign. Lázaro de la Garza, one of Villa's advisors, assured Carothers that there had been a trial. The next day the American agent received a copy of the trial proceedings. The legal transcript indicated that a court-martial had convicted Benton of attempted murder and of actively assisting both Orozco and Huerta. The unanimous death sentence had been carried out immediately by firing squad. The American agent too readily accepted the trial records as fact and sent them to Washington without further investigation. He did not know that the transcript was fraudulent, designed to placate the State Department. In reality Benton, after quarreling with Villa, had been murdered, clubbed to death by Rudolfo Fierro, Villa's personal assassin.[79]

Despite persistent rumors that Benton had been a victim of foul play, the British cabinet was prepared to accept the trial report. Parliament and the press, on the other hand, remained skeptical and heaped vituperation on Foreign Secretary Grey for not adequately insuring the safety of British citizens abroad.[80] Under pressure, Grey, at length, did notify the Wilson administration that, although "His Majesty's Government . . . can take no measures against Villa at

Department, February 20, 1914, in *Foreign Relations, 1914*, 844; Carothers to State Department, February 21, 1914, in NA 312.41/127.

79. Carothers to State Department, February 21, 1914, in *Foreign Relations, 1914*, 845–46; Testimony of Carothers, *Senate Documents*, 66th Cong., 2nd Sess., No. 285, pp. 1784–85; Guzmán, *Memoirs of Pancho Villa*, 134–35. Months later Villa confessed that Benton had been taken to Samalayuca, just south of Juárez, where he was killed while watching his own grave being dug.

80. The *Times* (London), February 24, 1914, p. 9; New York *Times*, February 23, 1914, p. 2; *ibid.*, February 24, 1914, p. 1; "The British Press on Benton's Fate," *Literary Digest*, XLVIII, 481.

the present time . . . they will take whatever steps are possible to secure justice being done whenever the opportunity occurs." [81] While Grey's memorandum appeared to be a veiled threat to the Roosevelt Corollary to the Monroe Doctrine, it was probably more the case of a wounded lion trying to retain some pride.

Before the episode ended, it became still more complex. As soon as Carothers and Edwards found out that Benton was dead, they requested that his body be returned to the family. Villa, realizing that he would be caught in a lie, refused to release it. Otherwise he seemed quite cooperative. He agreed that Mrs. Benton could visit the grave site, which he promised would be well marked. [82]

The British government, meanwhile, requested an inspection of the body to determine the exact cause of death. Bryan, confident that a medical examination would vindicate Villa and the United States, directed Carothers to request permission for a commission of examiners, including a British subject, to inspect the body. Villa not only agreed to the medical examination but offered to arrange a special train to transport the commission to Chihuahua. [83] The rebel chieftain acceded to the investigation because he had arranged a rather naïve ruse. He sent a special train to bring Benton's body from Samalayuca to Chihuahua. Trying to hide the fact that Benton had been clubbed to death, Villa, thinking that bullet holes would fool the medical examiners, had a squad of men fire a volley into the decomposing cadaver. [84] Luckily for Villa,

81. British embassy to State Department, March 3, 1914, in *Foreign Relations, 1914*, 858–59.

82. Carothers to State Department, February 21, 23, 1914, in *Foreign Relations, 1914*, 846–49; Edwards to State Department, February 22, 24, 1914, *ibid.*, 847, 850.

83. British embassy to State Department, February 24, 1914, *ibid.*, 851–52; Carothers to State Department, February 26, 1914, *ibid.*, 853; State Department to Carothers, February 25, 1914, in NA 312.41/130a; El Paso *Morning Times*, February 26, 1914.

84. Testimony of Carothers, *Senate Documents*, 66th Cong., 2nd Sess., No. 285, p. 1785; Guzmán, *Memoirs of Pancho Villa*, 136–37.

his medical knowledge was never tested by the examining commission.

While Carothers was dealing with Villa, Bryan appealed to Carranza as well. On February 28, before plans for the medical examination of Benton's body were finalized, the secretary of state instructed Consul Simpich at Nogales to urge the First Chief to order the body released to the victim's family. Indignant at not being consulted at the outset, Carranza delayed his answer for four days. Then he replied through Foreign Minister Fabela, reminding Wilson and Bryan that he had earlier informed them that all representations in behalf of foreigners should be made directly to his headquarters, not to subordinates, and only by representatives of the nation concerned. It was improper, he insisted, especially since Mrs. Benton was Mexican, for the United States to involve itself in the Benton case. He announced, also, that officials of his government would make a full investigation. Accordingly, the investigating commission, which had been organized by Carothers and Edwards, was turned back by Carranza's officials as it attempted to board the train in Juárez.[85]

Again Carranza's pugnacity had prevented Wilson and Bryan from exercising an influence in Mexican affairs. The First Chief was motivated solely by a desire to have other nations respect the right of Mexicans to conduct their own investigations. He and his advisors definitely believed that a

85. State Department to Simpich, February 17, 24, 1914, in *Foreign Relations, 1914*, 849–50, 855–56; Simpich to State Department, February 26, 28, 1914, *ibid.*, 853, 856–57; El Paso *Morning Times*, March 1–2, 1914. Carranza's agents in Washington were greatly disappointed at their chief's refusal to cooperate with the United States and Great Britain in investigating the Benton case. Ever since Cabrera's arrival in Washington, they had been attempting to cultivate a favorable impression of the revolution. All their efforts, they felt, were being sacrificed for the First Chief's narrow-minded nationalism. Their differences precipitated a short but intense conflict between the diplomatic agents in Washington and Carranza and his cabinet. See Kenneth J. Grieb, "El Caso Benton y la diplomacia de la Revolución," *Historia Mexicana*, XVIII (October–December, 1969), 299–301.

blow had been struck for Mexican sovereignty and against
American interventionism under the auspices of the Monroe
Doctrine.[86] In the process, much of the onus for the Benton
murder was transferred to Carranza. Quite unwittingly, he
rescued Villa from a ticklish situation. Since the true nature
of the Benton killing was still not known in Washington,
Wilson's image of Carranza was again darkened, while Villa's
was hardly tarnished.

Until the Benton incident, Carothers had made El Paso his
headquarters. Afterwards Bryan deemed it advisable for the
agent to remain constantly at Villa's side. But Carranza's
recent declarations caused Carothers to pause. "I can see that
from now on conditions will be very different," he wrote to
Bryan. "I can do more good by having the good will of both
Carranza and Villa." He recommended, therefore, that he go
first to Sonora and, hopefully, obtain the First Chief's
permission before proceeding to Villa's headquarters. With
the secretary of state's approval, Carothers arranged for an
interview with Carranza at Nogales. Although officially the
First Chief continued to demand that all diplomatic representations be directed to his headquarters rather than to
subordinates, the Benton episode apparently opened his eyes
to the advisability of having someone to watch over Villa.
Having made his public pronouncements in defense of Mexican sovereignty, Carranza gave his permission. He even gave
Carothers a code book for facilitating communication with
Constitutionalist officials. After the meeting, the special
agent was confident that American relations with both Villa
and Carranza would be more cordial in the future.[87]

86. Fabela, *Historia Diplomática*, I, 277–84; Juan Barragán, "De las
memorias de Don Venustiano Carranza," *El Universal, Magazine para todos*
(Sunday magazine section), April 27, 1930, p. 1.
    87. State Department to Carothers, February 25, March 1, 1914, in NA
312.41/130a, 152; Carothers to State Department, March 1, 3, 6, 1914,
ibid./152, 166, 175; Carothers to State Department, March 4, 7, 1914, in NA
812.00/11048, 11093; El Paso *Morning Times*, March 3, 1914.

Despite the furor caused by the Benton affair, it did not alter the Wilson administration's policy. The nature of Carothers' mission, however, did change. Before the affair he had merely carried out the department's orders and reported the results. During the course of the incident, he began to exercise considerable initiative of his own. He, not Bryan, had seen the necessity of his establishing cordial relations with Carranza. At the same time he wrote to Bryan, revealing his own conception of what his job should entail: "I wish you to know that my desire to do this work is prompted by my sincere affection for the Mexican people, acquired during twenty-five years residence among them, and I expect to live the balance of my life in Mexico. I have realized that there is still hope for them to settle their difficulties without intervention, and it has been my desire to contribute my efforts to further that end." He also acknowledged that incidents like the Benton murder were lamentable, but that the revolutionaries, most of whom were peons, had so long been treated like savages that they responded in kind. He closed his letter by declaring his intention "to hold him [Villa] within bounds as far as possible." [88] Bryan apparently agreed with Carothers' view, because he relieved the agent of the responsibility of further investigating the Benton affair. "Your influence with Villa," wrote the secretary of state, "should not be jeopardized by [my] putting you in a position where you might offend him." [89]

Judging from their correspondence and actions, both of the agents in Mexico felt a responsibility for aiding the Constitutionalists. They differed significantly over means to that end: Lind, fearing revolutionary excesses and looking to large-scale American direction of Mexican affairs, demanded military intervention; Carothers, understanding the violence of

88. Carothers to State Department, February 23, 1914, in NA 812.00/11454.
89. State Department to Carothers, February 27, 1914, in NA 312.41/138.

the revolution and willing to give the Mexicans a chance to settle their own affairs, hoped only to restrain the revolutionaries enough to prevent intervention. As events were to prove, Wilson was leaning toward Lind's position but as yet had no plausible pretext for adopting it. For the time being, Carothers' position had to suffice.

Agent Reginaldo F. Del Valle

Special Agent William Bayard Hale

Special Agent John Lind

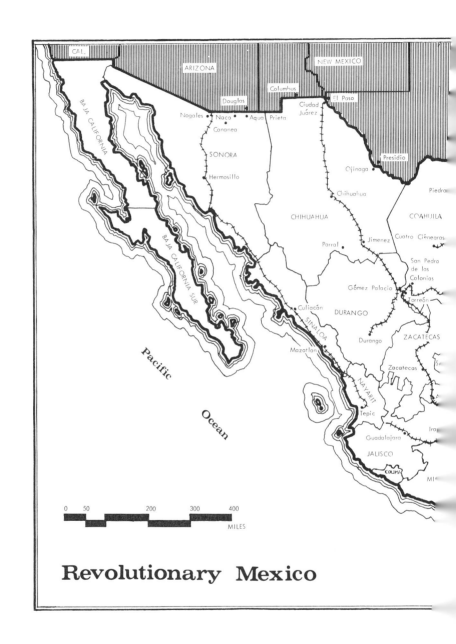

Revolutionary Mexico

Gulf of Mexico

TEXAS

Eagle Pass
San Antonio
Galveston

ra Negras

Nuevo Laredo
Laredo
Monclova

Brownsville
Matamoros

Monterre
Saltillo
NUEVO LEON
TAMAULIPAS

Dr Arroyo

LUIS POTOSI

San Luis Potosi

ascalientes
Valles

Tampico

GUANAJUATO
Leon
Querétaro

VERACRUZ

Progreso
Merida
YUCATAN

QUINTANA ROO

Celaya
HIDALGO

Campeche

CAMPECHE

MEXICO
Mexico City
Puebla
Veracruz

ACÁN
PUEBLA
Cordoba

TABASCO

BR.
HON.

Iguala

GUERRERO

Oaxaca

Acapulco

OAXACA

CHIAPAS

GUATEMALA

HONDURAS

Tapachula

Agent George C. Carothers, far left; General Hugh L. Scott, second from left

John W. Belt, assistant to Agent John R. Silliman, second from left; Silliman, third from left

Agent Duval West and General Emiliano Zapata, Tlaltizapan,
Mexico, April, 1915

CHAPTER VII

A Friend
Indeed

The months of March and April, 1914, were pregnant with events which determined the course of the Mexican revolution and the course of relations between the United States and Mexico. Given the nature of Wilson's Mexican policy, his agents inevitably became involved in these events. While John Lind was sweltering and seething in Vera Cruz, George Carothers was constantly on the move, accompanying General Villa's Division of the North. Villa provided the American agent with a passport which gave him access to the battle lines and allowed the two to be in constant contact. All revolutionary civil and military authorities were directed to give the American every assistance. Villa allowed him to use the Constitutionalists' telegraph lines and placed trains at his disposal. With Bryan's approval, Carothers established a communications system, using Zach L. Cobb, the customs collector at El Paso, as an intermediary. Cobb knew and maintained cordial relations with Constitutionalist officials on the border and was able to ascertain Villa's whereabouts at any time. With a minimum of delay, he was able to forward instructions from the department to Carothers and relay the agent's responses to Washington.[1]

While Villa massed his forces and stockpiled munitions for another assault on Torreón, Carothers busied himself ar-

1. Carothers to State Department, February 3, 10, 1914, in NA 812.00/10820, 10903.

ranging for the safety of foreigners who lived in the city. As early as January 30, the agent reported that Villa would not likely be too concerned for the safety of noncombatants. Then on February 4 the Associated Press quoted the general as declaring that the Spaniards in Torreón could expect no mercy. Troubled as much by the implied savagery in this pronouncement as by the possible diplomatic repercussions, Bryan again directed Carothers to remind Villa of the adverse world opinion that would result from his failure to observe "the rules of war and respect the person and property of foreigners." [2] The special agent replied that the press quoted Villa accurately but that the secretary of state should understand the context within which the general had made such comments. Carothers explained that Villa, being unsophisticated, was flattered when representatives of the press paid him so much attention. As a means of impressing reporters, the agent further explained, Villa was inclined to strut about and make bombastic pronouncements. Carothers also noted that Villa had revealed in confidence that he openly threatened the Spaniards as a means of frightening them into withholding support from the *Huertistas*. He pledged not to harm them unless he found substantial evidence that they had aided his enemies.[3]

Still not satisfied, Carothers sought the aid of General Hugh Lennox Scott, the commander at El Paso's Fort Bliss, whom Villa held in high esteem. After the War Department vetoed plans for a Villa-Scott conference in Ciudad Juárez, Carothers arranged for the two soldiers to rendezvous on the international bridge which linked Juárez and El Paso. For two hours on the night of February 18 Carothers, Scott, and

2. Carothers to State Department, January 30, 1914, in NA 312.11/3243; State Department to Carothers, February 6, 1914, in *Foreign Relations, 1914*, 790–91; New York *Times*, February 4, 1914, p. 2.

3. Carothers to State Department, February 8, 1914, in *Foreign Relations, 1914*, 791; Carothers to State Department, February 10, 1914, in NA 812.00/10903.

Villa sat in the back seat of an automobile and discussed the responsibilities of a civilized soldier. Scott impressed upon Villa that, for reasons of good politics and not merely for humanitarian ones, he should cease his harsh treatment of foreigners; otherwise, he would so prejudice foreign opinion that he would be unable to secure foreign support should he need it in the future. The American general also pointed up the favorable impression to be derived from humanitarian treatment of prisoners of war. At the conclusion of the conference, General Scott presented Villa with a facsimile of the Hague Convention's rules of civilized warfare, which some of his officers had roughly translated into Spanish. Carothers was elated at the generals' cordial relations and predicted optimistically that the meeting would produce "excellent results." [4]

Meanwhile, the special agent had also been attempting to establish a neutral zone for foreigners outside Torreón. Villa agreed to such an arrangement; so Carothers, choosing to remain constantly with Villa, sent a trusted friend, E. F. Fletcher, to Torreón to negotiate with leaders of the foreign colony. Arrested and detained temporarily as a Constitutionalist spy, Fletcher reported back that although the foreigners expressed relief at Villa's promises to protect their interests, most of them refused to leave the city, preferring to remain near their property.[5]

4. Carothers to State Department, February 3, 19, 1914, in NA 812.00/10775, 10917; State Department to Carothers, February 4, 1914, *ibid.*/10775; El Paso *Morning Times*, February 20, 1914; Testimony of Carothers, *Senate Documents*, 66th Cong., 2nd Sess., No. 285, p. 1766; Hugh Lenox Scott, *Some Memories of a Soldier* (New York, 1928), 500–502.

5. Carothers to State Department, February 8, 1914, in *Foreign Relations, 1914*, 791; Carothers to State Department, February 9, 1914, in NA 125.36582/58; State Department to Carothers, February 8, 1914, in NA 812.00/10820; Carothers to State Department, February 10, 13, 22, 23, 24, 1914, *ibid.*/10879, 10903, 10952, 10953, 10995; John R. Silliman (American consul, Saltillo) to State Department, February 21, 1914, *ibid.*/11044. Silliman, who was informed by an eyewitness, reported the details of Fletcher's arrest and detainment, which was apparently instigated by a suspicious Spaniard.

While Carothers dealt with Villa and the foreign colony at Torreón, Bryan directed O'Shaughnessy to secure Huerta's cooperation in establishing the neutral zone. After evading the issue for days, the dictator replied that, if he was informed when the attack was about to begin, he would instruct General José R. Velasco, his commander at Torreón, to take every precaution for the safety of foreigners. Although such notification would give the federals an advantage, Bryan, evidencing more concern for the safety of noncombatants than for a Constitutionalist victory, instructed Carothers to notify O'Shaughnessy on the eve of Villa's attack.[6]

Wishing to avoid any misunderstanding or possible interference with his efforts once the battle was joined, Carothers left Villa's side temporarily and again traveled to Sonora to confer with Carranza at Agua Prieta, across the border from Douglas, Arizona. Surprisingly cooperative, the First Chief promised to instruct Villa to give notice to foreigners before attacking Torreón. In order to facilitate communications with Constitutionalist headquarters, Carranza also gave the American agent an itinerary of his movements.[7]

On March 10, as Villa began his advance, Carothers did indeed notify O'Shaughnessy, who in turn informed Huerta. The usurper thereupon assured the chargé that General Velasco would be ordered to "spare no efforts" to insure the safety of foreigners.[8] Bryan, not satisfied with even these arrangements, again directed Carothers to attempt to arrange a neutral zone outside the city. Having discovered from friends in Torreón that General Velasco would likely arrest

6. State Department to O'Shaughnessy, February 14, 1914, in NA 812.00/10870; O'Shaughnessy to State Department, February 17, 25, March 3, 1914, *ibid.*/10913, 10983, 11040; State Department to Carothers, March 5, 1914, *ibid.*/11040.

7. Carothers to State Department, March 9, 10, 1914, *ibid.*/11103, 11117.

8. Carothers to State Department, conveying text of Carothers to O'Shaughnessy, March 10, 1914, *ibid.*/11121; O'Shaughnessy to State Department, March 11, 1914, *ibid.*/11150.

him if he entered the city, Carothers asked for detailed written instructions, so that the federals, if they took him into custody, would have no justifiable reason for detaining or prosecuting him. Armed with new instructions from Washington, Carothers joined Villa on March 19, as the Division of the North launched a massive assault on the suburbs of Torreón.[9]

On March 27, after Villa captured Gómez Palacio and was preparing his attack on Torreón proper, Carothers again attempted to establish a neutral zone. Instead of entering Torreón himself, he prudently sent the British vice consul at Gómez Palacio, H. Cunard Cummins, whose relations with the Federals were very friendly. At the same time, Villa forced the British consul to carry an unconditional surrender demand to General Velasco. The rebel general also promised that food and shelter would be provided for foreigners at the nearby villages of Aviles and Lerdo. Neither proposal was accepted. Velasco refused to surrender unless he was allowed to evacuate his men, and the foreigners, fearful of running a gauntlet between the opposing armies, chose to remain in the city and take refuge in the cellars of a few well-marked buildings. The following day the final attack began. On April 2 the surviving Federals evacuated under cover of a dust storm and the *Villistas* occupied the city. In the course of some of the fiercest fighting of the entire revolution, not one foreigner was killed or wounded.[10] Although no neutral zone was established, the American effort made both sides conscious of the welfare of noncombatants.

During the course of the Torreón campaign, Villa allowed

9. State Department to Carothers, February 18, March 13, 16, 1914, *ibid.*/10983, 10995, 11176; Carothers to State Department, March 15, 17, 1914, *ibid.*/11176, 11203.

10. Carothers to State Department, April 1, 1914, *ibid.*/11366; I. M. Ulmer, acting consular agent, Torreón, to Hamm, April 8, 1914, *ibid.*/11706; Hamm to State Department, April 13, 1914, *ibid.*/11706; New York *Times*, April 10, 1914, p. 2.

Carothers to periodically send brief accounts of the rebels' progress to Washington. These reports did not give details of the relative fighting ability of the opposing armies or the number of casualties suffered by either. Usually he merely reported the capture of small towns, such as Bermejillo, Tlahualilo, and Gómez Palacio, and finally the fall of Torreón itself. Since these reports often provided the most advanced information from the front, the State Department released the news to the press.[11] Huerta, on the other hand, did not allow the Mexico City press to reveal the magnitude of his defeats during the Torreón campaign. Consequently, the reports that appeared in the American press differed dramatically from those in Mexico City.[12] Puzzled by the American newspaper accounts, one of Huerta's consular officials in El Paso began searching for the source of the reports. On April 2, the day Torreón fell, he reported to Mexico City that one of his subordinates had intercepted a message from Carothers to Washington, imploring his superiors not to release any more news, since the outcome of the battle was still in the balance and any news might encourage the Federals to send in reinforcements.[13]

On April 5 Huerta released what he claimed was a translation of Carothers' dispatch. He charged that, as a consular agent accredited to his government, Carothers was guilty of unethical conduct, that he was openly siding with

11. Cobb (for Carothers) to State Department, March 23, 27, 28, April 1, 3, 1914, *ibid.*/11241, 11315, 11323, 11366, 11386; New York *Times*, March 22, 1914, II, p. 2; *ibid.*, March 24, 25, 27, April 2, 3, 1914, p. 1.

12. *Mexican Herald*, March 21–April 9, 1914; *El Imparcial*, March 22–April 9, 1914. During the seesaw of battle, Huerta reported minor reverses for the rebels as major victories for the Federals. Throughout the campaign he flatly denied that his forces were losing. As late as April 9, one week after the fall of Torreón, he had not admitted to the press that General Velasco had been defeated. He claimed, instead, that the Federal troops had evacuated the city only to take up more defensible positions in the highlands.

13. Inspección General de Consulados de México en Los Estados Unidos de America, El Paso, Texas, a Secretaría de Relaciones Exteriores, March 31, April 2, 1914, AGRE, L–E–795, Leg. 3, L–E–787, Leg. 8.

the revolutionaries. The dictator also insisted that the agent's claims of victory for Villa had been premature and had caused the reinforcements, which might have come to the aid of the Federals at Torreón, to turn back. He then withdrew Carothers' consular exequatur and declared him *persona non grata* in Mexico. The State Department promptly denied Huerta's charges but in the process was itself guilty of inaccuracy by insisting that Carothers had reported only information concerning the safety of foreigners.[14]

Huerta was even more erroneous in his claims. His consul in El Paso had misinterpreted Carothers' dispatch. In the note in question, sent on April 1, Carothers had reported on the status of foreigners in Torreón; but Cobb, in forwarding it to Washington, added a clause at the request of local Constitutionalist officials. They pointed out to him that they allowed Carothers' dispatches to come out of Mexico on their telegraph lines as a courtesy; now they requested that the State Department refrain from releasing their contents to the press, because the battle was at a critical stage.[15] Carothers, therefore, was not guilty of the charges leveled by Huerta. The usurper, well aware of the agent's increasingly friendly relations with Villa, had reason enough to want him removed from northern Mexico; his consul's misinterpretation of Carothers' note of April 1 provided the old general with an adequate pretext for recalling the agent's consular exequatur.[16] At any rate, the department paid no heed to Huerta's

14. O'Shaughnessy to State Department, April 5, 1914, in NA 125.36582/67; State Department to O'Shaughnessy, April 6, 1914, *ibid.*/71a; G. M. Courts to Admiral Fletcher, April 5, 1914, in NA 812.00/11459; War Department to State Department, April 7, 1914, *ibid.*/11459; New York *Times*, April 4, 6, 1914, p. 2; *Mexican Herald*, April 6, 1914. A consular exequatur is a statement of permission given to a consul, usually in the form of an executive order, which grants him authority to make representations in behalf of his nationals. See Stuart, *American Diplomatic and Consular Practice*, 298–301.

15. Cobb (for Carothers) to State Department, April 1, 1914, in NA 812.00/11366.

16. Before the Torreón campaign, Huerta's consuls along the border had

directive and Carothers continued as if he still had some recognized official status in Mexico.[17]

Villa's victory at Torreón, followed quickly by triumphs at San Pedro de las Colonias and Viesca, was by all odds his greatest. In terms of strategy and men and materials deployed, it was the most impressive Constitutionalist victory to date.[18] Not only did Villa cover himself with glory on the battlefield, but his humaneness in occupying the stricken city also caused his stock to rise in Washington and throughout the world. He maintained complete order, allowed no looting, and quickly established a civil government. He encouraged the local merchants to reopen their shops and to reprovision their depleted stocks via his railroad. Meanwhile, he fed the poor from his army's rations. For the first time in the revolution, the victor did not execute his prisoners, and the wounded received the same treatment as the wounded victors.[19]

A few days after the occupation of the city, Carothers wrote to General Hugh Scott, insisting that Villa's humane treatment of prisoners was a direct result of their conference on the El Paso–Juárez bridge. Scott, who recently had been appointed assistant chief of staff of the army, sent the letter to the president. Showing his own gratification for the rebel

reported Carothers' activities among the revolutionaries in northern Mexico. These consular dispatches may be found in AGRE, L–E–773, Leg. 12.

17. Bryan decided that since the administration had not acknowledged as legitimate any of Huerta's actions since October 10, 1913, there was no need to pay any heed to the revocation of Carothers' exequatur. See Bryan to Lansing, April 6, 1914, National Archives, Record Group 59, Papers of Robert Lansing, General Correspondence, Vol. 2.

18. Quirk, *Mexican Revolution*, 24–26. Quirk suggests that the victories at San Pedro and Viesca, where Villa caught and destroyed General Velasco's armies, were as important as the one at Torreón, because they eliminated any chance of counterattack.

19. Ulmer to Hamm, April 8, 1914, in NA 812.00/11706; Hamm to State Department, April 13, 19, 1914, *ibid.*/11703, 11706; Carothers to State Department, April 6, 1914, *ibid.*/11419; El Paso *Morning Times*, April 3–5, 1914; John Reed, *Insurgent Mexico* (New York, 1969), 144.

general's recently acquired humaneness, Wilson, in reply, conceded that "General Villa certainly seems capable of some good things." [20]

On the heels of these good reports, however, came disturbing news of Villa's renewed intimidation of the Spaniards. The day after he occupied Torreón, he had all the Spaniards congregated into three buildings. That afternoon he went before them and, in a lengthy harangue, again charged that they had openly aided the *Huertistas*. He insisted that he had enough evidence to execute several of them. Because of these few, he claimed, all would be in danger if he allowed them loose on the streets; therefore, he was going to deport all of them to El Paso for their own good. An investigating committee would be established in Juárez, and all who could establish their innocence would be allowed to return to Torreón. The property of those who could not return would be confiscated. Carothers and Acting Consular Agent I. M. Ulmer were present when Villa addressed the gathering. Both of them, along with Consul Hamm of Durango, British Consul Cunard Cummins of Gómez Palacio, and several members of Villa's staff, appealed to the *caudillo* to reverse his decree, but their pleas were unavailing.[21]

Carothers, his use of the telegraph restricted because of the Constitutionalists' military needs, hastened to El Paso to file his report on the battle of Torreón and the subsequent persecution of the Spaniards. In Juárez he found Carranza, who was in the process of moving his headquarters from Sonora to Chihuahua. Consequently, Bryan directed the agent to go over Villa's head and appeal directly to Carranza in behalf of the Spaniards. But the First Chief refused to

20. Carothers to Scott, April 9, 1914, and Wilson to Scott, April 16, 1914, in Hugh L. Scott Papers, Division of Manuscripts, Library of Congress, Box 15.

21. Carothers to State Department, April 6, 1914, in NA 812.00/11419; Ulmer to Hamm, April 8, 1914, *ibid.*/11706; Hamm to State Department, April 13, 1914, *ibid.*/11706; El Paso *Morning Times*, April 7, 1914.

countermand his general's orders. Instead, he, too, insisted that all Spaniards should leave Mexico before the Constitutionalists reached Mexico City. Echoing Villa, he charged them with supporting Huerta and warned that they could expect no mercy once the revolutionaries seized power. Hoping that General Scott could work his magic a second time, Carothers even arranged for him to meet with Carranza on the international bridge. This conference, however, induced no change of heart on the part of the flinty old First Chief. With Carranza's attitude coinciding with Villa's, Carothers warned that Washington should expect more depredations against Spaniards in the future and that he could do nothing to prevent them.[22]

In the meantime, trainloads of Spaniards began streaming into Juárez. Most of the refugees were destitute, having been forced to leave Torreón with nothing more than the clothes on their backs. Since they knew that Carothers had spoken in their behalf, they looked to him for aid and relief. When the special agent appealed to Washington for guidance in helping the unfortunates, the State Department secured Red Cross aid and relieved him of the responsibility of helping the refugees so that he might continue negotiating with the Constitutionalist leaders.[23]

When Carothers again approached Carranza, the First Chief fell back upon his earlier-issued directive in which, during the Benton affair, he had notified Washington that he would accept representations in behalf of foreigners only from the diplomatic representatives of the nations directly concerned. Puzzled by Carranza's hot-and-cold attitude, Ca-

22. State Department to Carothers, April 6, 1914, in *Foreign Relations, 1914*, 796; Carothers to State Department, April 7, 1914, *ibid.*, 798; Scott to Mrs. Scott, April 9, 1914, in Scott Papers, Box 4; New York *Times*, April 8, 1914, p. 7; El Paso *Morning Times*, April 8, 1914; *El País*, April 11, 1914.

23. Carothers to State Department, April 8, 1914, in *Foreign Relations, 1914*, 799; State Department to Carothers, April 8, 1914, *ibid.*, 799; El Paso *Morning Times*, April 9, 1914.

rothers made inquiries into the reasons for the First Chief's renewed recalcitrance and discovered that it resulted largely from the advice of his secretary of government, Rafael Zubarán Capmany, and of his secretary of foreign affairs, Isidro Fabela, both of whom were intensely anti-American. The special agent therefore approached Carranza through a lesser advisor, Roberto V. Pesquiera. By this means, on April 12 Carothers secured an unofficial agreement from Carranza: if the agent's instructions stated specifically that another nation had requested officially that the United States intercede in behalf of its nationals, Constitutionalist headquarters would act on such appeals. Two days later, Fabela officially notified the State Department that this procedure would be acceptable in the future.[24]

During the course of these negotiations, Carothers' reports pointed up the apparent reasons why Carranza's and Villa's attitudes toward the United States differed so markedly. He noted that the First Chief seemed to fear that if he was too friendly toward the United States he might in some way compromise himself in the eyes of his followers by seeming less than nationalistic. Villa, on the other hand, feared nothing, Carothers reported, and no matter what his followers thought, he acted according to his own sense of justice. But Carothers failed to perceive that the issue was more than mere nationalism or anti-Americanism. Carranza, Zubarán Capmany, and Fabela were, in fact, operating as if theirs was a viable government which should be accorded all rights of sovereignty. Villa, of course, was willing to follow whichever course—regardless of the consequences for Mexican sovereignty—would serve his own best interests. Carothers, then,

24. Carothers to State Department, April 9, 11, 12, 14, 1914, in *Foreign Relations, 1914*, 801, 804–806. Carothers did not state what positions the above-named Constitutionalist advisors held. For the nature of their offices, see Barragán Rodríguez, *Historia . . . de la Revolución Constitucionalista*, I, 219, 424.

was on the right track when he recommended that he make all his representations to Villa, adding that American consuls in northern Mexico could probably secure results faster by dealing with "authorities *de facto* in places where difficulties arise" rather than by referring them to Carranza.[25]

Although more important matters soon preoccupied him, Carothers, as part of his duties, continued to seek a favorable settlement for the Spaniards. He was not successful in every case, but by the end of June he had worked out an arrangement whereby most of the refugees were allowed to return to their property. Throughout the remainder of the year, nonetheless, there continued to be isolated cases of revolutionary depredations against Spaniards but there were no more instances, as in the Chihuahua and Torreón episodes, of mass confiscations and deportations.[26]

In no other sector had the Constitutionalist forces by this time achieved the success of Villa's Division of the North. Separated from Carranza's government by the Sierra Madre Occidental, Villa, although he repeatedly professed his loyalty to the First Chief, appeared to be a power unto himself. To forestall any thought of independent action by Villa and to take advantage of his victories, Carranza decided in March, 1914, to move the seat of his provisional government from Sonora to Chihuahua. The First Chief and the officials of his government arrived in the city of Chihuahua as Villa was mopping up the Federalist armies at San Pedro. The campaign completed, Villa returned to Chihuahua, and there the two *caudillos* met for the first time since the Madero revolution.[27]

25. Carothers to State Department, April 11, 12, 1914, in *Foreign Relations, 1914*, 804–805.

26. Carothers to State Department, June 21, 1914, in NA 312.52/335. The State Department's 312.52 (Protection by the United States of Spanish Subjects and Interests in Mexico) file contains accounts of all of Carothers' efforts in behalf of the Spaniards. For representative examples, see *Foreign Relations, 1914*, 806–38.

27. Barragán Rodríguez, *Historia . . . de la Revolución Constituciona-*

At first there was harmony; the First Chief commended Villa for his recent victories and Villa reaffirmed his loyalty to the First Chief. But Villa quickly became disenchanted with some of Carranza's appointees, particularly with General Manuel Chao, who was made governor of Chihuahua. As a soldier, moreover, Villa viewed with mounting suspicion the First Chief's "sweet-scented" civilian advisors. Because they did not fight, Villa considered them slackers and less than genuine revolutionaries. Carranza himself made the mistake of pointing out to Villa their differences in origin and political training. From this time on, Villa disliked the First Chief. He later reminisced: "I saw that I could not open my heart to him . . . There was nothing in common between that man and me." [28] The breach between the two rebel leaders as yet was small but it boded ill for the future of the revolution.

Carothers was greatly disappointed at the lack of cooperation between the two chieftains. "I had expected when Carranza arrived that complete fusion would result between him and Villa," he wrote to Bryan, "but such is not the case." Noting that Villa still went about his business raising men and money, purchasing munitions, and planning his next campaign without consulting the First Chief, Carothers further lamented, "Carranza has not assumed control of anything so far." [29] The American agent was even more disheartened when he realized the extent of their mutual antagonism. While in El Paso after the Torreón campaign, he found that the *Villista* officials and the newly arrived *Carrancista* officials quarreled constantly. One source of the antagonism, he discovered from conversations with some of Villa's advisors, was that Carranza resented their friendly

lista, I, 425, 433–41; Alamada, *La Revolución en el Estado de Chihuahua*, II, 86–88, 95; Quirk, *Mexican Revolution*, 16–19.

28. Guzmán, *Memoirs of Pancho Villa*, 189; Quirk, *Mexican Revolution*, 18.

29. Carothers to State Department, April 9, 1914, in NA 812.00/11461; copy in Wilson Papers, Ser. 2, Box 50.

attitude toward the United States. The reason for his own refusal to be more friendly, they charged, was to make himself appear more nationalistic than they. When Carothers asked what would happen if Carranza openly offended the United States, Lázaro de la Garza, an intimate of Villa, replied that "Villa would not stand for it" and would "instruct Carranza to change his policy or get out." [30]

Whether de la Garza's comments were designed purely to discredit Carranza or were a sincere statement of the *Villistas'* attitude toward the United States, they were about to be put to the test by a drastic turn in the relations between Wilson and Huerta. Meanwhile, the administration was gravely concerned over the estrangement between Villa and Carranza and directed Carothers to secure as much information as possible bearing on the relations between the two and to determine the "probable alignment of subordinates in the event of an open rupture. . . ." [31]

In Vera Cruz, meanwhile, John Lind was allowing his anxieties to drive him to the brink of paranoia. His trepidations began in February with the appearance of a scurrilous cartoon journal entitled *Mister Lind,* which seemed to focus anti-Americanism in *Huertista* Mexico directly at him. The March issue was even more vituperative than the first. They both pictured him as the personification of everything that was bad in Yankee imperialism. In February, also, John R. Silliman, the American consul in Saltillo, reported that Lind was the subject of a very popular anti-American satire being dramatized in a local theater. That same month, James Creelman, an American journalist who had earlier gained fame by reporting a personal interview with President Porfirio Díaz which helped to spawn the revolution, published an article in a New York newspaper, the contents of which were widely circulated in Mexico. It was intensely critical of

30. Carothers to State Department, April 12, 1914, in NA 812.00/11755.
31. State Department to Carothers, April 13, 1914, *ibid.*/11479.

Lind's clandestine encouragement of the revolutionaries and, by implication, blamed him for the death of hundreds killed in the civil war. Not surprisingly, Admiral Fletcher reported that Lind seemed "disturbed and not in the best of health and shows fear for his personal safety." Edith O'Shaughnessy, wife of the American chargé, also commented on the special agent's disturbed state of mind. Because of Lind's anxiety, Admiral Fletcher dispatched a permanent guard of seamen and marines to the consulate.[32]

Allowing his emotions to rule, Lind, in his hatred for Huerta, refused to seek any settlement with the dictator save the destruction of his regime by military force. In mid-March he shunned an opportunity to reopen peaceful talks when Huerta, aware that his sources of credit were not inexhausti-ble, sent his recently appointed minister of foreign relations, José López Portillo y Rojas, to speak with Lind in Vera Cruz. Portillo y Rojas promised that if Wilson would lift the "money embargo" and restore the "arms embargo," Huerta would resign after elections to be held in July. Lind, in reply, stated his conviction that President Wilson "would not recede one iota" from his previously stated demand that Huerta eliminate himself immediately. In reporting the Mexican diplomat's proposal to Washington, Lind urged that it be rejected outright. He insisted that Huerta could not be trusted to deal in good faith and that the offer for renewed negotiations was designed only to "induce non-action by the United States." Wilson and Bryan agreed. Despite the fact that Wilson informed the press that Portillo y Rojas was an honorable man and his proposals were worthy of considera-tion, he did not even instruct Lind to pursue the parleys past the initial conversation. Portillo y Rojas, therefore, returned

32. Fletcher to Daniels, February 4, 1914, in Daniels Papers, Box 39; Silliman to State Department, February 11, 1914, in NA 812.00/10928; O'Shaughnessy, *A Diplomat's Wife in Mexico*, 194, 229–30; Stephenson, *John Lind*, 257; *Mister Lind*, I (February, March, 1914), in Lind Papers.

to Mexico City without a formal response to Huerta's latest proposition.[33]

Shortly after the departure of Portillo y Rojas, Nelson O'Shaughnessy, suffering from sciatica, came to the warmer climate of Vera Cruz on his doctor's instructions. Unable to eliminate his frustrations by direct action against Huerta, Lind displaced them by attacking O'Shaughnessy. Ever since his own failure in November to secure Huerta's resignation by diplomatic pressure, Lind had resented the fact that O'Shaughnessy had continued to seek a more honorable way for the dictator to eliminate himself. At the time, the special agent had warned Washington that the chargé was being duped. After that he grew increasingly suspicious of O'Shaughnessy's continued friendly relations with Huerta and his officials. Lind was particularly chagrined by the fact that Mrs. O'Shaughnessy was so fond of the old dictator. Huerta, moreover, returned their friendship and, at official receptions and other social occasions, went out of his way to give them his attention.[34]

Lind saw sinister implications in all this, but especially in O'Shaughnessy's arrival in Vera Cruz so soon after the departure of Portillo y Rojas. In a personal letter to Bryan, Lind insisted that the chargé's stated claim for coming—to mend his health—was a subterfuge, that he was actually there as Huerta's spy. He had come at the dictator's behest to ferret out Washington's true response to his recent over-

33. Lind to State Department, March 19, 1914, in NA 812.00/11218; New York *Times*, March 19–23, 1914, p. 1. Neither Wilson nor Bryan revealed publicly that they would not negotiate with Huerta, but when the British ambassador inquired of their intentions Wilson replied that he would not. See Grieb, *United States and Huerta*, 119.

34. Lind to State Department, November 15, 1913, February 17, 22, 1914, in NA 812.00/9760, 17169, 10954; Lind to Wilson, January 10, 1914, in Wilson Papers, Ser. 2, Box 101. At the Pass Christian conference, Lind must have revealed his displeasure at the O'Shaughnessys' friendship with Huerta. In the last item cited above, Lind explains at length the suspicions he had expressed verbally.

ture.[35] Despite his suspicions, Lind did not think O'Shaughnessy was intentionally disloyal but rather that somehow his Catholic background was betraying him into supporting the Church-backed dictator. "I guess," he wrote to Bryan, "the explanation is that he was raised by Tammany, educated by the Jesuits and . . . corresponds with Cardinal Gibbons." The special agent also concluded that the chargé had been corrupted by long residence abroad. "He has never drawn a breath of American air," Lind lamented. With O'Shaughnessy's arrival in Vera Cruz, Lind's enmity became so pronounced that reporters noticed the strained relations between the two diplomats. O'Shaughnessy, still in pain, was so distressed by the agent's attitude that he returned to Mexico City after only two days' convalescence. The day of his departure, Lind recommended to Washington that the chargé be recalled immediately.[36]

But Wilson did not recall O'Shaughnessy[37] nor did he give

35. Lind to State Department, March 22, 23, 1914, in NA 812.00/11237, 11248. Before O'Shaughnessy went to Vera Cruz, the New York *Times* reported that he was bedridden with his illness. Mrs. O'Shaughnessy noted in a letter to her mother that a physician recommended that her husband go to the coast. See New York *Times*, March 20, 1914, p. 1; O'Shaughnessy, *A Diplomat's Wife in Mexico*, 229.

36. Lind to Bryan (personal), March 23, 1914, in NA 812.00/27482; New York *Times*, March 23, 1914, p. 1; *ibid.*, March 24, 1914, p. 2. James Cardinal Gibbons was a severe critic of the anticlerical Mexican revolutionaries; hence, of the Wilson administration's Mexican policy as well. See Arthur S. Link, *Wilson: The Struggle for Neutrality, 1914–1915* (Princeton, N.J., 1960), 468.

37. Wilson never recalled O'Shaughnessy; but after American marines invaded Vera Cruz in late April, Huerta handed the chargé his passports and directed him to leave Mexico. Meanwhile, Lind had returned to the United States and continued to criticize O'Shaughnessy. His relations with Huerta were friendly to the end, but the former chargé found nothing but scorn awaiting him when he arrived in Washington. He was thoroughly chastised and never again given a post commensurate with his abilities or experience. After a brief stint in a minor post at Vienna, he was dropped from the diplomatic service. See Robert E. Quirk, *An Affair of Honor* (Louisville, Ky., 1962), 109; New York *Times*, April 16, 1914, p. 2; *ibid.*, September 9, 1914, p. 9; *ibid.*, June 15, 1915, August 27, 1915, p. 5; *Mexican Herald*, May 1, 16, 1914.

any indication that, in the near future, he would adopt a more vigorous policy. By the end of March, with Villa's victory at Torreón yet to be accomplished, Lind was certain that the civil war in Mexico had reached a stalemate. Certain also that his pleas for intervention had been ignored in Washington, he became openly critical, almost condemnatory, of the administration's failure to accept more responsibility for ending the strife. "It seems to me," he wrote to Bryan, "that the time has passed for being overly scrupulous." [38] Believing that further efforts to move the president would be useless, he asked for and received permission to return to the United States. On April 3 he departed for New York aboard one of the presidential yachts, the *Mayflower*.[39] As he sailed, he had no reason to suspect that he still had a critical role to play in the contest between Wilson and Huerta.

As Lind prepared to depart from Vera Cruz, Carranza directed General Pablo González, commander of the Army Corps of the Northeast, to commence the attack against the oil-rich Tampico region held by the Federal forces. On April 9, two days after the battle for the port city began, a whaleboat from the American gunboat *Dolphin* put ashore to procure gasoline. The crew, because they landed in a combat zone, were arrested by Federal soldiers. The sailors were soon released by the commander, General Ignacio Morelos Zaragoza, who immediately sent his regrets to Admiral Henry T. Mayo aboard the *Dolphin*. Admiral Mayo, however, was not satisfied. Knowing of Wilson's attitude toward Huerta, he felt that he would be expected to uphold American prestige to the utmost. Mayo, therefore, demanded a twenty-one gun salute to the American flag within twenty-four hours. When Wilson was notified of the incident, he commented: "Mayo could not have done otherwise." [40]

38. Lind to State Department, March 27, 1914, in NA 812.00/11313.
39. Lind to State Department, March 29, 1914, and State Department to Lind, March 31, 1914, *ibid.*/11327; New York *Times*, April 3, 1914, p. 2.
40. Quirk, *Affair of Honor*, 1–32; Ted C. Hinckley, "Wilson, Huerta and

Lind's arrival in Washington on April 13 came precisely at the time when Wilson needed moral support. The day before, Huerta refused to fire the salute, claiming that to do so would be to offend Mexico's national dignity. On April 14, before the president met with his cabinet to discuss possible punitive measures, he had a conference with Lind. If Wilson needed any assurance that forceful action was needed, he surely received it from his special agent.[41] Although there is no record of what Lind said, the British ambassador reported that he used "very violent language." [42] He probably insisted that the ports of Tampico and Vera Cruz be seized. Even more important, as salve for Wilson's sense of humanity, Lind probably suggested, as he had in his dispatches, that the people of those cities so despised Huerta's exhorbitant taxes and military impressment that they would not offer much resistance and might even welcome the invasion.[43] Later that same day, Wilson ordered the Atlantic fleet to Mexican waters.[44]

The situation was soon blown entirely out of proportion. Huerta agreed to the salute, but only if Admiral Mayo responded with a shot-for-shot salute to the Mexican flag. Rejecting this solution, Wilson went before Congress on April 20 to secure its approval for the use of armed force to induce Huerta to recognize "the rights and dignity of the United

the Twenty-one Gun Salute," *The Historian*, XXII (February, 1960), 201–202.

41. Quirk, *Affair of Honor*, 49–50; Stephenson, *John Lind*, 263.

42. British ambassador quoted in Grieb, *United States and Huerta*, 147.

43. Lind to State Department, February 4, March 12, 23, 1914, in NA 812.00/10965, 11227, 27482. Under oath before the Fall committee in 1920, Lind denied ever having suggested the taking of Vera Cruz or Tampico, either in his dispatches or verbally. He also denied having claimed that American troops might be welcomed in Vera Cruz. See testimony of Lind, *Senate Documents*, 66th Cong., 2nd Sess., No. 285, p. 2363. Lind's biographer, George M. Stephenson, accepts this testimony. See Stephenson, *John Lind*, 264. Yet, the above-cited dispatches reveal that he did make such claims.

44. Quirk, *Affair of Honor*, 50–68; Hinckley, "Wilson, Huerta and the Twenty-one Gun Salute," 203–205.

States." [45] That evening, Lind, along with the secretaries of state, war, and navy, and the chiefs of staff of the army and navy, met with Wilson at the White House to detail plans for a possible naval blockade and invasion of Tampico and Vera Cruz.[46] Familiar with both ports and the surrounding military installations, and having already given considerable thought to possible military operations in Mexico, Lind doubtless contributed his views to this counsel of war.

Before Congress could act on Wilson's request, completely different circumstances prompted him to take immediate action. On April 20, the day Wilson addressed Congress, Consul Canada at Vera Cruz reported that the German freighter *Ypiranga*, laden with arms and ammunition for Huerta, was due to arrive the next day and discharge its deadly cargo. The arms of the *Ypiranga* completely distracted the president from his point of honor. He seized upon the ship's arrival at Vera Cruz as a pretext to do what Lind had been advising for weeks. In the early morning hours of April 21, without congressional sanction, he ordered Admiral Fletcher to seize the Vera Cruz customs house. Since he was only attempting to thwart Huerta and meant the Mexican people no harm, Wilson, accepting Lind's counsels, anticipated little or no resistance. But naval cadets and civilians did resist and the fighting cost Mexico over two hundred lives, the United States only nineteen. The day following the invasion, Congress gave its consent for the president to uphold the nation's honor by force, to what was now a sham *fait accompli*.[47]

45. *Ibid.*
46. Stephenson, *John Lind*, 263–64; Baker, *Woodrow Wilson*, IV, 328–29.
47. Quirk, *Affair of Honor*, 78–103; Hinckley, "Wilson, Huerta and the Twenty-one Gun Salute," 205–206; Meyer, "Arms of the *Ypiranga*," 546–56. Just prior to the Vera Cruz invasion, the Treasury Department had discovered that the arms aboard the *Ypiranga* had been purchased for Huerta in the United States and, in order to conceal their ultimate destination, had been shipped to Mexico by way of Odessa, Russia, and Hamburg, Germany. Anger over Huerta's attempted trickery may well have

Wilson was shaken and horrified by the unexpected spilling of blood in Vera Cruz. His plans for a large-scale invasion of Mexico to give Huerta the *coup de grace* were abandoned when, on April 25, Argentina, Brazil, and Chile offered to mediate the conflict and Wilson accepted. A number of factors besides the natural revulsion to death and violence prompted this decision. American and world opinion had been shocked and outraged by the aggression in Vera Cruz. Having explained that his sole purpose was to uphold national honor, Wilson could see that by continuing military operations until Huerta was eliminated he would run further afoul of public opinion. By using ABC mediators as his pawns, he hoped not only to eliminate Huerta at the negotiating table but, at the same time, to allay Latin American suspicions of Yankee imperialism. Huerta, now cut off from his main sources of revenue, was also willing to accept mediation.[48]

Another development that caused Wilson to stop short of a full-scale invasion was the violent reaction of Venustiano Carranza. After the *Dolphin* incident at Tampico, and during the diplomatic impasse that followed, the State Department paid little attention to what the Constitutionalists' attitude might be. The War Department, however, did alert its garrisons on the Mexican border and sent Brigadier General John J. Pershing to Fort Bliss at El Paso.[49] On the day the marines landed in Vera Cruz, Huerta forced Wilson to concern himself with the attitude of the rebels when he issued an amnesty decree and invited them to join with him in defending Mexico's sovereignty. Before the fighting in Vera Cruz ended, therefore, the president directed Bryan to have

contributed to Wilson's decision to seize the Vera Cruz customs house. Further proof that Wilson was merely looking for a pretext to intervene is provided by the fact that later the *Ypiranga* discharged its cargo at Puerto México, some two hundred miles south of Vera Cruz.

48. Quirk, *Affair of Honor*, 114–20; Link, *New Freedom*, 401–407.
49. Paul S. Horgan, *Great River: The Rio Grande in North American History* (New York, 1954), II, 916.

Carothers inform Carranza that the actions of the United
States should not be construed as war against the Mexican
people but as merely—and here he was not entirely truthful
—an attempt to force Huerta "to make proper reparation for
the arrest of the American sailors." [50]

On the morning of April 22, Carothers, from El Paso,
telegraphed Wilson's message to Carranza in Chihuahua.[51]
The First Chief's reply, which reached the special agent later
that day, bristled with anger. In characteristic fashion,
Carranza declared that since Huerta was a usurper, he had no
constitutional power to accept demands for redress of grievances or make reparations to any foreign government. The
constitution of Mexico, he continued, clearly stated that the
acts of a usurper, whether they be domestic or international
in nature, were punishable by the constitutional authorities
of Mexico, and no one else. He concluded his reply with an
open threat of war: "The invasion of our territory and the
stay of your forces in the port of Vera Cruz, violating the
rights that constitute our existence as a free and independent
sovereign entity, may indeed drag us into an unequal war
. . . which until today we have desired to avoid." [52]

The prospect of war electrified the city of El Paso. Even
before receiving Carranza's reply, Carothers detected "a very
strong undercurrent of resentment" among the Constitutionalist authorities in Juárez. Tension mounted when rumors
reached El Paso that Constitutionalist and American troops

50. State Department to Carothers, April 21, 1914, in *Foreign Relations,
1914*, 480.
51. Carothers to State Department, April 22, 1914, in NA 812.00/11596;
El Paso *Morning Times*, April 23, 1914.
52. Carothers (containing Carranza's reply) to State Department, April
22, 1914, in *Foreign Relations, 1914*, 483–84. This document is probably a
State Department translation of Carranza's telegraphic message to Carothers, the original of which was sent to Washington by mail after Carothers
telegraphed his own translation. The original must have been cited in
Foreign Relations, because it differs slightly from Carothers' translation. See
Carothers to State Department, April 22, 1914, in NA 812.00/11618; copy in
Wilson Papers, Ser. 2, Box 51.

had already clashed farther down the Rio Grande at Ojinaga. Then came the news that Villa was on his way to the border with twelve thousand troops and a trainload of artillery. Every hardware store sold out of firearms and ammunition within hours of the first rumors. Every train leaving El Paso, to the east, west, and north, was loaded to capacity. General Pershing placed his troops at the international bridge and all possible fords near the city. Reinforcements were sent speeding from Fort Sam Houston in San Antonio and from Fort Huachuca in southeast Arizona.[53] Tension also mounted in Washington. Bryan issued instructions for all consuls in Mexico to encourage Americans to leave as soon as possible, and Wilson promptly reimposed the arms embargo.[54]

When Villa arrived in Juárez, Carothers immediately crossed the river to determine the Mexicans' intentions. Villa greeted him cordially with the traditional Mexican *abrazo* for all the reporters to see and exclaimed aloud that "there would be no war between the United States and the Constitutionalists." To emphasize his friendship for the United States, he proclaimed that the Marines "could keep Vera Cruz and hold it so tight that not even water could get in to Huerta." His trip to the border, Villa further revealed, was designed only to restore confidence between himself and the United States. Then he asked Carothers to dine with him.[55] So as to ease the tension in El Paso, Carothers first telephoned Zach Cobb, the customs collector, and asked him to inform authorities that Villa was not belligerent and that all was well. That night, Carothers was a hero in El Paso.[56]

53. Carothers to State Department, April 21, 22, 1914, in NA 812.00/11587, 11596; General Tasker Bliss to War Department, April 23, 1914, Wilson Papers, Ser. 2, Box 106; El Paso *Morning Times*, April 23, 1914.

54. State Department to all American consuls in Mexico, April 22, 1914, in *Foreign Relations, 1914*, 671; New York *Times*, April 24, 1914, p. 1.

55. Carothers to State Department, April 23, 1914, in NA 812.00/11654; New York *Times*, April 24, 1914, p. 1; El Paso *Morning Times*, April 24, 1914; "Our Debt to Villa," *Literary Digest*, XLVIII (May 16, 1914), 1166; Guzmán, *Memoirs of Pancho Villa*, 190–91.

56. Cobb to State Department, April 23, 1914, in NA 812.00/11656;

Villa alone among the Constitutionalist generals took a peaceful stance following the Vera Cruz invasion. Indeed, the others encouraged Carranza to make his bellicose pronouncement.[57] Villa, in his conversations with Carothers, claimed that he had openly disagreed with Carranza's advisors and had hastened to disassociate himself from them by coming to the border to make his own views known.[58] He may, as he claimed, have realized that a perpetual arms embargo—which would result from the rebels taking a hard line against the United States—would stall the war against Huerta. On the other hand, he may simply have realized how valuable Wilson's good will might be in the future. At any rate, Carothers was confident of Villa's sincerity. Bryan was ecstatic. Referring to the general's independent stand, he urged Carothers to inform Villa that "it shows a largeness of view on his part and a comprehension of the whole situation which is greatly to his credit." Bryan also directed his agent to reveal that "public opinion in the United States has been greatly disturbed by General Carranza's attitude. . . ."[59] If this was an invitation for Villa to challenge Carranza's obdurate stand, it was not long in being accepted.

On April 25 Villa, through Carothers, sent a personal letter to President Wilson in which he reiterated what he had told the special agent two days before. He also disavowed Carranza's stand and rather apologetically assured the American president that he could disregard the First Chief's warlike tones, that they were just his means of defending the dignity of the republic.[60] Villa also told Carothers confidentially that

---

Raymond G. Carroll, "United States Agents Powerful in Mexico," New York *Sun*, August 15, 1915.

57. Letcher to State Department, April 22, 1914, in *Foreign Relations, 1914*, 484; Barragán, "De las memorias de Don Venustiano Carranza," *El Universal, Magazine para todos*, June 22, 1931, p. 1.

58. Carothers to State Department, April 23, 1914, in NA 812.00/11654; Guzmán, *Memoirs of Pancho Villa*, 190–91.

59. State Department to Carothers, April 24, 1914, in NA, 812.00/11654.

60. Villa to Wilson, April 25, 1914, *ibid.*/11714; copy in Wilson Papers, Ser. 4, Box 51.

he would force Carranza to change his attitude. In a letter to General Scott, the special agent stated his firm conviction that "if Carranza is not careful, Villa will overthrow him." [61] When, shortly thereafter, Villa returned to Chihuahua and Carranza's attitude began to soften, Carothers and the American press naturally assumed that Villa had forced the First Chief's hand.[62]

The possibility of his forces splitting was, no doubt, a sobering thought and helped persuade Carranza to modify his stand. Actually he had already notified Washington through Consul Letcher that he wished to avoid armed conflict. Carothers also received word that some of the other Constitutionalist generals had wavered and were now urging moderation.[63] Carranza, moreover, began receiving messages from one of his Anglo-American agents in the United States, Sherbourne G. Hopkins, who advised that American public opinion was greatly inflamed by the First Chief's recent warlike pronouncement. Hopkins counseled that, when the time seemed opportune, Carranza should issue a statement to the effect that, since the United States had occupied only Vera Cruz, the Constitutionalists were satisfied that Mexican sovereignty would be respected. On May 4, after Wilson had accepted the ABC mediation, Zubarán, who was now serving as Carranza's agent in Washington, addressed a note to Bryan which embodied the suggestions that Hopkins had made.[64]

During the last days of April and the first weeks of May,

61. Carothers to State Department, April 25, 1914, in NA 812.00/11704; Carothers to Scott, April 25, 1914, in Scott Papers, Box 15.

62. Carothers to State Department, April 27, 29, 1914, in NA 812.00/11731, 11770; "Our Debt to Villa," *Literary Digest*, XLVIII, 1166–67.

63. Letcher to State Department, April 22, 1914, in *Foreign Relations, 1914*, 484; Carothers to State Department, April 25, 1914, in NA 812.00/11704; copy in Wilson Papers, Ser. 4, Box 51.

64. S. Gil Herrera (Hopkins) a Carranza, April 23, 1914, AGRE, L–E–861, Leg. 5; Hopkins to Carranza, April 24, 1914, copy in Scott Papers, Box 15; Zubarán Capmany to State Department, in *Foreign Relations, 1914*, 496–97.

preparations went on for the ABC mediation. The mediators at first assumed that the only matter under consideration was the settling of the conflict between the United States and Huerta. But before the deliberations got under way on May 20, Wilson made it clear that he meant for the conferees to arrange the establishment of a new provisional government which he could recognize. Since the American president insisted upon delving into Mexico's internal affairs, the mediators extended an invitation to the Constitutionalists to participate in the conferences. Although Carranza accepted these good offices "in principle," he refused to send delegates unless he received prior assurances that his nation's internal affairs would not be the matter under consideration.

After laboring manfully under the handicaps imposed by Carranza and Wilson, on July 1 the conferees proposed the creation of a new provisional government through Carranza-Huerta negotiations. But the First Chief would accept nothing less than Huerta's unconditional surrender and declared his intentions to continue fighting until all vestiges of the usurper's regime were destroyed. Having settled nothing, the conference adjourned the next day.[65] Again Carranza's refusal to accept a negotiated peace thwarted Wilson's plans for guiding the reconstruction of Mexico.

Government and public opinion in the United States, disturbed by Carranza's initial response to the Vera Cruz landings, was little assuaged by his attitude toward mediation. For this John Lind was partially responsible. Paradoxically, the special agent's sympathies were with the *Carrancistas*. Having established contacts with Carranza's agents in the United States—Zubarán Capmany, Cabrera, and Juan F. Urquidi—during and after the Vera Cruz incident, he found them well-educated and as thoroughly middle-class as he. As a result, his earlier stated fears of their possible revolutionary excesses evaporated. His suspicions of more radical revolu-

65. Link, *New Freedom*, 405–13; Grieb, *United States and Huerta*, 159–77.

tionaries, such as Villa, whom he had earlier boosted, and Zapata, never disappeared. Little time passed, however, before he accepted the *Carrancistas'* goals for Mexico as his own. His trust in them was such that he no longer saw a need for the United States to intervene and aid in the reconstruction of Mexico.[66]

Equally significant, the *Carrancista* agents in Washington and New York placed their trust in Lind. As Zubarán Capmany put it in a letter to the First Chief, "the most loyal and important friend that we have among the Americans is Mr. Lind." [67] Before the end of the ABC mediation conferences, even Carranza accepted him as such. Thereafter the *Carrancista* press, denying that he had ever been an interventionist, periodically reminded the Mexican people that John Lind was their most trustworthy and sympathetic American ally.[68]

Lind played a curious dual role during the ABC proceedings. Wilson retained him in Washington as an advisor to the secretary of state and the American delegation to the mediation conference. As the deliberations progressed, however, he increasingly advised the *Carrancistas,* and, more and more, his ideas coincided with theirs. Even before the negotiations began, in a memorandum to the president, he prophesied the results: "I am fully convinced . . . that the mediation will result in nothing. Its greatest value, so far as the Mexican situation is concerned, is in the fact that

66. Stephenson, *John Lind,* 266–69; Lind to Bryan, April 16, 1915, in Bryan Papers, Box 43; Lind to Bryan, April 21, 1915, in Wilson Papers, Ser. 2, Box 129; Lind to Wilson, August 2, 1915, *ibid.,* Ser. 4, Box 125.

67. Zubarán Capmany a Carranza, June 19, 1914, Isidro Fabela (ed.), *Documentos históricos de la Revolución Mexicana* (México, D.F., 1962), III, 127–28.

68. *El Pueblo* (Mexico City), March 21, 27, 1915; *El Demócrata* (Mexico City), September 11, 1915. Isidro Fabela, in his *Historia Diplomática,* I, 367–71, acknowledged the *Carrancistas'* trust in Lind and suggests that the agent's sympathy for the Mexican revolution was shared by more Americans than was the hostility of the interventionists.

it has afforded the Americans an opportunity to escape." [69]

Lind was disturbed when he discovered that Wilson hoped to promote a new provisional government in Mexico. "The Mexicans of the north are, as you already appreciate, very sensitive about doing anything that smacks of taking orders from outside," he wrote to Bryan. Insisting that a military victory by the rebels was the only solution, he noted further, "The problem we have to deal with is a victorious army with a score of politically inexperienced but ambitious chiefs— every one including Zapata a potential candidate for the dictatorship. The only safe course for us in the mediation proceedings is to remain as listeners." [70]

Before the mediation conferences had proceeded far, Lind found himself in almost total disagreement with Wilson and Bryan. He spent more and more time in consultation with the Constitutionalist junta.[71] In fact, when Carranza declared that the Constitutionalists would not recognize the right of the mediators to involve themselves in Mexico's internal affairs, Lind helped draft the statement.[72] Almost simultaneously he sent Bryan a cautiously worded protest against the administration's continued attempts to create a new provisional government through mediation, since according to the Mexican Constitution Huerta, a usurper, could not legally be

69. Lind, Memorandum, April 30, 1914, in Wilson Papers, Ser. 2, Box 108.
70. Lind to Bryan, [n.d.], *ibid.*
71. New York *Times*, May 27, 28, 1914, p. 1; *ibid.*, June 10, 1914, p. 2; *Mexican Herald*, May 31, 1914; New York *Sun*, July 18, 1914.
72. Draft of the memorandum with notations to the effect that Lind helped prepare it, [n.d.], in Lind Papers. Portions of this draft are identical to Zubarán Capmany a los plenipotenciarios del ABC, May 27, 1914, in Fabela, *Documentos históricos de la Revolución Mexicana*, III, 43–44. See also Zubarán Capmany, representing General Carranza, to the mediators, May 28, 1914, enclosure no. 8 of the special commissioners to State Department, May 31, 1914, in *Foreign Relations, 1914*, 519. The different dates assigned to Zubarán Capmany's note by the above cited publications results from the fact that the first citation represents the date when Zubarán Capmany sent the note to Juan F. Urquidi with instructions for him to present it to the mediators, while the second citation represents the actual date that the mediators received the document.

a party to arranging his successor. "We should not worry about the succession," he counseled. "That will take care of itself." [73]

That there was no open break between Lind and the administration was owing to the fact that the administration's policy, despite the fact that Carranza refused to accept it, was designed to aid the revolutionists. To the casual observer, therefore, Lind and Wilson seemed to be in basic agreement. Indeed, the Huerta delegation at Niagara Falls assumed that Wilson's policy resulted largely from Lind's counsels.[74] The president, meanwhile, conveniently turned his back while the rebels procured arms in the United States in violation of the embargo and shipped them to Tampico, which had been captured by the Constitutionalists on May 13. When Huerta's delegates protested to the mediators, Wilson apologized, claiming ignorance of the illicit arms trade, but Lind made no excuses. Instead, he informed Sherbourne Hopkins, who was purchasing arms for the rebels, that the arms traffic would attract less unfavorable attention if the illicit cargoes were first shipped to Havana, where new ship's papers could be secured, then delivered to Tampico.[75] Despite their common sympathy for the Constitutionalists, Wilson never endorsed Carranza as enthusiastically as did Lind.

Although his services were not officially terminated until August—probably to enable him to draw a full year's salary—Lind returned to Minnesota in early June. Although he continued to communicate with Wilson and Bryan on Mexican affairs, his advice was virtually ignored for the remainder of 1914 and most of 1915, because the administra-

73. Lind to Bryan, May 29, 1914, in Bryan Papers, Box 30.
74. New York *Times*, July 3, 1914, p. 3.
75. Grieb, *United States and Huerta*, 172–75; Buckley, conversation with Sherbourne Hopkins, October 4, 1919, in Buckley Papers, File no. 233; Testimony of Sherbourne G. Hopkins, April 29, 1920, *Senate Documents*, 66th Cong., 2nd Sess., No. 285, pp. 2412–14; New York *Times*, July 10, 1914, p. 2. For details of the taking of Tampico, see Barragán Rodríguez, *Historia . . . de la Revolución Constitucionalista*, I, 471–75.

tion tended to favor Villa and Zapata over Carranza during that time. Lind's steadfast support of the First Chief ultimately drew charges from the anti-administration New York *Sun* to the effect that he was a paid agent of the *Carrancista* faction. He denied ever receiving money or any other compensation from Carranza, and there is little reason to doubt his word. He was such an unabashed supporter of the First Chief that, once he left the employ of the Wilson administration, he would have seen nothing unethical about receiving compensation from the revolutionaries.[76]

During World War I Lind again served the Wilson administration, first as a commissioner of conciliation in the Department of Labor, then as an umpire for the National War Labor Board. As did so many reformers of the Progressive era, he also served on his state's Commission on Public Safety, which was dedicated to promoting patriotism, ferreting out supposedly dangerous aliens, and suppressing wouldbe opponents of the war effort.[77] Even in his old age, Lind was politically active and remained true to his midwestern progressive heritage.[78] Certainly he had been the most publicized and controversial, and at times the most influential, of Wilson's special agents in Mexico.

All of Lind's diplomatic efforts in Mexico had met with failure. Indeed, his protracted stay may have served to harden Huerta's will to remain in power. But as a gatherer of information and as a propagandist he was much more

76. Stephenson, *John Lind*, 284–305; New York *Times*, June 10, 12, 1914, p. 2; New York *Sun*, July 16, 1914, November 5, 1915; Testimony of Lind and Buckley, *Senate Documents*, 66th Cong., 2nd Sess., No. 285, pp. 812, 2364.

77. Stephenson, *John Lind*, 332–33; William J. Preston, Jr., *Aliens and Dissenters: Federal Suppression of Radicals, 1903–1933* (New York, 1966), 126–28. Lind was largely responsible for the suppression of the syndicalist Industrial Workers of the World in Minnesota. Upon his recommendation, moreover, the United States Justice Department, by trying local I.W.W. leaders on criminal conspiracy charges, broke the power of the union throughout the Midwest.

78. Stephenson, *John Lind*, 342–66.

successful. Even before his departure, his promptings had influenced the president to establish permanent contacts with the Constitutionalists and to lift the arms embargo. The military intervention he so often pleaded for doubtless resulted, in part, from his counsels.

He left Mexico believing that his efforts had gone for naught. But Wilson must have been pleased with his overall performance. Lind had pursued his task with the zeal of a Progressive reformer, and the principles he strove to uphold mirrored Wilson's own New Freedom. In the Minnesotan's mind, Mexico contained all the same evils he had sought to eradicate in the United States during his political career: a corrupt political regime (in this case, Huerta's provisional government) sustained by a privileged group of business interests (in this case, *hacendados* and British concessionaries) who did not have the public interest at heart. He had a progressive's faith that such malignant political and economic conditions could be eliminated by an enlightened elite (in this case, the Constitutionalists of the North) working through democratic institutions. Since free elections, the traditional Anglo-American technique of eliminating such evils seemed temporarily unworkable in Mexico, Lind accepted as axiomatic the assumption that intervention by the United States would advance Mexico toward the establishment of a Progressive capitalist democracy.[79] Only after he returned to the United States did he realize that the price of such advancement—control of the Mexican revolution by the United States—was greater than the revolutionary leaders, at least Carranza, were willing to pay. In the process, he learned something that had escaped his president—that the Mexicans were capable of solving their own problems.

79. Larry D. Hill, "The Progressive Politician as a Diplomat: The Case of John Lind in Mexico," *The Americas*, XXVII (April, 1971), 372.

CHAPTER VIII

Holding the Lid On

Wilson's disappointment at his failure to influence Carranza through the ABC powers was alleviated somewhat by the more encouraging results of George Carothers' efforts. The longtime resident of Mexico had proved himself a capable diplomat, and several who witnessed him in action praised his work. Suggesting that the special agent was responsible for easing the border crisis which followed the Vera Cruz incident, General Pershing reported to his superiors that "Carothers has so far succeeded in directing the Constitutionalists along rational lines."[1] British Vice Consul Cunard Cummins of Gómez Palacio marveled at Carothers' ability to deal with the revolutionaries. In a letter to Zach Cobb, which he asked be forwarded to Bryan, the Englishman noted: "Mr. Carothers has displayed wisdom and tact, and produced such excellent and often unhoped-for results, that all observers have been deeply impressed, seeing in him a man exceptionally gifted to fill the highest duties in the calling of diplomacy."[2] Zach Cobb himself offered even more encouragement for the future. In a letter to General Scott, he wrote: "I see a splendid possibility, through the diplomatic work of Carothers, to get the Constitutionalists to agree to the President's program as it develops."[3]

1. Pershing to General Tasker H. Bliss, June 2, 1914, John J. Pershing Papers, Division of Manuscripts, Library of Congress, Box 372.
2. Cunard Cummins to Cobb, April 30, 1914, in NA 125.36582/85.
3. Cobb to Scott, May 2, 1914, Scott Papers, Box 15.

Yet Carothers continued to enjoy only mixed success in his relations with Carranza. The special agent's efforts to protect American oil interests at Tampico, for example, pointed up again the difficulty in securing a completely satisfactory agreement from the First Chief. Fearing reprisals from the Federal armies, most Americans fled Tampico following the Vera Cruz invasion. Other foreigners left the area because of the fighting between the Constitutionalists and the Federals. With millions of dollars worth of oil properties left to the caprice of the contesting forces, Bryan assigned Carothers the task of persuading Carranza to enter into an agreement with the Federals for neutralizing the oil producing areas. In his own inimitable way, Carranza replied that the Constitutionalists had not driven the foreign oil field workers from their jobs and that neutralization of the oil fields was not necessary, since his troops controlled the area and would insure the protection of foreigners and their interests. This arrangement was not precisely what Washington had requested but it was acceptable to the oil men. Several minor irritants resulted from the Constitutionalists' occupation of Tampico, but by the end of May most of the oil workers were back on the job and, at least temporarily, the oil companies had little with which to quarrel.[4]

Carothers' relations with Villa provided the administration with its greatest source of encouragement. Officially their relationship remained the same; Carothers' primary responsibility, at least until July, 1914, was to protect the interests of foreigners. But privately the two became fast friends. Villa provided Carothers with a private rail car—actually a converted boxcar with sleeping and kitchen facilities. Carothers also had two Chinese servants, one of whom the agent

4. State Department to Carothers, April 28, May 8, 14, 1914, in *Foreign Relations, 1914*, 690–91, 700, 702; Carothers to State Department, May 1, 20, 1914, *ibid.*, 695, 700; State Department to Clarence Miller, American consul, Tampico, May 6, 14, 1914, *ibid.*, 697, 701–702; Miller to State Department, May 8, 14, 15, 17, 21, 1914, *ibid.*, 698–99, 702–704.

claimed could cook as well as the best New York chef.[5] Villa and Carothers spent many hours discussing the nature of the revolution and America's response to it. In this respect, the friendship served Villa better than the United States, because he was always aware of what behavior would have the most favorable impact north of the border.

Whether the result of Carothers' counsels or of those offered by his Mexican advisors, Villa definitely sought to cultivate a favorable image in the United States. During the early months of 1914, before the outbreak of war in Europe, he received tremendous press coverage. He provided newspaper and magazine correspondents with a railroad car of their own. At least a dozen reporters were with him most of the time, and he made himself readily available for interviews. A motion picture crew from the United States even traveled with him and filmed his army in action.[6] For the most part these correspondents wrote glowing accounts of Villa's exploits and character. In the popular parlance of the day, he had become the "Mexican man of the hour." [7] Probably the reporter most enamored with Villa was a young socialist recently graduated from Harvard—John Reed of the New York *World* and *Metropolitan* magazine. His romanticized accounts pictured the rebel chieftain as combining the best qualities of Robin Hood and Napoleon.[8]

5. Edward L. Tinker, "Campaigning With Villa," *Southwest Review*, XXX (Winter, 1945), 150–52. Tinker was a journalist who traveled with Carothers in the private car during one of Villa's campaigns.

6. Herman Whitaker, "Villa—Bandit-Patriot," *Independent*, LXXVII (June 8, 1914), 450–51. For an analysis of Villa's relations with the press and motion picture industry and the myths that resulted, see Nancy Brandt, "Pancho Villa: The Making of a Modern Legend," *The Americas*, XXI (October, 1964), 146–62.

7. Gregory Mason, "The Mexican Man of the Hour," *Outlook*, CVII (June 6, 1914), 292.

8. Drewey Wayne Gunn, "Three Radicals and a Revolution: Reed, London, and Steffens on Mexico," *Southwest Review*, LV (Autumn, 1970), 394–99. John Reed incorporated his newspaper and magazine accounts into his previously cited book, *Insurgent Mexico*. He was so impressed by Villa

All of the correspondents were not as impressed with Villa as was Reed. Even the most hostile commentators admitted, nonetheless, that while Villa's professions of friendship for the United States were designed to further his own self-interest, he had eased Wilson's embarrassment following the Vera Cruz invasion. An editorial in the New York *World* probably came closest to expressing the president's own view: "We have many remarkable proofs of this man's [Villa's] capacity for leadership but not one of them has been more conclusive than his willingness to be advised and assisted by the United States." [9] Certainly Villa, among the Constitutionalist leaders, seemed most willing to accept American guidance. The State Department had chosen Carothers because of his ability to influence Villa; the decision had already paid dividends. In President Wilson's own words, "General Villa . . . often shows some susceptibilities of the best influences." [10]

The summer of 1914 found Carothers serving in still another role—that of mediator between Villa and Carranza. The antagonism between the two *caudillos*, first manifested during the Vera Cruz incident, continued to grow as Villa prepared to assault Zacatecas, the one remaining Federal stronghold between him and Mexico City. Determined to beat all other Constitutionalist armies to the capital, Villa planned his campaign without consulting Carranza, but the First Chief would not be ignored. He and his advisors decided that it was time to curb their impetuous colleague. Rather than allow Villa to march rapidly southward, Carranza ordered him to the East to capture Saltillo, a mission which logically

that when he returned to the United States he sought to pass on his impressions firsthand to President Wilson. After first meeting with Wilson's private secretary, Joseph P. Tumulty, and Assistant Secretary of State William Phillips, Reed did have an interview with the president. See Reed to Tumulty, April 8, 1914, in Wilson Papers, Ser. 4, Box 121; Wilson to Reed, June 17, 1914, *ibid.*, Ser. 2, Box 111; Tumulty, Memorandum, June 22, 1914, *ibid.*; Phillips to Bryan, April 24, 1914, in NA 812.00/24262.

9. New York *World*, June 20, 1914.

10. Wilson to Scott, April 16, 1914, in Scott Papers, Box 15.

should have been assigned to General Pablo González, commander of the Army Corps of the Northeast. The First Chief's stratagem was to sidetrack Villa long enough for General Obregón to strike across the mountains of Tepic and Jalisco, through Guadalajara, and arrive in Mexico City first.

As Villa marched on Saltillo, Carranza entrusted the Zacatecas campaign to General Pánfilo Natera, who proved unequal to the task. Three times his armies were repulsed with heavy casualties. Villa, meanwhile, took Paredón and marched into Saltillo unhindered, as the Federals fled before his arrival. Villa might then have struck southward, pursuing the retreating *Huertistas* toward San Luis Potosí, but he did not trust General González, who, sitting in nearby Monterrey, could menace his lines of communications out of Chihuahua. In the first days of June, therefore, Villa turned Saltillo over to González and returned to the more cordial surroundings of Torreón.[11]

Shortly after Villa's return to Torreón, Carothers journeyed to El Paso to file a lengthy report on the Saltillo campaign. While he was at the border, relations between Villa and Carranza reached a breaking point. Consul Letcher reported from Chihuahua that he had received information from *Carrancista* officials that the First Chief had arranged to deny the Division of the North ammunition and supplies and was determined to limit Villa's authority to the state of Chihuahua.[12] Carothers, puzzled by similar reports that appeared in the El Paso newspapers, reported his own belief that there was "no serious trouble between Carranza and Villa."[13] He was shocked, therefore, when he returned to Torreón and discovered that relations between the two

11. Quirk, *Mexican Revolution*, 28–30; Barragán Rodríguez, *Historia* . . . *de la Revolución Constitucionalista*, I, 475–83.
12. Letcher to State Department, June 4, 1914, in NA 812.00/12160; copy in Wilson Papers, Ser. 2, Box 54.
13. Carothers to State Department, June 6, 1914, in NA 812.00/12170; El Paso *Morning Times*, June 4, 5, 1914.

revolutionary chiefs had indeed deteriorated during his absence from Villa's side.

Villa was in a rage. The First Chief, he charged, was attempting to curtail the operations of the Division of the North by censoring communications and tying up all the railroad rolling stock. Villa also told Carothers that a shipment of ammunition, which he had personally paid for, had arrived in Tampico from Havana and that the *Carrancistas* were holding it. He warned that unless it was delivered immediately, he would break with Carranza. Carothers tried to calm Villa, urging patience and promising to personally intercede with the First Chief. But in his report to Washington, the special agent confided that he was not at all certain that he could prevent a split in the Constitutionalists' ranks.[14]

With the ABC mediation failing to oust Huerta as planned, Wilson was naturally concerned over any falling out among the revolutionaries that might in any way slow the pace of the war against the usurper. Carothers was urgently directed to use every means to prevent a split.[15] By the time these instructions reached him, the agent, attempting to appease Villa, had already made his way to the First Chief's headquarters, which was now located in Saltillo. On June 13 he interviewed Carranza, who reported that conditions were "improving." Carranza knew better; the next day he gleefully informed Carothers that after a heated six-hour telegraphic conversation, Villa had angrily resigned as commander of the Division of the North. Carranza insisted that Villa's arbitrary exercise of powers that belonged only to the First Chief had precipitated the break. The special agent was dismayed by Carranza's attitude and later recalled that the First Chief "appeared to be overjoyed that the breach had come, and would not listen to my reasoning." [16]

14. Cobb (for Carothers) to State Department, June 12, 1914, in NA 812.00/12219; copy in Wilson Papers, Ser. 2, Box 55.
15. State Department to Carothers, June 13, 1914, in NA 812.00/12219.
16. Carothers to State Department, June 11, 1914, in NA 125.36582/88;

Hoping to influence Villa to change his mind and be more cooperative, Carothers returned immediately to Torreón. There he discovered that Carranza had not been entirely candid. The break, as Consul Edwards of Juárez had already reported to Washington, had resulted when the First Chief ordered Villa to detach five thousand of his troops to General Natera. Villa and his advisors, both civilian and military, had interpreted the order as a deliberate attempt to split and weaken the Division of the North. The *Villistas* attempted through hours of telegraphic communication to explain their reluctance to break up their highly successful army and even offered to march en masse on Zacatecas, but Carranza refused to revoke his order. In a fit of pique, Villa then tendered his resignation.[17]

By the time Carothers reached Torreón, however, the officers of the Division of the North, having been forced to choose between their general and the First Chief, had refused to accept Villa's resignation and had declared their intention to stand by him. Feeling more righteous than ever, Villa took charge of the railroads and telegraphs in the area he controlled. His men also quietly removed the *Carrancistas* from their offices in Juárez and Chihuahua. Then, in open defiance of Carranza, Villa began his own campaign against Zacatecas.[18]

Since telegraphic communications were made uncertain by the break, Carothers was again forced to travel to El Paso to make his report and get new instructions. Villa had asked him to impress upon President Wilson the fact that the *Villistas* would engage in no hostile action against Carranza. He

Carothers to State Department, June 13, 14, 1914, in NA 812.00/12226, 12228; copies of both in Wilson Papers, Ser. 2, Box 55; Testimony of Carothers, *Senate Documents*, 66th Cong., 2nd Sess., No. 285, p. 1771.

17. Edwards to State Department, June 16, 1914, in *Foreign Relations, 1914*, 541–42; Carothers to State Department, June 18, 1914, *ibid.*; Testimony of Carothers, *Senate Documents*, 66th Cong., 2nd Sess., No. 285, p. 1771.

18. *Ibid.*; El Paso *Morning Times*, June 17, 18, 1914.

wanted Washington to know that he planned to proceed south alone, but if he met other revolutionary armies he would encourage them to join him. Villa especially wanted Carothers to make clear that his actions would speed the progress of the revolution. The American agent also noted that the Chihuahua strong man would gladly accept mediation by American officials. Carothers had not been in El Paso a day when news arrived that seemingly made mediation unnecessary. *Villista* officials reported that Carranza had "graciously" consented for Villa to "proceed south to Mexico City" and had agreed "to postpone settlement of differences between them until later." [19]

On June 20 Villa began his attack on Zacatecas, and within four days the city was his. Carothers, who was in Juárez at the time, relied upon information provided by the *Villistas* and reported that, as in the case of Torreón and Saltillo, Villa promptly restored order, established a civil government, and tended to the poor. Foreign lives and property, according to the *Villistas*, were carefully guarded. The only prisoners executed were snipers who continued to fire after the surrender. The wounded prisoners again received medical attention. As a result of such humane treatment, the *Villistas* claimed that two thousand prisoners had joined their ranks.[20]

Although distressed by the rift between Villa and Carranza, Wilson and Bryan must have been pleased by Villa's growing strength—strength that had earned him the nickname of Centaur of the North—and his continued humaneness and cooperation. Villa, for his part, was receiving ample cooperation from Carothers. The special agent's dispatches revealed that he sympathized overwhelmingly with the *Vil-*

19. Carothers to State Department, June 18, 1914, in NA 812.00/12294; El Paso *Morning Times*, June 19, 1914.

20. Carothers to State Department, July 5, 1914, in NA 812.00/12473; Quirk, *Mexican Revolution*, 32–33; Barragán Rodríguez, *Historia . . . de la Revolución Constitucionalista*, I, 536–37.

lista faction. Many of his diplomatic efforts which were directed to the State Department and to Carranza were made in Villa's behalf.

Those who criticized the Wilson administration's Mexican policy naturally gave the Villa-Carothers relationship close scrutiny. Senator Fall, a constant critic, upbraided the State Department for bypassing Marion Letcher (an old friend), the regular consular representative in Chihuahua. Fall claimed that Carothers would serve the interests of the United States only to a degree, then would do what was necessary to protect his own property interests in Torreón. Fall further maintained that Carothers had admitted as much.[21] Frank Mondell of Wyoming, a leading Republican critic in the House, found the relationship between Villa and Carothers disgusting. Referring to the *abrazo* Villa had given Carothers at Juárez following the Vera Cruz incident, Mondell said that the American agent could "fondle" Mexican bandits if he chose to, but that he should not imply in his public comments that the United States approved of Villa's activities.[22]

In Mexico, Carranza had become increasingly dissatisfied with the Villa-Carothers friendship. On June 28, at the First Chief's direction, Alfredo Breceda and Rafael Zubarán Capmany, Constitutionalist agents in Washington, issued a statement to the press condemning Carothers' activities. They charged that while Carothers "posed . . . as the confidential agent of the State Department," he was, in fact, serving as "a political attache and adviser of Villa in international matters."[23] Similarly they charged that Carothers' dispatches contained pro-Villa propaganda and that Villa's insubordination was prompted by the agent's promises of support from the Wilson administration.[24]

21. *Congressional Record*, 63rd Cong., 2nd Sess., 4519–20.
22. *Ibid.*, 7331.
23. New York *World*, June 28, 1914.
24. *Ibid.*; New York *Times*, June 28, 1914, II, p. 1; New York *Sun*, June 28, 1914. The *Sun*, which was extremely anti-administration, tended to expand the criticism of Carothers more than the other newspapers.

The most serious charges came from one of the administration's friends, Republican congressman William Kent of California. In early June, Kent brought to the attention of the president several letters sent him by René León of El Paso and Maurice León of New York. The Leóns, who professed to be Constitutionalist sympathizers, charged that Carothers was accepting lucrative business opportunities from Villa. Kent thought the charges worthy of an investigation.[25]

Considering their own reliance upon morality in the conduct of diplomacy, Wilson and Bryan would certainly have insisted upon an investigation had not Carothers himself earlier reported the business proposal. According to the agent, however, the offer came not from Villa but from a wealthy *hacendado*, who wanted Carothers to manage his large cotton plantation near Torreón. Previously, Carothers noted, Villa had confiscated the cotton from the plantation, and it was no longer in production. Under arrangements made with Villa, Carothers proposed to return the land to cotton production and pay the revolutionary army a tax of fifteen dollars per bale. The special agent also reported that Villa was willing to allow the other *hacendados* the same privilege. In this way the land would again produce and the armies would have a steady income. Well aware that such an activity might draw criticism to himself and to the administration, Carothers asked if his brother could operate the plantation until the Constitutionalists were victorious. If this arrangement were not satisfactory, he regretfully reported, he would be forced to resign from the service of the department.[26]

25. René León to Kent, June 5, 1914, in Bryan-Wilson Correspondence; Kent to Wilson, June 10, 1914, *ibid.*; copies of all these in Bryan Papers, Box 43; Wilson to Bryan, June 12, 1914, in Wilson Papers, Ser. 4, Box 124; Kent to Wilson, June 17, 18, 1914, *ibid.* Wilson was interested enough in the León-Kent correspondence that, before passing it on to Bryan, he prepared a condensation of the letters on his own portable typewriter.

26. Carothers to State Department, May 27, 1914, in NA 812.00/12343.

Wilson would not accept Carothers' proposed arrangement and directed Bryan to inform the special agent that if he accepted the business offer, he would have to resign from the department.[27] When Bryan telegraphed the president's decision, Zach Cobb interceded in the agent's behalf. Carothers "is the best diplomat I ever saw in dealing with the Mexican people," he wired the secretary of state, "and is patriotic in placing his duty to the government above personal interests." [28] Carothers, meanwhile, reported that he was prepared to accept the business opportunity unless the department specifically requested him not to. With the tension between Villa and Carranza mounting in early June, Bryan decided that Carothers would be needed. On June 5 he asked the agent to forego the business offer and continue his work with Villa. The following day, the special agent replied that he had declined the overseer job and would immediately turn his efforts toward conciliating Villa and Carranza.[29]

Since the president knew of Carothers' business opportunity, he exhibited no alarm in his return correspondence to Congressman Kent. When the Leóns persisted in their accusations later in June, Kent himself investigated further and determined that they were representing a group of French capitalists who were inclined to support Carranza in hopes of securing concessions.[30] Bryan, nonetheless, remained suspicious enough to carry through a plan that he had initiated earlier—to send a second special agent into Constitutionalist territory.

As early as April 24, 1914, when the antagonism between

27. Wilson to Bryan, June 5, 1914, *ibid.*

28. State Department to Carothers, June 4, 1914, *ibid.*; Cobb to State Department, June 4, 1914, in NA 125.36582/83.

29. Carothers to State Department, June 4, 1914, in NA 125.36582/83; State Department to Carothers, June 5, 1914, *ibid.*; Carothers to State Department, June 6, 1914, *ibid.*/84.

30. Kent to Wilson, June 29, 1914, in Wilson Papers, Ser. 2, Box 56; Wilson to Kent, June 30, 1914, *ibid.*; Wilson to Kent, June 22, 1914, *ibid.*, Ser. 4, Box 124.

Villa and Carranza was first manifested, Boaz Long, chief of the department's Division of Latin American Affairs, suggested such a move.[31] Nothing was done about his suggestion until the department was presented with the prospect of Carothers' possible resignation. Then Long suggested to the secretary of state that several Spanish-speaking agents, who knew Mexican politics and were sympathetic to the administration's designs for the future of Mexico, be sent to deal with the rebel leaders. In pursuance of this proposal, Long nominated Leon J. Canova to be sent immediately to Mexico to work with Carothers until he was thoroughly familiar with the Constitutionalist leaders. If he proved capable, he might then be attached to Carranza's headquarters or, if Carothers resigned, take his place.[32]

As was the custom under Wilson, Secretary Bryan submitted the proposal to the president for approval before taking action. Wilson heartily agreed with the wisdom of Long's plan but preferred to get an expert opinion of Canova's qualifications before tendering an appointment. Consequently, he directed Bryan to have Canova call upon General Hugh L. Scott, currently deputy chief of staff of the army, for an interview. On June 8 Canova met with Scott at Princeton, New Jersey. Afterwards, the general reported that Canova's credentials were quite satisfactory. At the same time, Scott, who admired Carothers and approved of his work, urged Bryan to designate carefully the duties of both Carothers and Canova so as to prevent any possibility of their working at cross-purposes. He also recommended that Carothers approve of the new agent before the appointment was finalized. Both

31. Long to Bryan, April 24, 1914, in Wilson Papers, Ser. 2, Box 107. At this time Long actually nominated one William A. McLaren, whom Counselor Robert Lansing, Assistant Secretary William Phillips, and John Lind all recommended, to serve as an agent. I was not able to determine why McLaren did not receive an appointment.

32. Long to Bryan, June 1, 1914, in NA 812.00/12342.

John Lind and Robert Lansing added their endorsements to Scott's. The decision was made, therefore, to send a second agent among the Constitutionalists.[33]

Canova's State Department dossier reveals that he had wide experience among Latin American people. Born of Spanish-speaking parents in St. Augustine, Florida, on February 22, 1866, and orphaned at an early age, Canova moved about Florida working at various jobs until Henry George, Jr., befriended him in 1893 and gave him a job with a Jacksonville newspaper. Canova was soon doing special work for the New York *World* and later became the Associated Press representative for southern Florida. While serving as a reporter, he became sympathetic with Cuban revolutionaries and assisted them in planning and launching filibuster expeditions from the Florida coast. When the Spanish-American War broke out, he went to Cuba to cover the war for the Associated Press. After the war, he remained in Cuba to serve as correspondent for the New York *World*. He soon found better opportunities with the Cuban press and served successively as managing editor of two of Havana's leading newspapers, the *Herald* and *La Lucha*. In 1909, when the Cuban government created an official information bureau, the president named Canova to head it. He served in that capacity until September, 1913, when he returned to the United States to allow his children to attend American schools. While in Cuba, Canova wrote two books that were published in the United States, *Cuba's New Government* (1909) and *Cuba* (1910).[34]

33. Wilson to Bryan, June 5, 1914, in Wilson Papers, Ser. 2, Box 56; Bryan to Scott, June 8, 1914, in Scott Papers, Box 15; Scott to Bryan, June 9, 1914, in Bryan-Wilson Correspondence; Bryan to Wilson, June 13, 1914, in Bryan Papers, Box 43.

34. Memorandum attached to Long to Bryan, June 1, 1914, in NA 812.00/12342; *Register of the Department of State, 1917*, 80; *Who's Who In America*, XII (1922–23), 612. During and after the Spanish-American War, Canova must have become acquainted with many officers of the United States Army, because he offered a list of officers' names as references. See

In need of a job, Canova, short and round-faced, had actively sought a position with the State Department. On May 24 he addressed a letter of application to the department in which he revealed, among other things, a great sympathy for the Mexican revolutionaries. If they were to avoid the chaos that free Cuba had experienced, he warned, they might well look to the United States for guidance. To lay the foundation for such an arrangement, he believed it necessary for the State Department to send to Mexico a number of representatives who spoke Spanish and understood the nature of Latin American characteristics, customs, and politics. If the United States was to successfully back the "right" revolutionary leaders, these agents, thought Canova, should not only scrutinize the professed purposes and aims of the various leaders but should "go deeper—and fathom their intentions and ambitions; to eat, sleep, and live with these men, so as to better be enabled to analyze their general intelligence, their qualifications to govern, their sense of responsibility, and, in fact, to take their exact moral measure." [35] Certainly Canova's expressions were fully in keeping with Wilsonian foreign policy, and they must have caught the eye of both the president and the secretary of state.

Canova may well have purposely designed his remarks to impress Bryan and Wilson. Future events were to prove that he was an opportunist. In fact, he may have been coached by Boaz Long to make such pleasing comments. Except for his interview with Scott, Canova's dealings had been with the chief of the department's Division of Latin American Affairs. Long had never sympathized with the administration's Mexican policy. A "deserving Democrat" from New Mexico, Long

Canova to Bryan, June 9, 1914, in NA 812.00/12252. He may well have known Bryan during the war, because the salutations of his letters to the secretary of state usually read, "My Dear Colonel." During the war, Bryan was a colonel in the Nebraska volunteers. See Paolo E. Coletta, *William Jennings Bryan: Political Evangelist, 1860–1908* (Lincoln, Neb., 1964), 226.

35. Canova to State Department, May 24, 1914, in NA 812.00/12342.

had received his appointment in May, 1913, because he was a friend of Vice-President Thomas R. Marshall. His sole claim to experience in Latin America rested with the fact that he ran a commission business with a branch office in Mexico City. He had Wall Street connections and, from the beginning, was an advocate of "dollar diplomacy." At every opportunity he sought to promote the security of American investments in Latin America. For that reason he had been ill at ease while such agents as Hale and Lind served in Mexico. He had no quarrels with Carothers' work, since, before June, 1914, Carothers was engaged primarily in protecting foreign-owned property. Canova, who in time was to reveal that he shared Long's attitudes, was the only agent actively recruited by the division chief. Long desired to recruit others; but his disagreements with Bryan became so pronounced by June, 1914, that he was relieved as division chief and appointed minister to El Salvador. There he continued to promote American business interests and, from time to time, express views on Mexican affairs.[36]

Despite his association with Long, Canova's credentials, plus the endorsement from Scott, seemed to mark him as an ideal candidate to serve in Mexico. The growing rift between Villa and Carranza, moreover, cried for the increased attention of the State Department. Accordingly, on June 19 Canova received an assignment as "special representative on roving mission" with instructions to join Carothers. Granted a salary of two hundred dollars per month and all legitimate expenses, his primary duty was to make an exhaustive study of conditions in Mexico and to familiarize himself with all the principal leaders. Nothing was said about a later assignment to Carranza's headquarters. The only restriction placed on him was that he was to remain with Carothers until he was

36. Grieb, *United States and Huerta*, 72; Link, *New Freedom*, 97–98; Coletta, *Progressive Politician*, 112; Link, *Struggle for Neutrality*, 498–99.

deemed experienced enough to go on his own.[37] Although it was not stated in his written instructions, his dispatches from Mexico reveal that he was also to determine if there was any validity to the charges recently leveled at Carothers.

Since, on the very day Canova received his appointment, Carothers had requested that the department provide funds for an assistant, he was more than pleased to welcome Canova when he arrived in El Paso on June 25. Carothers quickly took a liking to the new agent. Canova, for his part, reported within days that all the department had heard of Carothers' effectiveness was true. Their immediate friendship allowed them to work in harmony from the beginning. After spending two days in El Paso and Juárez, during which Canova familiarized himself with Constitutionalist activity in the area and met local officials, the two American agents set out to join Villa, who only days before had captured Zacatecas.[38]

Since the rail lines south of Juárez were damaged by washouts caused by unusually heavy rains, the two Americans were forced to take a roundabout route by way of San Antonio and Saltillo. This long detour, however, was not an inconvenience, since Saltillo was Carranza's headquarters, and Canova gained an excellent opportunity to meet the First Chief and his cabinet.[39] But trouble loomed in their path. While Canova and Carothers were conferring in El Paso, Carranza, determined to slow Villa's southward march and to punish his insubordination, immobilized the Division of the North by cutting off all supplies of fuel and ammunition. Denied access to supplies from the border by the arms embargo and by washouts on the rail lines, Villa could do

37. State Department to Canova, June 19, 1914, and State Department to Carothers, June 20, 1914, in NA 812.00/12343.
38. Carothers to State Department, June 19, 1914, NA 125.35682/93; Carothers to State Department, June 25, 1914, in NA 812.00/12348; Canova to State Department, June 28, 1914, *ibid.*/12386; Cobb to Scott, in Scott Papers, Box 15; El Paso *Morning Times*, June 27, 1914.
39. Carothers to State Department, June 26, 1914, NA 125.36582/93.

nothing but watch other Constitutionalist armies sweep southward toward Mexico City and ultimate victory. With each mile of victorious march by Generals González and Obregón, Villa's resentment toward the First Chief mounted. The schism between the two revolutionary leaders now seemed irreparable.[40]

Still hopeful of maintaining revolutionary solidarity, Bryan directed Carothers and Canova to "urgently appeal" to both Carranza and Villa "to forget their differences and cooperate for the securing of reforms necessary to the restoration of peace."[41] In order to avert any misunderstanding between the agents and the regularly accredited consuls (as had arisen between Carothers and Letcher) in northern Mexico, the department issued a directive informing the consuls that they should coordinate their efforts with those of the two agents.[42]

The main obstacle to the effectiveness of the agents was not likely to be the American consuls but Carranza's suspicions of Carothers. Noting that it was widely assumed among *Carrancista* officials that the American agent was responsible for Villa's insubordinate attitude, reporters along the border speculated that, at worst, the two agents would be turned back at Laredo or, at best, that Carranza would ignore them if they were allowed to proceed to Saltillo.[43]

There were no incidents. In fact, Carothers and Canova were invited to join Carranza's party at Monterrey and rode the same train to Saltillo. The trip gave Carothers an

40. Quirk, *Mexican Revolution*, 33–34.

41. State Department to Carothers, June 30, 1914, in NA 812.00/12381a.

42. Secretary of state to certain American consuls, July 1, 1914, in *Foreign Relations, 1914*, 553. Just prior to the issuance of this directive, Consul Letcher of Chihuahua had explained that his failure to cooperate with Carothers was due mainly to the department's failure to clarify the responsibilities of the agents. See Silliman to State Department, June 11, 1914, in NA 125.36582/131.

43. New York *World*, June 28, 1914; El Paso *Morning Times*, June 30, 1914.

opportunity to introduce Canova to the First Chief's advisors. The day of their arrival, July 1, they sought a conference with the First Chief. Despite the fact that a large crowd of people was waiting to see Carranza, the two Americans were ushered in ahead of them and granted a half-hour interview. After being introduced and exchanging pleasantries with the First Chief, Canova allowed Carothers to do all the talking while he took detailed notes on the conversation. Here, at the first opportunity, Canova exhibited a talent for describing and capturing detail that none of the other agents in Mexico ever mastered. As Carranza ranted about his insubordinate general, Canova noted every facial expression and gesture and described even changes in tone of voice.

While en route to Saltillo, the two agents were informed that General González had arranged for a commission of *Carrancista* generals to go to Torreón to meet with a commission of *Villista* generals in an attempt to hammer out some accommodation between the two factions. This conference of generals, then, was the main topic of Carothers' interview with Carranza. The First Chief quickly made clear that his generals were going on their own initiative and not at his instruction. When Carothers urged him to cooperate in arranging a solution, the old chieftain replied that if the trouble between the two continued, it would be Villa's fault. "Villa thinks he is indispensable to the Constitutionalist cause," Carranza stormed. "Well, he is mistaken. No individual who defies constituted authorities is indispensable." He ended his harangue by indicating that there could be no conciliation unless Villa agreed to be obedient in the future.[44]

After the interview, the two Americans discussed the

44. Canova to State Department, July 2, 1914, in NA 812.00/12462; Carothers to State Department, July 5, 1914, *ibid.*/12472. Canova's dispatches evidence his newspaper training. He was a keen observer, and in pursuance of his instructions he described in detail all that he saw. His reports are a veritable storehouse of information about the personalities and conditions in revolutionary Mexico.

Carranza-Villa dispute with Heriberto Barrón, an influential newspaper editor. Barrón indicated that if the breach was not healed soon, many of the *Carrancistas* would go over to Villa, since he was accomplishing more militarily than anyone else. With the situation so critical, Carothers decided to accompany the *Carrancista* generals to Torreón. Taking a chance on Canova's inexperience, he also decided to leave the new agent in Saltillo. This way, he hoped, Carranza would not feel slighted, and, with Canova pressuring the *Carrancistas*, and himself the *Villistas*, there was a chance of aiding the estranged parties to a conciliation.[45]

In Torreón Carothers found Villa unrepentant. When the special agent revealed that his government wished above all for Villa to settle his differences with the First Chief, the general replied: "Is it possible that a great nation like yours cannot see what kind of man Carranza is?" He then insisted that the First Chief was surrounding himself with politicians and slackers who were primarily concerned about their own futures and would, in the long run, establish a regime as despotic as those of the past. Villa claimed that the armies were beginning to see that Carranza was not seeking reform and that he was not the leader who could save the country from further revolution. As a temporary expedient, however, Villa agreed to conciliate the First Chief, since a break could only help Huerta.[46]

Conciliation did, indeed, reign at Torreón. On July 8, after five days of wrangling, the *Villista* and *Carrancista* generals worked out an apparently satisfactory settlement. The Pact of Torreón, as the agreement was called, stipulated that the Division of the North recognize Carranza as First Chief, but that Villa should remain in command of the division. Carranza was to supply Villa with all the fuel and ammunition he

45. *Ibid.*; Carothers to State Department, July 2, 1914, in NA 125.36582/96; Carothers to State Department, July 5, 1914, in NA 812.00/12472.
46. Carothers to State Department, July 5, 1914, *ibid.*/12472.

needed, and Villa was to report all his actions to the First Chief for acceptance. The conferees also drew up a list of twelve men from which Carranza was to pick his cabinet when he became interim president following the victorious revolution. This clause was inserted to insure that some *Villistas* were included. The interim president, upon taking office, was to call a convention, the delegates to be chosen by the division commanders on the basis of one delegate for every thousand troops in the ranks. The convention was to be a preconstitutional device which would decide upon a plan of government, institute needed reforms, and call elections for the regular government. In addition, the agreement stated that no member of the army could be a candidate for the presidency, nor could the interim president seek the permanent office.[47]

Carothers reported that the agreement was even more of a diplomatic victory for Villa than appeared on the surface. In addition to the formal pact, the *Carrancistas* agreed to two informal provisions: that General Felipe Angeles, who was Villa's closest advisor, would be commander of all the Constitutionalist armies, and that the railroads would be administered by Eusébio Calzado, also Villa's man. Carothers thought it significant that the generals of the Northeast had allied with those of the North in calling for a convention and in eliminating Carranza from possible contention for the elective presidency.[48] Both provisions were counter to the First Chief's Plan of Guadalupe.

From Saltillo, Canova reported that Carranza showed signs of relief upon hearing that the generals in Torreón were working toward an agreement. But when he received the finished pact, he refused to ratify it. He did tell Canova, however, that as far as he was concerned the difficulties with

47. "Pacto de Torreón," Gonazález Ramírez, *Planes políticos*, 152–57; Carothers to State Department, July 8, 9, 1914, in NA 812.00/12470, 12717.
48. *Ibid.*

Villa were settled. He also told the American agent that if another rupture occurred, "it will come through some act of Villa." [49] Despite Carranza's refusal to accept the letter of the Pact of Torreón, the Constitutionalists once again presented a facade of solidarity.

Canova, meanwhile, had studied Carranza and his advisors carefully and had begun to report his impressions. His assessment of the First Chief was, perhaps, the most balanced yet received by the State Department. Carranza, he revealed, was "an able man, a good executive who maintains exceptional order in his district." [50] He also noted that Carranza was a gentle man who loved flowers and was uncommonly affectionate toward his wife and two daughters. Canova found that the First Chief, when satisfied that all was going well, could be a most pleasant companion. The special agent was especially impressed by Carranza's honesty and integrity. [51]

Canova's reports from Saltillo also tended to promote another dark image of Carranza. Canova was surprised that the First Chief was not greeted by the people with adulation. Instead, when he walked among them, "a deep hush prevailed." They seemed more embarrassed than pleased by his presence. [52] Canova also noted, as had others before him, that Carranza was rigid in his beliefs and was inclined to take offense at even the slightest difference of opinion; hence, he was inclined to make "pets" of those who agreed with him. [53]

Canova was cordially received by Carranza's advisors, and he established a number of friendships in Saltillo that were to last the duration of his mission. A number of the *Carrancis-*

49. Canova to State Department, July 10, 14, 1914, in NA 812.00/27406, 12501, 12564.
50. Canova to State Department, July 10, 1914, *ibid.*/27406.
51. *Ibid.*; Canova to State Department, July 5, 8, 14, 1914, in NA 812.00/12495, 12474, 12564.
52. Canova to State Department, July 2, 1914, *ibid.*/12462.
53. Canova to State Department, July 5, 8, 1914, *ibid.*/12495, 12474.

tas took the American into their confidence; some were apparently influenced by his appeals. He was particularly proud of one incident. After he had impressed upon one of Carranza's anti-Villa cabinet members the necessity of disposing of personal jealousies and of maintaining harmony within the Constitutionalist camp for the sake of the revolution, the official rose, clutched Canova in an *abrazo*, and exclaimed, *"Que simpática"* (how understanding). Shortly thereafter, that same official sent Villa a personal note of conciliation.[54]

The *Carrancistas*, Canova found, went out of their way to downgrade Villa's achievements. The victories of other generals were celebrated with speeches and the ringing of church bells, while those of the Division of the North were only grudgingly mentioned to the people. Even those who were willing to acknowledge that Villa was a good soldier, true to the revolutionary cause, believed that he was too susceptible to the influences of certain members of the Madero family. Having failed to win prominence in politics through martyred President Madero, they now sought to use Villa. After many conversations with the *Carrancistas*, and even before meeting Villa, Canova was inclined to believe that their criticisms were prompted primarily by jealousy of Villa's success and his popularity with the people.[55]

54. *Ibid.*; Canova to State Department, July 14, 1914, in NA 812.00/12654.

55. Canova to State Department, July 8, 10, 14, 1914, *ibid.*/12474, 27406, 12564. The letter dated July 10, bearing the file number 27406, was not received by the Index Bureau of the Department of State until July, 1924. Perhaps the explanation for the delay in its being placed in the regular department files is that it was withheld by Bryan, as were some of the reports of Del Valle and Hale. The July 10 letter and several others from Canova were not addressed to the department but to Bryan at Thirteenth and Clifton Streets, Washington, D.C. These letters were much more intimate and opinionated than regular ones received by the department.

The charges that the Maderos were politically ambitious may have resulted from the high degree of nepotism practiced by Francisco Madero when he was president. Eleven different members of the Madero family held government offices during his administration. This led to charges, justified or

His experience in Carranza's camp also gave Canova some definite ideas about the future of the revolution. The agent believed that the spirit of revolution was so ingrained in the Mexican people that the slightest dissatisfaction with the results of the current revolution would sprout a new one. "The only salvation for this country," he wrote to Bryan, "is a supervision over its affairs by the United States." Lacking the confidence in the Constitutionalists that Lind had exhibited, Canova insisted that the United States should insist upon a supervisory plan similar to the Platt Amendment. He acknowledged that the Constitutionalists might resist, but he thought they might also acquiesce if the United States offered a hundred-million-dollar loan, which they could use to speedily implement their program of reform. With such funds at their disposal, the Constitutionalists could rest assured that their revolution would be complete.[56]

Certainly Canova's proposal fit within the framework of Wilson's Mexican policy. Considering his cordial relations with the *Carrancistas* and his faith that he could persuade them to accept American supervision, Canova seemed to be the ideal agent to accompany Carranza. In fact, he asked for permission to accompany the First Chief, first to Tampico, then southward through San Luis Potosí as he advanced on Mexico City. Carothers agreed that Canova should remain with the First Chief. But Bryan overrode his agents' advice because he and Wilson had already decided to try another agent in Carranza's camp, one who was on even more friendly terms with the First Chief.[57]

Until recently the vice and deputy consul at Saltillo, John

not, that they were using their kinsman-president to further their own ambitions. See Ross, *Madero*, 223; González Ramírez, *Las Ideas—La Violencia*, 312–16. During the Constitutionalist revolution several members of the Madero family (notably brother Raúl who was a colonel in the Division of the North) and other members of the Madero clique (notably Miguel Díaz Lombardo, Madero's minister of public instruction) joined forces with Villa or supported him in one way or another. See Guzmán, *Memoirs of Pancho Villa*, 121, 147, 223, 282.

56. Canova to State Department, July 10, 1914, in NA 812.00/27406.
57. Canova to State Department, July 18, 1914, *ibid.*/12554; Carothers to

Reid Silliman, the new agent, received his appointment through the most extraordinary circumstances. On April 21, at the time of the Vera Cruz intervention, he, along with his wife, consular clerk Joseph R. Marchani, and most of the other Americans in Saltillo, was arrested by the federal commander, a nephew of Huerta, General Joaquín Maass. Having quarreled with Maass in the past, Silliman expected the worst. The consulate was sacked and the possessions, including a copy of the State Department's "red code," were confiscated. When some of the consul's dispatches, which contained comments concerning both rebel and federal military activities, were decoded by General Maas's officers, Silliman was charged with espionage. Although Mrs. Silliman was released to the custody of the British vice consul, Silliman was held incommunicado in a vermin-infested prison for twenty-one days. During that time, while his health began to fail, he was repeatedly threatened with execution.[58] Meanwhile, the Brazilian minister in Mexico City, José M. Cardoso de Oliveira, who had been representing the interests of the United States since the Vera Cruz incident, made an earnest appeal in Silliman's behalf and on May 11 finally secured his release. After a harrowing train ride and only two days' rest in Mexico City, the unfortunate consul was ordered to Washington.[59]

State Department, July 18, 1914, *ibid.* 125.36582; State Department to Carothers, July 18, 1914, *ibid.*/12554.

58. Silliman to State Department, February 13, 1914, *ibid.* 125.8276/11; H. Booth to Bryan, May 5, 1914, *ibid.*, 125.8273/28; Canada to State Department, May 11, 1914, *ibid.*/14; Dr. J. Franklin Moore to State Department, including transcript of an interview with Boaz Long, May 22, 1914, *ibid.*/60; Silliman to Bryan, June 18, 1914, *ibid.*/88; *Mexican Herald*, April 28, May 12, 13, 1914; New York *Times*, May 5, 6, 1914, p. 2; *ibid.*, May 8, 9, 1914, p. 1. At the same time of Silliman's arrest Phillip Hanna, the American consul general at Monterrey, and William Bonney, the American consular agent at San Luis Potosí, were arrested. They were quickly released. See Hanna to State Department, in *Foreign Relations, 1914*, 656–60; New York *Times*, May 6, 1914, p. 2.

59. State Department to Cardoso de Oliveira, May 4, 5, 15, 22, 1914, in *Foreign Relations, 1914*, 660–62, 664–65; Cardoso de Oliveira to State

Both Silliman and Wilson had been members of the Princeton class of 1879, and Silliman returned to a hero's welcome at the class reunion held June 13. Although he did not see the president at the reunion, Silliman journeyed to Washington shortly thereafter and, on more than one occasion, discussed his trepidations with his old classmate. In the process, he urged that the vice consular post at Saltillo be elevated to a higher grade. Wilson, as a gesture of solace for Silliman's ordeal, gave his old friend a verbal agreement that he would receive a promotion. The lone obstacle to his return to Mexico was the charge of espionage still hanging over his head. This impediment was removed, however, when Cardoso de Oliveira reported, on June 8, that the charge had been dropped.[60]

Alabama-born and reared, Silliman, white-haired and dignified in appearance, was fifty-nine years old in 1914. Slow and deliberate in his speech and movements, he had moved to Texas after graduating from Princeton and had worked first as a railroad clerk, then as an insurance agent. Moving to the Mexican state of Coahuila in 1897, he engaged in farming and dairying. In 1907 he was appointed vice and deputy consul at Saltillo. During his residence in that city, he was befriended by Carranza, who was governor of the state, and by Isidro Fabela, who later became Carranza's foreign minister.[61]

Department, May 5, 10, 11, 22, 1914, *ibid.*, 662–65; *Mexican Herald*, May 23, 25, 27, 29, 1914; New York *Times*, May 12, 1914, p. 1; *ibid.*, May 13, 1914, p. 2; *ibid.*, May 14, 1914, p. 3; *ibid.*, May 23, 1914, p. 4.

60. Silliman to Wilson, April 16, 1915, in Wilson Papers, Ser. 2, Box 129; Silliman to Bryan, June 20, 1914, in Bryan Papers, Box 30; Wilson to Bryan, July 20, 1914, in Wilson Papers, Ser. 2, Box 111; Bryan to Wilson, July 2, 1914, in Bryan-Wilson Correspondence; State Department to Cardoso de Oliveira, June 6, 1914, in *Foreign Relations, 1914*, 666; Cardoso de Oliveira to State Department, June 8, 1914, *ibid.*, 667; New York *Times*, June 7, 1914, p. 9; New York *Sun*, July 14, 1914.

61. *Register of the Department of State, 1917*, 137; Carroll, "United States Special Agents Powerful in Mexico," New York *Sun*, August 15, 1915; New York *Times*, May 5, 1914, p. 2; New York *World*, July 3, 1914; Testimony of Buckley, *Senate Documents*, 66th Cong., 2nd Sess., No. 285, p. 812; Fabela, *Historia Diplomática*, I, 229.

While in Washington in June, 1914, Silliman professed to be on intimate terms with Carranza. When Bryan showed an interest in the relationship, the consul prepared a memorandum for the secretary of state, depicting the First Chief's character in glowing terms.[62] Lind, meanwhile, suggested that Silliman would be an ideal agent to assign to Carranza's headquarters. The decision was made, therefore, to send Silliman back to Saltillo as a full consul.[63] His past friendship with Carranza, Bryan and Wilson hoped, would allow Silliman to establish a relationship such as Carothers enjoyed with Villa. The *Carrancistas* were pleased with the appointment for similar reasons. After conversing with Silliman, Zubarán Capmany reported that the newly designated agent would likely serve their interests well, since he was obviously sympathetic to their cause and was on intimate terms with President Wilson.[64]

Silliman returned to Saltillo on July 8 and, according to his own testimony, "No American should have hoped for a more friendly personal reception." He apparently bore no written instructions and, at first, was considered only a consul. But from the tenor of his first report, it is clear that he had been directed to make a last-ditch appeal for Carranza to follow the ABC mediators' recommendations and enter into negotiations with Huerta for the creation of a new provisional government. On July 9, accompanied by Canova, Silliman

62. Bryan to Wilson, January 22, 1915, in Bryan Papers, Box 43; Bryan to Wilson, June 11, 1914, in Wilson Papers, Ser. 4, Box 49. The first letter cited above reveals that Silliman definitely claimed to be on intimate terms with Carranza. In the second letter, Bryan conveys to Wilson Silliman's estimate of Carranza's character. The letter describes the memorandum, but the memorandum itself was not to be found.

63. *Ibid.; Register of the State Department, 1917,* 137; New York *Times,* July 3, 1914, p. 3. The position of consul at Saltillo was not created until January, 1915. By executive order of July 3, 1914, Silliman was made a full consul, but served at a vice-consular post.

64. Zubarán Capmany a Carranza, July 3, 1914, in Josefina E. de Fabela (ed.), *Documentos históricos de la Revolución Mexicana* (México, D.F., 1969), XV, 119–20.

conferred with Carranza and Fabela. As an incentive for cooperation with the *Huertistas*, the consul held out the prospect of immediate diplomatic recognition by the United States and the ABC powers. But Silliman's appeals proved no more effective than those previously made by other representatives of the Wilson administration. The First Chief replied that the only matter he would discuss with anyone was Huerta's unconditional surrender.[65]

Wilson and Bryan must have been disappointed that even an old friend could not move Carranza to cooperate with the United States. They would have also been disappointed in their new agent had they been in Saltillo to witness his first confrontation with the First Chief. Canova reported that he had "never listened to anything so distressing." Silliman, he revealed, was not competent in expressing himself in Spanish. It took him two hours and forty-five minutes to say what should have taken fifteen minutes. Every few words, he had to ask for guidance from Foreign Minister Fabela. He often wandered from the subject at hand and interjected his personal experiences. When he told the First Chief of his imprisonment by General Maass, his voice broke and his eyes filled with tears. During Silliman's lengthy dissertation, Canova reported, Carranza and Fabela exchanged embarrassed glances, rolling their eyes upward in a sign of impatience.[66]

During this meeting, Silliman also gave another clue as to what his unwritten instructions included. His reception by the First Chief would obviously determine his future status, because he asked Carranza and Fabela for letters of recommendation that he might forward to Washington. Canova, thoroughly disgusted by Silliman's pandering after the approval of the First Chief, recommended that Consul General Phillip Hanna of Monterrey be assigned to Carranza's head-

---

65. Silliman to State Department, July 10, 1914, in NA 812.00/12469.
66. Canova to State Department, July 22, 1914, *ibid.*/27426.

quarters instead. When Canova's report was received in Washington, President Wilson was, indeed, disturbed, but only at Silliman's lack of fluency in Spanish. He apparently was more impressed by Silliman's own report of the cordial reception given him by the *Carrancistas*. He therefore recommended no change in Silliman's status.[67] Bryan, meanwhile, moved to remedy the agent's most obvious deficiency— his poor Spanish. The secretary of state arranged for an employee of the Pan-American Union, John W. Belt, who spoke and wrote fluent Spanish, and who was about to visit Mexico in the company of Luis Cabrera, to call upon Silliman and offer his services as a stenographer. Silliman found Belt quite satisfactory and employed him as a consular assistant.[68]

While the revolutionary leaders in northern Mexico quarreled and Wilson's agents scurried about attempting to promote revolutionary solidarity, Victoriano Huerta's power steadily deteriorated. During the spring and summer of 1914, the provisional president gradually became estranged from his cabinet and the legislature. Militarily he was sorely pressed by Villa from Zacatecas; by Obregón, who had captured Guadalajara on July 8; and by General Jesús Carranza, who was driving toward San Luis Potosí. Zapata, moreover, controlled the countryside around the national capital and, from time to time, made forays into the suburbs. The port of Vera Cruz was still occupied by American forces, and Tampico was in the hands of the rebels. Cut off from his main sources of revenue and unable to obtain arms or credit, Huerta resigned on July 15, turned over the government to his secretary of foreign relations, Francisco Carbajal, and fled the country.[69]

67. Wilson to Bryan, July 30, 1914, *ibid.*/27480.

68. Silliman to State Department, July 25, 1914, NA 125.8273/100; Department to Silliman, July 27, 1914, *ibid.;* Silliman to State Department, July 30, 31, 1914, *ibid.*/103, 104.

69. Meyer, *Huerta*, 204–209; Quirk, *Mexican Revolution*, 45–48; Barragán Rodríguez, *Historia . . . de la Revolución Constitucionalista*, I, 564–71;

The dictator had fallen, and Wilson's intervention had been a decisive factor in his elimination. Months of a steadily applied policy had finally borne fruit. But there were still potential pitfalls in the way of the president's design for the renovation of Mexico. The continued success of his policy now depended upon the maintenance of solidarity within the Constitutionalist camp. Wilson and Bryan were encouraged, therefore, when Carranza, upon receiving the news of Huerta's flight, asked Canova to go to Torreón and assure Villa that the *Carrancistas* wanted peace within the revolutionary family. Accordingly, Bryan directed the agent to join Villa as Carranza had suggested and to impress upon him the folly of further discord. He was also to remind the Centaur of the North that his actions in the future would have a great bearing on the manner in which the new revolutionary government was received by the world powers. Carothers was directed to do the same, while Silliman was ordered to remain constantly with Carranza and make similar representations. Silliman's new instructions constituted the first official designation of his status as an executive agent.[70] The demise of Huerta, therefore, saw no slackening in the activities of the special agents.

Canova's journey to Torreón was as arduous as it was fruitless. Traveling by rail, he was forced to stand in an overcrowded passenger coach. When he arrived on July 19, he was suffering from the malady—diarrhea and severe abdomi-

---

Womack, *Zapata*, 186–88. Huerta having gone into exile in Europe, returned to the United States in June, 1915, to arrange a counterrevolution with Pascual Orozco. Arrested in El Paso for conspiracy to violate the neutrality laws of the United States, he died in custody on January 13, 1916, of cirrhosis of the liver and complications following gall-bladder surgery. See George J. Rausch, Jr., "The Exile and Death of Victoriano Huerta," *Hispanic American Historical Review*, XLII (February, 1962), 131–51.

70. Canova to State Department, July 14, 1914, in NA 812.00/12564; State Department to Canova, July 16, 1914, *ibid.*/12501; State Department to Carothers, July 20, 1914, in *Foreign Relations, 1914*, 567; State Department to Silliman, July 16, 1914, *ibid.*, 564.

nal pains—that so often plagues newcomers to Mexico. Finding that both Villa and Carothers had gone to Juárez, and feeling too ill to remain there alone without medical attention, Canova decided to return to Monterrey, where Carranza had moved his headquarters. After a bone-jarring return ride on the floor of a boxcar, Canova's illness was so acute that he required over a week to recuperate.[71]

Even while Special Agent Canova was convalescing in Monterrey, he received orders on July 22 to proceed to Zacatecas and investigate reports of atrocities committed against the Roman Catholic clergy in that city. Among the other acts of cruelty, the French chargé d'affaires in Washington reported that two French Christian Brothers had been executed. Coincidentally, General Natera, whose forces were occupying Zacatecas, was in Monterrey meeting with the First Chief when Canova received his orders. Carranza, obviously well disposed toward Canova, directed Natera to cooperate fully with the American agent. The First Chief also wired the acting governor of the state of Zacatecas to assist Canova.[72]

The trip to Zacatecas exposed Canova to even more of the hazards of diplomacy in revolutionary Mexico. When the agent arrived at the depot at the previously arranged time of departure, Natera was not to be found. Canova and Fabela then spent hours searching the houses of prostitution until they found the general, dead drunk. Having discovered from his recent trip to Torreón that traveling in a crowded passenger coach on a Mexican train was an experience to avoid, Canova decided to ride a boxcar to Zacatecas. Taking a folding cot, which was now part of his "necessary" equipment, the special agent found himself a large enough spot

71. Canova to State Department, July 22, 25, 1914, in NA 812.00/12588, 27426, 12650.
72. Clausse, chargé d'affaires of the Republic of France, to State Department, July 16, 1914, in NA 312.51/57; State Department to Canova, July 22, 1914, *ibid.*/63a; Canova to State Department, July 27, 1914, *ibid.*/73.

between boxes of dynamite and ammunition and, preferring
the company of high explosives to the crowds in the passenger coaches, enjoyed a relatively comfortable trip to Zacatecas.[73]

Arriving there on August 1, Canova, for the first time,
seems to have become fully aware of the horrors of the
revolutionary war. Zacatecas was the first city he visited that
had only recently been ravaged by war. Accustomed to the
relative prosperity of the farming areas around Saltillo and
Torreón, the special agent was appalled by the physical
damage done to this mining town and by the suffering of the
people. Having associated with the upper classes in Cuba and
with the gentlemen in Carranza's camp, Canova naturally
gravitated toward the same type of people in Zacatecas.
From what was left of the upper- and middle-class element,
he received an entirely different account of the battle and
occupation of the city from the one Carothers had reported.
Carothers had relied upon the word of the *Villistas*; Canova
upon those who claimed to be victims of Villa's justice. They
insisted that there had been wholesale despoliation of private
property and that there had been unspeakable acts of cruelty
committed against the Federals and the clergy. Canova also
reported that the "better" element of Zacatecas begged for
intervention by the United States. The peons, he continued,
were happy with the course of the revolution and enjoyed
"lording it over the more intelligent people." [74]

As directed, Canova appealed to General Natera to ease his
persecution of the clergy. The general would do nothing to
prevent the forced taxation and confiscation of Church

73. Canova to State Department, August 4, 1914, in NA 812.00/12826.
74. *Ibid.;* Canova to State Department, August 10, 14, 1914, in NA
812.00/12888, 12979; Canova to State Department, August 3, 1914, *ibid.*
312.51/80. Canova's reconstruction of the battle of Zacatecas and the
occupation that followed was so vividly gory that Bryan directed him to be
more factual and to delete "opinion" from his official reports. Bryan to
Canova, August 15, 1914, in NA 812.00/12826.

property, but on August 7 he did allow one church to reopen
for mass. That day literally thousands crowded before the
church to celebrate their first mass in over a month. Afterwards Canova was not sure whether it was his pleas or those
of the thousands of devout Roman Catholics in the city that
persuaded the harsh Mexican general to moderate his stand
against the church.[75]

Canova had been in Zacatecas ten days when he received
orders to join General Obregón. With Carranza refusing to
accept any terms from Provisional President Carbajal other
than unconditional surrender, there was grave concern in
Washington that Obregón might carry the fighting into the
heart of Mexico City. Wilson and Bryan, therefore, wanted
one of their agents to accompany the general and plead
clemency for the hapless populace of the capital.[76] Although
Canova was nearer to Obregón's advancing army than any of
the other agents, he was unable to rendezvous with Obregón
before he reached the capital because the rail lines between
Zacatecas and Mexico City had been heavily damaged by the
retreating *Huertistas*.[77]

Silliman, meanwhile, had been ordered to urge the First
Chief to receive representatives from Carbajal and to use his
influence in arranging the transfer of the capital into the
hands of the revolutionaries. Joined by Consul General
Hanna, Silliman called upon Carranza in Monterrey on July
19 and handed him the department's note. The First Chief
expressed appreciation for the "good offices" extended by the
United States and agreed to meet with any "duly accredited
and fully authorized representatives" of the Mexico City
government. He insisted, however, that the only terms he
would discuss were the unconditional delivery of the capital
to the Constitutionalists and the unconditional surrender of

75. Canova to State Department, August 10, 1914, in NA 812.00/12888.
76. State Department to Canova, August 11, 1914, *ibid.*/12832b.
77. Canova to State Department, August 14, 16, 1914, *ibid.*/12863, 12880.

the Federal armies. He also suggested Saltillo as a meeting place and recommended that Carbajal's delegates come directly north by way of San Luis Potosí.[78]

Carranza's proposal was forwarded to Carbajal through Cardoso de Oliveira, the Brazilian minister to Mexico City. Carbajal at first balked at sending representatives into the enemy's territory; but when the Wilson administration refused to support his request for a conference in neutral New York, he relented and agreed to the meeting in Saltillo. In an apparent effort to preserve some dignity, the delegates, General Lauro Villar, chief justice of the Supreme Military Court, and David Gutiérrez Allende, associate justice of the Supreme Court, instead of taking Carranza's proposed route to Saltillo, journeyed by way of Vera Cruz and Tampico.[79]

While these arrangements were being made, fear gripped Mexico City. Cardoso de Oliveira reported that the *Zapatistas'* attacks on the suburbs had increased since Huerta's resignation. The populace feared, moreover, that the army might disband, leaving the city to the mercy of looters. Most frightening of all, the Brazilian minister informed Washington, the city newspapers were reporting Carranza as having declared that he would "resort to reprisals and bloodshed" upon occupying the capital.[80]

On July 23, with such threats weighing on his mind, Wilson, through Silliman, warned the First Chief that the United States (and hence other powers also) might withhold recognition of a government established by the Constitutionalists unless guarantees were given on several accounts.

78. State Department to Silliman, July 16, 1914, in *Foreign Relations, 1914*, 564; Silliman to State Department, July 19, 1914, *ibid.*, 566.
79. State Department to Cardoso de Oliveira, July 20, 23, 1914, in *Foreign Relations, 1914*, 566, 568; Cardoso de Oliveira to State Department, July 22, 24, 26, 27, 1914, *ibid.*, 567–68, 570, 572–73.
80. Cardoso de Oliveira to State Department, July 22, 1914, *ibid.*, 567–68; New York *Times*, July 10, 1914, p. 1; *ibid.*, July 22, 1914, p. 3; *ibid.*, July 24, 1914, p. 5.

The president again demanded respect for foreign lives, property, and debt obligations. He then insisted upon a "most generous amnesty" for "political and military opponents." Recalling the depredations against the church and clergy in Zacatecas, he also insisted that there be no "punitive or vindictive action toward priests or ministers of any church, whether Catholic or Protestant." [81]

Silliman, meanwhile, had accompanied Carranza to Tampico, and Wilson's note found him in the port city. The agent must have been certain what the First Chief's response would be, because prior to delivering it he cabled Washington, informing the administration of the factors that would condition the reply. Recognizing what Wilson and Bryan often chose to ignore, Silliman reminded them that the Constitutionalists were bent on social revolution. The revolutionaries, he pointed out, blamed the aristocrats and large landowners for the failure of Madero's revolutionary government. These same elements had also supported Huerta's regime. He felt certain that the rebels would insist upon punishing them. He also reported that the Constitutionalists believed that the Church and priesthood had foresaken their spiritual mission and, for their own self-interest, had allied with Huerta against the interests of the people. Severe restrictions on the activities of the Church could, therefore, be expected.[82]

Foreign Minister Fabela, in replying for the First Chief, was not as explicit as Silliman had been, but his message was clear. He promised that the lives and property of foreigners would be "protected in the future as they have been in the past." As for the other points in Wilson's note, Fabela declared that they would be "decided according to the best interests of justice and our national interests." [83] But Wilson

81. State Department to Silliman, July 23, 1914, in *Foreign Relations, 1914*, 568–69.
82. Silliman to State Department, July 27, 1914, in NA 812.00/12634.
83. Fabela to Silliman, July 27, 1914, in *Foreign Relations, 1914*, 575.

was just as unyielding as Carranza. He directed Silliman to remind the First Chief that "our advice offered, and everything in our telegram of the 23d, cannot be modified nor can we recede from it in the least." He further warned that without recognition from the United States, a Constitutionalist government "could obtain no loans and must speedily break down." [84]

Such threats from the president of the United States might have deterred a lesser man, but Carranza calmly proceeded to arrange the surrender of Mexico City on his own terms. He was careful enough, however, not to cut off his lines of communication with Washington. Silliman was accorded every courtesy. He attended all social functions with the First Chief. Fabela introduced him to the crowds in flattering terms, while President Wilson was toasted as the friend of the Constitutionalists. [85]

The agent soon discovered that this courtesy did not include a voice in arranging a peace with the Federals. Determined that the Federal representatives should come to him on his own terms, Carranza, when he discovered that they were on their way to Tampico, refused to meet them at the port city and insisted that they adhere to his original proposal by meeting in Saltillo. Reporters who accompanied Carbajal's representatives were turned back at Tampico, while the representatives themselves were herded aboard a military train like prisoners of war and whisked incognito to Monterrey. Dumped from the train with no directions, they attempted to persuade Consul Hanna to escort them to the Texas border; but he persuaded them to press on to Saltillo. [86]

When Silliman discovered that the envoys had arrived in

84. State Department to Silliman, July 31, 1914, *ibid.*, 576–77.
85. Silliman to State Department, July 23, 25, 26, 1914, in NA 812.00/12519, 12619, 12620; New York *Times*, July 24, 1914, p. 5.
86. Hanna to State Department, August 1, 1914, in NA 812.00/12704; Quirk, *Mexican Revolution*, 51–52.

Saltillo, he offered to help them arrange an interview with Carranza. He discovered that the envoys' secretary, Salvador Urbina, was an old friend of Cabrera and Fabela and arranged through them for Urbina to meet with the First Chief. Carranza insisted that Carbajal's representatives first meet with two of his own underlings to determine if they were prepared to discuss peace on his terms. When it became apparent that they wanted assurances that certain officials of the Huerta regime would be given amnesty, Carranza broke off the conferences before they really began. Now more fearful than ever for their own safety, the Federalist commissioners asked Silliman to escort them to the United States, but the First Chief insisted that they return by the way they came. Silliman then could do no more than provide them with enough money to pay their return fares to Tampico.[87]

Failing to secure an unconditional surrender agreement from Carbajal, and determined to personally supervise the siege of Mexico City, Carranza, accompanied by Silliman, departed from Saltillo on August 6. While they journeyed southward, the Brazilian minister worked feverishly to prevent the destruction of the beautiful city. By the time Carranza was nearing Obregón's headquarters at Teoloyucán, Cardoso de Oliveira met with Obregón and Silliman, who had hastened ahead of the First Chief in order to be at the conference. Soon joined by Carranza, the Constitutionalist leaders again refused to make any accommodation with Carbajal; but they did agree to a formula for the peaceful occupation of the capital. By the terms of this agreement and another made the following day between Obregón and representatives of the Federal army, Carbajal resigned and fled to Vera Cruz, the Federal army evacuated the city piecemeal, and the Constitutionalist army took its place. On August 15

87. Silliman to State Department, August 1, 2, 3, 4, 1914, in NA 812.00/12700, 12716, 12721, 12727, 12733, 12746, 12735.

the occupation was peacefully accomplished as Eduardo Iturbide, governor of the Federal District, turned over to Obregón control of the capital city's police force. With both Silliman and Canova on hand, Carranza made his grand and triumphal entry into the city on August 20.[88]

The Constitutionalists were triumphant. Silliman thought it a most encouraging sign for future cordial relations with the Constitutionalists that when he entered the city alone on August 18, with the stars and stripes fluttering on a make-shift staff connected to the front bumper of his automobile, the Constitutionalist soldiers stood and cheered as he passed.[89] But Mexico's problems were not solved, and more troubled times lay ahead. Pancho Villa was noticeably absent from the coterie of generals that surrounded the First Chief during his impressive entry into Mexico City. The Chihuahua strong man was not one to be slighted. Nor was the puritan in the White House one to be ignored. Together, these two, with the help of the special agents, were to seek their own solution for Mexico's problems.

88. Cardoso de Oliveira to State Department, August 8, 9, 12, 13, 1914, in *Foreign Relations, 1914*, 582–86; Silliman to State Department, August 13, 20, 1914, *ibid.*, 586–88; *El Sol* (Mexico City), August 18, 1914; New York *Times*, August 12, 13, 1914, p. 9; *ibid.*, August 16, 1914, II, p. 8; *ibid.*, August 31, 1914, p. 10.
89. Silliman to State Department, August 18, 1914, NA 125.8276/15.

CHAPTER IX

Searching for the
Right Combination

In Washington it appeared by mid-August, 1914, that the demise of Huerta had only contributed to the rise of another *caudillo*—Carranza. As the armies of Obregón and González approached Mexico City, the First Chief had them arrayed so as to prevent either Villa or Zapata from sharing in the triumph or challenging his authority in the national capital. After occupying the city, he made no move to create a more representative provisional government. Prefacing his invitation with a demand for submission to the Plan of Guadalupe, Carranza did offer to confer with Zapata and even sent representatives into Morelos. But Zapata refused to submit to the First Chief's authority. Carranza was so contemptuous of the foreign colony and diplomatic corps that many of them left the capital.[1]

State Department agent Leon Canova was on hand as the Constitutionalists invested the capital. He described the scenes as the *Carrancistas*, either by military tribunal or outright murder, began eliminating their enemies. The generals occupied the sumptuous mansions on the most exclusive boulevards and avenues, while their soldiers seized their own booty.[2] "Soldiers openly state that they were promised loot,"

1. Quirk, *Mexican Revolution*, 58–66; Womack, *Zapata*, 203–10; Francisco Ramírez Plancarte, *La Ciudad de México durante la Revolución Constitucionalista* (México, D.F., 1941), 70–71.
2. Canova to State Department, August 25, 26, 27, 1914, in NA 812.00/13129, 13013, 13020.

Canova reported, "and they want it now."³ Wilson looked southward at the situation that he had helped to create and decided that still more changes were in order.

The president's plans began to evolve well before Carranza's armies occupied Mexico City, and they were initiated by Pancho Villa. In late July reports from northern Mexico and the border indicated that Villa was busy recruiting men, confiscating everything he could get his hands on, and arranging to sell the goods in the United States. The reports also indicated that he was buying large quantities of arms, dynamite, and fuel in the United States and smuggling it into Mexico.⁴ With only other revolutionary armies to fight, Villa's military preparations seemed ominous. Any southward advance might bring him into conflict with Obregón or González.

Actually Villa did not contemplate warfare except as a last resort. On about July 25 he called in his friend, State Department agent George Carothers, outlined his future plans, and urged the American to go to Washington and personally explain the situation to President Wilson. Zach Cobb, who had great faith in Carothers' ability to direct Villa's energies into constructive channels, urged that the Chihuahua strong man's request be honored. Accordingly, on July 28 Bryan directed Carothers first to secure Villa's pledge to maintain the peace in his absence, then to come at once to Washington. Having already secured such a pledge, Carothers departed from El Paso the next day.⁵ At this stage he was as much the agent of Pancho Villa as the agent of the United States.

3. Canova to State Department, August 29, 1914, in NA 812.00/13039.
4. Bliss to War Department, July 20, 1914, *ibid.*/12559; Cobb to State Department, July 24, 1914, *ibid.*/12601; Letcher to State Department, July 25, 1914, *ibid.*/12614.
5. Carothers to State Department, July 27, 1914, in NA 125.36582/101, 102; State Department to Carothers, *ibid.*/101; Cobb to State Department, July 27, 1914, in Wilson Papers, Ser. 2, Box 58; El Paso *Morning Times*, July 28, 1914; *El Sol*, July 31, 1914; *El País*, August 1, 1914.

Bryan had another reason to confer with Carothers; namely, the persistent charges of his misconduct while serving the department. Although Bryan had been inclined to pass off as *Carrancista* propaganda the earlier charges leveled by the León brothers, he could not ignore similar claims made by special agent Canova. As part of his duties, Canova had made inquiries into the Carothers-Villa relationship. His confidential reports to Bryan were devastating. "Since I have been in Mexico," he wrote in late July, "I have heard him (Carothers) described as a 'crook,' 'blackmailer,' 'gambler,' and 'woman-chaser.'" Canova insisted that it was an "accepted fact" that while Carothers "is Special Agent of the State Department, he represents Villa with far greater zeal." Carothers' "zeal" could be accounted for, Canova explained, by the fact that he had received lucrative business opportunities from the Mexican general, including gambling concessions in Chihuahua and Juárez. Word also reached Canova that Carothers had arranged through contacts in the United States for Villa to dispose of confiscated goods, including large amounts of foreign-owned cotton from the Torreón district. Equally damaging, Canova reported that Carothers might be encouraging the antagonism between Villa and Carranza.[6]

Canova's informants, whom he never named, also claimed that Carothers had, indeed, taken over a cotton plantation near Torreón. The opportunity had been presented him, not by the owner, but by Villa, who had confiscated the land. Canova's informants also indicated that Carothers had arranged with J. F. Brittingham, a Gómez Palacio soapmaker, for the *hacienda* to be temporarily managed by one of Brittingham's associates. Brittingham had agreed to help Carothers in return for a contract to take all the plantation's cottonseed at a reduced price. Carothers' family, meanwhile,

6. Canova to Bryan, July 22, 1914, in NA 111.70022/48. This report was not turned over to the department's Index Bureau until November 14, 1916.

was living in Brittingham's home in Gómez Palacio. All these
activities, Canova noted, reportedly allowed Carothers to
"spend money like a prince."[7]

On August 1 Carothers met with the secretary of state and
was personally confronted with the charges. He categorically
denied each. Describing the conference for the president,
Bryan wrote that he was inclined to believe Carothers.[8]
Several days later, the agent penned a memorandum for the
secretary. Again denying any wrongdoing, he insisted that he
had no income except from his salary paid by the department,
and that his real estate and mining properties in and around
Torreón, which were valued at only 25,000 pesos, were not
currently earning him any income.[9] Since similar charges had
been leveled at Carothers by such a variety of sources, it
seems unlikely that Bryan and Wilson dismissed them entirely. Nonetheless, they returned him to his duties a few
days later. They probably reasoned that Carothers' ability to
influence Villa was an asset that overbalanced any of the
debits that his alleged shady dealings might produce. Even
Canova admitted that Carothers was extremely capable, that
he had that "shade of dignity with a democratic spirit," that
commended him so highly for his kind of work. Canova later
admitted, moreover, that he had "yet to witness a single act
of his (Carothers) which has not been for the good of the
service."[10]

Carothers, meanwhile, held out hope for a peaceful solution to Mexico's problems. Villa's plan, as Carothers explained
it to Bryan, called for the rebel general to remain in
Chihuahua and increase the size of his army to sixty thousand
men. He would not interfere with Carranza in the capital, but
would insist upon the convention of revolutionary generals as

7. *Ibid.*; Canova to Bryan, August 6, 1914, in NA 812.00/27407.

8. Bryan to Wilson, August 2, 1914, in Wilson Papers, Ser. 4, Box 254;
New York *Times*, August 7, 1914, p. 8.

9. Carothers to Bryan, August 11, 1914, in NA 125.36582/111.

10. Canova to Bryan, October 20, 1914, in NA 812.00/13611.

provided for in the Pact of Torreón. Under the formula of representation—one representative per thousand troops— stipulated by the pact, he hoped to control half of the convention delegates. Villa disclaimed any personal ambitions and insisted only upon a program of agrarian reform to benefit his followers. If chosen by the convention, he would accept an able civilian as provisional president but would prefer to see General Felipe Angeles, a reform-minded professional soldier, receive the office. Although the First Chief had not ratified the Pact of Torreón, Villa believed that since he had abided by parts of it, he would accept the convention, too, if the United States applied enough pressure. If Carranza refused, Carothers revealed, renewed warfare was a certainty.[11]

Carothers' report gave Wilson and Bryan food for thought. A new avenue for influencing the revolution and at the same time neutralizing the power of the pugnacious First Chief seemed to be opening. Their immediate task, as they saw it after two or three days of discussion, was to insure that Villa did not engage in any hostile actions that would jeopardize the workability of his own formula. With Carothers' reputa- tion somewhat under a cloud, they decided to send a new agent, a personal representative from the president, to appeal to Villa. They considered John Lind, but Wilson ruled him out because of the "violent prejudice" directed at him by certain representatives of the Roman Catholic Church. Instead, he chose Paul Fuller, a prominent New York attorney. "I formed a most delightful impression of Mr. Fuller," Wilson wrote to Bryan. "He is a Democrat, is full of sympathy with the purposes of the administration, and is accustomed by long habit to deal with our friends in Latin America." [12]

At age sixty-five, Paul Fuller was a frail man in poor

11. Bryan to Wilson, August 2, 1914, in Wilson Papers, Ser. 4, Box 254.
12. Wilson to Bryan, August 5, 1914, in Bryan-Wilson Correspondence; copy in Bryan Papers, Box 43.

health when he accepted the mission and had to be accompanied by his physician during his travels. He had a deep sense
of responsibility to the administration and served without
salary.[13] His parents being Forty-niners, he was said to have
been born aboard a clipper ship as it sailed through San
Francisco's Golden Gate. Orphaned by the age of ten, he had
wandered eastward to New York City. There he was befriended by Charles Coubert, a French schoolteacher. After
reading law and being admitted to the bar, Fuller had
married his benefactor's daughter and joined the old man's
sons' law firm—Coubert Brothers. Through the firm, one of
the most prominent in the country, Fuller made numerous
international contacts and was reputed to be one of America's
foremost experts on foreign law. During his career he learned
Spanish and enjoyed great success in his dealings with Latin
American clients. It was this experience, no doubt, that
commended him to Wilson. Even before his appointment, he
had discussed Latin American policy with the president and
had been considered a prospective emissary to Santo Domingo. A possible conflict of interest prevented this appointment. A Roman Catholic, he was, perhaps, the best qualified
and most able of Wilson's personal agents.[14]

At a White House conference on August 9, Wilson presumably directed his new agent to urge Villa to remain at peace
and to allow the proposed convention to establish a new
government through free elections. There is no record of
their conversation, but Fuller's reports indicated that this
was the primary concern of his mission. They also reveal that
Fuller was probably instructed to either confirm or refute

13. The terms of Fuller's service are revealed in Bryan to Wilson, August
24, 1914, in Wilson Papers. Ser. 2, Box 114.
14. *Ibid.*; New York *Times*, November 30, 1915, p. 6. Biographical data on
Fuller is extremely sketchy. Most of the above information comes from his
obituary. For one who was reputed to be internationally famous, his name
rarely appeared in the newspapers and does not appear at all in the popular
biographical registers.

Carothers' overwhelmingly favorable impressions of Villa. Departing immediately for the border, the new agent bore a personal letter from Wilson asking Villa to explain his hopes for the future of Mexico.[15]

When Fuller arrived in El Paso on August 12, he was greeted by Zach Cobb, who promptly introduced the New Yorker to the local *Villista* leaders. Since Villa's whereabouts were unknown at the time, the local chieftain, General Juan Medina, in order to avoid delay, escorted the envoy south, while others attempted to locate their leader. Arriving in Chihuahua on August 14, the party was informed that Villa was in an inaccessible village hundreds of miles away. Only after two days of constant attempts at telegraphic communications was Villa reached and a rendezvous arranged at Santa Rosalía, some six hours from Chihuahua by rail.[16]

The delay allowed Fuller to take the measure of Villa's subordinates, especially of General Felipe Angeles, whom Villa had marked as a candidate for provisional president. The American agent was favorably impressed. He reported that the general was "a friend of free government" and had a "warm appreciation for President Wilson's attitude." When Fuller queried Angeles about Villa's abilities, the professional soldier replied frankly that because of a lack of "early training" his chieftain was still an "incomplete man," but that he was dedicated to his followers and their welfare.

15. Since there is no copy available, Wilson must have prepared the letter to Villa on his own portable typewriter. The content of the letter, as in the case of Fuller's instructions, must be inferred from the information in Fuller's report and Villa's return letter to Wilson. See Fuller, Memorandum for the President, August 20, 1914, in Wilson Papers, Ser. 2, Box 114; Villa to Wilson, August 18, 1914, *ibid*. The New York *World*, August 18, 1914, wildly exaggerated the purpose of Fuller's mission, claiming that he had been sent to warn Villa that American troops would march inland from Vera Cruz if he and Carranza fought over the occupation of Mexico City. Fuller was supposedly to warn Villa to keep away from the capital.

16. Cobb to State Department, August 13, 14, 1914, in NA 812.00/12844, 12851; Fuller, Memorandum for the President, August 20, 1914, in Wilson Papers, Ser. 2, Box 114.

Angeles insisted that Villa had no political ambitions but that Carranza did. He described the First Chief, whom he had served before joining Villa's camp, as "arbitrary and suspicious in manner and act," a potential dictator.[17]

On August 16, after suitable introductions, Fuller conferred alone with Villa. The special envoy emphasized that Wilson desired Villa to avoid any armed conflict with Carranza's forces that might ruin the chances of the early formation of a constitutional government. After expressing a like desire, Villa warned that it might not be possible if Carranza continued to consolidate all political power into his own hands. He also expressed fear that the United States or some other foreign power, in order to protect its private interests in Mexico, might encourage this trend by extending diplomatic recognition to the First Chief's provisional government. Sensing that he had found a bargaining point, Fuller, half asking and half demanding, told Villa: "If recognition should be withheld . . . you will be held responsible for the preservation of peace throughout Northern Mexico." In all apparent sincerity, Villa accepted the responsibility.

Fuller then inquired into the authenticity of a statement attributed to Villa, and recently published in the El Paso *Times*, in which the general supposedly declared that military men should not serve in the elected government and that agrarian reform should be accomplished by constitutional means. When Villa acknowledged that he had made the statement, Fuller asked the general to set forth in writing the objectives of his followers.[18]

The next day Fuller joined Villa and several of his advisors in the general's private rail car for a return trip to Chihuahua. In a relaxed atmosphere, the revolutionaries opened up and explained their fears and ambitions. Again Villa disclaimed any ambitions save to promote the welfare of his

17. *Ibid.*; Fuller to State Department, August 17, 1914, *ibid.*
18. *Ibid.*

men. In order to insure justice for the common people, he and his subordinates insisted that all inequalities in the law must be eliminated. Insisting that he was forced into outlawry because he had defended his sister's virtue against the carnal lusts of a rich landowner, Villa claimed to be just one of many victims of such inequalities. The *Villistas* also insisted upon land reform, claiming that the land would not be confiscated but that compensation would be made. But above all they seemed to want a government which would be more truly representative of all the people.

Inevitably the group got around to discussing Carranza. The consensus was that the strained relations between the revolutionary factions resulted primarily from a lack of trust on the part of the First Chief. They cited as an example the conduct of the Zacatecas campaign. Carranza's lack of trust in the Division of the North had needlessly cost the Constitutionalists hundreds of lives and had created hostility between the *Villistas* and the *Carrancistas*. Fuller then asked if it might be advisable for him to go to Mexico City and, in behalf of peace, make similar representations to Carranza. Unanimously, the *Villistas* replied that he should.[19]

In Chihuahua on August 18, Villa presented Fuller with a lengthy memorandum for President Wilson, outlining the desires of his faction. The preamble might have been penned by Wilson himself: "The principal aspiration of the Division of the North . . . is the establishment of a democratic government, elected freely and without official pressure." Neither the First Chief nor his Plan of Gaudalupe, the document continued, held out such guarantees. The Division of the North, nonetheless, conceded that it would accept a provisional government, even if headed by Carranza, provided that he was not eligible for the elective presidency. As a guarantee for elections, the Division of the North was to

19. Fuller, Memorandum for the President, August 20, 1914, in Wilson Papers, Ser. 2, Box 114.

remain intact. Fuller added his own penciled comments to Villa's memorandum. If Carranza followed his Plan of Guadalupe and became provisional president, Fuller scribbled, he would become ineligible for the constitutional presidency. By his own declaration, Villa, a military leader, was also ineligible. Thus, if all bargains were kept, neither should despair that his chief antagonist would rule the country.[20]

Taking his leave, Fuller made two additional appeals to Villa: that there should be no vindictive treatment of the defeated and that the Catholic Church, its priests and property, be treated with justice. By special train, Fuller then traveled to El Paso, where he boarded another train for the East Coast. He apparently intended to go to his home in New York and report by mail, but, while en route, he received a wire from Bryan directing him to come directly to Washington.[21]

While journeying eastward, Fuller set forth his impressions in a lengthy memorandum. Villa, he reminisced, was "an unusually quiet man, gentle in manner, low voiced, slow of speech, earnest and occasionally emotional in expression but always subdued with an undercurrent of sadness." He also noted that the rebel chieftain showed "no outward manifestation of vanity or self-sufficiency, is conscious of his own shortcomings." Fuller formed no less favorable impressions of Villa's subordinates. He admired their frankness, apparent sincerity and dedication, and willingness to accept guidance from the United States. His written report could hardly have been more complimentary to the *Villistas*.[22]

20. Villa to Wilson, August 18, 1914, in NA 812.00/27437; English translation in Wilson Papers, Ser. 2, Box 114.

21. Fuller, Memorandum for the President, August 20, 1914, *ibid.*; State Department to Fuller aboard Train 22, Manhattan Limited, Pennsylvania Railroad, August 21, 1914, in NA 812.00/12959a; New York *Times*, August 20, 1914, p. 7.

22. Fuller, Memorandum for the President, August 20, 1914, in Wilson Papers, Ser. 2, Box 114.

While Fuller was in Santa Rosalía, Carothers rejoined Villa. Fuller's report indicates that the State Department agent did not attempt to exert any influence in favor of Villa. Instead, he traveled alone in his own private car and did not enter into the discussions. Villa, however, did praise Carothers. The agent, he insisted, was an honest, straightforward man who never hesitated to speak his mind, no matter what the consequences. Those who charged that Carothers was trying to feather his nest through him, declared Villa, should come forward with some proof.[23]

If Wilson did not share this view, he still saw the Carothers-Villa relationship as an advantage to be exploited. The president had planned to meet with the special agent and discuss his work, but the grave illness of Mrs. Wilson prevented him from doing so. Thus Carothers never met President Wilson.[24] He returned to Villa's side bearing instructions to make representations similar to those already made by Fuller.[25] But future events indicated that his mission involved much more: through Villa, the promotion of a provisional government that would neutralize Carranza's power.

Conditions in the state of Sonora offered Carothers an opportunity. Back from his self-imposed exile, Governor José M. Maytorena began ousting governmental officials that Carranza had left behind in Sonora. Maytorena soon besieged Carranza's forces, commanded by Colonel Plutarco Elías Calles, in the border hamlet of Naco. During the fighting, shots from the attackers rained on the American side of the border. At the same time, Americans and other foreigners in Sonora were complaining about the daily depredations com-

23. *Ibid.*
24. Bryan to Wilson, August 2, 1914, in Wilson Papers, Ser. 4, Box 254; Testimony of Carothers, *Senate Documents*, 66th Cong., 2nd Sess., No. 285, p. 1771.
25. State Department to Carothers, August 11, 1914, in *Foreign Relations, 1914*, 584.

mitted by the Yaqui Indians, who made up the bulk of Maytorena's troops.[26]

Fuller had spoken to Villa about the Sonora disturbance, and the rebel general had promised to do all he could to promote peace.[27] Carothers, however, was specifically charged with the responsibility of pressuring Villa to arrange a peace settlement.[28] Accordingly, on about August 20 or 21, Villa invited General Obregón, whose home state was Sonora, to join him and aid in mediating the differences between Maytorena and Calles. Accepting the invitation with Carranza's permission, Obregón left Mexico City on August 21 to join Villa in Chihuahua.[29] Was the invitation to Obregón the fruit of Villa's mind or was it proposed by Carothers as part of a plan to check Carranza? The records do not reveal concrete answers to this question. One thing is certain: regardless of the origin of the invitation, Villa had more than peace in Sonora on his mind when he extended it.

The Villa-Obregón conferences went smoothly from the beginning. From Chihuahua Carothers reported that he believed the two generals would "act in accord. Conditions look favorable to me." [30] Travel to Nogales, where the conference with Maytorena was to be held, was very difficult because no rail line crossed northern Mexico from Chihuahua to Sonora. By appealing to General Pershing and Customs Collector Cobb, Villa's officials in Juárez arranged for the Mexican generals to use the American rail line between El Paso and Nogales.[31]

26. Frederick Simpich (American counsul, Nogales) to State Department, August 15, 18, 19, 23, 24, 1914, in NA 812.00/12875, 12913, 12937, 12968, 12984; El Paso *Morning Times*, August 15–24, 1914.

27. Fuller, Memorandum for the President, August 20, 1914, in Wilson Papers, Ser. 2, Box 114.

28. State Department to Carothers, August 13, 1914, in NA 812.00/12836.

29. Canova to State Department, August 21, 22, 1914, *ibid.*/12959, 12960.

30. Cobb (for Carothers) to State Department, August 26, 1914, *ibid.*/13003.

31. Bliss to War Department, August 23, 1914, in NA 812.2311/138; Cobb to State Department, August 25, 1914, *ibid.*/153.

Exuberant Villa partisans almost sabotaged the whole proceedings. While Cobb was busy arranging a smooth passage for the two generals, the *Villistas* persuaded General Pershing to publicly greet them when they arrived in El Paso. While Pershing was most courteous, some of the *Villistas* staged a pro-Villa demonstration that was obviously intended to deride Obregón. Showing no resentment, Obregón remained cordial and continued with Villa to Nogales. Delayed temporarily, Carothers arrived in El Paso after the incident and was greatly disturbed when he discovered what had happened. In a jointly prepared telegram, he and Cobb recommended that since more demonstrations might have an adverse effect on the existing rapport between Villa and Obregón, on the return trip they should not stop in El Paso for a banquet being planned in their honor.[32]

Early in the morning of August 28, Villa and Carothers went to Nogales, Sonora, to confer with Maytorena, while Obregón, somewhat apprehensive of the attitude of the governor and his followers, remained on the Arizona side and breakfasted with his fiancée, who had come to meet him. Later that day, after Villa and Carothers had arranged a tentative agreement, Obregón joined the conference, and the three revolutionary leaders, aided by the American agent, hammered out an agreement for the pacification of northwestern Mexico. Despite Carothers' efforts to prevent it, Villa's partisans continued to slight Obregón. Throughout the proceedings, however, Obregón conducted himself like a statesman.[33]

32. Cobb to State Department, August 26, 1914, *ibid.*/149; Cobb (joint telegram with Carothers) to State Department, August 27, 1914, *ibid.*/157; Carothers to State Department, August 27, 1914, in NA 812.00/13018; Cobb to Bryan, personal, August 29, 1914, *ibid.*/27428; El Paso *Morning Times*, August 27, 1914.

33. Carothers to State Department, August 28, 1914, in NA 812.2311/160; Carothers to State Department, August 30, 1914, in NA 812.00/13042; Tucson *Daily Citizen*, August 28, 29, 1914; El Paso *Morning Times*, August 30, 1914; Guzmán, *Memoirs of Pancho Villa*, 293–304; Alvaro Obregón, *Ocho mil kilómetros en campaña* (México, D.F., 1917), 266.

On their return trip to El Paso, Villa and Obregón asked Carothers to secure permission for General Pershing to join them on the Mexican side of the border. Although wanting to avoid the possibility of further incidents, Carothers dutifully acceded to request the meeting. For one reason or another, possibly at the request of the State Department, the War Department had already ordered Pershing not to meet again with the two Mexican generals.[34] Instead, when they arrived back in El Paso, Cobb had contrived to have identical telegrams of commendation from Secretary Bryan presented to them.[35] The American customs collector later reported that the notes relieved much of the embarrassment which might have resulted from the cancellation of the festivities that had been scheduled in the generals' honor.[36]

All the signs must have been encouraging in Washington. Obregón addressed a note to Bryan, thanking the administration for its interest in Mexico and its aid in establishing peace.[37] Carothers saw encouraging signs for the future. "Villa and Obregón are working in harmony and friendship," he wired the secretary of state.[38] More prone to emotional expressions, Cobb wrote to Bryan that the Villa-Obregón relationship had taken on the "effect of a love feast." [39] He also praised Carothers, claiming that the rapprochement between the generals was largely the result of his efforts.[40]

34. Carothers to State Department, September 1, 1914, in NA 812.2311/165; Adjutant General's Office to Commanding General, Southern Department, August 31, 1914, *ibid.*/169.

35. Cobb to State Department, August 30, 1914, and State Department to Cobb, September 1, 1914, in NA 812.00/13043.

36. Cobb to State Department, September 1, 1914, *ibid.*/13065; copy in Wilson Papers, Ser. 2, Box 115.

37. Obregón to Cobb (for Bryan), September 1, 1914, in *Foreign Relations, 1914*, 593.

38. Carothers to State Department, September 1, 1914, in NA 812.00/13063.

39. Cobb to Bryan, personal, August 29, 1914, *ibid.*/27428.

40. Cobb to State Department, September 1, 1914, *ibid.*/13065; copy in Wilson Papers, Ser. 2, Box 115.

Carothers continued to shepherd the two generals, returning with them to Chihuahua. There his efforts paid more dividends. Villa and Obregón expanded their discussion to include measures to prevent further revolutionary discord and promote a government acceptable to all factions. On September 3 they agreed to a nine-point program that was essentially the same as the one Villa had outlined in the memorandum which Fuller took to Washington. Although Obregón was a loyal *Carrancista*, he agreed with the wisdom of the First Chief's becoming provisional president, thus eliminating him from the elective presidency. The Villa-Obregón agreement also provided for free elections and the exclusion of military men from civil offices.[41] Whether by contrivance or pure coincidence, a Villa-Obregón axis had seemingly emerged.

After remaining in Chihuahua for several days to solidify his friendship with Villa, Obregón asked Carothers to return with him to Mexico City. Carothers interpreted the invitation as more evidence of Obregón's cordiality toward Villa and the United States. Sensing that Carothers' acceptance of the invitation would lend an aura of American support to the recently negotiated pact, Villa also urged the agent to go to Mexico City. Bryan was only too pleased to grant permission.[42] Things were beginning to fall into place. Villa and Obregón had expressed a desire for peace and representative government. If their coalition was maintained, Carranza would be checked.

Paul Fuller, meanwhile, had returned to Washington, submitted his report and Villa's memorandum, and agreed to go to Mexico City to meet with Carranza. Again no written instructions may be found, but several months later Fuller confided the nature of his mission to a group of friends. "He

41. Quirk, *Mexican Revolution*, 69–70; Barragán Rodríguez, *Historia . . . de la Revolución Constitucionalista*, II, 67–70.
42. Cobb (for Carothers) to State Department, September 4, 1914, in NA 812.00/13111; State Department to Carothers, September 7, 1914, *ibid.*

stated confidentially," recalled Chandler P. Anderson, a special assistant in the State Department, "that the object of his mission was conciliation and mediation between hostile elements, directed chiefly to bringing about a convention which would place Villa in control." [43] Fuller's mission, then, complemented Carothers' and vice versa.

On returning to Mexico, Fuller, this time accompanied by his wife, journeyed to Galveston by rail where he caught a steamer to Vera Cruz. Arriving on September 4, he was met by Silliman and Isidro Fabela, Carranza's foreign minister. En route to the capital, the special envoy conferred with Fabela. He suggested to the foreign minister that the duration of the revolutionary interim government should be short and that early provision should be made for free elections. Fabela scoffed at this suggestion, insisting that the interim government could carry out reforms more efficiently. When the American agent replied that only the elected representatives of all the people should presume to inaugurate reforms, Fabela insisted that elections would take time and that a legislature would debate for months. Recalling Madero's experience, he noted that such delays would only lead to renewed rebellions. The best way to insure tranquility in Mexico, he contended, was for the United States to extend diplomatic recognition to the interim government and thus invest it with an official status. If the elected representatives of the people wanted to change the policies adopted by the interim government, they could do so later.

Abruptly, Fabela changed the subject. He urged that the American troops be withdrawn from Vera Cruz. President Wilson, he reminded Fuller, had declared that the invasion was directed only at Huerta, yet the troops remained. He claimed that the Mexican people were unified in their desire

43. Diary of Chandler P. Anderson, February 20, 1915, in Papers and Diaries of Chandler P. Anderson, Division of Manuscripts, Library of Congress, Box 21.

to see the Americans leave. Then he claimed that the apparent signs of dissension among his people were misleading. He maintained that most of the governors and generals were devotedly loyal to Carranza. Zapata, he noted, was an exception. He also admitted that force might be necessary to subdue the revolutionaries of the South.[44]

The regimen in Mexico City had abated somewhat by the time of Fuller's arrival. Taking steps to quiet the criticism of his arbitrary rule, on September 5 Carranza issued a call for a *junta* of Constitutionalist governors and generals to meet in the capital on October 1. His action was prompted no doubt by rumors of growing accord between Obregón and Villa, who were still conferring in Chihuahua. At any rate, Fuller thought the proposed *junta* an encouraging step and commended the First Chief when they met later that same day. But he also reminded Carranza that President Wilson desired the early establishment of a constitutional government.[45]

In reply, the First Chief, echoing Fabela, claimed that an interim military government was necessary for instituting reforms. He blamed meddling by the United States for much of the disunity among the revolutionary factions. Denying that this was the intention of his president, Fuller offered to promote unity. He suggested that President Wilson address a note to Zapata through Silliman, urging him to renew negotiations with the Constitutionalists and notifying him that his refusal to do so would displease the United States. Carranza was caught off guard by Fuller's counterplay. At first he hedged, suggesting that he could not ask an alien to restore internal order in Mexico. But under Fabela's prodding he acceded to the proposal. Fuller then promptly wired

44. Fuller, Memorandum for the President, September 18, 1914, in Wilson Papers, Ser. 2, Box 117.
45. *Ibid.*; Fuller to State Department, September 5, 1914, in *Foreign Relations, 1914*, 594; Silliman to State Department, September 5, 1914, in NA 812.00/13119; *El Liberal* (Mexico City), September 5, 6, 1914.

Bryan, requesting that the overture be made to Zapata. Two days later, Silliman received instructions to do so.[46]

On September 7, while Fuller was still in Mexico City, Obregón, accompanied by Carothers and two of Villa's aids, returned from Chihuahua. The *Villistas*, both of whom Fuller had met earlier, searched him out and explained the agreement their chief had made with Obregón. They were fearful that Carranza would not accept it and asked Fuller to intercede. The New Yorker also discussed the pact with Obregón, who was just as reluctant to assure the First Chief's acceptance.[47]

Turning next to the First Chief, Fuller urged acceptance of the Villa-Obregón agreement. He told Carranza that the pact was "in consonance with the views" of President Wilson and that "its early realization would enlist the sympathy and approval" of the United States. Carranza gave no reply; instead, he took up the question of the evacuation of Vera Cruz. Again wielding a deft hand at diplomacy, Fuller inquired: "To what organized government could we make any transfer of so important a port?" There was currently "not even a provisional government in existence," he continued, "but only a revolutionary body in military occupation of the capital." Fuller then indicated that when a satisfactory provisional government was established, he was certain that President Wilson would be most willing to evacuate Vera Cruz.

Carranza was enraged. He took out his wrath on Silliman, who had accompanied Fuller but had lingered behind in an attempt to soothe the First Chief. Turning on the weaker of the two agents, he told Silliman that unless he had authority

46. Fuller, Memorandum for the President, September 18, 1914, in Wilson Papers, Ser. 2, Box 117; Fuller to State Department, September 5, 1914, in *Foreign Relations, 1914*, 594; State Department to Silliman, September 7, 1914, *ibid.*

47. Fuller, Memorandum for the President, September 18, 1914, in Wilson Papers, Ser. 2, Box 117; Fuller to State Department, September 8, 1914, in NA 812.00/13133.

to negotiate the evacuation of Vera Cruz, he should leave the country with Fuller. His rage intensifying, he complained that he was tired of dealing with envoys who were supposedly clothed with authority to discuss important international questions yet did nothing but delve into Mexico's internal affairs.[48] Silliman was so intimidated by Carranza's outburst that he was reluctant to even pursue attempts to bring the First Chief and Zapata together.[49]

The *Carrancistas* were not in the least cowed by Fuller. The day after his encounter with the First Chief, the special agent dined with Fabela and Carranza's private secretary, Gustavo Espinoza. Fuller expressed dismay at the revolutionaries' vengeful attitude toward officials of the defunct Huerta regime. He suggested that some distinction should be made between those who had definitely committed crimes and those who had done their duty as they saw it. Both Fabela and Espinoza insisted that no such distinction would be made, that it would only encourage those who might be treated with leniency to again plot against legally constituted authority. Fuller came away from the meeting with the impression that, unless their power was curbed, the *Carrancistas* would make "proscription and confiscation . . . a settled policy." [50]

Just as Villa had done, before Fuller departed, Carranza presented the agent with a letter for President Wilson. The letters, however, differed greatly. Villa's had been lengthy and cordial and had urged the United States to aid in promoting peace in Mexico. It had also outlined a plan for the creation of a new government. Carranza's letter was short and businesslike; it simply notified Wilson that Rafael Zubarán Capmany, the Constitutionalist agent in Washington,

48. *Ibid.*
49. Silliman to State Department, September 12, 1914, in NA 812.00/13166.
50. Fuller, Memorandum for the President, September 18, 1914, in Wilson Papers, Ser. 2, Box 117.

had been directed to immediately pursue negotiations leading to the evacuation of Vera Cruz.[51]

En Route to Washington, Fuller prepared another lengthy memorandum describing the *Carrancistas* and his relations with them. As might be expected, he had little of a complimentary nature to report. "Fabela I consider a retrograde influence," he wrote. "Carranza impressed me as a man of good intentions but without any sufficient force to dominate his petty surroundings, and greatly hampered by the fear of lowering his prestige which hinders him from adopting conciliating measures or correcting mistakes." He suggested, moreover, that the only apparent solution to Mexico's difficulties lay in adherence to a plan such as that proposed by Villa and Obregón. Significantly, he suggested that further bloodshed was preferable to allowing Mexico to return to prerevolutionary conditions, which he indicated might result if Carranza's rule continued unrestricted.[52]

It is difficult to surmise with certainty what Fuller said to Wilson when they met privately in late September, but a reporter who claimed to know suggested that the agent warned that Carranza could never restore order to his country.[53] Certainly there is no reason to think that his verbal report was any less critical than his written memorandum. After making his report, Fuller returned to his law practice and did not visit Mexico again. But he remained a close associate of the president and from time to time was called upon to give advice on Latin American affairs.

On September 9 prospects for cooperation among the revolutionary factions were given another boost by Obregón. Attempting to enlist Carranza's support in forming a new provisional government as provided for in his agreement with

51. *Ibid.*; Carranza to Wilson, September 7, 1914, *ibid.*, Box 116.

52. Fuller, Memorandum for the President, September 18, 1914, *ibid.*, Box 117.

53. New York *World*, November 14, 1914, cited in Link, *Struggle for Neutrality*, 248.

Villa, Obregón issued a public appeal for an American withdrawal from Vera Cruz. He also urged Villa to do the same, and Villa accommodated his newly found friend in the *Carrancista* camp by replying that he would lend his support to such an appeal.[54] Hoping to abet this budding revolutionary unity, Wilson directed Silliman to ask Carranza to designate "responsible officials" to whom the port might be surrendered. Receiving the president's note on September 15, Silliman, with a dramatic flare, delayed delivering the message until the sixteenth, the anniversary of Mexican independence.[55] At almost the same time, Silliman reported discouraging news to Washington. Carranza and Zapata, he cabled, were hopelessly rent, and there seemed to be little hope of averting armed conflict between the two. Having discussed the situation with Carothers, who was then in Mexico City, Silliman also revealed that Villa would probably not approve of an attack on Zapata.[56]

Zapata now appeared to be the fly in the ointment. Of all the revolutionary leaders, the Wilson administration had had the fewest contacts with Zapata. Even those contacts had proved unsatisfactory. Indeed, the circumstances surrounding the attempts were, to say the least, bizarre. To fully understand them, moreover, we must digress several months to March, 1914, when Hubert L. Hall first appeared in Vera Cruz and attempted to arrange contacts between the *Zapatistas* and John Lind.

54. Silliman (enclosing Obregón to Villa, September 9, 1914) to State Department, September 11, 1914, in *Foreign Relations, 1914*, 595; Silliman (enclosing Villa to Obregón, September 9, 1914), to State Department, September 12, 1914, *ibid.*, 596; *El Liberal*, September 9, 10, 1914.

55. State Department to Cardoso de Oliveira, September 15, 1914, in *Foreign Relations, 1914*, 598; Silliman to State Department, September 16, 1914, *ibid.*; Silliman to Carranza, September 15, 1914, AGRE, L–E–861, Leg. 5. Wilson's proposal to withdraw the troops from Vera Cruz was made in good faith. The same day he addressed the note to Silliman, he also discussed with Secretary of War Garrison plans for the evacuation. See Garrison to Bryan, September 15, 1914, in NA 812.00/13225.

56. Silliman to State Department, September 14, 1914, in *Foreign Relations, 1914*, 596.

A longtime resident of Mexico, Hall was born a New Englander but moved to Utah in his youth and was converted to Mormonism. Around 1890 he migrated to one of the Mormon colonies in northern Mexico, where he remained for two years before making his permanent home in Morelos. For a time he operated a hotel in the city of Cuernavaca. After the *Zapatistas* occupied the city, the hotel business was no longer profitable, so he turned to other pursuits. When the agrarian reform program of the Madero administration foundered, Hall and several businessmen of Mexican nationality attempted to organize one of their own. The plan, which was to dominate Hall's thoughts for years to come, was to borrow enough capital from the national agricultural bank, *La Caja de Préstamos*, to purchase land for a colony, then sell shares on easy terms to the landless. But the bank's funds were exhausted, and Hall's colonizing plans were temporarily abandoned.[57] He claimed that he then devoted time to relief work in the service of *La Cruz Blanca Neutral* (an organization similar to the Red Cross) in Cuernavaca and Mexico City. In this capacity, he treated the wounded of both the loyal and insurgent armies during the *Decena Trágica*.[58] How he sustained himself otherwise is a mystery.

Hall never blamed Zapata for his losses. Rather, he blamed the oppressive conditions in Morelos which had spawned the revolution. In fact, he became absolutely enamored of Zapata.

57. Lind to Bryan, March 23, 1914, in Lind Papers; Hall to Bryan, May 21, 1914, in Wilson Papers, Ser. 2, Box 109; Rosa E. King, *Tempest Over Mexico: A Personal Chronicle* (Boston, 1935), 136–37. Mrs. King, herself a notable Cuernavaca hotel-owner, named Mrs. Hall as proprietor of the Hotel Morelos.

Hall claimed that Jorge Vera Estañol and Alberto García Granados, both government officials and well known throughout Mexico, were among the backers of his colonizing scheme. *La Caja de Préstamos* was created in 1908, during the Díaz regime, to underwrite privately sponsored reclamation and irrigation projects such as Hall's. See González Ramírez, *El Problema agrario*, 171–73.

58. Hall to Ben G. Davis, chief clerk of the Department of State, September 5, 26, 1914, in NA 812.00/20609½.

His devotion to the revolutionary leader made him prey for a huckster named Jacobo Ramos Martínez, a clever lawyer who had served in various official capacities in Morelos and had ample opportunity to mark Hall as a perfect accomplice.[59] Sometime in February or March, 1914, Ramos Martínez gained the confidence of Hall and Arnold Shanklin, the American consul general in Mexico City. Bearing bogus credentials which granted him sole authority to represent Zapata to officials of the United States, and claiming that he was seeking arms and supplies for the revolutionaries in Morelos, the charlatan persuaded Hall to serve as intermediary between himself and Lind, who was still in Vera Cruz. Although he distrusted the *Zapatistas*, Lind embraced the scheme for a variety of reasons. First, it might hasten the fall of Huerta. And, as Hall suggested, it might enable the United States to exert some influence on Zapata. Finally, Lind had taken a liking to Hall when the two met several months earlier in Mexico City. Reminiscing on that first meeting, Lind wrote to Bryan that Hall "impressed me at once as a man of keen powers of observation and of excellent judgment." Further investigation had satisfied Lind that the Mormon was "entirely trustworthy and a man of high character." [60]

59. During Madero's administration, Ramos Martínez served in Morelos as lieutenant governor and commandant of the *Rurales*. Hall may or may not have known him at that time. Twice Ramos Martínez was commissioned (one time each by Madero and Huerta) to negotiate a peace with Zapata. During the second parleys, conducted in March, 1913, Hall offered to both Ramos Martínez and Zapata, as inducement for the successful arrangement of peace, shares in his proposed colony. This move may have been instigated by Minister of Government Alberto García Granados, who had commissioned Ramos Martínez and was also one of the original planners of Hall's colony. The proposal came to naught, but it may well have given Ramos Martínez an opportunity to fathom the depths of the Mormon's naïveté. See Gildardo Magaña and Carlos Pérez Guerrero, *Emiliano Zapata y el agrarismo en Mexico* (México, D.F., 1951–52), III, 105–106; Baltasar Dromundo, *Vida de Emiliano Zapata* (Mexico, D.F., 1961), 170–71.

60. Lind to Bryan, March 23, 1914, in NA 812.00/20609½. Since he claimed to be in constant danger, a system of code names was adopted by the

Since the whole plot began to emerge only days before Lind's departure from Mexico, the Minnesotan was not able to see it through. On the eve of his departure, Hall appeared in Vera Cruz a second time. This time he was accompanied by Ramos Martínez, who, claiming to be in great danger, pleaded for asylum. Before Lind could arrange it, his ship sailed for home. When Consul Canada of Vera Cruz expressed doubt that asylum was in order, Ramos Martínez hastily departed the city, claiming that he had been dealt with in bad faith. Before leaving, however, he persuaded Hall to go to Washington in his place. Hall, being an American, had little trouble in securing funds for his passage from Canada.[61]

Until Hall appeared in Washington in April, 1914, the Wilson administration had given scant attention to Zapata. Endeavoring to inform Wilson and Bryan of the revolution in the South, Hall appeared almost daily at the State Department throughout the summer of 1914. Although he met periodically with Bryan and prepared a lengthy memorandum for the president, he conferred mainly with Chief Clerk Ben G. Davis, who took the Mormon under his wing and introduced him to others in the department and to the Constitutionalist agents in Washington. Hall described Zapata in near rapturous terms as a born leader of the common people, and his sympathetic views of the southern revolutionaries were the most flattering the administration had yet

---

conspirators to shield Ramos Martínez and preserve the secrecy of the plot to aid Zapata. The code names of those involved were as follows: Lind, "Juárez"; Shanklin, "Paz"; Ramos Martínez, "Brady"; and Hall, "Clark." Although Zapata was not a party to the conspiracy, he was given the code name "Dix." See Lind to Canada, April 5, 1914, in Lind Papers; copy in Buckley Papers, File no. 233.

61. *Ibid.*; Lind to State Department, April 6, 1914, in NA 812.00/11409, 11415; Canada to State Department, April 9, 17, 1914, *ibid.*/11457, 11539; State Department to Canada, April 13, 16, 1914, *ibid.*/11457, 11539; Shanklin to Lind, April 11, 12, 1914, *ibid.*/27474. Bryan ultimately approved his asylum request, but Ramos Martínez refused to accept it unless Consul General Shanklin accompanied him to the United States. Bryan would not approve this request.

received. Hall's accounts definitely shed new light on the *Zapatistas* and made the administration temporarily well disposed toward them. In August, Davis reported to Bryan that Hall had even won friends for Zapata from among the Constitutionalist agents.[62]

Throughout the summer of 1914, Hall and State Department officials maintained communications with Ramos Martínez, who still claimed to be seeking aid for Zapata. The available evidence indicates that what he really wanted was money—twenty-five to fifty thousand dollars—ostensibly to purchase medical supplies but actually for his own pocket. Ramos Martínez's attitude, initially cordial, grew menacing when Bryan refused to supply funds. The would-be extortionist warned that only his personal restraints prevented Zapata from overrunning and pillaging Mexico City. He also reminded Hall that his property in Cuernavaca had not yet been

---

62. Hall to Bryan, May 14, 1914, enclosed in Bryan to Wilson, May 19, 1914, in Wilson Papers, Ser. 4, Box 254; Davis to Bryan, August 22, 1914, *ibid.*, Box 124. Hall describes his activities during the summer of 1914 in the voluminous correspondence that he sent back to Washington after his return to Mexico. One must consult many letters to reconstruct his activities. They are too numerous to cite individually, but are all filed under document number 812.00/10609½.

While in Washington, Hall, with Bryan's support, also tried to persuade the department of agriculture to make an exhaustive study of Mexico's agricultural potential. He believed that Zapata could use such a study in formulating his program of agrarian reform. But Secretary of Agriculture David F. Houston claimed that the project would require a greater expenditure of time and money than Zapata's gratitude could justify and refused to commit his department to the study. Still Hall took advantage of Bryan's introduction and continued meeting with experts in the department of agriculture. By the time he returned to Mexico, he had received considerable instruction on advanced methods and technology. See Bryan to Houston, June 30, 1914, Records of the Secretary of Agriculture, 1904–64, National Archives, Record Group 16; William A. Taylor, Chief of the Bureau of Plant Industry, to Houston, July 10, 1914, *ibid.*; Houston to Bryan, July 13, 1914, *ibid.*; Hall to Frederick V. Coville, September 20, October 22, 1914, General Correspondence, 1889–1934, of the Records of the Division of Botany, Bureau of Plant Industry, Soils, and Agricultural Engineering, Department of Agriculture, *ibid.*, Record Group 54.

molested, but that there could be no guarantees against future destruction unless the money was forthcoming.[63]

As the antagonism between Zapata and Carranza intensified in late August, Bryan, suspicious of further dealings with Ramos Martínez, decided to send a State Department agent to deal directly with Zapata. Chief Clerk Davis recommended Hall for the mission, suggesting that he more than any other American might be able to exert some influence in Morelos. Davis also intimated that the Mormon would be willing to perform this service with nothing more than his expenses being paid by the State Department. Bryan passed on this recommendation to the White House and added that Hall had "shown more interest . . . [in Mexico] than any other American." He also noted with considerable exaggeration that Hall was "an intimate friend of Zapata." [64] There is no evidence that Hall ever claimed such intimacy, but the president accepted Bryan's recommendations. "I think that your suggestion about paying his [Hall's] expenses to go down and confer with Zapata is an excellent one," Wilson replied. "He may be extremely useful to us." [65]

Bryan was notoriously clumsy in making appointments, but never more so than in Hall's case. A busy schedule prevented him from conferring at any length with his newly designated agent. Hall later reported that he and Bryan had discussed his mission during a brief carriage ride from the State Department to the secretary's home. Fatefully, Hall was sent back to Mexico with nothing more than verbal

63. The documents relating to the State Department's dealings with Ramos Martínez are too numerous to cite individually, but may be found in file 812.00/27474. A detailed account of the affair may be found in Teitelbaum, *Wilson and the Mexican Revolution*, 143–57.

64. Davis to Bryan, August 22, 1914, in Wilson Papers, Ser. 4, Box 124; Bryan to Wilson, August, 1914, *ibid.* In his written memoranda to Secretary Bryan, Hall never claimed the friendship of Zapata, but merely that they had met and that he had observed Zapata on several occasions.

65. Wilson to Bryan, August 25, 1914, in Bryan-Wilson Correspondence.

instructions and five hundred dollars to cover his expenses.[66] He journeyed as far as Vera Cruz with Paul Fuller. By the time he arrived there on September 4, the situation had changed. At the urging of the State Department, the Red Cross had sent a representative named Charles Jenkinson into Morelos to determine Zapata's need for medical supplies. Besides bearing personal felicitations from Zapata to President Wilson, Jenkinson emerged from Morelos with the news that Ramos Martínez was a fraud. Zapata, believing that Hall, like Ramos Martínez, was nothing more than an extortionist, had also told Jenkinson that the Mormon was no longer welcome in Morelos. Anxious not to alienate Zapata, Bryan ordered Hall to remain in Vera Cruz.[67]

At first Hall accepted his plight as the result of a simple misunderstanding. Within a few days, however, he had convinced himself that Jenkinson and Silliman, who had come to Vera Cruz to meet Fuller, had contrived to keep him from joining Zapata. Jenkinson and the Red Cross, Hall insisted, were trying to supercede the Wilson administration in promoting peace in Mexico and would derive great satisfaction from succeeding where the State Department was failing. Silliman, the irate Mormon charged, was so sympathetic to Carranza that he did not want another agent offering advice to Zapata. This latter charge was accurate to a point. Carranza had in fact told Silliman that he did not want the United States meddling in his relations with Zapata,

66. Hall to Davis, September 5, October 21, 1914, September 11, 1916, in NA 812.00/20609½; New York *Times*, September 4, 1914, p. 6.

67. Jenkinson to Wilson, September 8, 1914, in Wilson Papers, Ser. 2, Box 116; Silliman to Bryan, August 26, 29, 1914 in NA 812.00/12015, 13040; Bryan to Canada, August 30, 1914, *ibid.*/13040. Jenkinson made an earlier trip into Morelos in December, 1913. At that time he also brought out a letter from Zapata to Wilson, but it was never answered. See Teitelbaum, *Wilson and the Mexican Revolution*, 152–53. For Jenkinson's own comments on his Red Cross service among the *Zapatistas*, see Charles Jenkinson, "Vera Cruz, What American Occupation Has Meant to a Mexican Community," *The Survey*, XXXIII (November 7, 1914), 133–34.

and the agent had recommended that Hall's mission be scrapped.[68]

Hall spent three agonizing weeks in Vera Cruz, during which time he sent repeated pleas to Bryan for permission to go inland and face his accusers. He received no further word from Washington. He sent even more urgent appeals to Ramos Martínez in Mexico City, imploring his former collaborator to clear up the misunderstanding surrounding their recent attempts to aid Zapata. Hall's anxiety ultimately got the best of him and he journeyed to the capital without State Department permission. Unable to persuade Silliman that he could be of service to the department or even to locate Ramos Martínez, he resolved to return to Cuernavaca and seek vindication.

Hall spent two more weeks in Mexico City, attempting to establish contacts in Zapata's country. During that time he sent to Washington lengthy and extremely critical reports of Carranza's regime. At length, a friend came to escort him to Cuernavaca; but before leaving Mexico City, Hall appealed for formal State Department credentials. When none were forthcoming, he returned to Morelos without formal authority.[69]

Back in Cuernavaca, the pertinacious Mormon was highly suspected. Zapata's officials demanded to see his credentials. He, of course, had none. The *Zapatistas* were distressed over their relations with the United States. Through Jenkinson they had attempted to establish official relations with Washington but had received no reply. They resented the fact that Carranza and Villa were accorded special representatives and they were not. But most embarrassing of all for Hall, the day after his arrival in Cuernavaca he received a letter from Zapata which revealed that Ramos Martínez had never

68. Hall to Davis, September 5, 8, 12, 13, 14, 15, 16, 1914, in NA 812.00/20609½; Silliman to Bryan, August 29, 1914, *ibid.*/13040.
69. Hall to Davis, September, 5, 8, 12, 13, 14, 15, 16, 18, 19, 20, 26, 28, 30, October 1, 3, 5, 8, 1914, *ibid.*/20609½, 27430, 27431, 27432, 27433; Shanklin (for Hall) to State Department, September 21, 1914, *ibid.*/13242.

legitimately represented the *Zapatistas* and that he was currently a wanted man. At first refusing to believe this news, the gullible American recovered his perspective after several days and reported to Washington what the administration had long since suspected: "Ramos Martínez has deceived us." [70]

Despite the *Zapatistas'* suspicions, Hall reported that he was treated cordially. He nonetheless renewed his pleas for official credentials. While he waited vainly, he continued his descriptive correspondence to Washington. In contrast to conditions in Mexico City, he reported, Morelos was quiet and the people were living in peace and harmony. There was no looting, the government was functioning to everyone's satisfaction, a program for breaking up the large *haciendas* and distributing the land to the peasants had been inaugurated, and the crops were being harvested. In short, the *Zapatistas* were carrying out their own tidy revolution.[71]

Once in Zapata's mountains, Hall had great difficulty communicating with the outside world. Occasionally, when other messages were sent out, he was allowed to send a letter to Washington, but he received no return correspondence. Bryan waited until October 22 before even attempting to communicate with Hall. Having received Hall's plea for credentials, and possibly fearing for his safety, Bryan directed Davis to send a message to Hall through Consul General Shanklin. It was not the letter of credentials that Hall had asked for. Addressed "to whom it may concern," the letter reviewed Hall's activities in Washington in behalf of the *Zapatistas*, then stated that the department had been "pleased to place its facilities, unofficially, at Mr. Hall's disposal" and had permitted him "to transmit and receive

70. Zapata to Hall, October 12, 1914, *ibid.*/27453; Hall to Davis, October 11, 12, 21, 1914, *ibid.*/20609½, 27436, 27424.

71. *Ibid.*; John Womack, Jr., using different sources, largely substantiated Hall's descriptions of the *Zapatistas* and their local revolution. See Womack, *Zapata*, 211.

information through its agents." The note closed by endorsing Hall's character, but it said nothing about his future
relations with the department.[72]

Even this innocuous letter might have been of some
comfort to Hall, had Shanklin known how to get it to him. So
Hall remained in Cuernavaca and brooded because his
country had forgotten him. In time the *Zapatistas'* suspicions
of him dissipated, and he got along quite well. Certainly the
administration had no compelling reason to claim him. With
Hall periodically sending lengthy and informative letters to
Washington, the State Department enjoyed all the benefits of
his efforts without facing any liabilities.

The administration, meanwhile, read off as hopeless any
attempt by the United States to bring Zapata and Carranza
together. But Jenkinson had reported seeing *Villista* agents
in Morelos and claimed that Zapata and Villa were working
in harmony. If Villa and Obregón could come to some
agreement with the First Chief, it was hoped Zapata would
accept it.[73] The promotion of the Villa-Obregón axis, then,
seemed to offer the best avenue for the adjustment of all
grievances.

The Washington-inspired coalition, however, was enduring
severe trials. On September 13 Carranza notified Obregón
that the provisions of the pact he and Villa had agreed to
some ten days before were too momentous to be decided upon
by two or three men and that they would be reviewed by the
revolutionary *junta* which was scheduled for the capital on
October 1.[74] The most serious test of the coalition's strength,
however, came from within. Renewed conflict in Sonora
between Maytorena and the *Carrancistas*, now led by General Benjamín Hill, again provided Obregón with a pretext to

72. State Department to Shanklin, October 22, 1914, *ibid.*/27474.
73. Silliman to State Department, August 26, 1914, in *Foreign Relations,
1914*, 591.
74. Barragán Rodríguez, *Historia . . . de la Revolución Constitucionalista*, II, 71.

travel north to meet with Villa. Departing from Mexico City on September 13, he was accompanied by Carothers, Canova, and General Juan Cabral, who earlier had been designated to replace Maytorena as governor of Sonora. Since Carranza's occupation of the capital, Canova had been relatively idle. He had distressed the Brazilian minister, who was still officially in charge of American affairs in Mexico City, because he operated independently and had not even called at the legation. Feeling that Canova was surplus in the Mexican capital, Bryan had directed the agent to return to Washington for reassignment. Taking advantage of the comfort of Carothers' private car, he traveled north with the Obregón party.[75]

Carothers had been directed to proceed to the border with General Cabral and lend his effort to the repacification of Sonora. Aware that Obregón bore an invitation for Villa and his chiefs to attend the *junta* in Mexico City, the agent paused in Chihuahua long enough to discuss the matter with the Centaur of the North. The rebel leader was beside himself with rage because Carranza had not accepted outright the Villa-Obregón pact. The First Chief's *junta* would be rigged, he warned. The State Department agent pleaded that Obregón was an honorable man and that he and the other generals would enforce justice. Forced to leave for the border before he could pacify the strong man of the North, Carothers persuaded Canova to remain behind and continue the effort.[76]

When Carothers arrived in El Paso, a wire from Canova awaited him. Canova and Obregón had again spoken to Villa, and Villa had agreed to send representatives to the *junta* if

75. Simpich to State Department, September 9, 10, 1914, in NA 812.00/13137, 13153; Cobb to State Department, September 10, 1914, *ibid.*/13146; State Department to Silliman, September 11, 12, 1914, *ibid.*/ 13153, 13167; State Department to Canova, September 10, 1914, *ibid.*/13174a; Canova to State Department, September 11, 1914, *ibid.*/13164.

76. Carothers to State Department, September 19, 1914, *ibid.*/13227; copy in Wilson Papers, Ser. 2, Box 63; Canova to State Department, September 22, 1914, in NA 812.00/13323.

Carranza would agree to immediate elections and the establishment of a civil government. The *junta*, he demanded,
must be short and to the point and must not act as a
governing body. Canova despaired that a complete break
would result if Carranza refused to accede to Villa's provisos.[77]

On the afternoon of September 19, Canova had another
appointment with Villa, but when he arrived at the general's
headquarters he found that Villa and Obregón were quarreling violently. The American agent quickly moved to a
courtyard adjoining the headquarters building, where he
could hear the conversation without appearing to be eaves-
dropping. Villa had just received a telegram from Sonora
which, to his way of thinking, laid the blame for the renewed
hostilities on the *Carrancistas*. Suspicious of Obregón because he had compromised with Carranza on the matter of
the revolutionary convention, Villa now charged the general
with dealing in bad faith on the pacification of Sonora. Villa
called in a squad of soldiers and threatened to kill Obregón
unless he ordered General Hill's troops to evacuate Sonora.
Although Obregón refused, Villa's temper subsided and, after
some discussion, Obregón wired Hill to withdraw a short
distance from the trouble spot. Their friendship apparently
restored, the two generals went dancing together that
night.[78] The incident seemed to have passed, but a series of
resulting misunderstandings brought Mexico again to the
brink of civil war.

Rumors reached Mexico City that Villa was holding
Obregón prisoner in Chihuahua. Carranza, fearing renewal of
hostilities, not only suspended rail traffic south of Torreón but

77. Carothers to State Department, September 19, 1914, in NA
812.00/13227.

78. *Ibid.*; Canova to State Department, September 11, 1914, *ibid.*/13323;
Guzmán, *Memoirs of Pancho Villa*, 312–18; Obregón, *Ocho mil kilómetros*,
312–14. Villa's and Obregón's accounts of the incident differ greatly. Canova
offers a more balanced treatment.

countermanded Obregón's withdrawal order to General Hill.[79] Villa, meanwhile, had arranged for his delegates to accompany Obregón to the *junta*. On September 21 the two generals sent a joint telegram warning Carranza not to attempt to control the proposed meeting. Carranza refused to accept it as authentic. When Villa's delegates, accompanied by Obregón, were stopped at Torreón, Villa interpreted this as an attempt by Carranza to prevent him from being represented. Obregón was returned to Chihuahua, where he became a virtual prisoner.[80]

Carothers, who had been sitting in El Paso attempting to deal with the troubles in Sonora and Chihuahua and unable to treat either satisfactorily, received new orders from Washington to hasten to Villa's side and use his influence to calm the rebel chieftain.[81] He arrived too late. Villa had withdrawn any recognition of Carranza and declared his intention to move at once on the capital to oust the "dictator." Canova, who witnessed the whole turn of events, reported that Villa, "his eyes dancing and his face smiling," was delighted at the opportunity to fight Carranza.[82]

The entire impasse was most unfortunate since it resulted from a series of misunderstandings. It pointed out a weakness in the State Department's representation in Mexico. One of the primary responsibilities of the agents was to make every effort to prevent a renewal of warfare. Yet, during this time of crisis, there was absolutely no communication be-

79. Silliman to State Department, September 21, 22, 1914, in NA 812.00/13243, 13268; Silliman to State Department, September 23, 1914, in *Foreign Relations, 1914*, 605; Belt to State Department, September 25, 1914, in NA 812.00/13292.

80. Canova to State Department, September 22, 25, 1914, *ibid.*/13247, 13326; Carothers to State Department, September 22, 23, 1914, *ibid.*/13217, 13247; El Paso *Morning Times*, September 24, 1914.

81. Carothers to State Department and State Department to Carothers, September 23, 1914, in NA 812.00/13271.

82. Canova to State Department, September 23, 25, 1914, *ibid.*/13275, 13326.

tween Silliman in Mexico City and Canova and Carothers in northern Mexico. Each was allowed by the department to become so engrossed with one factional leader that the positive benefits of close coordination between all the agents was ignored. Had there been some planned liaison between them, the misunderstanding might well have been detected and the breach prevented.

In the long run, it was Obregón, not the American agents, who averted war. The general's staff, meanwhile, was distraught, fearful for their commander's safety. They urged him to remain with Canova at all times, and they pleaded with the agent to intercede in his behalf. Canova did speak first to one of Villa's closest advisors, Eugenio Aguirre Benavides, then to Villa himself. Obregón, he argued, was anxious to find a settlement suitable to the *Villistas* and, if allowed to go to Mexico City, would attempt to pressure Carranza into making concessions. After one long interview, Villa abruptly revealed that Obregón would be sent to El Paso. Canova again argued the necessity of sending Obregón directly to Mexico City, but Villa said that his decision would stand. Carothers had not yet arrived to lend his influence.[83]

Dejected, Canova revealed Villa's plans to Obregón. He assured the Mexican general that he would accompany him to the border to insure his safety. But Obregón was more despondent over the prospect of renewed warfare than he was concerned for his own safety. "This situation is criminal, Mr. Canova," he lamented, "for everything possible should be done by both sides to avoid another revolution." [84] Just before Obregón and Canova were to depart for El Paso, Villa reversed his decision and sent word that Obregón would be allowed to go directly to Mexico City. Obregón thanked

83. Canova to State Department, September 25, 1914, *ibid.*/13326; Canova to Bryan, personal, October 9, 1914, *ibid.*/27411.

84. Canova to State Department, September 25, 1914, *ibid.*/13326; Obregón, *Ocho mil kilómetros*, 315–16.

Canova for his efforts and promised to do everything in his power to persuade Carranza to relent so that a reconciliation might be accomplished. Only weeks later did Canova discover that Villa had sent ahead a train with an officer and some soldiers who were supposed to stop Obregón's train, take him off, and assassinate him. When Aguirre Benavides, who also wished to avoid further bloodshed, discovered the plot, he braved Villa's wrath, intervened without Villa's knowledge, and allowed Obregón to pass unharmed to Mexico City.[85]

The combined pressures of Carothers, who arrived shortly from the border, Canova, Aguirre Benavides, and others of Villa's staff eventually had their effect on Villa. Carothers' influence appears to have been crucial. Before his arrival in Chihuahua, Villa had been anxious to fight. Within a day after Carothers' arrival, Villa agreed to call off his advance on Mexico City and seek a peaceful solution.[86]

Back in Mexico City, Obregón persuaded Carranza to send representatives to meet with Villa's at Zacatecas. Villa also agreed to send delegates to this conciliation conference. With Carothers in attendance, the conference, which was dominated by Obregón, agreed that Carranza's *junta* should meet in Mexico City only to issue a call for a larger revolutionary convention to be held at Aguascalientes. It was to convene on October 10, all factions were to be represented on the basis provided for in the Pact of Torreón, and Carranza was to relinquish his authority as First Chief to this larger body.

---

85. *Ibid.*; Canova to Bryan, personal, October 9, 1914, in NA 812.00/27411.

86. Carothers to State Department, September 26, 1914, in *Foreign Relations, 1914*, 605. Villa at first suggested that Fernando Iglesias Calderón, who was not a revolutionary but had the reputation of being a liberal reformer, should assume control of a provisional government. When Carranza rejected this proposal, Villa on September 30 issued a "Manifesto to the Mexican People," setting forth his grievances and urging the people to join him in demanding a more representative government. See Belt to State Department, September 29, 1914, *ibid.*, 606; Francisco Villa, "Manifesto to the Mexican People," *ibid.*, 607–608.

When the *junta* met in Mexico City, the generals lived up to their bargain. More encouragingly, Carranza accepted their decision.[87]

The Wilson administration's friendly relations with Villa seemed to have paid dividends. Even Canova, who had seen Villa at his worst, conceded that the Centaur of the North was "a great man, in a way. He has genius, and there is much to admire in him, but at heart he is plainly a savage . . . With proper training and counseling," he prophesied, "Villa can be developed into a great character." [88] But even as Canova penned these all-too-optimistic words, it was becoming daily more apparent that Alvaro Obregón was the more likely instrument for promoting a stable representative government in Mexico. Although neither the special agents nor their president had yet recognized Obregón's full potential, events of the immediate future proved that they would be wise to look to him, and not to Villa, for the solutions to Mexico's problems.

87. Cobb (for Carothers) to State Department, October 1, 1914, in NA 812.00/13353; Testimony of Carothers, *Senate Documents*, 66th Cong., 2nd Sess., No. 285, p. 1774; Quirk, *Mexican Revolution*, 84–97.
88. Canova to Bryan, personal, October 9, 1914, in NA 812.00/27411.

CHAPTER X

The Retreat Begins

The fall and winter of 1914 witnessed still another shift in Wilson's Mexican policy: if not the emergence of neutrality, then certainly a growing reluctance to become further involved in the revolutionaries' factional squabbles. As the delegates assembled for the revolutionary Convention of Aguascalientes, Secretary of State Bryan suggested to the president that he personally urge both Villa and Carranza to cooperate with the convention in creating a constitutional government.[1] Wilson neither replied to Bryan nor made such an appeal to the factional leaders. Once the convention began its deliberations, he made no attempt to influence its decisions. Perhaps his mind was occupied more with the problems of war-torn Europe. He may well have been satisfied that the Villa-Obregón coalition had matters well in hand and, working through the convention, would promote a constitutional regime. On the other hand, he may have reasoned that interference by the United States would alienate the apparently cooperative *Carrancistas* and give their chief a pretext for scuttling the convention. Or he may have just assumed that, having aided in raising Villa to a pinnacle of power, it was time to give him an opportunity to sink or swim alone. Yet Villa's actions in nearly assassinating Obregón may have caused Wilson to pause before extending further support.[2] Such a shift in policy at this particular

1. Bryan to Wilson, October 7, 1914, in Bryan-Wilson Correspondence.
2. The documents give no clues as to the reasons for Wilson's policy shift.

juncture was uncharacteristic of Wilson, since the deliberations at Aguascalientes seemingly offered him tantalizing
opportunities for molding Mexican institutions more along
Anglo-Saxon lines.

Whatever Wilson's attitude might have been, it was not
always shared by his special agents. While the convention
met, the agents received no extraordinary instructions. It was
a time of relative inactivity for George Carothers. He
remained with Villa, who was encamped at Guadalupe, a rail
center some hundred miles north of Aguascalientes, and
merely reported the general's impressions (which were almost
entirely favorable) of the convention's proceedings. Noticeably missing were the constant reminders and suggestions
from the State Department, which aimed at guiding Villa in a
proper course of action. Carothers later complained at the
lack of guidance from Washington.[3] The only request that the
administration made of Villa during this time was that he aid
in ending the fighting on the Sonora-Arizona border between
Maytorena and the *Carrancistas*. At Carothers' suggestion,
Villa referred the matter to the convention, which sent
General Ramón V. Sosa to Sonora to put an end to the
conflict. Sosa's efforts proved unavailing and the fighting
continued.[4]

For his part, Villa made only one significant request of
Carothers—that he ask the administration to suppress the
various revolutionary *juntas* in New Orleans, San Antonio,
and El Paso, because they were hostile to his interests. True
to the administration's emerging policy of noninvolvement,
Bryan directed Carothers to reply that unless Villa could give

In fact, the exchange of expressions between the White House and the State
Department concerning Mexican affairs decreased markedly in October and
November.

3. Testimony of Carothers, *Senate Documents*, 66th Cong., 2nd Sess., No.
285, p. 1770.

4. State Department to Carothers, October 16, 1914, in NA
812.00/13547a; Cobb (for Carothers) to State Department, October 21, 1914,
ibid./13548.

specific evidence that these organizations were violating the neutrality laws of the United States, the Justice Department could not move against them.[5]

The period of the Convention of Aguascalientes was Leon Canova's busiest time in Mexico. The administration, having recalled him in September, reconsidered its decision because of Canova's efforts during the Villa-Obregón quarrel in Chihuahua and decided to retain him in Mexico. At first he was directed to accompany Villa and assist Carothers. After the calling of the Convention of Aguascalientes, he was directed to observe the sessions and report.[6] Sending as many as four coded messages daily by Mexican telegraph was job enough in itself. The telegraphers so butchered the messages that Canova often had to repeat them two or three times before Zach Cobb, who relayed them from El Paso, could understand them. In order to insure that Washington got an accurate account, Canova periodically codified the briefer telegraphic dispatches into letters that ran up to twenty pages. Even his telegraphic messages became so lengthy and vivid that Acting Secretary of State Robert Lansing directed him to leave all unnecessary detail and opinion to his letters.[7]

Canova's early reports may well have encouraged Wilson's hands-off policy. On the eve of the convention, the special agent was apprehensive. Villa marched his troops into Zacatecas. Carranza's armies surrounded the convention city to

5. Cobb (for Carothers) to State Department, October 6, 1914, and State Department to Cobb (for Carothers), October 8, 1914, *ibid.*/13417.

6. State Department to Canova, September 23, 1914, *ibid.*/13272; State Department to Canova, October 4, 1914, *ibid.*/13391; El Paso *Morning Times*, October 5, 7, 1914.

7. Lansing to Canova, October 19, 1914, in NA 812.00/13619. Many of Canova's dispatches from Aguascalientes are found in *Foreign Relations, 1914,* 610–27; but these are only a small portion of his reports. Collectively, his messages constitute one of the richest and most colorful sources for reconstructing the events of the revolutionary convention. Robert E. Quirk, who has written the standard monograph on the convention, relies as heavily upon Canova's accounts as those of Vito Alessio Robles, the recording secretary of the convention. See Quirk, *Mexican Revolution*, 101–31.

the South. Canova reported from Aguascalientes that the arriving delegates were fearful for their safety. But when the convention convened, these anxieties evaporated. Villa, true to his promise, kept his troops one hundred miles away at Guadalupe. General Natera remained neutral, and his troops protected the convention. The delegates, Canova reported, mingled in "a spirit of cordiality and good fellowship." [8] Previously antagonistic personalities found themselves applauding one another's comments. The delegates, however, were in no mood to humor the factional leaders. Even the *Carrancistas*, Canova noted, were determined that the First Chief should "take a back seat" to the convention. Nor would Villa, who had lost prestige because of his treatment of Obregón, be allowed to dominate the proceedings.[9]

Canova quickly developed a close affinity for the convention delegates as they assembled and began deliberations in the Morelos Theatre. "Few of the men attending the convention," the special agent wrote to Washington, "have any knowledge of parliamentary proceedings, many are men of limited education and, it must be admitted, some are of most unsavory reputations and are dangerous in extreme." Then almost proudly he added that their "proceedings have been so well conducted and so orderly, that I . . . cannot but compliment them." [10]

The special agent mingled freely, almost as if he were a

8. Canova to State Department, letter, October 9, 1914, in NA 812.00/17411.

9. Canova to State Department, letters, October 5, 8, 9, 1914, *ibid.*/27410, 13518, 27411; Cobb (for Canova) to State Department, October 6, 8, 12, 1914, *ibid.*/13415, 13437, 13490. The traditional historical view of the Convention of Aguascalientes is that it was dominated by the *Villistas* and that Villa, with thousands of troops nearby, intimidated the *Carrancistas*. The whole affair, therefore, was a sham. Robert E. Quirk applied a corrective in his previously cited work, *Mexican Revolution*, 105–106, 114. Citing convention records, he substantiates Canova's view that the convention was at first independent of factional control. Only after the *Carrancistas* withdrew did the *Villistas* and *Zapatistas* dominate.

10. Canova to State Department, October 14, 1914, in NA 812.00/13572.

delegate. He was frequently photographed with the conventioneers, including chairman Antonio J. Villarreal.[11] Canova renewed old acquaintanceships among the *Carrancistas* and brought them together with his newly found friends among the *Villistas*. Instead of heaping recriminations upon the other faction's leaders, each side was almost maudlin in bemoaning the shortcomings of its own leaders. Not realizing how prophetic they were, members of each faction suggested to Canova that peace might be easier achieved if Villa and Carranza were sent abroad on diplomatic missions.[12] The American did not become well acquainted with Zapata's delegates, who were the most radical at the convention. Although he remained suspicious of them for that reason, he did compliment them for their persuasiveness.[13]

Canova often involved himself emotionally in the proceedings of the convention, especially in two notable instances. On October 17 Villa created a temporary stir by appearing in Aguascalientes. He kissed and signed the Mexican flag, as the delegates had previously done, and Canova revealed that he shared the convention's delirious joy when Villa and Obregón met at the front of the theater and locked arms in an *abrazo*. For the remainder of the day, Canova reported, exhortations of patriotism flowed like wine.[14]

11. Gustavo Casasola, *Historia gráfica de la Revolución Mexicana, 1910–1960* (México, D.F., 1960), II, 905–908.

12. Cobb (for Canova) to State Department, October 12, 1914, in NA 812.00/13469, 13474; Canova to Bryan, personal, October 21, 1914, *ibid./*13633.

13. Canova to State Department, October 28, November 10, 1914, *ibid./*13619, 13924. Zapata's delegation was led by the intellectual elite of the revolution of the South. Among them were Antonio Díaz Soto y Gama, a onetime anarchist who was thoroughly conversant in the ideas of Kropotkin, Bukanin, and Marx; and Otilio E. Montaño, an advocate of agrarian reform who had collaborated with Zapata in drafting the Plan of Ayala. For the nature of their ideas, see Womack, *Zapata*, 193, 396; Cockroft, *Intellectual Precursors of the Mexican Revolution*, 71–73.

14. Cobb (for Canova) to State Department, October 18, 1914, in NA 812.00/13529; *El Liberal*, October 18, 1914.

An even more lively scene resulted when one of Zapata's delegates, Antonio Díaz Soto y Gama, condemned the flag to which the other delegates had paid homage. Crumpling it in his fist and waving it tauntingly at the crowd, he declared that it was not a symbol of liberty but a banner of tyrants, such as Díaz and Huerta. Again pandemonium reigned in the Morelos Theatre. But whereas Canova had found the excitement produced by Villa and Obregón's embrace exhilarating, he was frightened by the uproar created by Díaz Soto y Gama. "The members of the Convention rose to their feet, their faces livid with indignation, trembling, and shaking their fists at the speaker," Canova wrote to Bryan afterward. "The delegates screamed at one another, with left hands pounding their chests, and their right hands on their pistols, for all were mad." Ready to flee himself, the special agent confided that "from the crowded boxes and galleries of the theatre, humanity was tumbling over itself in a mad effort to escape imminent danger." [15]

Although there were other emotional outbursts, the important work of the convention was conducted in the spirit of compromise. As previously arranged by the *junta* in Mexico City, the convention declared itself sovereign and adopted the formula of representation prescribed by the Pact of Torreón. The body accorded Zapata a concession when it adopted the Plan of Ayala "in principle," but retained the right to reject those clauses that did not comform to the ideals of the convention. On November 1 the convention chose Eulalio Gutiérrez, a mild *Carrancista* but one who was acceptable to both the *Villistas* and *Zapatistas*, as the temporary provisional president.[16] Canova was ecstatic. "Surely, the Republic of Mexico was born again last night by the selection of a man [around] whom all factions and elements could center without

15. Cobb (for Canova) to State Department, October 28, 29, 1914, *ibid.*/13619, 13702.
16. Quirk, *Mexican Revolution*, 101–118.

discord," he wrote to Bryan.[17] The American agent was certain that Mexico was well on the way to solving its problems. Regardless of his overall optimism, he was forced to interject one discouraging note. Carranza not only refused to attend the convention, or send a delegate to represent him, but absolutely refused to acknowledge the assembly's right to declare itself sovereign.[18]

Ominously, Carothers reported from Guadalupe that Villa was furious over Carranza's recalcitrance. Villa promised the special agent that he would apply no pressure on the convention to take punitive action, that he would wait patiently, but if he was ordered to take the field against the First Chief, he would "do so with keen pleasure." [19] Even Villa became hopeful when the convention chose Gutiérrez as provisional president. He immediately wired the convention of his satisfaction and, to Carothers, he pledged his full support of the new provisional president. Speaking for himself, Villa, and Villa's staff, Carothers optimistically telegraphed the department: "We all believe end of trouble is in sight." [20]

John Silliman, meanwhile, had gone to Washington at Carranza's behest to confer personally with President Wilson. Well aware that Carothers had earlier visited Bryan in Villa's behalf, Carranza, on September 23, placed a special train at Silliman's disposal and requested that the American agent take a message to Washington. Leaving his assistant, John W. Belt, to represent the State Department in the First Chief's headquarters, Silliman departed immediately for the

17. Canova to Bryan, personal, November 2, 1914, in NA 812.00/13738.
18. Canova to State Department, October 23, 1914, in *Foreign Relations, 1914*, 612; Cobb (for Canova) to State Department, October 30, 1914, in NA 812.00/13638.
19. Carothers to State Department, October 23, 1914, in *Foreign Relations, 1914*, 611–12.
20. Cobb (for Carothers) to State Department, November 3, 1914, in NA 812.00/13671.

border, even before receiving authority from his superiors.[21] The special agent was, therefore, not available to lend any influence during the critical period while Obregón and the other conciliatory *Carrancista* generals were arranging the Convention of Aguascalientes. It is doubtful that he could have been of much service, since Carranza ignored him except when it was convenient to do otherwise.

Wilson and Bryan were not at all satisfied with Silliman's service to the State Department. In August they had even considered replacing him. In the end, they decided that because he was Wilson's old friend he at least presented an aura of personally representing the president of the United States.[22] This decision signaled their admission that they could do little to influence Carranza. Although they had retained Silliman's services, Wilson and Bryan did not wish to confer with him in October, especially since the agent's coming would be counter to their emerging policy of noninvolvement. When Silliman arrived in San Antonio, he received a telegram from Bryan, directing him not to proceed further unless he thought it absolutely necessary. Replying that he thought a conference with the president was "desirable," the special agent continued on to the capital.[23]

At no time before his arrival in Washington did Silliman reveal his reasons for coming. Since he departed before the calling of the Convention of Aguascalientes, while Villa and Carranza were still very much at odds, the special agent had, more than likely, been asked to present Carranza's view of the conflict. More definitely, he had been requested to renew

21. Silliman to State Department, September 23, 1914, in *Foreign Relations, 1914*, 605; Silliman to State Department, September 25, 1914, in NA 125.8273/120; *Nueva Patria* (Mexico City), September 16, 1914.
22. Bryan to Wilson, August 17, 1914, in Wilson Papers, Ser. 2, Box 114; Wilson to Bryan, August 18, 1914, in Bryan Papers, Box 43.
23. State Department to Silliman, October 1, 1914, in NA 125.8273/125; Silliman to State Department, October 2, 1914, in NA 812.00/13363; New York *Times*, September 27, 1914, II, p. 11; *ibid.*, October 5, 1914, p. 11.

the First Chief's demand for the evacuation of American troops from Vera Cruz.[24]

On September 15 Wilson had offered in good faith to evacuate American troops from Vera Cruz. But at the time he was not aware of all the implications involved in the evacuation. General Frederick Funston, the American commander in Vera Cruz, revealed, for example, that the local merchants feared that the Constitutionalists might force them to pay extra import duties on items for which they had already paid duties to the American authorities. He also indicated that Mexicans, who had served the American military government, feared reprisals at the hands of the Constitutionalists, as did the hundreds of refugees, including priests and nuns and former *Huertistas*, who had crowded into the port city. These revelations had prompted Wilson, on September 22, to direct Robert Lansing, the acting secretary of state, to notify Carranza that the evacuation would not take place until he specifically guaranteed that there would be no punitive measures of this nature.[25] The receipt of this message may well have prompted Carranza to send Silliman to Washington.

Anticipating help from the American agent, the First Chief was slow in replying to Lansing's note of September 22. Impatiently, Bryan, on October 1, renewed the request for guarantees. Four days later, Foreign Minister Fabela finally delivered a note to the Brazilian minister, Cardoso de Oliveira, which ignored the demand for guarantees and merely notified Washington that General Cándido Aguilar

24. Silliman never revealed in his correspondence the exact nature of his visit, nor is there a record of his conversations with either Wilson or Bryan. There is little reason to doubt the accuracy of an account of his visit in the Washington *Post*, October 9, 1914, which revealed that the Vera Cruz evacuation was the primary subject of his discussions with the president.

25. War Department to State Department, September 21, 1914, in *Foreign Relations, 1914*, 601–602; State Department to Cardoso de Oliveira, September 22, 1914, *ibid.*, 603.

had been designated to receive the port of Vera Cruz from General Funston.[26] When Silliman arrived in Washington at approximately the same time, he walked into a hornets' nest. Wilson and Bryan were in no mood to listen to any pro-Carranza propaganda. They directed their agent to inform Fabela by wire that his note had not been "sufficiently explicit" on the matter of guarantees. When, again, no reply was immediately forthcoming, Bryan sent Silliman packing back to Mexico to extract the guarantees from the First Chief.[27]

En route to Vera Cruz, Silliman told reporters in Havana that he was confident the evacuation problems could be "straightened out."[28] He also sent encouraging news from Vera Cruz. He spoke to General Aguilar, who was quite willing to issue a proclamation embodying the guarantees requested by President Wilson.[29] Upon returning to Mexico City, Silliman reported that even the convention had instructed Carranza to adhere to the demands of the United States.[30] Knowing well Silliman's pro-Carranza attitude, the capital city press, meanwhile, had interpreted the agent's conversations with Aguilar as preliminaries to the immediate withdrawal of American troops. His return to Mexico was heralded as evidence of growing cordiality between the United States and Carranza.[31]

Following his instructions, Silliman was forced to dispel this impression. He again pressed the First Chief for guarantees that no punitive action would be taken against the

26. State Department to Cardoso de Oliveira, October 1, 1914, *ibid.*, 608; Cardoso de Oliveira to State Department, October 5, 1914, *ibid.*, 609.

27. State Department to Cardoso de Oliveira (conveying Silliman to Fabela, October 7, 1914), October 7, 1914, *ibid.*, 609–10; Washington *Post*, October 9, 1914.

28. New York *Times*, October 13, 1914, p. 7.

29. Canada (for Silliman) to State Department, October 16, 1914, in NA 812.00/13514.

30. Silliman to State Department, October 19, 1914, *ibid.*/13537.

31. *El Pueblo*, October 18, 20, 1914; *El Liberal*, October 18, 1914.

people of Vera Cruz. In reply Carranza acknowledged that if such guarantees could be given by a Mexican government without coercion from an outside power, they would be honorable and just, but to offer them as a result of pressure from the United States would be dishonorable.[32] Carranza's insistence upon upholding the abstract principle of Mexican sovereignty again proved a stumbling block, and the Vera Cruz matter remained unsettled until late November. The First Chief still considered himself the only legitimate authority in Mexico. By taking this stand, he defied not only Wilson but the convention, which demanded with equal vigor that it was the guardian of Mexican sovereignty.

Carranza set himself against the convention as soon as it adopted measures that were counter to his Plan of Guadalupe. Silliman reported that the First Chief was convinced of his own rectitude and preferred renewed civil war to compromising his principles.[33] On the other hand, the convention had become almost as intractable as Carranza. In making their decisions, most of the delegates seemed more intent upon subjecting their former chief to their will than upon promoting the welfare of the Mexican people. In the last days of October and the first days of November, the convention attempted a complete transfer of power from Carranza to its own provisional president. The First Chief, who had taken refuge with General Francisco Coss in Córdoba, refused even to receive a commission which had been sent to accept his resignation. After most of the *Carrancistas* had bolted the convention, on November 10 the assembly declared Carranza a rebel. Gutiérrez then called upon Villa, who had supposedly accepted the convention's request for a resignation, to assume command of the Conventionist forces and take the field against the First Chief. Attempting to avert more bloodshed,

32. Silliman to State Department, October 19, 1914, in NA 812.00/13537.
33. Silliman to State Department, October 19, 20, 22, November 3, 4, 1914, *ibid.*/13535, 13547, 13570, 13571, 13675, 13689.

generals from both camps proposed various plans for exiling
both Carranza and Villa. The two chief antagonists even
professed willingness to accept one or more of the plans if the
other first gave evidence of compliance. While these tragi-
comedies were being enacted, with none of the performers
showing the divine spark necessary to bring them to a happy
conclusion, Villa was driving southward.[34]

Canova remained convinced that the convention was
making the right decisions. Literally smitten by the atmosphere of this assemblage, he could find no fault with its
actions. At the same time, Carranza became an arch-villain in
his eyes. "The continuance of General Carranza in power," he
wrote to Bryan shortly after the First Chief refused to turn
over the executive power to Guitiérrez, "would in no manner
symbolize the triumph of the revolution, for it would only
mean the overthrow of one dictator to place another in
power." The First Chief, Canova insisted, had forgotten all
the altruism that moved him when they first met in Monterrey during the month of June. Now, only personal ambition
directed his actions.[35]

Carranza's generals also drew Canova's ire. When many of
them broke with the convention and sided with the First
Chief, Canova too readily assumed that they did so because of
disappointed political ambitions. Generals Eduardo Hay, Antonio Villarreal, and Alvaro Obregón, he insisted, had all
"hoped that presidential lightening [sic] would strike
them." [36] The other delegates, however, had recognized their
ambitions and had eliminated them as presidential prospects.[37]

Villarreal and Hay, Canova believed, had then sought to
salvage some measure of preeminence by promoting the

34. Quirk, *Mexican Revolution*, 114–25.
35. Canova to State Department, November 6, 1914, in NA 812.00/13788.
36. Canova to State Department, November 12, 1914, *ibid.*/13923.
37. Canova to State Department, November 10, 17, 1914, *ibid.*/13924,
13935.

interests of their close confederate, Lucio Blanco. The plot was actually initiated by a group of unscrupulous Americans, which Canova called the "Brownsville syndicate." The syndicate was headed by Frank W. Rabb, U.S. customs collector at Brownsville, Texas; M. J. Slatter, publisher of a Brownsville newspaper; and Edwin Brodix of San Antonio. Canova thought that Senator Morris Sheppard of Texas might also be implicated. Although Canova did not suggest it in his dispatches, the syndicate members may well have been acquainted with Blanco, Hay, and Villarreal for some time, since all three were from northern Mexico. Although he only supposed that Hay and Villarreal were involved, the special agent claimed to have proof that Blanco was receiving financial support from the syndicate. In return the syndicate members expected land grants and business concessions from Blanco if he attained power.[38]

In September Canova reported Rabb's presence in Mexico City but made no mention of the syndicate. In late October, Rabb came to Canova in Aguascalientes and hinted that the special agent would be richly rewarded if he used his influence with the members of the convention to promote Blanco for the provisional presidency. According to his report of the episode, Canova declined to support Blanco. The syndicate, nonetheless, had continued to direct pro-Blanco propaganda at the delegates. After Gutiérrez was elected provisional president, the syndicate's plans changed. Hay and Villarreal supposedly became involved. Their scheme now called for Blanco to perform some act of heroism against Carranza that would endear him to the Conventionists; then, when Gutiérrez's temporary term expired, Blanco would be in a position to succeed him.[39]

38. Canova to Bryan, November 12, 1914, *ibid.*/27413.
39. *Ibid.*; Canova to State Department, September 2, 1914, in NA 812.00/27409. In September Canova assumed that Rabb was merely on vacation in Mexico. The special agent had even sent one of his lengthy reports to the border with Rabb. The syndicate's conspiracy may well have

After Carranza showed irrevocably that he would not
support the convention, Canova, although claiming that he
was not a party to the Brownsville syndicate's machinations,
decided, on his own, to encourage the conspirators as a means
of eliminating the First Chief. Pointing out that Blanco's
troops occupied Mexico City, the special agent suggested to
Slattery and Brodix that their hero could demonstrate his
devotion to the convention by seizing Carranza and holding
him hostage. The *Carrancista* opposition would, he hoped,
falter, the convention would be grateful, and Blanco would
certainly stand in line to succeed Gutiérrez as provisional
president or, possibly better, be a logical candidate for the
elective presidency. According to Canova's report of the
incident, the two American conspirators left immediately for
the capital. But before the plot was consummated, Carranza
grew wary of Blanco and fled to Córdoba. Although the
syndicate continued to plot Blanco's rise to power, the
ambitious general was never able to fulfill their ambitions.[40]

been operational at that time. In the month of September, Blanco played a
critical role in persuading the other *Carrancista* generals to agree to the
Convention of Aguascalientes. His subsequent actions revealed that he was
extremely ambitious. See Quirk, *Mexican Revolution*, 84–85, 89.

40. Canova to Bryan, personal, November 12, 1914, in NA 812.00/27413.
Before Bryan received the above letter, M. J. Slattery, Senator Sheppard,
and one Henry Borden telegraphed Secretary of Treasury McAdoo and
requested that Customs Collector Rabb's leave of absence be extended. Each
insisted that Rabb was performing valuable service in promoting peace in
Mexico. When McAdoo brought the matter to Bryan's attention, the
secretary of state replied that he knew of no service Rabb could provide in
Mexico. See McAdoo to Bryan (conveying Sheppard to McAdoo, November 3,
1914; Borden to McAdoo, November 6, 1914; and Slattery to McAdoo,
November 8, 1914), November 9, 1914, and Bryan to McAdoo, November 11,
1914, in NA 812.00/13765. Later, Blanco asked Silliman to appeal for an
extension of Rabb's leave. With Bryan absent from Washington, Acting
Secretary of State Robert Lansing handled the matter and did not request
the customs collector's recall. Not until December, when Carothers became
aware of Rabb's activities, did he and Canova request that Rabb's leave be
canceled. Even then the Treasury Department requested proof of wrongdoing before recalling him. See Silliman to State Department, November 14,
1914, and Lansing to McAdoo, November 16, 1914, in NA 812.00/13778;

The upshot of these fruitless connivances was to again point out to Washington how the personal ambitions of many Mexican leaders took precedence over statesmanship.

While Canova pilloried Carranza and his generals, he also extolled Villa's virtues, picturing him as the most stable influence in Mexico. "General Villa is the only individual who can put the country on a peaceful footing and establish confidence," he wrote to Bryan. "Were he to leave the country at this time, or before a duly elected Administration is inaugurated in office, Mexico would witness, and be the victim of anarchy." [41] Canova also sanctioned the Conventionist war against Carranza. "Sometimes it is necessary that a painful surgical operation has to be undergone in order that the body may return to good health," he concluded. "And while I regret to say it, a clash of arms will be in the end the best thing for the country, for it will clarify the political atmosphere." [42]

More than Carothers, Canova had become Villa's champion in the State Department. More accurately reflecting the administration's current attitude, Carothers remained noncommittal. He neither justified nor advocated the Conventionist, hence the *Villista*, cause. He merely reported the general's actions to Washington. When Carranza was de-

---

McAdoo to Lansing, November 23, 1914, *ibid.*/13893; Carothers to State Department, December 9, 1914, and Bryan to McAdoo, December 10, 1914, *ibid.*/13985; A. Peters, assistant secretary of treasury, to Bryan, December 15, 1914, *ibid.*/14035; Testimony of Carothers, *Senate Documents*, 66th Cong., 2nd Sess., No. 285, pp. 1779–80.

Lucio Blanco defied Carranza's orders and remained in Mexico City after the other Constitutionalist forces evacuated. No doubt he was still looking for an opportunity to establish a reputation for gallantry, but his courage ultimately failed him as attacks by the *Zapatistas* intensified, and he too fled the city. Retiring to Michoacán, Blanco maintained a precarious neutrality for about a week before casting his lot with the convention. He never again made a serious bid for power. See Quirk, *Mexican Revolution*, 128–29, 144, 166–67, 175.

41. Canova to State Department, letter, November 12, 1914, in NA 812.00/13923.

42. Canova to State Department, November 16, 1914, *ibid.*/13866.

clared a rebel, Carothers, in businesslike fashion, informed Bryan that he had designated Canova to remain with Provisional President Gutiérrez, while he accompanied Villa and the Conventionist armies. In the process, he would see to the protection of foreign lives and property.[43]

Among the American agents, Carothers remained the main target of *Carrancista* rancor. Even before the convention disowned the First Chief, the Constitutionalist agents in the United States issued a press release declaring that Carothers' efforts had always been designed to undercut Carranza's authority and elevate Villa to power.[44] Commenting satirically on these *Carrancista* outbursts, the New York *Herald* suggested in an editorial, entitled "Venustiano Makes His Will," that the First Chief offer as an epitaph to his political demise: "Here lies Venustiano Carranza who died of a State Department agent." [45]

After Carranza broke with the convention, the Constitutionalist daily, *El Pueblo*, attacked Carothers repeatedly. He was particularly condemned in a November 12 editorial for having gone to Washington to plead Villa's case to Wilson and Bryan (the editorial failed to mention that Silliman had just returned from a similar mission in Carranza's behalf). Branding Carothers "an active agent of discord" and a "propagandist of rebellion," the editorial demanded his recall.[46] During the remainder of his service in Mexico, Carothers was a favorite target of the *Carrancista* press, the most persistent charges being that Villa had given him lucrative concessions and that he sought to prolong the civil war in order to protect his profits.[47]

43. Cobb (for Carothers) to State Department, November 4, 8, 11, 17, 18, 19, 20, 1914, *ibid.*/13692, 13714, 13745, 13807, 13814, 13833, 13838.
44. New York *Times*, October 19, 1914, p. 4.
45. New York *Herald*, December 21, 1914.
46. "Carothers," *El Pueblo*, November 12, 1914, p. 3.
47. *El Pueblo*, January 9, March 8, April 3, 1915; *El Demócrata*, September 8, 9, October 24, 28, 1915.

Only incidently did the *Carrancistas* criticize Canova. They accused him of allying with Carothers to present a far too optimistic view of the proceedings at Aguascalientes.[48] On the other hand, press comments concerning special agent Silliman were uniformly complimentary. On November 5 *El Pueblo* made it clear that Silliman did not share the views of the other agents in Mexico. Even during the negotiations for the evacuation of Vera Cruz, when Silliman was supposedly dictating Wilson's terms, the Mexico City press depicted him as a fair-minded diplomat.[49]

As Villa mounted his campaign on Mexico City, the *Carrancista* generals made agonizing decisions. The Conventionist armies were larger and better equipped. Yet the near assassination of Obregón revealed that an alliance with Villa could be hazardous. Obregón was the key figure. He had exercised great influence at the convention and had worked diligently for compromise. He had even been willing to support Gutiérrez until the provisional president turned Conventionist forces over to Villa. Choosing between the lesser of two evils, Obregón sided with Carranza. González preceded him, and their decisions swayed others. Without their support, Carranza would have been no match for the Conventionists. As it turned out, he was a formidable foe.[50]

At the outset of the fighting, the First Chief's situation was precarious to say the least. His forces hemmed in at Córdoba and Puebla, he had no access to the North nor to the nearby port of Vera Cruz. Since mid-October he had remained immovable in his refusal to disavow punitive measures against the people of Vera Cruz. After his break with the convention, prudence dictated that he give in to Wilson's demands. On November 9 he issued a proclamation of

48. *El Pueblo*, October 26, November 4, 1914; New York *World*, November 20, 1914.
49. *El Pueblo*, October 20, 30, November 5, 1914; *El Sol*, November 12, 23, 30, 1914.
50. Quirk, *Mexican Revolution*, 123–26.

amnesty for all Mexicans who had served the American government in the port city. The next day Fabela notified the Brazilian minister that the Constitutionalists would levy no additional import duties in cases where they had already been paid.[51] Villa, meanwhile, sent word to Washington through Carothers that the port should be turned over to authorities designated by Gutiérrez.[52] Holding the port for the Conventionists was fraught with danger, because the Constitutionalists now looked upon the possession of the city as necessary to their very survival. The possibility of clashes between American and Constitutionalist troops, therefore, seemed a distinct possibility.

True to his recently adopted policy of nonentanglement, Wilson, on November 13, directed Bryan to send word to the Brazilian minister, Carothers, and Canova, who, in turn, were to notify Carranza, Villa, and Gutiérrez that the United States would begin evacuating her troops from Vera Cruz in ten days. No authorities were designated to receive the port. Nothing more than an official notice of evacuation was given. Orders were sent to General Funston that he was to make no arrangements with representatives of any faction.[53] By early afternoon of November 23, the last troops had embarked, and shortly thereafter General Aguilar, who was waiting nearby, occupied the city in the name of the Constitutionalists. Carranza's possession of Vera Cruz proved a decisive factor in his war against the Conventionists. The city became the seat of his provisional government and the port proved invaluable as an access to outside sources of supply.[54]

51. Silliman to State Department, November 9, 1914, in *Foreign Relations, 1914*, 618; Cardoso de Oliveira to State Department, November 10, 1914, *ibid.*, 618–20.
52. Cobb (for Carothers) to State Department, November 10, 1914, in NA 812.00/13734.
53. Wilson to Bryan, November 13, 1914, *ibid.*/13766; State Department to Cardoso de Oliveira, Carothers, Canova, and various United States embassies, November 13, 1914, in *Foreign Relations, 1914*, 621–22; War Department to Funston, November 20, 1914, *ibid.*, 625.
54. Quirk, *Affair of Honor*, 169–70.

With Villa driving relentlessly toward Mexico City, Carranza ordered his remaining troops evacuated on November 19. Silliman and Cardoso de Oliveira reported widespread terror among the populace, as the Constitutionalists looted the city before departing. They took all automobiles, horses, and other items that could be utilized by the army. Causing even greater alarm was the prospect of a Hun-like descent upon the city by the Conventionists. Rumor spread that Villa and Zapata had promised their troops two hours of unrestricted looting upon entering the capital. Although Silliman and Cardoso de Oliveira suspected the Constitutionalists of spreading the rumor in order to discredit their opponents, Acting Secretary of State Lansing directed Carothers to look into the matter. The special agent replied promptly that Villa had issued orders to the effect that anyone caught looting or molesting civilians would be executed on the spot. Carothers further revealed that Villa was maintaining excellent order in the cities and towns he occupied.[55]

On November 20 *Carrancista* officials invited the diplomatic corps to follow the retreating armies to Puebla; otherwise, the Constitutionalists would accept no responsibility for their safety. Realizing that such a move would imply at least moral support of Carranza, the diplomatic corps unanimously declined the invitation.[56] Although admitting that he had "been able to accomplish very little with Carranza," Silliman, nonetheless, believed that he should rejoin the First Chief. The Brazilian minister, anticipating an increase in his activities with the arrival of the Conventionists, recommended to Washington that the special agent be

55. Silliman to State Department, November 19, 20, 21, 1914, in NA 812.00/13829, 13832, 13844, 13848, 13854; Cardoso de Oliveira to State Department, November 20, 21, 1914, *ibid.*/13845, 13863; State Department to Carothers, November 21, 1914, *ibid.*/13845; Cobb (for Carothers) to State Department, November 21, 25, 1914, *ibid.*/13856, 13906.

56. Cardoso de Oliveira to State Department, November 20, 1914, *ibid.*/13848.

retained in Mexico City to lend assistance to the Brazilian legation. Considering all of Cardoso de Oliveira's work in behalf of the United States, Bryan was pleased to partially repay the minister for his efforts by directing Silliman to remain in Mexico City.[57]

On the evening of November 24, the *Zapatistas* began occupying the capital. Contrary to expectations, they were more timid than fearsome. Allene Tupper Wilkes, daughter of Dr. Henry Allen Tupper of the International Peace Forum, who was present at the time, wrote that the soldiers from the South, instead of looting, went quietly from door to door begging for food. There were only a few incidents of violence.[58] Zapata himself arrived in the capital on November 26. Ever wary, he remained near the railway station and refused to attend ceremonies held in his honor at the National Palace. Silliman personally called upon the revolutionary chieftain and thanked him for the peaceful conditions enjoyed by the city's inhabitants. Zapata was most cordial, and prospects for friendly relations seemed good. But on November 28, as Villa's armies approached, Zapata again disappeared into his mountain retreat.[59]

Bryan was cheered by the recent events in Mexico City. "The situation seems to be clearing up," he wrote to the

57. Canada (for Silliman) to State Department, November 24, 1914, *ibid.*/13886; Cardoso de Oliveira to State Department, November 25, 1914, and State Department to Cardoso de Oliveira, November 27, 1914, in NA 125.8273/131.

58. Canada (for Silliman) to State Department, November 24, 1914, in NA 812.00/13888; Silliman to State Department, November 25, 30, 1914, *ibid.*/13896, 13939; Cardoso de Oliveira to State Department, November 25, 27, 1914, *ibid.*/13898, 13919; Allene Tupper Wilkes, "The Gentle Zapatistas," *Harper's Weekly*, LX (January 16, 1915), 56–57; New York *Times*, November 25, 1914, p. 1; Ramírez Plancarte, *La Ciudad de México*, 255–56.

59. Silliman to State Department, November 30, 1914, in NA 812.00/13939; Cardoso de Oliveira to State Department, November 29, 1914, in *Foreign Relations, 1914*, 627; *El Pueblo* (Vera Cruz), December 3, 1914. The staff of *El Pueblo* evacuated Mexico City along with the *Carrancista* forces and reestablished themselves in Vera Cruz as the principal organ of the Constitutionalist faction.

president. Assuming that the Conventionists would make short work of Carranza and that Gutiérrez's government would soon be the power to reckon with, Bryan recommended that a note be sent to the provisional president offering congratulations and restating the position of the United States on the matters of protecting foreign interests and the granting of amnesty to political enemies. Wilson refused to be drawn into even the slightest association with the Conventionists. He told Bryan that such a note should be sent only "through some person known to be *persona grata* to those now in charge of affairs in Mexico City and who can convey it confidentially and unofficially." [60] Gutiérrez received no encouragement from Washington.

By December 1 Villa was in the suburbs of Mexico City. There Carothers, who accompanied Villa, and Canova, who accompanied Gutiérrez and the Permanent Commission chosen by the convention, were reunited. The two American agents entered the city ahead of the armies. Establishing liaison with Cardoso de Oliveira and Silliman, they all agreed that each agent should have a specific sphere of authority. Carothers was to handle matters involving Villa, while Canova was to continue making representations to Gutiérrez and the Permanent Commission of the convention. Cardoso de Oliveira was to be informed of and accede to all important decisions. When Gutiérrez chose a foreign minister, Cardoso de Oliveira would conduct official relations between Washington and the convention. Silliman was to remain at the disposal of the Brazilian legation.[61]

These matters having been decided, Carothers and Canova were presented to the diplomatic corps at a reception given

60. Bryan to Wilson, December 2, 1914, and Wilson to Bryan, December 3, 1914, in Bryan-Wilson Correspondence.

61. Cardoso de Oliveira to State Department, December 1, 1914, NA 125.36582/114; Cobb (for Carothers) to State Department, December 5, 1914, in NA 812.00/13965; Canova to State Department, December 8, 1914, *ibid.*/14048.

by Minister Cardoso de Oliveira. The diplomats were unanimous in their concern for continued peace in the capital. The currently quiet conditions had not overcome Villa and Zapata's bloodthirsty reputations. The ministers complained that there were still rumors current that Villa and Zapata planned murder, pillage, and rape upon entering the city in force. The two American agents assured the diplomats that their fears were unfounded, but added that they would again appeal to the two generals for renewed guarantees of clemency.[62]

The next day Carothers went on a mission for Villa, an action that was more characteristic of his past activities. He joined Roque González Garza, who also represented Villa, and two *Zapatistas* who had accompanied Villa from Aguascalientes, in journeying to Cuernavaca. Their purpose was to draw Zapata out of his stronghold. Until now Villa had not coordinated his military effort with Zapata's. As a result, the chieftain of the South had become wary of Villa. He feared that the Conventionists might occupy Mexico City as Carranza had in August and completely ignore the interests of the people of the South. Carothers and González Garza hoped to dispel those fears. After being cordially received, they presented Zapata with a letter from Villa and attempted to persuade him that he would be safe in Mexico City. Zapata told Carothers that Villa alone, among the revolutionary leaders, had ever commanded his slightest confidence. Still he refused to leave his sanctuary altogether. He would agree only to hold a preliminary conference with Villa in Xochimilco at the edge of his domain.[63]

Canova, meanwhile, accompanied Gutiérrez and Villa into Mexico City. They entered with no fanfare, and few people

62. *Ibid.*; Testimony of Carothers, *Senate Documents*, 66th Cong. 2nd Sess., No. 285, p. 1775.
63. Cobb (for Carothers) to State Department, December 6, 1914, in NA 812.00/13966; Carothers to State Department, December 16, 1914, *ibid.*/14061; *El Monitor* (Mexico City), December 6, 1914; El Paso *Morning Times*, December 8, 1914.

even knew that Villa was present. This was as Villa wanted it. He did not want to alienate Zapata by giving the slightest appearance of occupying the city. He remained only to attend the ceremony establishing Guitiérrez and the Permanent Commission in the National Palace, then he retired to Tacuba.[64]

On December 4 both Carothers and Canova took part in one of the most dramatic and picturesque events of the entire revolution, the first meeting of Pancho Villa and Emiliano Zapata. In a borrowed automobile, the two agents motored out to Xochimilco. Upon arriving they found no activity. Fearful that the conference had been abandoned, they sped back toward Mexico City. While en route, they came upon Villa and his party leisurely trotting along on horseback, taking in the scenery as they went. When they returned to the city of the floating gardens at midday, a great throng had gathered to see the two already legendary leaders. Zapata greeted Villa warmly. He was deeply appreciative that Villa had ventured into *Zapatista* territory. The Centaur of the North accepted him as an equal, quite a change from the treatment Zapata had received from Carranza.[65]

The two Americans joined in a conference held in the municipal school building. Canova reported that, at first, Villa and Zapata "sat in an embarrassed silence, occasionally broken by some insignificant remark, like two country sweethearts." Finally, someone called Carranza an old *"cabron."* The ice broken, the room erupted with profanity. Canova captured the color of the meeting. His characterizations are well worth quoting in length. Pointing out the distinct contrast between the two chieftains, the special agent noted:

> General Villa, tall, robust, weighing about 180 pounds, with a complexion almost as florid as a German, was wearing an English

64. Cobb (for Canova) to State Department, December 7, 8, 1914, in NA 812.00/13974, 14048; *El Monitor*, December 4, 1914.

65. Canova to State Department, December 8, 1914, in NA 812.00/14048; *El Monitor*, December 5, 1914; Womack, *Zapata*, 220; Edgcomb Pinchon, *Zapata the Unconquerable* (New York, 1941), 298–300.

(pith) helmet, a heavy brown sweater, khaki trousers, leggings and heavy riding shoes. Zapata to his left, with his immense sombrero shading his eyes so that they could not be seen, had dark complexion, thin face, a man much shorter in stature than Villa and weighing about 130 pounds. He wore a short black coat, a large blue silk neckerchief, pronounced lavender shirt and used alternately a white handkerchief with a green border and another with all the colors of the flowers. He had on a pair of black, tight-fitting Mexican trousers with silver buttons down the outside seam of each leg. . . . Sitting in the semi-circle as we were, and watching every play of his [Villa's] and Zapata's countenance, I could not but measure Villa as the highest type of warrior, a man of great energy and unbounded self-confidence. Zapata . . . seemed to be studying Villa all the time. . . . He is an idealist. One may say a dreamer, like the ill-fated José Martí of Cuba. . . . One wonders in looking at him where his qualities of a leader are hidden, but it seems to have been his honesty of purpose, his constancy to the interests of his people and his unfailing kindness to them, which have made him the great leader he is.[66]

After they had dined, the two leaders retired to an adjoining room for a private conference, at which time they agreed on future military campaigns against Carranza.[67] When Carothers considered that enough time had elapsed for an adequate exchange of expressions, he entered the room. With no current instructions from Washington to guide him, the special agent let his past experience be his guide. He told the revolutionary chieftains that "the world was watching their actions" and that "the peace of Mexico depended upon their joint cooperation." He also intimated that they could expect the continued friendship of the Wilson administration. The two generals, in turn, expressed their gratitude for the moral support accorded them by the United States. They

66. Canova to State Department, December 8, 1914, in NA 812.00/14048. The passage quoted above, plus other portions of Canova's report, are often quoted by scholars. For example, see Link, *Struggle for Neutrality*, 264; Quirk, *Mexican Revolution*, 135–36; Womack, *Zapata*, 220–21; Atkin, *Revolution! Mexico, 1910–1920*, 232–33.

67. "Pacto de Xochimilco," González Ramírez, *Planes políticos*, 113–21.

insisted that they expected no other form of assistance and would attempt to vindicate Wilson's faith in their previous efforts. They also revealed that their armies would enter Mexico City jointly on December 6 and pledged that it would be a peaceful occupation. The American agents were relieved. Ever optimistic, Canova reported to Bryan that the union affected at Xochimilco offered "great promise for the early establishment of peace in Mexico." [68] Receiving an Associated Press account of the Xochimilco conference even before the reports of his agents, Bryan was equally optimistic. He again proclaimed to President Wilson that the end of their troubles in Mexico seemed to be in sight.[69]

At first Bryan's optimism seemed justified. On December 6, Villa and Zapata, side by side at the head of their unified armies, made their triumphal entry into the capital. Neither Carothers, who had worked to promote the union, nor Canova, who had so ably described the chieftains' first encounter, witnessed the colorful procession. Both were ill, Carothers delirious with fever from a severe case of tonsillitis, Canova with a bad cold. The historian could well use the account of the entry which might have come from Canova's pen. Fortunately, photographers caught the scenes for posterity.[70] From accounts of the entry that reached them, the two agents were able to determine that it was entirely peaceful. When Carothers was well enough, he made an investigation and found that the populace of the city was welcoming the Conventionist armies with open arms.[71]

68. Canova to State Department, December 8, 1914, in NA 812.00/14048; Carothers to State Department, December 16, 1914, *ibid.*/14061.
69. Bryan to Wilson, December 7, 1914, in Wilson Papers, Ser. 2, Box 69.
70. Cardoso de Oliveira to State Department, December 9, 1914, in NA 125.36582/116; Cobb (for Carothers), December 15, 1914, in NA 812.00/14017; Casasola, *Historia gráfica*, II, 940–48. Canova did prepare a brief account of the entry which he reconstructed secondhand; see Canova to State Department, December 8, 1914, in NA 812.00/14048.
71. Carothers to State Department, December 16, 1914, in NA 812.00/14061.

On December 10 Villa sent word to Carothers that he was leaving for the North. Still quite ill, Carothers struggled to his railcar and made the journey. As they traveled northward, Villa informed the special agent of his and Zapata's plans for the defeat of Carranza. The Conventionist forces were to be divided into three armies: one under Cabral, to clean up Sonora; one under Zapata, to take Puebla and Vera Cruz; and his own, to conquer all northeastern Mexico, including Monterrey, Saltillo, Tampico, and Matamoros. The months of riding in a converted boxcar had taken their toll of Carothers' health. On the advice of his physician, he requested a two-week leave of absence. In doing so, he assured Bryan that "nothing of importance" would happen before January 1.[72]

Carothers was allowed no respite. Upon his arrival in El Paso, he was directed to proceed to Naco on the Sonora-Arizona border and attempt to end the strife that had raged there since September.[73] During the months in which Governor Maytorena had beseiged General Hill in the small border town, a number of Americans had been killed or wounded by stray bullets that crossed the border. The War Department, meanwhile, sent some five thousand troops under the command of General Tasker H. Bliss to watch over the troubled area.[74] On December 9 Bryan addressed identical notes to Carranza and Gutiérrez, warning that unless the firing across the border ceased, the U. S. Army would "take such steps as may be necessary to protect American lives." [75] Gutiérrez immediately wired Maytorena to do everything possible, including the suspension of hostilities, if necessary,

72. *Ibid.*; Carothers to State Department, December 16, 1914, in NA 125.36582/117.
73. Carothers to State Department, December 17, 1914, in NA 812.00/14030. No copy of orders to Carothers was found, only his acknowledgement of receipt of the orders.
74. Clendenen, *United States and Pancho Villa*, 141–42.
75. State Department to Canada and Silliman, December 9, 1914, in *Foreign Relations, 1914*, 649.

to prevent further firing across the border. In characteristic fashion, Carranza denied any responsibility. He claimed that the *Carrancista* troops, with their backs to the border, were not firing at the United States. He also denied that there was any justification for United States involvement in the Naco affair.[76]

Carothers' job, then, was to secure a cease-fire agreement from the local commanders. The special agent conferred at length with Maytorena on December 18. Maytorena, anxious to avoid a clash with American troops, suggested that he withdraw his forces five or ten miles inland from Naco and that the port of Naco, Arizona, be closed to General Hill. Without access to supplies from across the border, Maytorena revealed, the *Carrancistas* would be forced to evacuate the town. With Hill being forced inland for supplies, the fighting between the two forces would take place away from the border. Since General Tasker H. Bliss endorsed this move, Carothers recommended that the port of Naco be closed.[77] Bryan also endorsed Carothers' suggestion. Although Wilson expressed sympathy for such a policy, he wrote to Bryan that he was not certain that he had the legal right to close the port on such a pretext.[78] Whereas months before he would have cast aside such legal subtleties, he now insisted upon consulting the law before taking action.

While Bryan looked into the legality of the matter, General Hugh L. Scott, who had also been ordered to the border to aid in arranging a cease-fire, joined Carothers, and on December 24, they announced that they had negotiated a satisfactory settlement. *Carrancista* generals Hill and Calles,

76. Silliman to State Department (conveying copy of Gutiérrez to Maytorena, December 10, 1914), December 10, 1914, *ibid.*, 649–50; Zubarán Capmany to State Department, December 12, 1914, *ibid.*, 650–51; Canada to State Department, December 13, 1914, in NA 812.00/13997.

77. Carothers to State Department, December 19, 1914, in *Foreign Relations, 1914*, 652–53; El Paso *Morning Times*, December 19, 1914.

78. Bryan to Wilson, December 21, 1914, and Wilson to Bryan, December 23, 1914, in Bryan-Wilson Correspondence.

as well as the First Chief's personal representative, Roberto V. Pesqueira, signed the agreement, but Maytorena refused, claiming that he first had to have orders from Provisional President Gutiérrez. Both Gutiérrez and Villa signified their acceptance of the arrangement, but Maytorena still hedged. Through Felix Sommerfeld, one of Villa's commercial agents on the border, Scott even secured a special order from Villa, directing Maytorena to evacuate the border town. On December 26 Maytorena began withdrawing his forces, but he either could not control his Yaqui Indian troops or only started the evacuation as a ruse. When some of Hill's troops moved out into the open, their opponents opened fire. By December 30 the seige was on again in earnest.[79]

On January 2 Villa announced that he would settle the matter once and for all. Through Sommerfeld he notified Scott and Carothers that eight thousand troops were on their way to Naco and, if allowed eight hours of fighting, they would take the border town. The two American negotiators vetoed this scheme because it would inevitably mean more shooting across the border. Finally, at their urging, Villa agreed to come to the border and help negotiate a cease-fire.[80]

Villa was again in Mexico City when he agreed to aid Scott and Carothers. During his brief absence, conditions in the capital had changed drastically. Zapata had also vacated the city to begin preparations for his campaign on Puebla. They had left the city in the hands of their more ruthless henchmen, who began a wholesale liquidation of political enemies. On December 14 Canova reported that as many as

79. Scott to War Department, December 24, 1914, in NA 812.00/14100; Scott to Mrs. Scott, December 26, 27, 1914, in Scott Papers, Box 4; Scott to Mrs. Scott, January 1, 1915, *ibid.*, Box 5; Enrique Llorente (confidential agent of the provisional government of Mexico) to State Department, December 26, 1914, in *Foreign Relations, 1914*, 654.

80. Scott to Mrs. Scott, January 1, 1915, in Scott Papers, Box 5; Happer (for Scott) to Carothers, January 3, 1915, *ibid.*, Box 16; Carothers to State Department, January 3, 1915, in NA 812.00/14128.

150 had already been executed.[81] Conveniently, neither Villa nor Zapata were on hand to bear the onus for the killings. When, at Bryan's request, Silliman urged Gutiérrez to halt the reign of terror, the provisional president replied that he had not ordered any executions, that the *Villistas* and the *Zapatistas* had not consulted him in the matter.[82] And it was obvious that he could do nothing to prevent more killings.

The purge was only one of several incidents which made Gutiérrez realize that Villa and Zapata intended to do as they pleased. Even though he was the convention's chief executive, Gutiérrez had no army of his own, no means of compelling them to submit to his will. Seeking an escape from his dilemma, Gutiérrez renewed communication with Obregón, González, and other Constitutionalist generals. He urged them to join him in organizing another convention in San Luis Potosí, which would eliminate Villa, Zapata, and Carranza. Since he was not at all secretive about his plans, Villa got wind of them in Guadalajara, where he was planning a campaign into Jalisco. Returning to the capital, he at first put Gutiérrez under close surveillance, then quarreled violently with him, and ultimately placed him under house arrest. As usual, Villa's rage did not last long. With the intercession of General José I. Robles, he and Gutiérrez were apparently reconciled.[83]

Having set things in order in Mexico City, Villa joined Scott and Carothers in Juárez on January 8, 1915. He had a friendly chat with the two Americans that evening on the international bridge between El Paso and Juárez. The next

81. Silliman to State Department, December 12, 1914, in NA 812.00/13999; Canova to State Department, December 14, 15, 1914, *ibid.*/14008, 14018.
82. Bryan to Silliman, December 13, 1914, in *Foreign Relations, 1914*, 628–29; Silliman to State Department, December 15, 1914, in NA 812.00/14019.
83. Silliman to State Department, December 23, 26, 29, 30, 31, 1914, in *Foreign Relations, 1914*, 634–35; Silliman to State Department, December 22, 28, 1914, in NA 812.00/14070, 14095.

day, at a formal conference held in El Paso, Villa again asked for permission to make massive assaults on Naco and Agua Prieta, after first giving American citizens an opportunity to withdraw a safe distance away. When Scott replied that he could not accede to such a proposal, Villa insisted that the United States was being unreasonable. Carothers and Scott held fast and their perserverance paid off. Later that day, Villa agreed to order Maytorena to sign the agreement made in December. All parties were to evacuate Naco. The *Carrancistas* were allowed to occupy Agua Prieta, nearby to the East. Maytorena might occupy Nogales, on the border west of Naco. Neither side was to attack the other in its border bastion. On January 11 Scott and Carothers brought together Maytorena and General Calles, who had replaced Hill, to sign the formal agreement. The evacuation of Naco began shortly thereafter.[84]

Whatever Wilson's motives, his noninvolvement policy had done nothing to diminish Villa's ascendency. However coarse Villa's methods, he had proved his resourcefulness and his continued willingness to cooperate with American officials. If Wilson's policy was designed to give Villa a chance to prove himself, the Chihuahua strong man certainly presented a facade of success. But many Mexicans, some who had trusted and supported him, were beginning to look beneath the veneer and abhor what they saw. The seeds of discord, sown by his high-handed methods in Mexico City, were already bearing bitter fruit. Although he appeared to be at his zenith—a position he had gained with the help of the United States—his power was already declining.

84. Scott to Mrs. Scott, January 9, 11, 1915, in Scott Papers, Box 5; Carothers to State Department, January 9, 1914, U.S. Department of State, *Papers Relating to the Foreign Relations of the United States, 1915* (Washington, D.C., 1924), 789; Agreement of January 11, 1915, between Governor Maytorena and General Calles, *ibid.*, 789–90; Testimony of Carothers, *Senate Documents*, 66th Cong., 2nd Sess., No. 285, p. 1776; El Paso *Morning Times*, January 9, 10, 1915; Scott, *Some Memories of a Soldier*, 505–13.

CHAPTER XI

A Steady
Disintegration

In his Jackson Day address delivered at Indianapolis on
January 8, 1915, Wilson reaffirmed his policy of noninvolvement in Mexico. In terms that would later give so much hope
to millions in Europe, he proclaimed: "I hold it is a fundamen-
tal principle . . . that every people has the right to determine
its own form of government." Insisting that the revolutionaries in Mexico were slowly working toward that end, he
further declared: "And so far as my influence goes, while I
am President nobody shall interfere with them." [1] Wilson
probably meant each of these words when he spoke them. At
the time, however, conditions in Mexico seemed to be vindica-
ting his noninvolvement policy. Within a very short time,
conditions deteriorated and the president's policy was repeatedly put to the test.

The special agents were inextricably involved in the events
that marked this deterioration. The system of diplomatic
representation in Mexico caused the administration numerous
difficulties during the early months of 1915. Only in George
Carothers did the State Department have an agent who
carried on effective relations with a Mexican leader. Carothers understood Villa's moods. He knew when best to confront
the general directly and when to use the services of influential intermediaries, such as General Scott and certain Villa
subordinates. The total result was that Villa continued to

1. New York *Times*, January 9, 1915, p. 4.

express a willingness to cooperate with the Wilson administration.

Villa did cause anxious moments. However strong he appeared to be during the early months of 1915, he was operating at a disadvantage. The Constitutionalists commanded greater financial resources because they controlled the ports of Vera Cruz and Tampico, along with the oil fields surrounding the latter. Villa depended solely on income from the sale of confiscated goods and taxes, particularly those on mining properties. As the civil war intensified, the number of depredatory incidents in northern Mexico involving foreigners increased. Repeatedly the State Department called upon Carothers to make representations in their behalf, and Villa usually responded favorably.[2]

The civil war, by causing many of the mines to close, ultimately cut off such a share of income that Villa was forced to take drastic steps. On March 19 he decreed that all mining property abandoned in northern Mexico, if not reclaimed and put into operation within four months, would be confiscated. Those mine operators whose taxes were in arrears were given ninety days to pay in full.[3] With the foreign-owned mining industry up in arms over the decree, Bryan directed Carothers to remind Villa that many of the mines had been abandoned, and the miners forced to flee, because of the dangers presented by the civil war. Easing fears slightly, Villa revealed that the decree was not designed to pressure legitimate mine operators. He told Carothers that it was meant to prevent speculators from taking advantage

2. Carothers to State Department, January 2, 7, March 18, 1915, in NA 812.00/14130, 14160, 14731; Cobb (for Carothers), March 18, 1915, *ibid.*/14626; State Department to Carothers, February 5, 1915, in NA 125.1236/22; Cobb (for Carothers) to State Department, February 12, 1915, *ibid.*/25. For representative cases involving forced loans levied against foreigners and satisfactory settlements of these problems, see *Foreign Relations, 1915*, 983–96.

3. Mining decree issued by Francisco Villa at Monterrey, March 19, 1915, *ibid.*, 894–95.

of the war by purchasing abandoned mines at a fraction of their values and later attempting to sell them to Mexican investors at an undeserved profit. When this reply did not satisfy Bryan, Carothers again pressed for repeal of the decree. Villa ultimately capitulated. He told the American agent that the decree would not be enforced until he could guarantee tranquility in northern Mexico and adequate rail facilities to service the mines. Villa also assured Carothers that he would not allow the decree to cause any international embarrassments for the United States.[4]

The other agents did not enjoy such success. John Silliman, who was never very effective in his relations with Carranza, was no longer even attached to the First Chief's headquarters. He remained in Mexico City, assisting the Brazilian minister. Cool and calculating, Leon Canova had revealed a pragmatic ability to deal effectively with all factions. However, the administration forfeited Canova's potential influence with members of the convention by involving him in attempts to save the lives of the Mexicans being purged by the *Villistas* and *Zapatistas*. Bryan directed Canova and Silliman to appeal for the lives of all political prisoners, but the secretary of state was most interested in the plight of Eduardo Iturbide. It may be recalled that Iturbide, as governor of the Federal District, had arranged the transfer of Mexico City into the hands of the Constitutionalists following the fall of Huerta. At the urging of the diplomatic corps, he again assumed control of the city after the *Carrancistas* evacuated in late November. In both instances he had done much to maintain order and had earned the gratitude of the foreign colony. Upon entering the city, the *Zapatistas* showed no gratitude for his efforts. Instead, they charged him with crimes against the peasant population of Morelos, including the execution of some laborers on his

4. State Department to Carothers, April 7, 15, 1915, *ibid.*, 895–96, 899; Carothers to State Department, April 12, 16, 1915, *ibid.*, 899, 901.

hacienda and the impressment of many others into Huerta's army.[5]

Canova was not immediately involved. In fact, Iturbide took refuge in the home of a British subject, H. A. Cunard Cummins, where Carothers was also staying. Presenting Carothers with a testimonial signed by several members of the diplomatic corps, the British chargé d'affaires, Thomas B. Hohler, urged the special agent to intercede in Iturbide's behalf. Luckily, Carothers was never implicated in the affair. Shortly after Iturbide applied for asylum, the American agent left the city with Villa.[6] Bryan then directed Silliman to "do everything in your power to save Iturbide."[7] Bryan's determination to protect Iturbide was predicated, no doubt, by reports from Cardoso de Oliveira and Silliman to the effect that the charges against the former Mexican official were not valid and that he was being persecuted for political reasons.[8]

Interpreting his instructions liberally, Silliman, along with Cardoso de Oliveira and Hohler, first planned to send Iturbide to Vera Cruz in the company of John W. Belt, Silliman's assistant, who had recently been granted a leave. This plan was foiled when Cardoso de Oliveira and Silliman took Conventionist Secretary of War José I. Robles into their confidence and asked that Iturbide be granted a *salvo conducto* (safe-conduct passport). Sympathetic, but not willing to risk involvement, Robles refused.[9] Assuming that

5. State Department to Silliman, December 8, 1914, in NA 312.12/94a; Silliman to State Department, December 14, 1914, in NA 812.00/14010; El Paso *Morning Times*, December 23, 1914; New York *World*, December 24, 1914.

6. Cardoso de Oliveira to State Department, December 9, 1914, in NA 312.12/95; Carothers to State Department, December 26, 1914, *ibid.*/164.

7. State Department to Silliman, December 13, 1914, in *Foreign Relations, 1914*, 628–29.

8. Cardoso de Oliveira to State Department, December 9, 1914, in NA 312.12/95; Silliman to State Department, December 16, 1914, *ibid.*/100.

9. Silliman to State Department, December 9, 1914, and State Department to Silliman, December 11, 1914, in NA 125.8273/136; Silliman to State Department, December 16, 1914, in NA 312.12/100, 104; Canova to State Department, December 16, 1914, in NA 812.00/14097.

Silliman, who was not attached to any faction, was the one to
conduct the unfortunate Mexican to safety, Canova used his
influence with the Conventionists to secure *salvos conductos*
for Silliman and an unnamed friend. According to Canova's
report of the incident, this plan fell through because Silliman
lacked the courage to carry it out.[10]

With Silliman faltering and Bryan appealing for someone
to help Iturbide, Minister Cardoso de Oliveira took matters in
hand. He asked Canova to escort Iturbide to the border.
Securing *salvos conductos* directly from Provisional President
Gutiérrez, who was sickened by the purge, Canova spirited
Iturbide aboard a northbound train early in the morning of
December 22. When the departure was delayed, Canova went
to inquire about the difficulty. There he came face to face
with General Villa. Covering his nervousness, the special
agent struck up a conversation. Villa asked Canova where he
was going. When the agent replied that he was going to the
border to get his wife, Villa insisted that, upon their return to
Mexico City, they should dine with him. Thus Canova left
Mexico City still on the best of terms with the Conventionist
leaders.[11]

Canova was no sooner out of the capital than the storm
broke. The day of his departure it was common knowledge
that he and Iturbide were on their way to El Paso. Silliman
blamed Canova's indiscreet relations with reporters for the
exposure, but Silliman was just as likely at fault. Unwilling
to approach the *Zapatistas* himself, he had asked a reporter

10. Silliman to State Department, December 19, 21, 1914, in NA
312.12/106, 108; Cardoso de Oliveira to State Department, December 22,
1914, *ibid.*/115; Canova to State Department, December 27, 1914, *ibid.*/131;
Canova to State Department, December 20, 1914, in NA 812.00/27415.
11. State Department to Silliman, December 17, 1914, in NA 312.12/103;
Cardoso de Oliveira to State Department, December 22, 1914, *ibid.*/115;
Silliman to State Department, December 22, 1914, *ibid.*/112; Canova to State
Department, December 20, 1914, in NA 812.00/27415; New York *Sun*,
December 28, 1914. Canova started his letter on December 20, but did not
complete it until December 23, as his train approached Zacatecas.

friend, John W. Roberts of the Hearst chain, to intercede in
Iturbide's behalf. Roberts, who often mingled with the
agents, was not always candid in his dealings with them. The
very day of Canova's departure, the reporter filed his story on
the escape. It was accurate in almost every detail.[12]

The *Zapatistas* were furious at Iturbide's escape. The most
vocal among them was Manuel Palafox, who served virtually
as Zapata's secretary of state, but who currently was the
Conventionist secretary of agriculture. Without consulting
Gutiérrez, he issued orders for Iturbide to be removed from
the northbound train and returned to stand trial. At the same
time, he issued a statement to the press condemning Silliman
and Canova and charging that each had received a 500,000
peso bribe from Iturbide. After consulting with Palafox,
Villa, too, sent an order for Iturbide's arrest.[13]

Canova's and Iturbide's experiences as they traveled
northward could scarcely have been more exciting had they
been described in a dime novel. Soldiers and secret police
repeatedly attempted to enter their compartment. Each time,
Canova feigned ignorance of Iturbide's whereabouts and
claimed diplomatic immunity to prevent entry. Claiming
further that upholding the dignity of his country prevented
him from submitting to a search, he warned of the dire

12. Silliman to State Department, December 21, 1914, in NA 312.12/108,
110; El Paso *Morning Times*, December 23, 1914. An intimate of Carothers,
Canova, and Silliman, Roberts witnessed and reported much of their activity.
In August, 1916, during the presidential election campaign, he tried to sell his
information to the Republican National Committee. If the committee chose
to attack the Wilson administration's Mexican policy, he claimed that he
could provide a great deal of information concerning the activities of the
special agents. See Roberts to G. R. Scrugham, August 29, 1916, in Albert B.
Fall Papers, microfilm copies, Zimmermann Library, University of New
Mexico, Reel no. 33.

13. Silliman to State Department, December 23, 1914, in NA 312.12/117;
Cardoso de Oliveira to State Department, December 24, 1914, *ibid.*/119, 120;
El Paso *Morning Times*, December 23, 25, 1914; New York *World*, December
24, 27, 1914. Silliman suspected Roberts of being responsible for the bribery
charge.

consequences that would result from forceful entry and maltreatment of a representative of the United States government. Thoroughly terror-stricken by the time the train approached Chihuahua, Iturbide decided to leave the coach and strike off on his own. When the train was again stopped just south of Chihuahua, Iturbide made his escape through a window under the cover of darkness, while Canova shouted warnings through the closed compartment door.[14]

When Canova was informed in Chihuahua that the car in which he was riding would be detached and left for repairs, the special agent made no protest and serenely exited his compartment. Astonished when they did not find Iturbide, the soldiers declared the car to be fit to continue the journey. After again lecturing the searchers on the necessity of upholding the dignity of his government, Canova continued on to Juárez in the same compartment. At Juárez reporters were also astonished to find that Iturbide was not accompanying Canova. The special agent gave the press a detailed account of his trip, emphasizing every indignity that he had endured but steadfastly denying that Iturbide had ever been with him.[15]

On December 29 the New York *Times* reported on good authority that Canova had, indeed, aided Iturbide's escape, and by January 2 it was known in El Paso that Iturbide had safely crossed the border near Presidio, Texas.[16] Villa knew

14. Canova to State Department, December 19, 20, 1914, in NA 812.00/27415, 27418; El Paso *Morning Times*, December 28, 1914; New York *Times*, December 28, 1914, p. 4.

15. Canova to State Department, December 28, 29, 30, 1914, in NA 812.00/27417, 27418, 27419; El Paso *Morning Times*, December 27, 1914; New York *World*, December 29, 1914. A more detailed account of Iturbide's escape may be found in Robert E. Quirk, "Cómo se salvó Eduardo Iturbide," *Historia Mexicana*, VI (Julio–Septiembre, 1956), 39–58.

16. New York *Times*, December 29, 1914, p. 1; El Paso *Morning Times*, January 2, 1915. Before leaving the train, Iturbide told Canova that he planned to hire a horse and guide and make for the border near Presidio. Canova learned that Iturbide crossed the border on December 31. Appearing incognito in El Paso shortly afterward, Iturbide took a train to the East

very well what had happened. At Gómez Palacio, during his perilous journey northward, Canova conferred with Carothers and asked him to plead with Villa by wire to uphold the *salvos conductos*. Incorrectly assuming that Villa would sustain his actions, Canova told Carothers to be completely candid with the general. Contrary to expectations, Villa did not uphold the *salvos conductos*. Instead he continued to condemn Canova's complicity in Iturbide's escape. At first, Carothers did not take Villa seriously. He reported to Bryan that Villa had probably condemned Canova in order to mollify the *Zapatistas*.[17] Even Canova did not take Villa seriously. He wrote to Bryan that he believed the episode would serve to enhance his reputation for bravery in Villa's eyes. Villa, he assumed, would applaud acts of gallantry regardless of what prompted them. "I really believe General Villa will chuckle over the whole matter," he concluded.[18]

Both agents were wrong. Villa continued to denounce Canova and demand his recall. He remained immovable even to explanations that the special agent had merely acted on orders from his superiors. Carothers made another appeal when the general came north to settle the problems at Naco. Villa softened his attitude somewhat in Carothers' presence, but suggested that feelings were running so strongly against Canova in Mexico City that, if he returned, embarrassing and potentially dangerous incidents might result. Although Canova still requested permission to return to his duties, Bryan directed him to come to Washington for reassignment.[19] Thus the department lost one of its agents in Mexico.

Coast of the United States. See Canova to State Department, January 1, 4, 1915, in NA 312.12/150, 157.

17. Carothers to State Department, December 26, 1914, January 8, 1915, *ibid.*/164, 174; Canova to State Department, December 29, 1914, in NA 812.00/27418.

18. Canova to State Department, December 30, 1914, NA 812.00/27419.

19. Cardoso de Oliveira to State Department, December 26, 1914, in NA 312.12/126, 127; Carothers to State Department, January 2, 8, 1915, *ibid.*/154, 174; State Department to Canova, January 4, 1915, *ibid.*/157; Canova to State Department, January 4, 1915, in NA 812.00/27420; El Paso *Morning Times*, January 6, 1915.

Minister Cardoso de Oliveira was disappointed at losing Canova's services, especially since he was the only one with influence among the Conventionists. "[I] have not enough words to emphasize his merits to you," he wrote to Bryan. Noting that he was personally responsible for the orders which directed Canova to aid Iturbide, Cardoso de Oliveira apologized to the secretary of state for having denied the department so valuable a representative. Carothers was similarly saddened by Canova's recall.[20] Bryan had no intention of allowing Canova's gallantry to go unrewarded. In February he recommended to the president that the former agent be given a clerical post in the Latin American Division of the State Department. In April Canova became assistant chief of the division; in July, the chief.[21] In that post, which he held until 1918, he continued to reveal an immense capacity for intrigue.

Denied Canova's services in Mexico, Bryan sought to vindicate him, as well as Silliman. He directed Cardoso de Oliveira to secure proof of the bribery charges or a complete retraction. Palafox, a tough, swarthy little revolutionary, at first refused to do either. Instead, he demanded that Silliman also be recalled. He claimed that the agent's association with Carranza made him an enemy of the revolution. Cardoso de Oliveira refused to be cowed. In a memorandum addressed to Zapata and Villa, instead of Palafox, he set forth the reasons why the United States and other foreign powers had wanted Iturbide's life spared. He included copies of Bryan's instructions on this score. As a result, Palafox made a partial

20. Cardoso de Oliveira to State Department, December 26, 1914, in NA 312.12/126; Carothers to State Department, January 8, 1915, *ibid.*/174.
21. Bryan to Wilson, Bryan Papers, Box 43; *Register of the Department of State, 1917*, 93. While serving as chief of the Division of Latin American Affairs, Canova earned the reputation in Mexico of being an interventionist. An undated memorandum in the Archivo de la Secretaría de Relaciones Exteriores in Mexico City, which outlines his career, reveals that Canova was anathema in Mexico City. See "Información cerca de Leon J. Canova," AGRE, L–E–849, Leg. 1.

retraction of the charges, claiming that they had been based on secondhand information.[22]

Bryan refused to accept the partial retraction. If there was no absolute proof, he wrote to Cardoso de Oliveira, then Palafox must admit the innocence of the two agents. Under pressure from other ministers in the Conventionist provisional government, Palafox made a full retraction.[23] Bryan's headstrong behavior may have vindicated Canova and Silliman, but it heightened *Zapatista* resentment against the United States. On January 15, the day after Palafox withdrew his allegations, several members of the Zapata delegation to the convention (which began meeting again in Mexico City on January 1) denounced President Wilson as a meddler who lacked true sympathy for the objectives of the Mexican revolution.[24]

This attack upon the president would have been less portentous had not the *Zapatistas* seemed so determined to speak for all the Conventionists. In December and January, the followers of Zapata steadfastly strove to increase their influence. It became increasingly apparent, also, that the Villa-Zapata union was more marriage of convenience than holy wedlock. The purge in Mexico City witnessed *Zapatistas*

22. Silliman to State Department, December 24, 1914, in NA 312.12/118; Cardoso de Oliveira to State Department, December 29, 1914, January 3, 1915, *ibid.*/145, 156; State Department to Cardoso de Oliveira, December 27, 1914, ibid./127; Bryan to Wilson, December 24, 1914, in Bryan Papers, Box 43; "A Resume of the Case of Eduardo N. Iturbide, respectfully submitted to the consideration of Generals Francisco Villa and Emiliano Zapata," [n.d.], AGRE, L–E–847, Leg. 10; copy in Cardoso de Oliveira to State Department, December 28, 1914, in NA 312.12/137.

23. State Department to Cardoso de Oliveira, January 4, 1915, *ibid.*/156; Silliman to State Department, January 13, 1915, *ibid.*/175; New York *Times*, January 14, 1915, p. 6. In making his retraction, Palafox sought to save face by claiming that he had been so busy at the time he signed the statement of charges that he had not been aware of the exact nature of the document.

24. Silliman to State Department, January 16, 1915, in NA 812.00/14223; New York *Times*, January 16, 1915, p. 4.

killing *Villistas* and vice versa. Canova reported from El Paso that a potential estrangement between Villa and Zapata was likely because the *Zapatistas* were determined to "hold a balance of power" in the convention. From Mexico City, Silliman also reported that Zapata's followers were determined to dominate the proceedings.[25]

If Wilson and Bryan paid any attention to the reports of H. L. Hall, they must have been aware of this tendency long before Canova and Silliman reported it. Hall, of course, had no official connection with the State Department. The *Zapatistas* at Aguascalientes had been curious enough to make inquiries to Canova concerning the Mormon's status. At the direction of the department, Canova had replied that Hall served in no official capacity, but that he had championed the *Zapatistas* during his stay in Washington and through his correspondence from Cuernavaca. This statement, plus the fact that Hall gave much of his time to volunteer service at the *Cruz Blanca* hospital in Cuernavaca, apparently satisfied them that he was acting in their interests.[26]

Cloistered in Cuernavaca, Hall faithfully reported the attitudes of the *Zapatistas*. His rambling letters revealed that they at first had little faith in the convention; but after achieving more success than expected at Aguascalientes, including acceptance of the principles of their Plan of Ayala, they grew increasingly determined to dominate the convention, hence the revolution. He did not attribute these ambitions to Zapata personally, but to others, such as Díaz Soto y Gama and Palafox. The *Zapatistas'* greatest virtue, he implied, was their inflexibility; they did not compromise their principles. On the other hand, they thought Villa too worldly, too willing to compromise, because he consorted with holdovers of the Madero regime. Assuming that wealth inevitably

25. Canova to State Department, December 30, 1914, in NA 812.00/14131; Silliman to State Department, December 31, 1914, *ibid.*/14115.
26. Cobb (for Canova) to State Department, November 4, 1915, and State Department to Cobb (for Canova), November 5, 1914, *ibid.*/13679.

corrupts, they suspected the *Villistas* because they commanded such an abundance of munitions and supplies. The meeting at Xochimilco and the joint entry into Mexico City, Hall revealed, had served to confirm the *Zapatistas'* suspicions. The *Villistas* adorned themselves in gaudy uniforms and cruised about in automobiles. Their ostentation smacked of past reactionary regimes. As Hall put it, their behavior compromised their revolutionary virtue.[27]

For his part, Villa distrusted Zapata because he had allowed so many former Federals to join his revolutionary army. Carothers reported Villa as saying that many of these former Federals should be tried as criminals rather than treated as allies.[28] Nor was Villa satisfied that Zapata was prosecuting the war against Carranza vigorously enough. After capturing Puebla in December, Zapata withdrew most of his forces to Morelos. Obregón had little trouble in retaking Puebla in early January. Nothing stood between him and Mexico City. Villa was infuriated. He was beginning to learn that Zapata's first concern was always the protection of Morelos. On the other hand, Zapata complained because Villa had not made good his pledges to supply arms and munitions.

Gutiérrez was disenchanted with both Villa and Zapata. In addition to their factional disputes, the *Villistas* and *Zapatistas* subjected the provisional president to constant harassment. After failing a second time to establish an accord with Obregón to eliminate Carranza, Villa and Zapata, Gutiérrez gathered some of his loyal followers on January 15 and fled the capital with most of the funds in the Conventionist treasury. The convention then chose Roque González Garza, the body's presiding officer, to exercise executive power, but did not grant him the title of provisional president.[29]

27. Hall to State Department, October 21, 26, November 3, 6, 8, 9, 13, 25, December 2, 3, 1914, *ibid.*/27424, 27436, 20609½.

28. Carothers to State Department, December 16, 1914, *ibid.*/14061.

29. Barragán Rodríguez, *Historia . . . de la Revolución Constitucionalista*, II, 176–77; Quirk, *Mexican Revolution*, 154, 165–75; Womack, *Zapata*,

From the Wilson administration's point of view, the disintegration of Conventionist unity underlined the inadequacies of its representation in Mexico. Only through Carothers did the State Department have satisfactory communications with a factional leader. Until Gutiérrez fled the capital, Silliman maintained close relations with the provisional president.[30] González Garza, angling for the support of the United States, also made overtures to Silliman.[31] H. L. Hall, perhaps seeking the position for himself, pointed out that Silliman was the wrong person to serve as special agent to the convention. The Mormon revealed that the *Zapatistas* looked upon Silliman as Carranza's spy and would have no dealings with him.[32] Even Carothers complained of Silliman's inadequacy in this respect. "I do not believe he [Silliman] will do the Government any good in his position in Mexico City," Carothers complained to Bryan, "because he is a coward and absolutely biased in his opinions. . . . The Government needs a man in Mexico City who is not afraid of the devil, and at the same time has sufficient tact." [33]

Hall also presented a potential problem. It may be recalled that, in response to his request for written credentials, Bryan sent a letter to Consul General Shanklin on October 22, reviewing Hall's activities in Washington and indicating that the State Department had allowed him to "unofficially"

222–23. Gutiérrez attempted to establish rump conventions in San Luis Potosí and Nuevo León before renouncing all claims to the provisional presidency and retiring to private life in June, 1915.

30. Silliman to State Department, January 9, 12, 13, 1915, in NA 812.00/14173, 14188, 14195. On the eve of his defection, Gutiérrez poured out his woes to Silliman and even hinted that he was negotiating with Obregón.

31. Silliman to State Department, January 23, 1915, in NA 812.00/14271.

32. Hall to State Department, December 10, 17, 20, 23, 27, 1914, in NA 812.00/20609½.

33. Carothers to State Department, January 8, 1915, in NA 125.36582/129. When Silliman received word from a State Department source that both Canova and Carothers were criticizing him, he demanded an opportunity to refute the charges. Bryan did not even reply to Silliman's request. Silliman to State Department, January 9, 1915, in NA 125.8273/144.

report on conditions in Cuernavaca. Hall did not receive this letter until he came to Mexico City with the *Zapatistas* in early December. Although it was not the letter of credentials he had hoped for, Hall accepted it as such and went about passing himself off as a special agent of the State Department.[34] For their part, the *Zapatistas* either accepted the letter as sufficient credentials or, more likely, recognized his true status and sought merely to use him as a funnel through which to pass propaganda to Washington.

The legitimate agents resented Hall's activities. Silliman and Canova thought that he might have influenced Palafox against them. Before departing Mexico City, Canova urged Cardoso de Oliveira to secure a note from Washington which would clarify Hall's status. Carothers felt that the *Zapatistas* should be informed of Hall's status in order to prevent a possibly serious misunderstanding that would produce strained relations between them and the United States.[35] Bryan did direct Chief Clerk Ben Davis, to whom Hall addressed all his correspondence, to again inform the misguided Mormon that he was not an official representative of the State Department and that he should cease representing himself as one. The letter, addressed on January 19, did not arrive until after Hall left Mexico City when the *Zapatistas* evacuated in late January.[36]

Hall returned to his volunteer work with the *Cruz Blanca* hospital in Cuernavaca. He also revived and expanded his plan to establish an agricultural colony in Morelos. His lengthy reports of conditions in Zapata's stronghold continued to flow into Washington. In describing the tumultuous

34. *El Sol*, December 14, 1914.

35. Silliman to State Department, December 24, 1914, in NA 312.12/118; Canova to State Department, December 27, 1914, *ibid.*/131; Carothers to State Department, January 8, 1915, in NA 125.36582/129.

36. Davis to Hall, January 19, 1915, in NA 812.00/20609½. Hall did not receive this letter until he returned to Mexico City nearly three months later. See Hall to State Department, April 5, 1915, *ibid.*/20609½.

sessions of the convention, which met in Cuernavaca from early February to mid-April, he invariably depicted Zapata's delegates as disinterested patriots. Villa's delegates, on the other hand, were pictured as obstructionist remnants of the Madero regime. If the *Zapatistas* sought to use Hall for propaganda purposes, they did not err in their choice of organs.[37]

Events of late January and early February further revealed the State Department's need for more adequate representation in Mexico. The news of Gutiérrez's defection caused the *Zapatista* garrison to bolt the capital; whereupon the convention accepted Zapata's invitation to hold its sessions in Cuernavaca. On January 28, within hours after the Conventionists' departure, Obregón again occupied Mexico City in the name of the Constitutionalists. Shortly thereafter Carranza proclaimed Vera Cruz the new capital of the republic. Mexico City was reduced to the status of capital of the newly created state, Valle de México. Having no means of effectively communicating with the convention in Cuernavaca, on February 5 Villa declared Chihuahua the capital of his regime. He too created a provisional government, but promised to disband it when the convention could effectively assume control of civil affairs in northern Mexico.[38]

Rapid changes in the fortunes of the revolutionary factions followed these events. Carranza realized that his personal reform ideas were not sufficient to satisfy his generals, especially those who had attended the Convention of Aguas-

37. Hall to State Department, February 9, 17, 18, 27, March 3, 7, 12, April 4, 7, 13, 1915, *ibid.*/20609½.

38. Silliman to State Department, January 27, 28, 29, 1915, in *Foreign Relations, 1915*, 648–49; Cardoso de Oliveira to State Department, February 6, 1915, *ibid.*, 649–50; Enrique Llorente, confidential agent of the provisional government of Mexico (convention) to State Department, February 5, 1915, *ibid.*, 650–51; Silliman to State Department, January 28, 1915, in NA 812.00/14303; Cobb (for Carothers) to State Department, February 6, 1915, *ibid.*/14362; New York *Times*, January 28, 29, 1915, p. 1; Quirk, *Mexican Revolution*, 178.

calientes. To solidify his support and gain more, Carranza, with Obregón's wise counsel, promulgated additions to his Plan of Guadalupe, including provisions for land redistribution, equalization of tax loads, dissolution of industrial monopolies, and electoral, judicial, and municipal government reforms. In return for pledges to enact laws beneficial to labor, Obregón persuaded the syndicalist *Casa del Obrero Mundial* to form military units called "Red Battalions" and enter the war against Villa. As a result of these promises, Carranza garnered thousands of new supporters.[39]

Obregón's defeat of the *Zapatistas* at Puebla and his reoccupation of Mexico City were the first signs to indicate that the Constitutionalists would not be easily defeated and that Mexico was in for its bloodiest months of civil war. As far as Washington was concerned, the most alarming aspect of the internecine warfare was the fact that Carranza and Obregón seemed determined to punish the city of Mexico. Much as if it had a mind of its own and was responsible, the city was to be razed for having previously been the seat of reactionary regimes and the protector of wealthy exploiters. Besides stripping public buildings of usable equipment, suppressing the newspapers, and declaring valueless all currency save that issued by the Constitutionalists after December 1, 1914, Obregón reserved all railroads for military use. Thus the city was denied an important means of acquiring the necessities of life. Just securing food became the paramount concern for most of the people. When the *Zapatistas* destroyed the waterworks and public sanitation became a grave problem, Obregón refused to repair the damage. Carranza, meanwhile, ignored pleas for relief from Silliman and Cardoso de Oliveira.[40]

39. "Adiciones al Plan de Guadalupe y decretos dictados conforme a las mismas," González Ramírez, *Planes políticos,* 158–64; Quirk, *Mexican Revolution,* 151–52; González Ramírez, *El Problema agrario,* 214–15; Edwin Lieuwen, *Mexican Militarism, 1910–1940: The Political Rise and Fall of the Revolutionary Army* (Albuquerque, 1968), 31, 59.

40. Cardoso de Oliveira to State Department, February 3, 1915, in *Foreign Relations, 1915,* 649; Cardoso de Oliveira to State Department,

For obvious reasons, Secretary of State Bryan gave considerable thought to increasing the number of agents in Mexico. The search for new agents began early in January following Canova's recall to Washington. It intensified when Carothers temporarily threatened to resign. Offered a large retainer by several business firms to act as their counselor, Carothers wrote to Bryan that he owed it to his family to accept such a lucrative offer. At first, he agreed to continue in the service of the department only until a replacement could be found. Bryan did not lack for candidates. He proposed several midwesterners, all "deserving Democrats," but President Wilson was not impressed with their qualifications. He would have liked to send Paul Fuller to Mexico City, but thought the assignment lacked prestige enough for the New Yorker. Wilson did suggest that Bryan consult Fuller in choosing new State Department agents, and the former presidential agent recommended two New York acquaintances.[41]

At the same time, Bryan urged Carothers to postpone his resignation. "Owing to [the] limited number of persons possessing requisite qualifications, namely loyalty to the Administration, having friendship of Villa, and knowledge of the Spanish language," the secretary explained, it would be very difficult to find an adequate replacement.[42] General

February 5, 1915, in NA 812.00/14353; Silliman to State Department, January 30, February 1, 2, 4, 5, 8, 9, 12, 13, 16, 1915, *ibid.*/14316, 14325, 14329, 14337, 14352, 14356, 14357, 14371, 14375, 14385, 14387, 14402; Ramírez Plancarte, *La Ciudad de México*, 324–36.

41. Bryan to Wilson, January 6, 22, 1915, in Bryan-Wilson Correspondence; Bryan to Wilson, January 12, 1915, in Wilson Papers, Ser. 2, Box 124; Wilson to Bryan, January 14, 1915, *ibid.;* Bryan to Fuller, January 27, 1915, in Bryan Papers, Box 30; Carothers to State Department, January 7, 8, 1915, in NA 125.36582/121, 129; State Department to Carothers, January 7, 1915, *ibid.*/121; New York *Times,* January 10, 1915, II, p. 10. In the above correspondence, Bryan did not refer to the nominees by their first names. Those he mentioned were identified as D. J. Campeau of Detroit, Connally of Iowa, Graham of Illinois, and Hughes of Missouri. The two proposed by Fuller were referred to as Smith and Fearn.

42. State Department to Carothers, January 12, 1915, U.S. Department of State, *Papers Relating to the Foreign Relations of the United States, 1916*

Scott, meanwhile, was looking after Carothers' interests. He wrote to Bryan that Carothers was irreplaceable and that he deserved a raise in salary. Bryan responded by raising the agent's salary from three to five hundred dollars per month. The pay increase, plus the secretary's words of praise, persuaded Carothers to continue in the capacity of special agent as long as he was needed.[43]

Despite his search for additional State Department agents, Bryan made no new appointments. The convention and Zapata were ignored. In February, without enthusiasm, he reassigned Silliman to Carranza. On January 12 Bryan had suggested to Wilson that, since Silliman had never been very effective, he should be returned to his consular duties in Saltillo. Shortly afterward the secretary of state received a letter from Luis Cabrera, inquiring why Silliman had not been sent to Vera Cruz to represent the United States near the First Chief. Bryan thought Cabrera's inquiry adequate justification to send the agent to Vera Cruz; but before he acted on the suggestion, Carranza made it practically necessary. On February 15 the First Chief directed his military commanders in the field not to receive representations from "confidential or consular agents of foreign governments." Obviously referring to the activities of Canova and Carothers, he declared that dealing with such agents in the past had produced "the inconvenient effect of breaking up the unity which should prevail in all the acts of the Constitutionalist Government and tends to belittle the authority of the First Chief." Regardless of their nature, all diplomatic representa-

(Washington, D.C., 1925), 479. There is no explanation for this document appearing in the 1916 edition instead of the 1915 edition of *Foreign Relations.*

43. Carothers to State Department, January 12, 30, 1915, in NA 125.36582/124, 128; State Department to Carothers, January 30, February 3, 1915, *ibid.*/125, 128; Scott to Carothers, January 26, 1915, in Scott Papers, Box 17; Carothers to Bryan, February 5, 1915, in Bryan Papers, Box 43.

tions should be directed to the foreign minister in Vera Cruz.[44]

It was obvious that the administration required an agent in Vera Cruz. Consequently, the day after Carranza issued his directive, Silliman received orders to rejoin the First Chief. Belt, who had been on leave in the United States for almost two months, was again directed to join Silliman and act as his assistant. Regular passenger service between Vera Cruz and Mexico City having been disrupted by the *Zapatistas*, Carranza sent a special train to fetch Silliman. On February 21 Silliman received an enthusiastic welcome upon his arrival in Vera Cruz.[45]

Perhaps one reason why Bryan did not appoint more State Department agents was that Wilson had decided to send one of his own. The president was bewildered by the kaleidoscope of events in Mexico. As he indicated to Duval West, whom he had chosen as his new fact finder, "the situation there has become so complicated that I feel that I have lost the threads of it."[46] In choosing West, a San Antonio attorney, the administration was again rewarding a "deserving Democrat." But at least he had the reputation of being knowledgeable in Mexican affairs. The new agent owed his appointment to the two Texans in the Wilson cabinet, Attorney General Thomas W. Gregory and Postmaster General Albert S. Burleson. Indeed, it was Gregory, an old friend, rather than Bryan, who called the San Antonian to Washington.[47]

44. Bryan to Wilson, January 22, 1915, in Bryan-Wilson Correspondence; Elisio Arredondo, confidential agent of the Constitutionalist government of Mexico, to State Department (conveying copy of Carranza to all military commanders of the Constitutionalist army), February 15, 1915, in *Foreign Relations, 1915*, 652–53.

45. State Department to Cardoso de Oliveira (for Silliman), February 16, 1915, in NA 125.8273/157a; Silliman to State Department, February 18, 1915, *ibid.*/155; Silliman to State Department, February 19, 1915, in NA 812.00/14425; Canada to State Department, February 21, 1915, *ibid.*/14427; New York *Times*, February 19, 1915, p. 8; *El Pueblo*, February 21, 1915.

46. Wilson to West, February 10, 1915, in Wilson Papers, Ser. 2, Box 126.

47. Bryan to Wilson, February 3, 1915, in Bryan Papers, Box 43; San Antonio *Express*, February 1, 1915; New York *Times*, February 2, 1915, p. 4.

A slightly built man of fifty-four, Duval West was a product of the southwestern frontier. His father was one of the framers of Texas' first state constitution. A professional hunter at seventeen, young Duval killed meat for the Southern Pacific Railroad survey expedition. For a time he was a working cowboy. In 1888, as a deputy United States marshal, he gained a measure of fame by winning a shootout with a band of train robbers. Seeking the quieter life of a lawyer, he attended Cumberland University at Lebanon, Tennessee, before settling in San Antonio to practice his profession. Appointed assistant federal district attorney for the western district of Texas by President Grover Cleveland in 1893, West again gained notoriety by prosecuting author William S. Porter (who wrote under the pseudonym O. Henry) for embezzlement. Returning to private practice after serving as adjutant to the 1st Texas Infantry, U.S. Volunteers, during the Spanish-American War, he was one of San Antonio's most prominent citizens when called to the service of the Wilson administration.[48]

West met with the president on February 9. Wilson's purposes were aptly expressed in the instructions he gave the special agent:

> My wish is this: To have you meet and, as far as possible assess the character and purposes of the principle [sic] men down there of the several groups and factions, in the hope that you may be able to form a definite idea not only as to their relative strength and their relative prospects of success, but also as their real purposes.
>
> Above all, I want to find out just what prospects for a settlement there are and what sort of settlement it would be likely to be. If the settlement contemplated is not seriously intended for the benefit of the common people of the country, if the plans and ambitions of the leaders center upon themselves

48. *Ibid.*; "When Duval West Showed His Nerve," San Antonio *Express Sunday Magazine*, February 7, 1915, p. 17; Dallas *News*, May 15, 1949; Austin *American*, May 18, 1949; Biographical File, in Eugene C. Barker Collection, University of Texas.

and not upon the people they are trying to represent, of course it will not be a permanent settlement but will simply lead to further distress and disorder. I am very anxious to know just what the moral situation is, therefore, and just what it behooves us to do to check what is futile and what promises genuine reform and settled peace.[49]

These instructions indicate that the president was considering resuming an active role in the settlement of Mexican affairs, but he wanted fresh information to guide him.

Strangely, Wilson directed West to go first to Villa's country rather than to the South, the area which was currently causing the administration the greatest concern. Although the San Antonian reputedly spoke Spanish fluently, the State Department provided him an interpreter who also served as his secretary. Carothers met the new agent at the border but brought news that a meeting with Villa would be delayed, because the general was on an expedition in the western states organizing military campaigns. Carothers and Cobb, therefore, arranged conferences with Villa's subordinates. Availing himself of the comforts of Carothers' private car, West journeyed first to Chihuahua, then to Monterrey, before heading further south to join Villa at Guadalajara. In the process, he conferred with members of Villa's cabinet, the governors of Coahuila and Nuevo León, several important military officers, including General Felipe Angeles, and numerous municipal officials.[50]

For the most part, West was not favorably impressed with the *Villistas*. Most of them, he suggested, were "hoping for

49. Wilson to West, February 5, 1915, in Wilson Papers, Ser. 2, Box 126; Bryan to Wilson, February 9, 1915, *ibid.*

50. *Ibid.;* State Department to Cobb, February 13, 1915, in NA 111.70W52/44b; Cobb to State Department, February 13, 19, 1915, *ibid.*/44; West to State Department, February 19, March 2, 1915, *ibid.*/45, 47; Cobb (for Carothers) to State Department, February 15, 22, 1915, in NA 812.00/14391, 14431; Carothers to State Department, February 18, 1915, *ibid.*/14411; San Antonio *Express*, February 17, March 1, 1915; El Paso *Morning Times*, February 18, March 1, 1915.

benefits to themselves." In so characterizing them, he exhibited a personal aversion for the crude, uneducated revolutionaries who held most of the positions of authority under Villa. The officials he admired, General Angeles and Secretary of Foreign Relations Miguel Díaz Lombardo, were well-bred and educated. West noted that otherwise "the man with the white shirt has apparently disappeared." The very absence of educated men left him with doubts about Villa's ability "to secure the services of men of experience and loyalty in the formation and administration of a proper and just civil government" which could "carry into effect wise and proper financial, educational, and great reforms."

West was definitely distressed because these administrators seemed imbued with the idea "that the property of the rich should be administered by the Government for the benefit of the masses of people. . . . The socialist idea, without definite expression," he reported, "seems to prevail everywhere." West also complained that the law, as administered by the *Villistas*, was harsh and unfair. People were condemned to death without the semblance of a trial. Property was confiscated without judicial process. Although compensation was promised the former owners, even Díaz Lombardo was vague on just how this was to be accomplished.

West interviewed Villa twice: once in Guadalajara, when they dined together, and again in Carothers' private car as they traveled northward toward Aguascalientes. Villa exuded optimism. He claimed that he could establish complete control of northern Mexico within forty days. The Chihuahua strong man also insisted that he could control Zapata. When West queried him concerning his resources, Villa claimed to have a large stockpile of necessary staples— corn and beans—and an abundance of bullion. Pressing further, the American agent asked Villa if he could command the services of "men of matured judgement and experience," and Villa replied, " 'Yes, I have them—and can get them.' " West noted that he doubted if Villa could make good his claim.

Concerned for the sanctity of private property, West asked Villa if he would encourage foreigners to develop his country once it was pacified. The revolutionary chieftain's answer must have startled officials in Washington when they read it. He suggested that foreigners "should not, or would not, be permitted to own lands." He also indicated that he would prefer industry to be developed by Mexican capital. "I got the idea," West wrote in his report, "that he is standing upon the popular demand that 'Mexico should be for the Mexicans,' and that an open door to foreign investors means ultimate danger to the nation." West admitted, however, that Carothers disagreed with this interpretation of Villa's remarks.

In his impressions of Villa, West was complimentary to a point. As did virtually everyone who ever met him, the special agent was struck by Villa's robust personal magnetism. "He is much stronger in native mentality than given credit for," West wrote to Wilson. "There can be no doubt of his good hard common sense." Then he added a critical note: "His views of important governmental plans and policies to be undertaken by way of civil administration must be, for the present, considered entirely amateurish and tentative."

West's overall assessment of the *Villista* movement contained a contradiction. Making a tentative conclusion based on the briefing he received from Villa and Angeles, he indicated that they would probably win a military victory. While admitting, moreover, that perfect order prevailed everywhere he went, that in all municipalities the people seemed contented with their officials, and that the churches, schools, and markets were open and attended by great numbers of people, West still did not think the *Villistas* had the ability to establish a stable government and carry out reforms. Realistically, he concluded that the accomplishment of reforms would probably require the work of several generations.[51]

West planned to travel from Guadalajara to Zapata's country; but he could not arrange passage by this route. In view of the critical conditions in Mexico City, Wilson decided that West should go there next. Villa, however, could not guarantee safe conduct into the city, so the special agent was forced to travel all the way back to the Texas border. Pausing in San Antonio long enough to prepare a lengthy report, on March 15 West set out for Mexico City via Vera Cruz.[52]

Silliman, meanwhile, was wrestling with problems posed by the *Carrancistas* and was being repeatedly humiliated. The degeneration of conditions in Mexico City was Silliman's first concern. With business at a standstill and food extremely scarce, the populace grew panicky. Convinced that the suffering was induced by the city's merchants whose only reason for closing their doors was to avoid accepting Constitutionalist paper money, Obregón warned them that he would "not fire a single shot into any mob who may attempt to get what hunger has driven them to seize."[53] On March 4 he declared that all merchants who did not open their shops and accept paper money would receive "severe punishment."[54] Presumably, he meant this edict to apply even to foreigners. Silliman reported, moreover, that Carranza, who still claimed that the railroads were needed entirely for military use,

51. Preliminary report to the honorable secretary of state on the conditions in Mexico by Duval West, acting under authority conferred by the president, dated February 10, 1915, requesting him to investigate same [n.d.], in NA 812.00/14622.

52. *Ibid.*; West to State Department, March 11, 13, 1915, in NA 111.70W52/46, 48; State Department to Cardoso de Oliveira, March 3, 1915, *ibid.*/52; Cardoso de Oliveira to State Department, March 4, 1915, *ibid.*/3; State Department to West, March 12, 1915, *ibid.*/6; San Antonio *Express*, March 15, 1915.

53. Cardoso de Oliveira to State Department, March 2, 1915, in *Foreign Relations, 1915*, 654; Ramírez Plancarte, *La Ciudad de México*, 324–36.

54. Cardoso de Oliveira to State Department, March 4, 1915, in *Foreign Relations, 1915*, 657.

refused to allow provisioning of the stricken city via the rail lines.[55]

Wilson and Bryan viewed these conditions with mounting alarm. Convinced that only drastic measures could forestall a catastrophe, on March 6 they approved a strongly worded note drafted by Robert Lansing and sent it to Cardoso de Oliveira and Silliman. "When a factional leader preys on a starving city to compel obedience to its decrees by inciting outlawry and at the same time uses means to prevent the city from being supplied with food," it declared, "a situation is created which it is impossible for the United States to contemplate longer with patience." Carranza and Obregón were to be warned that "the Government of the United States will take such measures as are expedient to bring to account those who are personally responsible for what may occur." [56] Adding emphasis to the note, Wilson directed Secretary of the Navy Josephus Daniels to send the battleship *Georgia* and the cruiser *Washington* to join the small naval force already at Vera Cruz.[57]

When Cardoso de Oliveira presented the message to Obregón, the general replied that he was not authorized to deal in international matters. On March 8 Silliman presented the note directly to Carranza, who read it with mounting indignation. He turned to the American agent and declared that the tone was insulting. Losing his habitual reserve momentarily, he turned to his minister of foreign relations, Jesús Urueta, and stormed: "Do not reply to this note, which is unworthy of any chancery representing a true democracy." Then the First Chief and his advisors protested to Silliman that they should not be given sole responsibility for the suffering in Mexico City. Throughout the uproar Silliman

55. Silliman to State Department, March 3, 1915, *ibid.*, 654–55.
56. Bryan to Wilson, March 5, 1915, in NA 812.00/14496a; Wilson to Bryan, March 6, 1915, *ibid.*/14504½; State Department to Cardoso de Oliveira and Silliman, March 6, 1915, in *Foreign Relations, 1915*, 659–61.
57. Link, *Struggle for Neutrality*, 462.

remained silent. A Constitutionalist army officer, who witnessed the scene, later reminisced that the agent's reticence
probably prevented a complete break in relations, which, he
wisely noted, would have later been greatly regretted by the
Constitutionalists.[58]

Silliman was afraid that by his recalcitrance Carranza was
courting intervention. Seeking the support of Charles Douglas, Carranza's New York legal counsel, who had recently
come to Vera Cruz for conferences, the special agent called on
the First Chief the next day and repeated his appeal for the
use of the railway in relieving the hunger in Mexico City.
Carranza remained immovable.[59] Contrary to what he had
said earlier, on March 10 the First Chief gave Silliman a
written reply to Wilson's threat. Addressing himself directly
to the president in amiable terms, Carranza disclaimed
responsibility for the want and chaos in Mexico City. He
insisted that the United States was being misinformed by
"reactionaries" who were "attempting to bring about complications which may cause the failure of the ideals of the
Mexican revolution." [60] Privately, Carranza was more caustic.
He told Silliman confidentially that he felt a "great personal
resentment against the Secretary of State." He held Bryan,
alone, responsible for the note of the 6th and declared that
"the Secretary personally sooner or later must respond to him
for it." [61]

With conditions in Mexico City still deteriorating, Carranza realized that his denial of responsibility was not likely

58. Cardoso de Oliveira to State Department, March 7, 1915, in *Foreign Relations, 1915*, 661; Silliman to State Department, March 8, 1915, *ibid.*; Barragán, "De las memorias de Don Venustiano Carranza," *El Universal, Magazine para todos*, March 1, 1931, p. 1.

59. Silliman to State Department, March 9, 1915, in NA 812.00/14540, 14541.

60. Silliman to State Department (conveying Carranza to Wilson, March 9, 1915), March 10, 1915, in *Foreign Relations, 1915*, 666–68.

61. Silliman to State Department, March 11, 1915, in NA 812.00/14547.

to satisfy President Wilson. Rather than run the risk of a confrontation with the United States, he decided to abandon the city in order to avoid the onus Wilson had imposed upon him. On March 11 Obregón evacuated his troops, and conditions improved when the *Zapatistas* reoccupied the city.[62] But Wilson refused to let the matter rest. He sent a personal note to Carranza through Silliman, indicating that he had used stern language in the note of March 6 so that the gravity of his warning would be clear. Claiming that he did so as a friend, Wilson nonetheless left the impression that the warning still stood in the event of future incidents.[63] When Silliman delivered the note, Carranza asked him to read it aloud in Spanish. Knowing how poorly Silliman spoke the language, the First Chief was no doubt trying to save some pride by humiliating Wilson's representative. The agent reported that when he had finished, the First Chief made "no comment whatever." After a few embarrassingly silent moments, Silliman changed the subject.[64] A crisis had been averted.

The conflict with Carranza over Mexico City had prompted Wilson to ready his weapons; a controversy over the port of Progreso on the Yucatán Peninsula almost caused him to pull the trigger. In an attempt to pacify the peninsula, Carranza closed all the ports in late February. In the process he prevented the exportation of some 200,000 bales of sisal hemp, which threatened American manufacturers and farmers with a serious shortage of binding twine.[65] In Washington

62. Cardoso de Oliveira to State Department, March 11, 1915, in *Foreign Relations, 1915*, 669; Cardoso de Oliveira to State Department, March 15, 1915, in NA 812.00/14600.
63. State Department to Silliman, March 11, 1915, in *Foreign Relations, 1915*, 668–69.
64. Silliman to State Department, March 12, 1915, in NA 812.00/14577.
65. George A. Ranney, secretary of the International Harvester Company of New Jersey, to Joseph P. Tumulty, February 25, 1915, in Wilson Papers, Ser. 4, Box 385; Secretary of Commerce William C. Redfield to Wilson, March 9, 1915, *ibid.*; Houston to Wilson, March 14, 1915, *ibid.*

it appeared that the First Chief was prompted by no other
motive than to spite the United States. Under directions from
Bryan, Silliman asked Carranza to allow the exportation of
the badly needed hemp. The First Chief, believing that the
wealthy sisal planters of the peninsula had influenced the
State Department to come to their aid, refused even this
partial opening of the port of Progreso.[66]

Trying to assure Carranza that the United States was not
taking sides in the Yucatán conflict, Bryan directed Silliman
to propose that, in order to prevent the rebels from profiting
from the sisal trade, buyers in the United States would hold
in trust the purchase price of the amount of sisal they
exported. Luis Cabrera, the First Chief's secretary of the
treasury, told Silliman that this arrangement would be
satisfactory, if the United States would also agree not to
import supplies to the Yucatecans through the port of
Progreso. On March 10 Bryan replied that this arrangement
would be most satisfactory.[67] Considering past relations with
Carranza, this problem had apparently been settled with
relative ease.

The settlement did not last. For one thing, Bryan received
word from American sisal buyers and his consular agent at
Progreso that the Yucatecans were so desperate for food that
they might prevent the exportation of sisal unless they were
allowed to import food. Silliman reported, moreover, that
Carranza had refused to allow an American merchantman,
the *Morro Castle*, to sail from Vera Cruz bound for Progreso.
Naval authorities also reported from Vera Cruz that a
Constitutionalist gunboat was on its way to bombard the
port.[68] After a cabinet meeting on March 12, in which the

66. State Department to Silliman, February 24, 1915, in *Foreign Relations, 1915*, 821; Silliman to State Department, February 27, March 2, 1915,
ibid.; Barragán, "De las memorias de Don Venustiano Carranza," *El
Universal, Magazine para todos*, March 8, 1931, p. 1.
67. State Department to Silliman, March 8, 10, 1915, in *Foreign Relations, 1915*, 822, 823; Silliman to State Department, March 9, 1915, *ibid.*, 822.
68. W. P. Young (consular agent, Progreso) to State Department, [n.d.],
in Bryan-Wilson Correspondence; State Department to Silliman, March 11,

advisability of intervention was discussed, Wilson directed Bryan to inform Carranza that the United States did not recognize his right to blockade the port of Progreso. If he did not open the port of his own volition, American warships would be instructed to do so. As if it would give Carranza some reassurance, the secretary of state was also to say, "We are doing this in the interest of peace and amity between the two countries and with no wish or intention to interfere with her internal affairs." [69]

With more warships already on their way to the Mexican coast because of the Mexico City incidents, conditions were ripe for armed conflict. But Bryan was confident that there would be no bloody sequel to the Vera Cruz intervention, because the Yucatecans were anti-Carranza.[70] On the other hand, he would have been wise to recall that Lind had expected no shooting at Vera Cruz. As it turned out, U. S. Navy vessels were not deployed at Progreso, Carranza's blockade was never very effective, and American merchant ships began sailing intermittently with sisal cargoes. The tension was further abated when the Constitutionalist gunboat bound for Progreso ran into foul weather and was forced to return to Vera Cruz. By the time Silliman worked up enough courage to confront Carranza with Wilson's new ultimatum (it took two days), the Constitutionalists had nearly succeeded in defeating the rebels in the Yucatán and had gained control of Progreso. The Constitutionalist commander in the Yucatán, General Salvador Alvarado, was also wise enough to turn his back while American ships sailed.[71]

1915, in *Foreign Relations, 1915*, 823; Silliman to State Department, March 11, 1915, in NA 612.1123/66; State Department to Silliman, March 11, 1915, in NA 812.00/14584a.

69. Wilson to Bryan, March 12, 1915, in Bryan-Wilson Correspondence; State Department to Silliman, in *Foreign Relations, 1915*, 824.

70. Bryan to Wilson, March 13, 1915, in Bryan-Wilson Correspondence.

71. Silliman to State Department, March 13, 16, 18, 25, 1915, in NA 812.00/14585, 14586, 14607, 14623, 14693; Silliman to State Department, March 19, 1915, in NA 612.1123/57.

Silliman's timidity may well have been the most important factor in easing the crisis. He did not deliver Wilson's ultimatum as instructed. Instead, he merely told the First Chief and members of the cabinet that President Wilson had again requested the revocation of the Progreso blockade. The Mexican conferees seemed aware that Silliman had received extraordinary new instructions and played a cat-and-mouse game with him. Knowing well that the agent usually presented them with a copy of his instructions, they asked to see the text of the president's request. Fearful of the possible consequences, Silliman replied that he had been instructed to make the appeal verbally. The First Chief then asked what the response of the United States would be if he refused the request. The American agent again dodged the issue, claiming that he had not been instructed in this regard. A Mexican stenographer noted that when Carranza's secretaries pressed further for an answer to this question, Silliman conferred with Belt, then replied that he had been instructed to do no more than secure a positive or negative reply to his president's request. Apparently having known all along what his reply would be, Carranza abruptly announced that he would accede to the reopening of the port.[72]

Whether it was prudence or lack of courage that prompted him, Silliman had declined to court a crisis. In this regard he served both his country and Mexico well. In the process, he was forced to endure the bantering of Carranza's assistants. He also received a history lecture from the First Chief, who

72. Silliman to State Department, March 15, 1915, in *Foreign Relations, 1915*, 824; Memorandum de un conversación con El Sr. Silliman, March 15, 1915, AGRE, L–E–861, Leg. 5. Silliman's account of the conference gives no hint of the grilling he received. He merely noted that he "was not obliged to communicate in any way the President's intentions." *Carrancista* General Juan Barragán later claimed that Carranza opened the port of Progreso because Wilson threatened an arms embargo against the Constitutionalists. See Barragán, "De las memorias de Don Venustiano Carranza," *El Universal, Magazine para todos*, March 8, 1931, p. 1. State Department files record no such threat.

pointed out that had Great Britain insisted upon the exportation of cotton from New Orleans during the Civil War in the United States, it would have been comparable to the current demand of the United States for the right to export sisal from Progreso.[73]

Considering the gravity of the recent strained relations between the United States and Carranza, special agent Duval West enjoyed a remarkably cordial welcome when he arrived in Vera Cruz on March 24. Owing to illness, Carranza was unable to meet with West until five days later. Even then the First Chief was suffering from lumbago; consequently, the conference was short. In a cooperative mood, Carranza promised the San Antonian that his cabinet would provide any desired information. He also expressed hope that West's report would dispel many of the misconceptions currently held in Washington. As promised, Carranza's advisors, including Cabrera, Zubarán Capmany, and Urueta, were amply cooperative.[74]

West had little opportunity to assess Carranza's character but did note that the First Chief was a "man of few words and slow of thought, almost stolid." In comparing the personnel around Carranza with Villa's advisors, he suggested that "they are a much higher order." He thought most of them were actuated by patriotism and seemed surprised to find that they were "devoting much study and work toward formulating the laws and reforms referred to in the Plan of Guadalupe." Their conception of reform needs, West noted, was virtually the same as that of the *Villistas*. Taken as a group, he believed that the *Carrancistas* "would probably be

73. Silliman to State Department, March 16, 1915, in *Foreign Relations, 1915,* 824.
74. Silliman to State Department, March 24, 1915, in NA 111.70W52/8; Silliman to State Department, March 27, 1915, in NA 812.00/14716; West (enclosing Partial Report and Impressions Received at Vera Cruz, March 14, 1915–April 5, 1915) to State Department, April 5, 1915, in NA 812.00/20721; New York *Times,* March 30, 1915, p. 4.

able to develop the ability necessary to carry on a Civil Administration."

The Constitutionalists' weakness, West thought, was in military leadership. He noted that none of the civilian leaders would prophesy military victory. Apparently unaware that this was a war being fought along rail lines to control strategic points, West offered as evidence of the poor quality of military men the fact that so much of the countryside, supposedly under Constitutionalist control, was in constant turmoil. Admitting that his opinions had to be considered tentative because he had had no opportunity to meet the Constitutionalists' two foremost military men, Obregón and González, West concluded that "the Constitutionalist Government under its present leaders cannot establish peace in Mexico because of the failure of its military leaders." [75]

West's journey to Mexico City required rather elaborate arrangements. Carranza provided a special train and an escort for the agent as far as Ometusco. To avoid a possible clash with the *Zapatistas*, he requested the Brazilian minister to send certain designated individuals to meet the train in carefully marked automobiles. As it turned out, the tracks were destroyed well before the rendezvous point, and West and his secretary-interpreter were left alone in a detached car. After a long delay, a representative of the Brazilian legation arrived with horses. From there the party rode horseback to a point from which they boarded a *Zapatista* train and continued their journey to Mexico City. Minister Cardoso de Oliveira, meanwhile, had arranged a reception so that West could meet the diplomatic corps and officials of the Conventionist government.[76]

In his reports, West did not give much space to the

75. West, Partial Report and Impressions Received at Vera Cruz, March 14, 1915–April 5, 1915, in NA 812.00/20721.
76. Silliman to State Department, April 4, 1914, in NA 111.79W52/15; Oliveira to State Department, April 7, 1915, *ibid.*/18; Biographical File, Barker Collection.

Conventionist government. He described Roque González Garza, the president of the convention, as a "well intentioned man." West also noted correctly that González Garza was a Villa adherent, but that the convention was currently dominated by the *Zapatistas*. The cabinet was scarcely mentioned. He did indicate that the government maintained excellent order in Mexico City and had made every effort to protect the lives and property of foreigners.[77] He did not even mention the complete absence of cooperation and constant quarreling between the *Villista* and *Zapatista* factions of the convention. Perhaps he did not do so because Cardoso de Oliveira had already fully informed Washington of the imminent disintegration of the convention as an effective deliberative body.[78] By his minimal comments, West implied that the convention was incapable of promoting a stable government.

While making preparations to visit Zapata, West discovered that the chieftain of the South was distressed by the fact that he had not received replies to the two letters he had sent to President Wilson. In these letters, forwarded to Washington by Red Cross representative Charles Jenkinson, Zapata had urged Wilson to receive a group from Morelos who would explain the nature of the revolution in the South and seek guidance from the United States. Before journeying into Morelos, West, therefore, asked the president for clarification on this score. Wishing to pave the way for his agent, Wilson alibied that he had prepared a reply, but that, owing to a clerical misunderstanding, it was never sent. West was deputed to make apologies.[79]

77. Report to the president, through the honorable secretary of state, of conditions in Mexico by Duval West, acting under authority of the president, dated February 10, 1915, this report being supplemental to preliminary report on the Villa government and preliminary report on the Carranza government heretofore made, May 11, 1915, in NA 812.00/19181.
78. Cardoso de Oliveira to State Department, March 27, 29, 1915, in *Foreign Relations, 1915*, 682–83.
79. West to State Department, April 10, 1915, and State Department to West, April 12, 1915, in NA 812.00/14832; draft of reply in Wilson Papers, Ser. 2, Box 129.

Escorted by General Alfredo Serratos, West journeyed to Tlaltizapán on April 16 to meet with Zapata. The train ride through the mountains covered with lush foliage impressed the American agent more than any of the other scenes he had witnessed. Arriving in mid-afternoon, West was ushered into a hot, dimly lit room where Zapata was counseling with an advisor. West first apologized for Wilson's not having answered the general's letters; whereupon Zapata replied in the simplest of terms, "Esta bueno." The American then asked Zapata to explain the intent of his letters. With no copy to guide him, the general requested a delay while he conferred with his advisors. Seeking relief from the heat, West and his party took a short swim in a nearby stream while waiting for Zapata's reply. When the conference was resumed, the rebel chieftain asked if Wilson would receive a commission of *Zapatistas* in Washington. West could only reply that he would make inquiries. Zapata seemed reluctant to discuss any other matters with the special representative. He left West with the impression that he trusted only his own kind to adequately explain his purposes to President Wilson.[80]

Before leaving Tlaltizapán, West dined with Zapata on canned salmon and peaches, beans, chili, tortillas, and hot beer. Afterwards, they posed for photographs, strolled leisurely back to the train, and West departed. Despite the brevity of the meeting, West formed firm opinions. "I was agreeably disappointed in Zapata," he wrote in his report. Like most of the revolutionaries, "he believes that it is perfectly right that the property of the rich shall be taken and given to the poor." As far as his being able to influence a permanent settlement of affairs in Mexico, West wrote: "I do not think Zapata may be taken into account other than being

80. West, Mexico City to Tlaltizapán, April 16, 1915, in NA 812.00/24272a. West's description of his meeting with Zapata was apparently attached to his report of May 11, cited above. President Wilson was apparently so taken with the descriptions of the journey and the meeting that he detached it and later returned it to Bryan. See Wilson to Bryan, June 18, 1915, *ibid*.

the representative of the people in the hills and mountains of his own scope of country."[81]

Upon his return to Mexico City, West dutifully inquired if the president would receive a commission of *Zapatistas*. Bryan was inclined to accede, but Wilson was fearful that Zapata and the other factional leaders would interpret the move as connoting diplomatic recognition. Wilson directed Bryan to reply that since the president had not received commissions from the other factions, he must decline to receive one from Zapata. Zapata was to be informed, however, that President Wilson would welcome whatever explanatory documents the general would care to send.[82]

West made a good impression on the *Zapatistas*. Before he left the city, they held a banquet in his honor, and even Díaz Soto y Gama offered a toast of praise to the American agent.[83] His mission completed, West had difficulty leaving Mexico City. Fighting along the rail line that brought him to the city prevented his return by the same route. Delayed for nearly ten days, he was finally taken to Puebla by automobile, where he met Belt. Escorted to Vera Cruz, he just had time to dine with Silliman and Admiral William B. Caperton before sailing for home.[84]

While West was making his investigations in Vera Cruz, Mexico City, and Tlaltizapán, conditions elsewhere underwent a drastic change. After his meeting with West, Villa went north to direct the campaigns against Matamoros,

81. West, Mexico City to Tlaltizapán, April 16, 1915, *ibid.*
82. West to State Department, April 19, 1915, and State Department to West, April 22, 1915, in *Foreign Relations, 1915*, 688–89; Bryan to Wilson, April 20, 1915, and Wilson to Bryan, April 21, 1915, in Bryan-Wilson Correspondence. The *Zapatistas* did send several documents including a copy of the Plan of Ayala with West. These documents are filed in the State Department's Internal Affairs of Mexico file, 812.00/15166.
83. "El viaje de Mr. West," *La Verdad* (Mexico City), May 5, 1915; New York *Sun*, May 10, 1915.
84. Silliman to State Department, April 24, 27, 28, 29, 1915, in NA 111.70W52/24, 28, 29, 33, 36; *El Pueblo*, May 1, 1915; San Antonio *Express*, April 28, 29, 1915.

Nuevo Laredo, and Tampico. He hoped to defeat the Constitutionalists in the North before having to return southward for the inevitable showdown with Obregón.[85] Villa was unable to dislodge General González from Tampico, and his campaigns on the border also went badly. Because the *Carrancistas* were supplied by the United States, they were able to put up stiff resistance. Villa complained to Carothers about the lack of reciprocity in the demands of the State Department. He was expected to carry on his attacks without firing across the border, yet the Constitutionalists had complete access to supplies from the United States. Bryan only replied that the laws of the United States did not provide for the closing of the frontier in such instances.[86] At any rate, Villa had not been able to complete his border campaigns before Obregón began pushing northward.

The decisive battle of this phase of the revolution was at hand. On March 28 Carothers reported unusually heavy troop movements to the South. The next day Villa appeared in Torreón and asked Carothers to go south with him "for a couple of days." They did not stop until they reached Irapuato. Obregón was just thirty-five miles to the east in Celaya. Villa boasted that he would "annihilate the enemy." Carothers, never doubting that he would, left the scene and went to Guadalajara to investigate the complaints of some foreigners whose property had been confiscated.[87]

With the understanding that Zapata would hit Obregón's supply lines which stretched from Vera Cruz to Celaya, Villa attacked Obregón's main force on April 6 and was repulsed. Even though aid from Zapata did not materialize, the enraged Villa attacked again on April 13. Using a well-de-

85. Quirk, *Mexican Revolution*, 177, 214.
86. Carothers to State Department, March 27, 1915, and State Department to Carothers, April 10, 1915, in NA 812.00/14849.
87. Cobb (for Carothers) to State Department, March 29, April 3, 5, 6, 8, 12, 1915, in NA 812.00/14731, 14778, 14787, 14795, 14784, 14836; Cobb (for Carothers) to State Department, March 28, 1915, in NA 812.48/2152.

signed machine-gun cross fire, a maze of trenches, and barbed-wire entanglements, Obregón cut Villa's once-proud army to pieces and sent the Centaur of the North retreating all the way to Aguascalientes.[88] Carothers returned to Irapuato on April 12, the day before Villa's second defeat. Villa was at the front. His loyal subalterns did not inform the American of the true gravity of the situation. Consequently, his reports gave no hint. Silliman, on the other hand, was reporting from Vera Cruz that Obregón was winning.[89] When, even after it became apparent in Washington that Villa had been defeated, Carothers' reports indicated that Villa had the upper hand, the State Department directed him to make a more careful investigation.[90]

On April 20 Carothers suddenly appeared in El Paso. He reported that Villa had not revealed the true situation until three days after his defeat. The special agent claimed, moreover, that he telegraphed the news to the border, but Cobb never received the telegram. Carothers assumed that Villa's telegraphers destroyed the coded draft. Carothers' full-length report, written in El Paso, indicated that Villa had misled the agent even in admitting defeat. Villa told Carothers that he lost only six thousand men and had escaped with his rolling stock and other equipment intact. The Constitutionalist agency in Washington claimed that he had lost fourteen thousand men, part of his rolling stock, and most of

88. Quirk, *Mexican Revolution*, 221–25; Thord-Gray, *Gringo Rebel*, 462–63; Lieuwen, *Mexican Militarism*, 34; Barragán Rodríguez, *Historia . . . de la Revolución Constitucionalista*, II, 279–96.

89. Cobb (for Carothers) to State Department, April 12, 1915, in NA 812.00/14836; Silliman to State Department, April 7, 15, 1915, *ibid.*/14809, 14810; Tinker, "Campaigning With Villa," *Southwest Review*, XXX, 154. Tinker, a journalist who had accompanied Carothers to Irapuato, indicated that the *Villistas* withheld the fact that Villa had already been repulsed once with heavy losses.

90. Cobb (for Carothers) to State Department, April 15, 1915, in NA 812.00/14858; State Department to Cobb (for Carothers), April 19, 1915, *ibid.*/14893.

his artillery.[91] Regardless of the accuracy of either estimate, the defeat was decisive and marked the beginning of a disastrous decline for Villa. It also marked a change in the relationship between Villa and Carothers. No longer could the special agent trust the candor of the Mexican general.

Shortly after Celaya, Carothers reported that the pressure of defeat caused Villa to call in his forces from Jalisco and Michoacán.[92] At the same time, Obregón's success took much of the pressure off the Constitutionalist garrisons at Matamoros, Nuevo Laredo, and Tampico. By the end of April, the *Villista* seige on the border outposts collapsed.[93] Acknowledging Villa's eclipse, Bryan expressed his and Wilson's disappointment when he told reporters that "the failure of Villa . . . to capture Celaya and defeat Obregón has about convinced Administration officials here that the man upon whom hopes had been pinned for pacification of Mexico cannot be relied upon to save the situation." [94]

Following on the heels of Villa's decline came Duval West's final reports on his observations in southern Mexico. West arrived in Washington on May 9, in the midst of the *Lusitania* crisis. More than two weeks passed before the Texan was able to confer directly with the president.[95] On May 11, however, he submitted a written report to the secretary of state. He did not rehash what he had written before or amend his earlier reports to take into account the changes that had occurred since he had first entered Mexico some three months before. His most noteworthy conclusion was "that a condition of permanent peace and order and the establishment of stable government . . . cannot be brought

91. Carothers to State Department, April 20, 22, 1915, *ibid.*/14897, 14898, 14935; Arredondo to State Department, April 16, 1915, *ibid.*/14882.

92. Carothers to State Department, April 22, 1915, *ibid.*/14935.

93. Quirk, *Mexican Revolution,* 226; Barragán Rodríguez, *Historia* . . . *de la Revolución Constitucionalista,* II, 302–19.

94. New York *Times,* April 20, 1915, p. 1.

95. New York *Times,* May 10, 1915, p. 8; *ibid.,* May 25, 1915, p. 9; San Antonio *Express,* May 10, 11, 12, 1915.

about by any of the contending parties without the aid or assistance of the United States." If the president wanted a responsible government in Mexico, he would somehow have to aid in its creation. How could this be accomplished? West was not explicit. But he hinted, without specifying which ones should be considered, that the best way for the United States to help was to recognize one faction or a combination of factions and be prepared to support that government to the hilt.[96]

On May 24 West at last conferred with President Wilson. The press reported that West spoke disparagingly of all the factions, which was likely true. He supposedly warned the president not to support any faction.[97] If he did so, then he controverted his written recommendations. After the meeting, West returned to San Antonio. He did not serve the administration again in a diplomatic capacity. In December, 1916, however, he was appointed federal judge for the western district of Texas. He served in that capacity until his retirement in 1932.[98]

In assessing the conditions in Mexico, West erred in some respects. Most glaringly, he underestimated Carranza's military strength and overestimated Villa's. He no sooner reported the Constitutionalists' lack of quality military leadership than Obregón won his smashing triumph at Celaya. West too readily assumed that the Mexican leaders, except for Zapata, who advocated confiscation of private property did so only for pecuniary motives.

On the other hand, West's accounts were the most balanced and least biased yet received from a special agent. He was the first agent directed to call on Villa who was not absolutely smitten by the dynamic personality of the Chi-

96. West, Report to the President . . . May 11, 1915, in NA 812.00/19181.
97. New York *Times*, May 25, 1915, p. 9; *ibid.*, May 26, 1915, p. 5; San Antonio *Express*, May 29, 1915.
98. San Antonio *Express*, June 13, 1915; Austin *American*, May 18, 1949; Biographical File, Barker Collection.

huahua strong man. He was the first to indicate that Villa lacked the ability to peacefully administer to the needs of the Mexican nation. Other than Silliman and Lind, West was the only agent who did not find Carranza thoroughly obnoxious. He seemed to sense the First Chief's inner strength. He rightfully pointed out that Zapata's ideals did not embrace a sympathy or concern for the whole nation. By not associating agrarian reform with Zapata alone, West revealed how widespread the ideas, first espoused by the revolutionaries of the South, had become.

What would Wilson do with the information West had provided? The president must have asked himself the questions that an editorialist of the New York *Times* posed when West was first sent to Mexico: "Perhaps after a few weeks he [West] will be in a position to make wise suggestions, but will they be heeded? Can they be heeded?" [99] To answer these questions, Wilson would have to abandon his policy of nonintervention.

99. "Duval West's Mission," New York *Times*, February 12, 1915, p. 10.

CHAPTER XII

The Final
Accounting

During the first six months of 1915, Wilson faced near irresistible pressures for intervention in Mexico. His Republican opponents on Capitol Hill led the cry. The habitual critics, Senators Henry Cabot Lodge and Albert B. Fall, insisted that it was the president's responsibility to restore order in Mexico. Refining their arguments somewhat, Senator William E. Borah of Idaho, normally not an interventionist, reasoned that once Wilson intervened against the dictator Huerta, he should have insured that the successor acted responsibly.[1] Even more intense was the demand for intervention voiced by the hierarchy and laymen of the Roman Catholic Church, who decried the anticlerical sentiments of the revolutionaries. As pressure from American Catholics mounted, Bryan felt constrained on April 22 to issue a public statement declaring that, while the administration took note of every reported act of anticlericalism and lodged protests, it could not accept persecution of the Church in Mexico as grounds for military intervention.[2]

As already indicated, conditions in Mexico City between January and March had driven the president to consider intervention. The reoccupation of the city by the *Zapatistas* in March brought temporary relief; but shortly afterward

1. *Congressional Record*, 63rd Cong., 3rd Sess., 1016–21, 1500–1502, 4274–84.
2. Link, *Wilson and the Progressive Era*, 132; New York *Times*, April 22, 1915, p. 6.

Emissaries to a Revolution

332

conditions deteriorated again. In late March and throughout April and May, hunger, looting, and violence again resulted in appeals for intervention from the foreign colony of the city. Carranza continued to aggravate matters by denying the use of his railroads to supply the city. He enraged President Wilson in May by seizing some of the supplies purchased by the International Relief Committee.[3] Organized by members of the foreign colony, the ostensible purpose of the committee was to provide relief for Mexico City's suffering poor. John W. Belt, on the other hand, maintained in a personal letter to Bryan that this committee harbored a group of dissidents who were courting such incidents in order to provoke intervention. Mostly Americans, they were, he warned, in communication with business interests in the United States who also hoped for intervention.[4]

Villa was also causing the United States concern. Having modified his demands against foreign-owned mining interests, his main source of revenue for a time was the sale of cattle at El Paso. American stockmen's associations, protesting that many of the cattle were stolen from Americans, succeeded by late April in seriously curtailing Villa's sales in the United States. Villa then opened a slaughtering plant in Juárez and, through agreements with several American packing companies, began marketing processed beef. As a result, American stockmen appealed to the Department of Agriculture to stop this beef trade. Despite pledges from Carothers and the packing companies that Villa was not processing beef stolen from Americans, the Department of Agriculture did stop shipments of Villa's beef on the grounds that his abattoir did not meet sanitation requirements prescribed by the laws of the United States.[5] Carothers warned

3. Cardoso de Oliveira to State Department, March 26, 27, May 7, 21, 1915, in *Foreign Relations, 1915*, 682, 689–91; Cardoso de Oliveira to State Department, April 3, 1915, in NA 812.00/14775; New York *Times*, May 29, 1915, p. 1; *ibid.*, May 31, 1915, p. 4.
4. Belt to Bryan, May 21, 1915, in Bryan-Wilson Correspondence.
5. Senator Charles A. Culberson (Dem.-Tex.) to Bryan, January 8, 1915, in NA 312.114P19; Carothers to State Department, March 15, April 30, May

that Villa would be indignant over this turn of events and, in his opinion, "justly so." The special agent also indicated his fear that, as a result of the decision, Villa would not take favorable action on pending matters concerning foreign property.[6]

Carothers' prophecy held true. When, in mid-May, the Yaqui Indians of Sonora began raiding foreign-owned ranches, and three Americans were brutally murdered, Bryan urged Villa to send troops to put an end to the depredations. In response, Villa told Carothers that as long as the *Carrancistas* controlled the Sonoran border and he was expected to abide by the agreement made in January which forbade him to attack border towns, he could not guarantee the safety of foreigners in Sonora.[7]

Intrigue in the State Department also hastened the drift toward intervention. By the spring of 1915, there were several Mexican *juntas* in the United States either plotting counterrevolution or trying to win the support of the Wilson administration for plans to pacify Mexico.[8] The preeminent plot involved State Department support of Eduardo Iturbide as a third force to eliminate both Villa and Carranza. Hatched

---

6, 1915, *ibid.*/5, 6, 10. Carothers' letter of March 15 includes affidavits from American packing companies pledging that they were not trafficking in beef stolen from American ranches.

   6. Cobb (for Carothers) to State Department, May 9, 1915, *ibid.*/10.

   7. State Department to Carothers, May 17, 1915, in NA 312.11/5980; Carothers to State Department, May 19, 21, 1915, *ibid.*/6019, 6021.

   8. One such counterrevolutionary movement centered around Pascual Orozco and Victoriano Huerta, who came to the United States from exile in Spain. See Meyer, *Pascual Orozco*, 124–31; Meyer, *Huerta*, 210–22; Rausch, "Exile and Death of Huerta," 135–44. Federico Gamboa and other remnants of the Mexican Catholic party, with the support of Catholic elements in the United States, tried to interest Bryan in a plan of pacification. Both Bryan and Wilson thought they smelled counterrevolution in the plot. Wilson called it a "pig in a poke." See Bishop Charles Currier to Bryan, March 14, 1915, in NA 812.00/16810; Bryan to Wilson, March 16, 1915 and Wilson to Bryan, March 16, 1915, *ibid.*; Bryan to Currier, March 19, 1915, *ibid.* Felix Díaz was also plotting an uprising in the state of Oaxaca. See Memorandum of a conversation with Honorable Leslie M. Shaw, July 15, 1915, *ibid.*/23137.

by Leon J. Canova, Iturbide's guardian angel, the scheme was supported by Counselor Robert Lansing, Assistant Counselor Chandler P. Anderson, and Secretary of the Interior Franklin K. Lane. Bryan opposed the plot, and the upshot of the debate was a tumultuous cabinet meeting on June 1, at which Bryan and Lane argued over Iturbide's merits. Although the president did not take part in the argument, he accepted Bryan's advice that the plot smelled of reaction. The cabinet meeting, nonetheless, convinced Wilson that he must abandon noninvolvement and personally take a more active part in promoting a final settlement in Mexico.[9]

How could he become involved without courting a military confrontation? West had suggested recognizing one faction or a coalition of factions and supporting that government to the hilt. But which faction or factions? Even before the climactic cabinet meeting of June 1, David Lawrence, a young journalist friend of Wilson, suggested a means of narrowing the choices. A Princeton graduate of the class of 1910, Lawrence had known Wilson since he (Lawrence) had been a reporter assigned to the university president's office by the undergraduate newspaper. In 1911–1912 he had covered the Madero revolution for the Associated Press. A correspondent for the Washington bureau of the Associated Press since 1912, he was an intimate of the president and the leaders of the various Mexican *juntas* in the United States.[10]

Addressing a letter to the president on May 27, Lawrence warned that famine would sweep Mexico and the cries for intervention would intensify if the revolutionary factions in Mexico and the various *juntas* in the United States continued to work at cross purposes. He suggested that besides the great personalities of the revolution (Carranza, Villa, and Zapata), there were many leaders who would willingly enter

9. Lind, *Struggle for Neutrality*, 470–76; Teitelbaum, *Wilson and the Mexican Revolution*, 268–70.
10. *Current Biography, 1943 s.v.*, "Lawrence, David."

into a compromise agreement if it would mean peace. The president should appeal directly to them, as well as to the great personalities, to resolve their differences over the conference table. A provisional government created in such a manner, Lawrence proposed, should be accorded diplomatic recognition and given moral, financial, and military backing, while those who abstained from the conference should be denied such support.[11]

Wilson liked Lawrence's proposals so much that on June 2 he incorporated them into a note which he addressed to all Mexican leaders, both prominent and obscure. Wilson also added his own touch; he warned that if they did not settle their differences over the negotiating table, he would be "constrained to decide what means should be employed . . . to help Mexico save herself and serve her people." [12] Wilson had scrapped his nonintervention policy. But in once more striving to help solve Mexico's problems, he continued to reveal his naivete—as did his new advisor, David Lawrence. Wilson seems to have thought that after some five years of fighting the revolutionaries could get together around a conference table, shed their animosities, and end their revolution. At the same time, the special agents were called upon to play a very passive role in this peace endeavor; they merely distributed the president's note and waited for replies.

Remarkably, the first responses to the president's note were encouraging. Roque González Garza invited Villa and Carranza to join the convention in an armistice and negotiations leading to the creation of a provisional government.[13] The First Chief told Silliman that "he would disappoint any

11. Lawrence to Wilson, May 27, 1915, in Wilson Papers, Ser. 2, Box 130.
12. Statement by the president, sent to all American consuls and other special representatives in Mexico, June 2, 1915, in *Foreign Relations, 1915*, 694–95.
13. Cardoso de Oliveira to State Department (conveying González Garza to Carranza and Villa, June 3, 1915), June 4, 1914, *ibid.*, 697–98; State Department to Silliman and Carothers, June 5, 1915, *ibid.*, 698.

enemies of Mexico who expected defiance from him." [14] After
losing still another great battle to Obregón at León de las
Aldamas, Villa boasted that he still controlled the largest
part of Mexico, yet would humble himself for the sake of
peace and negotiate with his enemies.[15] It was all very
encouraging, to a point.

Washington was soon aware that any hope for a prompt
settlement was illusory. For one thing, the lesser chiefs did
not come forward and demand peace. They continued to defer
to their factional leaders. The *Zapatistas* did not support
González Garza's peace overtures. Zapata personally urged
the convention to ignore Wilson's demands.[16] In the convention, Díaz Soto y Gama denounced González Garza and
launched into a lengthy but apocryphal attack upon President
Wilson and the United States. He even claimed that Duval
West had demanded a bribe from Zapata in return for a
favorable report on his faction. When Zapata had refused,
Soto y Gama continued, West returned to Washington
supporting Carranza, who evidently had paid the bribe. Soto
y Gama warned that Wilson's newest proposal grew out of
West's visit (here, he was partially correct) and would, if
adhered to, benefit Carranza. The convention responded by
forcing González Garza out of office and ignoring Wilson's
plea.[17]

Carranza, meanwhile, did not even bother to answer
González Garza's overture. After Obregón's victory at León,

14. Silliman to State Department, June 7, 1915, in NA 812.00/15161.
15. Carothers to State Department (conveying Villa to Wilson, June 10,
1915), June 11, 1915, in *Foreign Relations, 1915*, 701–703; Carothers to State
Department (conveying Villa to González Garza and Carranza, June 10,
1915), June 11, 1915, *ibid.*, 703–704; Quirk, *Mexican Revolution*, 260–61;
Barragán Rodríguez, *Historia . . . de la Revolución Constitucionalista*, II,
341–47.
16. Quirk, *Mexican Revolution*, 258.
17. Cardoso de Oliveira to State Department, June 9, 1915, in *Foreign
Relations, 1915*, 699–700; Cardoso de Oliveira to State Department, June 11,
1915, in NA 812.00/15482.

moreover, he felt less constrained than ever to negotiate with his enemies. The First Chief did not even give Silliman a reply to Wilson's note. Instead, on June 11 he issued a "Manifesto to the Mexican People," which embodied his answer. He announced the near triumph of the Constitutionalist movement, called for his enemies to lay down their arms and submit to his authority, and promised the early establishment of a constitutional government through national elections. He promised law and order; protection to foreigners; separation of Church and state, but leniency to the clergy; and agrarian, judicial, and municipal reform. He also expressed hope that his government would soon be recognized by the world powers. A copy of this manifesto was sent to the State Department by Carranza's agent in Washington, but Silliman was allowed to learn of it as did the Mexican people—through the press.[18]

While Wilson awaited the answers from the revolutionary leaders, Secretary of State Bryan disagreed with the president's handling of the *Lusitania* crisis and resigned. To fill the vacancy Wilson, with some misgivings, chose Robert Lansing. Where Wilson and Bryan were intuitive and idealistic, Lansing tended to be more practical, coldly analytical, and realistic.[19] As the president became more embroiled in the affairs of Europe, the new secretary of state devoted much time to the solution of the Mexican puzzle. Since he feared that the Germans might use Mexico as a focal point to stir up trouble for the United States in Latin America, he was anxious to find a quick solution.[20]

18. Confidential agent of the Constitutionalist government of Mexico to State Department, June 12, 1915, in *Foreign Relations, 1915*, 705–707; Silliman to State Department, June 11, 1915, in NA 812.00/15202; *El Pueblo*, June 12, 1915.
19. Link, *Wilson the Diplomatist*, 27; Daniel M. Smith, "Robert Lansing," *An Uncertain Tradition*, 101–104.
20. Louis G. Kahle, "Robert Lansing and the Recognition of Venustiano Carranza," *Hispanic American Historical Review*, XXXVIII (August, 1958), 353.

With all peace feelers being spurned by the *Carrancistas*, Wilson concluded that he should make the bait more appealing. Again, it was David Lawrence who suggested a means for speeding the First Chief to a peaceful solution. After speaking to Charles Douglas, Carranza's New York attorney, Lawrence reported to Wilson on June 16 that "Carranza realizes that without the approval of the United States no government can stand in Mexico and while there will be resentment over any outside interference, it will be accepted and the best made of it." [21] Hoping that the prospect of recognition would move the First Chief, Wilson suggested to Lansing that he notify Carranza that the United States had not ruled out granting diplomatic recognition to his provisional regime. The First Chief should also be made to realize that the United States would be reluctant to do so unless every effort was made to conciliate the warring factions.[22]

Lansing quickly drafted the message embodying the president's suggestions and sent it to the White House for approval. Wilson was pleased with the document, but he was not sure Silliman could convey its intent with adequate forcefulness. "I fear he [Silliman] rather bores and irritates Carranza," he confided to Lansing. "I think, therefore, that we had better seek others in addition." Drawing from Lawrence's suggestions, Wilson proposed that Charles Douglas, who was again on his way to Vera Cruz, be asked to support Silliman's appeals to the First Chief.[23]

Silliman received the note on June 18 and presented it to the First Chief on June 21. If Douglas offered support, Silliman did not mention it. The headstrong First Chief

21. Lawrence to Wilson, June 16, 1915, in Wilson Papers, Ser. 2, Box 131.
22. Wilson to Lansing, June 17, 1915, U.S. Department of State, *Papers Relating to the Foreign Relations of the United States: The Lansing Papers, 1914–1920* (Washington, D.C., 1940), II, 535; hereinafter cited as *Lansing Papers*.
23. Lansing to Wilson, June 17, 1915, in NA 812.00/15285½; Wilson to Lansing, June 18, 1915, *ibid.*/15286½.

referred the American agent to his recently issued manifesto, claiming that by urging his enemies to submit, he was, in fact, offering conciliation. Silliman asked if he could go beyond this declaration and invite the factional leaders to a conference. Thereupon, Carranza replied that "under no circumstances" would he treat with Villa and Zapata. He told the special agent that President Wilson was shortsighted for seeking a solution through compromise, that a government so created would fail. "The determination of the United States to adopt any other measures than the recognition and support of the Constitutionalist cause would be a regrettable injustice," the First Chief declared. "If the Government of the United States will maintain a neutral attitude, the Constitutionalist cause will subdue the opposition and win recognition." Wilson was more than disappointed when he received the reply from Silliman. Admitting the failure of his conciliation effort, he wrote to Lansing: "I think I have never known a man more impossible to deal with on human principles than this man Carranza." [24]

Carranza's intransigence left Wilson in an embarrassing situation; he could intervene, as he had hinted that he would do in his note of June 2, or he could seek another peaceful solution. Consequently, he gratefully embraced a plan proposed by Secretary Lansing. In March, when Lansing was still counselor, he had suggested that, should the United States find it necessary to intervene in Mexico, she should endeavor to do so in cooperation with the ABC powers. In this way, Latin American resentment would be minimized and the action could be portrayed as a collective attempt by American nations to promote peace and stability in the Americas. At the time, Wilson had been favorably impressed with the idea. When Lansing revived it in a conversation in late June,

24. State Department to Silliman, June 18, 1915, in *Foreign Relations, 1915*, 715; Silliman to State Department, June 22, 1915, *ibid.*, 718–19; Wilson to Lansing, July 2, 1915, in NA 812.00/15409½.

Wilson eagerly urged him to arrange Pan-American cooperation for some kind of intervention to end the Mexican civil
war.[25] Having been given the initiative, Lansing took relations with Mexico into his own hands and, in the process,
began creating a milieu in which Pan-American intervention
would operate to the fullest benefit of the United States.

The Pan-American conference was slow in materializing.
Relations between the United States and Carranza, in the
meantime, remained strained. The First Chief was clearly
undermatched when he dealt with John Silliman, and this
encouraged him to be bold. In fairness to the American agent,
it must be admitted that his orders from Washington often
placed him in a compromising position. Such was the case
during an incident in July. Consul Canada of Vera Cruz
reported in May and June that General Cándido Aguilar,
Carranza's future son-in-law and Constitutionalist governor
of the state of Vera Cruz, was encouraging laborers to drive
foreign owners from their properties. Ever hostile to the
revolutionaries, Canada also indicated that depredations
against Americans were particularly on the increase. Stung
by the recent difficulties in dealing with Carranza, Lansing
decided that stern measures were in order. On July 3 he
directed Silliman to demand Aguilar's removal as governor of
Vera Cruz and to say that refusal to remove him would be
considered "an unfriendly act toward the United States." [26]

By demanding Aguilar's ouster, Lansing may well have
been courting an incident that would further reveal Carranza's uncompromising nature. Clearly it was a challenge to
Mexican sovereignty. As might be expected, Silliman shrank
from the prospect of obeying his orders to the utmost. If
Carranza refused, he warned Washington, it would create a

25. Lansing to Wilson, March 8, 1915, *Lansing Papers*, II, 529–31; Wilson
to Lansing, July 2, 1915, *ibid.*, 537; Wilson to Lansing, July 2, 1915, in NA
812.00/15409½.

26. Canada to State Department, May 27, June 18, 1915, in NA
812.00/15352, 15344; State Department to Silliman, July 3, 1915, *ibid.*/15344.

grave crisis. He asked permission to withhold the note temporarily and discuss the situation with Charles Douglas, who had just arrived in Vera Cruz. Silliman held the note for days before Lansing again directed him to present it to Carranza. This time Douglas interceded. He cabled the secretary of state that he was personally investigating the matter. Hinting that Canada might have exaggerated the dangers in Vera Cruz, Douglas insisted that conditions were improving and asked for the department's patience. Lansing accepted Douglas' counsel and informed Silliman that he need only bring the matter of depredations to Carranza's attention and urge that conditions be improved.[27] Lest Douglas become a cipher through which the department's full intentions were habitually commuted, Lansing directed Silliman to use "great discretion" in dealing with Carranza's paid counsel.[28]

Mexico City's ordeal remained an open sore, causing conflict between the United States and Carranza. By the end of June, the Constitutionalists had clamped a seige on the city so tightly that virtually all communications with the outside world were cut off. Again, shortages of the necessities of life threatened mass privation. Succumbing to the pressure, on July 9 the convention evacuated the city for the last time and the next day General González occupied the city. The *Carrancista* general proclaimed amnesty and promised that the railroads would give priority to supply trains. On July 13 Silliman reported that food was on its way from Vera Cruz.[29]

27. Silliman to State Department, July 4, 8, 12, 1915, *ibid.*/15364, 15395, 15420; State Department to Silliman, July 10, 1915, *ibid.*/15395; Douglas to State Department, July 9, 1915, and State Department to Douglas, July 10, 1915, *ibid.*/15398.
28. State Department to Silliman, July 14, 1915, *ibid.*/15439.
29. Cardoso de Oliveira to State Department, June 22, 25, 29, 1915, *ibid.*/15336, 15337, 15412; Cardoso de Oliveira to State Department, July 4, 11, 1915, in *Foreign Relations, 1915*, 721, 723–24; Silliman to State Department, June 27, 28, July 10, 11, 13, 1915, in NA 812.00/15318, 15322, 15403, 15406, 15427; Silliman to State Department, [n.d.], *ibid.*/15404.

The respite was short-lived. When the *Zapatistas* counter-attacked, González again evacuated, leaving the capital without an effective government. At the mercy of roving bands of *Zapatistas*, the people of the city suffered, perhaps, their severest two-week period of the revolution.[30] Ignoring the fact that most of the outrages were committed by Zapata's troops, Lansing addressed a stern note to Carranza. He demanded, in effect, that the Constitutionalists become more militarily effective. The secretary directed Silliman to insist that the Constitutionalists reoccupy the city, this time permanently, and keep open the lines of communication. Carranza and his ministers disdained to even reply to this latest threat from the United States.[31]

Tensions again eased when González reinvested the city on August 2 and reopened communications with Vera Cruz.[32] Mexico City's ordeal was over. The Constitutionalists were there to stay, although Carranza was not sure enough of that fact to make it his capital. Minister Cardoso de Oliveira caused a temporary stir when he announced, on August 9, that he was taking a well-earned leave from the beleaguered city. He reported to Washington that most foreigners thought that President Wilson's policy had caused most of their woes. Since he had represented the interests of the United States for so long, Cardoso de Oliveira felt that they held him partially responsible. Charles B. Parker, an embassy clerk who had been serving Cardoso de Oliveira at the Brazilian legation, was left to report on conditions in Mexico City.[33] Still ineffective despite the eased tensions, Silliman

30. Cardoso de Oliveira to State Department, July 18, 19, 22, 25, 29, 30, 1915, in *Foreign Relations, 1915*, 726–32; Silliman to State Department, July 21, 1915, *ibid.*, 727; Silliman to State Department, July 28, 1915, in NA 812.00/15568; Quirk, *Mexican Revolution*, 276.
31. State Department to Silliman, July 29, 1915, in NA 812.00/15572; Silliman to State Department, July 30, 1915, *ibid.*/15591.
32. Cardoso de Oliveira to State Department, August 3, 4, 1915, in *Foreign Relations, 1915*, 732–33; Silliman to State Department, August 7, 1915, in NA 812.00/15686.
33. Cardoso de Oliveira to State Department, July 29, 1915, in *Foreign Relations, 1915*, 731–32; Silliman to State Department, August 9, 1915,

The Final Accounting   343

reported that his representations were systematically ignored. The foreign minister told the American agent that the tone of the State Department's notes was insulting; hence, the First Chief had refrained from answering them and would continue to do so.[34]

Carothers was also having his troubles in the North. Villa misled the agent before and during the battle of León. Claiming victory when the battle was only in its early stages, Villa sent word to Carothers, who passed the information on to Washington. When, after his defeat at León, Villa prophesied victory in his next battle and Carothers so reported to Washington, the special agent drew an admonishment from the secretary of state. Lansing directed Carothers to report only the final outcome of military engagements. The department was not interested in Villa's prophecies.[35]

Zach Cobb also began to criticize Carothers' shortsightedness. Beginning in May, the customs collector sometimes added notes to Carothers' dispatches, claiming that Villa was misleading the special agent. While Carothers continued to be optimistic in early June, Cobb reported that Villa's military strength was steadily deteriorating.[36] Slowly Carothers overcame his feelings of loyalty and admiration for Villa and saw things as they really were. His change of heart probably began when General Angeles, who was on his way to visit his family in Boston, spoke to Carothers in El Paso. It was

in NA 812.00/15713; Silliman to State Department, August 11, 1915, in NA 701.3212/32; New York *Times*, August 11, 1915, p. 1. Cardoso de Oliveira came to Washington to confer with Lansing and Wilson before returning to Brazil. See *ibid.*, August 21, 1915, p. 9; *ibid.*, August 24, 1915, p. 6.

34. Silliman to State Department, August 9, 10, 12, 1915, in NA 812.00/15713, 15731, 15749.

35. Carothers to State Department, May 23, 26, 1915, *ibid.*/15063, 15080; Cobb (for Carothers) to State Department, May 31, June 2, 9, 1915, *ibid.*/15098, 15112, 15176; State Department to Carothers, June 10, 1915, *ibid.*/15176.

36. Cobb to State Department, May 31, June 7, 1915, *ibid.*/15098, 15155; Cobb (for Carothers) to State Department, May 31, June 2, 3, 1915, *ibid.*/15098, 15115.

rumored that the general and Villa had quarreled following their defeat at León. Angeles expressed doubts about Villa's future and asked Carothers to secure an interview for him with President Wilson, so that he might propose a plan to eliminate "certain elements" from both factions in order that the rest could come to some agreement.[37]

After the interview with Angeles, the American agent's expectations for Villa's ultimate victory disappeared from his dispatches. He began to report that conditions in the area under Villa's control were deplorable. The soldiers were taking everything, leaving large segments of the population destitute. For a time his attitude toward Villa personally did not change. He claimed that Villa was conscientious in his desire for peace. Carothers also insisted that the Department of Agriculture's refusal to allow Villa to export beef to the United States was partially responsible for the increased confiscations within the general's territory.[38]

During Wilson's attempt to conciliate the revolutionary factions, Carothers remained in El Paso in order to facilitate communications with Washington. Upon returning to Villa's side in mid-July, the metamorphosis of his opinions accelerated. Conditions were even worse than he suspected. "I see conditions very critical in all northern Mexico," he reported upon his return to the border. "While I do not see immediate signs of complete collapse, I cannot see how existing conditions can last much longer without it." Fearful that Villa would no longer confide in him if he knew what was being reported to Washington, Carothers urged the secre-

37. Carothers to State Department, June 18, 20, 1915, *ibid.*/15263, 15269. Angeles had urged Villa to make a defensive stand at León, but Villa ignored this advice and made another massed cavalry charge at Obregón. The result was another disastrous defeat. See Quirk, *Mexican Revolution*, 260–62; Barragán Rodríguez, *Historia . . . de la Revolución Constitucionalista*, II, 341–47.

38. Carothers to State Department, June 21, July 6, 1915, in NA 312.114P19/18, 812.48/258.

tary of state to withhold any public mention of his reports.[39]

A note of apprehension now crept into the special agent's notes. He reported that "Villa is becoming harder to deal with. He is sorely pressed for money." [40] He received information that Villa had executed a Mexican rancher who refused to pay a forced loan. Such incidents were likely to increase, he warned, and foreigners would probably be involved. Appeals for Villa to desist were liable to antagonize him to the point that life for foreigners in his bailiwick would become intolerable. Carothers hoped that his appeals, combined with those of Díaz Lombardo and Angeles, who would soon return to Mexico, would be able to at least minimize the danger.[41]

On July 26 Carothers reported that Villa had demanded a forced loan of $300,000 in gold from the mine operators of Chihuahua. Since the operators refused to pay, Carothers feared that Villa would invoke his confiscatory mining decree of March 19. When the special agent, joined by Díaz Lombardo and others of Villa's advisors, met with Villa in Torreón and asked for modification of his demands against the miners, Villa answered with more threats of confiscation. Journeying to Chihuahua, on July 31 he called a meeting of all the city's merchants. He charged that they were responsible for the shortages and resulting privation. They were demanding extortionate prices. Foreign merchants, he stormed, were the most felonious offenders. Because of their alleged treachery, he told them that he had decided to confiscate their stocks. He promised Carothers that foreign merchants would be compensated at the rate of cost plus 15 percent. At first he ordered all merchants expelled from Chihuahua but he later modified his decree to allow foreigners to stay.[42]

39. Carothers to State Department, July 19, 1915, in NA 812.00/15490.
40. Carothers to State Department, July 11, 1915, *ibid.*/15518.
41. *Ibid.*; Carothers to State Department, July 23, 1915, in NA 812.00/15530.
42. Carothers to State Department, July 26, 1915, in NA 812.63/143; Carothers to State Department, July 26, 29, August 1, 5, 1915, *ibid.*/

Prospectively more ominous, Carothers reported on August 2, was the fact that Villa had called a general meeting of mine operators at Chihuahua for August 9, supposedly to discuss regulation of the industry. At this announcement, the special agent hastened to the border where he could report more freely. He despondently wired the secretary of state that "Villa's ministers and diplomatic agents have been practically set aside in name and Villa is handling all matters himself according to his ideas." Carothers further noted that the rebel general was dead broke and would seize "everything in sight in order to raise money. . . . Unless he is curbed, I feel that he will stop at nothing." [43]

Villa still professed his friendship for Carothers. In a quiet conversation in Carothers' car just before the agent departed for the border, the Mexican general put his hand on Carothers' knee and said: "I believe you and I will be friends until death, I feel that way towards you and believe you feel the same towards me." Afterwards, Villa's ministers came to the agent, one by one, and told him that he had more influence over Villa than did any other man. They urged him not to give up his attempts to hold their chief in check.[44] Carothers was equally depressed. In a telegram to Lansing, he lamented that "Villa is now dedicating to extortion the cupidity he formerly used for military purposes." [45]

Still not willing to abandon his friend, Carothers once again turned to General Hugh Scott for help. In the past, because of his great admiration for the American general, Villa had accepted his direction. Shortly after Carothers made the appeal, Villa came to Juárez to confer with his

812.00/15540, 15582, 15606; Cobb to State Department, July 28, 1915, *ibid.*/15570; Letcher to State Department, August 1, 1915, *ibid.*/15607, 15610.

43. Cobb (for Carothers) to State Department, August 2, 1915, in NA 812.63/146; Carothers to State Department, August 3, 1915, in NA 812.00/15626.

44. *Ibid.*

45. Carothers to State Department, August 5, 1915, in NA 812.00/15658.

commercial agents. On August 6 the department directed the special agent to endeavor to hold Villa on the border, because General Scott was on his way. So that they might have some bargaining point, Carothers then requested that the secretary of agriculture give him and Scott authority to discuss conditions under which Villa's Juárez slaughterhouse might be reopened. With a legitimate source of revenue at his disposal, the agent reasoned, Villa might be persuaded to reverse his recent confiscatory decrees.[46]

In Washington, Secretary Lansing was concerned that Villa's power might completely collapse before the Pan-American nations could apply pressure on Carranza. With no effective force to counterbalance the First Chief, they would not likely secure any concessions. He, therefore, asked President Wilson to direct Secretary of Agriculture Houston to allow Villa to resume his meatpacking operation out of Juárez. At first the president was puzzled, unable to understand why Lansing would want to bolster Villa and prolong the conflict in Mexico. When the secretary explained his purposes, Wilson agreed that Villa should be allowed to export beef. As a result, Lansing conferred with Houston, made arrangements, and notified Carothers that, if Villa's abattoir could meet inspection requirements, it could resume operations.[47]

When Carothers and Scott met with Villa on August 10, they had a concession to offer. The two American negotiators were encouraged after the first meeting. They reported that Villa had agreed not only to call off the proposed meeting of miners in Chihuahua but to return all goods confiscated from the merchants of that city.[48] Two days later a committee of

46. Carothers to State Department, August 3, 5, 1915, *ibid.*/15627, 15630; State Department to Carothers, August 6, 1915, *ibid.*/15757a.

47. Lansing to Wilson, August 6, 7, 1915, in *Lansing Papers*, II, 545–47; Wilson to Lansing, August 7, 1915, *ibid.*, 546; State Department to Carothers, August 9, 1915, in NA 312.114P19/29a.

48. Carothers to State Department, August 10, 1915, in *Foreign Rela-*

mine operators from Chihuahua joined the conferences. Carothers and Scott convinced Villa that his demand for forced loans from the miners was impracticable. Since he needed their coal to fuel his railroads, the Americans counseled, he should be more cooperative with the mine operators. As a practical matter, therefore, Villa agreed to allow them to use his railroads to import whatever equipment they needed to put their mines in operation and also promised military protection. The miners, for their part, pledged a thousand tons of coal to assist in the operation of the railroad. After the conference was over, Carothers reported that Villa balked at the settlement of several other matters. He and Scott had agreed that they should not press their luck and make more demands.[49]

Carothers and Scott had secured more than they had reason to hope for. The miners were quite pleased with the arrangements. Writing in behalf of the Mine and Smelter Operators Association, A. J. McQuatters praised the two American negotiators. He especially singled out Carothers, noting that there were few Anglo-Americans who could confront the Mexicans day in and day out with demands and still maintain cordial relations with them.[50] Ever Carothers' champion, Scott added his own words of commendation: "No one but Carothers could accomplish what he has." [51] Certainly Carothers had not erred in calling for the aid of General

tions, 1915, 934; Scott to State Department, August 10, 1915, ibid., 935; El Paso Morning Times, August 11, 1915.

49. Carothers to State Department, August 12, 1915, in NA 812.00/15739; incomplete version of this document in Foreign Relations, 1915, 935; El Paso Morning Times, August 13, 1915.

50. McQuatters to Lansing, August 13, 1915, in NA 812.00/15815.

51. Scott to Lansing, August 14, 1915/no document number. Scott also requested that Carothers be given stenographic help. In a pencilled note attached to Scott's telegram, Canova indicated to the secretary of state that Carothers did not need a stenographer, since most of his correspondence was by telegraph. Canova further suggested that Carothers probably wanted a stenographer merely to enhance his image. See Scott to Lansing, August 14, 1915, in NA 111.70C22/11.

Scott. Villa's awe of Scott is inexplicable. He was not similarly impressed with other American soldiers. Again Carothers had taken advantage of that special chemistry, and the results were not disappointing.

Neither Scott nor Carothers were particularly sanguine about their accomplishment. They realized that they had only bought some time. In order to extend that time as long as possible, Scott remained on the border temporarily to continue aiding Carothers.[52] Even with the reopening of his slaughterhouse, Villa's strength continued to wane. Carothers urged, therefore, that Washington make every effort to promote some peaceful accommodation between the factions. He warned the secretary of state that if Villa met with more defeats and his faction degenerated into small bands, their confiscatory measures would increase.[53] Privately Carothers admitted to Scott that the dissolution of the *Villistas* was near at hand.[54]

Villa also saw the handwriting on the wall. While conferring with Scott, he made a last-ditch attempt to end the civil war before he was defeated. He authorized the general to negotiate an armistice with the *Carrancistas*, in order that a conciliation conference could be held. Through the American consul in Monterrey, the State Department attempted to arrange a meeting between Scott and Obregón, but the *Carrancista* general refused to confer under the aegis of the United States.[55]

In Washington, Lansing had completed arrangements for a conference with the diplomatic representatives from Argentina, Brazil, Chile, Uraguay, Bolivia, and Guatemala. At

52. Carothers to State Department, August 24, 27, 1915, in NA 812.00/15900, 15942. Scott remained in El Paso until August 27.
53. Carothers to State Department, August 13, 1915, in NA 812.00/15756.
54. Carothers to Scott, September 9, 1915, in Scott Papers, Box 20.
55. Carothers to State Department, August 10, 1915, in NA 812.00/15717; State Department to Hanna, August 13, 1915, *ibid.*; Bonnet to State Department, August 20, 1915, *ibid.*/15864; Scott to Mrs. Scott, August 14, 16, 17, 1915, in Scott Papers, Box 5.

the same time others in the State Department were commu-
nicating with the leaders of the various Mexican *juntas* in the
United States, all of whom claimed that they could pacify
their homeland. Canova intensified his support of Iturbide.
Even the president showed considerable interest in General
Felipe Angeles, who appeared briefly in Washington in July.
Aware that Paul Fuller had previously reported very favorably on Angeles, Wilson urged Lansing to bring the former
special agent into consultation in preparing for the Pan-
American conference. In constant communication with *Carrancista* agents, former agent John Lind suggested immediate recognition of Carranza. When the Pan-American diplomats assembled on August 5, Lansing, Fuller, Canova, and
others in the State Department were prepared to present an
array of candidates to head a provisional government in
Mexico.[56]

Lansing and Fuller met with the six Latin American
diplomats in the secretary's office on August 5 and 6. Suave
and persuasive, Lansing appealed for their aid in ending the
strife in Mexico. Their task, as he saw it, was to promote the
establishment of a regime that would leave the revolutionaries in power. Otherwise, the peace would not last. The Latin
American conferees agreed. They concluded, also, that all the
current factional leaders should be eliminated. They then
decided upon a two-step plan of action that was wholly in
keeping with Lansing's line of thought. First, they would
send a communication to all the factions, inviting them to a
peace conference. Second, they chose a committee of three,
including Fuller, to work out an arrangement for selecting a
government they could recognize, even if the first step
failed.[57]

56. Lind to Lansing, July 23, 1915, in NA 812.00/17050; Lind to Wilson,
August 2, 1915, in Wilson Papers, Ser. 4, Box 125; Link, *Struggle for
Neutrality*, 481–87; Teitelbaum, *Wilson and the Mexican Revolution*, 270–76.
Lind began appealing for the recognition of Carranza several months earlier.
See Lind to Bryan, April 21, 1915, in Wilson Papers, Ser. 4, Box 129.
57. Lansing to Wilson, August 6, 1915, in *Lansing Papers*, II, 543–45.

By the time President Wilson received Lansing's report of the Pan-American conference, his thinking had undergone a metamorphosis. He wrote to Lansing that the conferees should not expect immediate elections but should be prepared to accept a provisional government that would inaugurate reforms by decree. Obviously impressed with Carranza's growing strength, he also notified Lansing that he and the Latin American diplomats should not rule out Carranza as a possible head of that provisional regime. To do so, he warned, "would be to ignore some very big facts."[58] As the foremost of Wilson biographers has suggested, Woodrow Wilson had finally accepted the Mexican revolution on Venustiano Carranza's terms.[59]

Conferring again with the Latin American diplomats in New York on August 11, Lansing launched into a discourse that embodied Wilson's ideas. The conferees, including Fuller, at first balked, but finally agreed to go ahead with the first step of their plan and invite the revolutionaries to a conference. Discussion of the second step was postponed until they received the answers to their invitation.[60] On August 13, Lansing and the six Latin American diplomats made the following appeal to all the civil and military leaders of Mexico: "We, the undersigned, believe that . . . the men directing the armed movements in Mexico—whether political or military chiefs—should agree to meet, either in person or by delegates, far from the sound of cannon, and with no other

58. Wilson to Lansing, July 8, 10, 1915, *ibid.*, 547, 549.

59. Link, *Struggle for Neutrality*, 491. Arthur S. Link suggests that Wilson's response to the Latin American diplomats' proposals initiated the trend which resulted in the recognition of Carranza. Louis G. Kahle speculates that Lansing anticipated the recognition of Carranza from the beginning of the conferences and used tactics designed to make the Latin American diplomats believe that they had come to the decision of their own volition. See Kahle, "Robert Lansing and the Recognition of Carranza," 361–64.

60. "Continuation of the Conference on Mexican Affairs," August 11, 1915, in NA 812.00/15754½.

inspiration save the thought of their afflicted land, there to exchange ideas and to determine the fate of and unyielding agreement requisite to the creation of a provisional government." The diplomats offered to serve as mediators and to arrange a neutral site within Mexico's borders. They indicated that they expected an answer within a reasonable time, hopefully in ten days.[61]

Since the notes were dispersed so widely throughout Mexico, Carothers and Silliman played only a minor role in securing answers. Carothers did no more than deliver the note to *Villista* authorities in Juárez, who passed it on to Villa. Carothers did report on August 16 that "the joint note has caused a very favorable impression, both in El Paso and northern Mexico. The soldiers, as well as the people, are tired of war and want peace." [62] Villa's personal reply was sent to the Pan-American conferees through his agent in Washington. As might be expected, he responded favorably. Still referring to himself as a Conventionist, Zapata also agreed to the conference. At the same time, virtually all the leading *Villistas* and *Zapatistas* accepted the invitation.[63]

Carranza responded in typical fashion. He began by denouncing the Pan-American conferees even before he received their message. He made it clear that he would no sooner endure interference from other Latin American nations than he would from the United States.[64] Waiting one

61. A communication, made severally and independently, to all prominent civil and military authorities in Mexico, from the secretary of state and the diplomatic representatives at Washington of Brazil, Chile, Argentina, Bolivia, Uraguay, and Guatemala, August 11 (sent August 13), 1915, in *Foreign Relations, 1915,* 735–36.

62. Carothers to State Department, August 15, 16, 1915, in NA 812.00/15763, 15800.

63. Llorente to State Department (conveying Villa's reply), August 19, 1915, in *Foreign Relations, 1915,* 737–38; Parker to State Department (conveying Zapata's reply), August 29, 1915, *ibid.,* 739–40; List of replies to Pan-American diplomats' message of August 11, 1915, *ibid.,* 753–54.

64. Arredondo to State Department, August 10, 1915, *ibid.,* 734–35.

day past the requested ten-day deadline, on August 24, the First Chief, implying that the Latin American diplomats had been pressured into agreeing to the note, sent word to Silliman that he would not reply until he received some guarantee that they acted in an official capacity in affixing their signatures. By September 3 all six diplomats had sent official statements through Silliman that they had, indeed, acted in an official capacity, and with the full knowledge of their governments.[65] Still Carranza procrastinated.

It soon became apparent (as it usually did) that the First Chief's obstinacy was prompted by more important reasons than merely that of antagonizing the United States. His forces having taken Aguascalientes, Zacatecas, and San Luis Potosí in July, Carranza sent Obregón attacking further northward in late August. By September 10 Saltillo, Durango, and Villa's greatest prize, Torreón, had fallen to the Constitutionalist armies. Once again Villa's hegemony was restricted to the state of Chihuahua.[66] What the First Chief planned was to present the Pan-American diplomats with the *fait accompli* of his supremacy.

Wilson and Lansing, meanwhile, were secretly working to prevent the Pan-American effort from becoming an embarrassing failure. They arranged for David Lawrence, who was currently on vacation, to join with the Chilean ambassador, Eduardo Suárez Mujica, in conferring with Eliseo Arredondo, Carranza's agent in Washington. Meeting with Arredondo at Ashbury Park, New Jersey, on August 15 Lawrence and Suárez Mujica revealed that the Pan-American nations had not ruled out the possibility of recognizing Carranza, but that they were not likely to do so unless his provisional government grew out of the proposed peace conference. The

65. Silliman to State Department, August 24, 26, 1915, in NA 812.00/15898, 15935; Lansing to Pan-American diplomats, September 1, 1915, *ibid.*/16251a; State Department to Silliman, September 3, 1915, *ibid.*/15898.

66. Quirk, *Mexican Revolution*, 275–76, 287; Barragán Rodríguez, *Historia . . . de la Revolución Constitucionalista*, II, 393–96, 466–69.

Constitutionalist agent suggested that Carranza might be inclined to accept their invitation if they first "cleared the air" and indicated what conditions would have to be met at the peace conference. Hinting that such a conference would reach conclusions not unfavorable to the First Chief, Lawrence told Arredondo that, for now, all the conferees wanted was for Carranza to accept the peace conference "in principle." The American journalist left Ashbury Park with the impression that Arredondo would urge the First Chief to accept this proposition.[67]

The events that followed the Ashbury Park meeting were shrouded in secrecy. Encouraged by Arredondo's response, Lansing and Wilson decided to make a secret unilateral appeal directly to the First Chief. At their suggestion, Lawrence contrived to have the Associated Press send him to Vera Cruz to interview Carranza concerning the Pan-American proposal. As far as the public or the Latin American diplomats knew, he was just another journalist. Once in Vera Cruz, Lawrence reported directly to Lansing under the code name "Laguirre."[68] Wilson's and Lansing's bent for secrecy in this case indicates that they had about made up their minds to recognize Carranza, but that they preferred to do it as painlessly as possible and without making it appear that they

67. Lawrence to Lansing, August 15, 1915, in NA 812.00/15866½.

68. Lansing to Lawrence, August 17, 1915, ibid./15867½; Canada (for Laguirre) to State Department, CONFIDENTIAL, for the secretary only, August 29, 1915, ibid./16014½; Lawrence to Wilson, September 11, 1915, ibid./16189½; David Lawrence, The True Story of Woodrow Wilson (New York, 1924), 104–105. The nature of Lawrence's sojourn must be pieced together from fragments. Lansing, in the above-cited letter to Lawrence, did not specifically mention a secret mission, but he did include the following statement: "I do not wish to interrupt your vacation, but I do think that you might be of very great service if you are here Thursday or Friday, as you suggest." In his own reminiscences, Lawrence states that he went to Vera Cruz as the joint representative of the president and the Associated Press, but mentions nothing about secrecy. Without mentioning Lawrence's real name, Canada reported that "Laguirre" had information for the secretary. In his letter to the president, dated September 11, Lawrence referred to his "conversations at Vera Cruz."

were imposing their will upon the Latin American diplomats.
Only twenty-six years old, Lawrence substituted brass for
experience in his conversations with the First Chief. Meeting
Carranza for the first time on August 29, Lawrence presented
himself as having no official character. This way, he revealed,
he could be of service to both sides. He explained that the
United States preferred to recognize a provisional government which grew out of a peace conference, because granting
recognition to only one faction would leave the others
resentful and only encourage continued fighting. Carranza
replied that within three weeks he would completely dominate the country. The remaining rebels would be so few and
weak that their resentment would cause no dire consequences. He rejected the idea of accepting a peace conference
"in principle," whether it ever met or not, because it would
imply acceptance of foreign involvement in Mexico's internal
affairs. Lawrence then suggested that the First Chief himself
initiate a peace conference. After the meeting, the American
journalist reported to Lansing that Carranza seemed impressed by this suggestion but would not state specifically if
he would act upon it.

Perhaps revealing Wilson's ultimate intentions, Lawrence
outlined for the First Chief a method by which he could
probably obtain recognition. He suggested that Carranza
reply to the Latin American conferees in terms that would
give no offense and that he should agree to some form of
peace conference, self-initiated or otherwise. If no satisfactory agreement came from that conference, the most powerful faction would likely be recognized, provided it gave
promise of living up to international obligations. This proposal definitely interested Carranza. Like a tiger stalking its
prey, he replied that if Lawrence was invested with official
character, and offered such a proposition, he would be willing
to phrase his reply to the Latin American diplomats as
Lawrence had suggested. Retreating, the American said that
this was not possible, because his government was acting in

conjunction with other governments and President Wilson could not alone decide the issue. The First Chief was still interested. Wanting at least semi-official assurance, he urged that Silliman be instructed from Washington to say that Lawrence "spoke in the name of the Secretary of State." [69]

When Wilson read Lawrence's dispatch, he wrote to Lansing: "It does not seem to me that our friend has got anywhere in particular in his representations to the stiff-necked First Chief or made any impressions on him that is likely, if confirmed, to lead to cooperation on his part with the United States." Wary of giving Carranza the impression that the United States would make a unilateral agreement with him, the president instructed the secretary to "send word to Silliman that our friend does come fresh from conversations with you and is in a position to know what the real sentiments and purposes of the Government of the United States are. Any official recognition of him would be a mistake." On August 31 Lansing sent the substance of the president's suggestion to Silliman. [70]

In Vera Cruz, Lawrence was making some investigations of his own. Drawing information from what he called "authoritative and well-informed persons," he reported what was already well known in Washington—that the administration's representation in Vera Cruz was ineffective. "Our influence is virtually zero," he indignantly informed the secretary of state. "We do not even get our protests and messages before Carranza." The First Chief, he added, took advantage of Silliman's friendship, while Consul Canada was absolutely ignored because he was considered an enemy of the revolution. He proposed that a new representative, one who would be more firm in his relations with Carranza, be sent to Vera Cruz. This new representative should again

69. Canada (for Laguirre) to State Department, CONFIDENTIAL, for the secretary only, August 29, 1915, in NA 812.00/16014½.
70. Wilson to Lansing, August 31, 1915, *ibid.*/16015½; State Department to Silliman, August 31, 1915, *ibid.*

recommend a peace conference; but if Carranza refused to confer, the United States should recognize him anyway.[71]

Wilson would have none of Lawrence's suggestions. "I do not think any part of this good advice," he wrote to the secretary of state. "The usual thing has happened: a man is sent down to explain our exact position and purpose and within a day or two sends a comprehensive plan of his own. . . . I think it best to make no reply at all to this." [72] Lansing was similarly dissatisfied. Having committed himself to Pan-American cooperation, he could not accept the journalist's advice regarding recognition. As far as the administration's representation in Vera Cruz was concerned, he admitted that neither Silliman nor Canada alone was adequate. They had opposite points of view and were extremely biased. But if their reports were juxtaposed, he informed the president, they struck a neat balance and gave the department a "reasonably correct idea of the situation." No one was likely to be successful in dealing with the First Chief. Lansing suggested, therefore, that neither be replaced.[73]

Lawrence met with Carranza again on September 1. The quasi agent could not change the First Chief's attitude toward the peace conference. After the meeting, Lawrence reported that he felt certain he had convinced Carranza that Wilson and Lansing were not personally prejudiced against him and that, from then on, the First Chief would be "better disposed" toward the United States. Carranza convinced Lawrence that he was only trying to prevent the revolution from being deprived of its triumph. He also pointed out that the spirit of nationalism was so imbued in his people that,

71. Canada (for Laguirre) to State Department, CONFIDENTIAL, for the secretary only, August 30, 1915, *ibid.*/16016½.

72. Wilson to Lansing, August 31, 1915, *ibid.*/16017½.

73. Lansing to Wilson, August 30, 1915, National Archives, Record Group 59, Personal and Confidential Letters from Secretary of State Lansing to President Wilson, 1915–1918/875; Lansing to Wilson, August 31, 1915, in NA 812.00/16016½.

even if he did not uphold it, others would. After this second meeting, Lawrence left Vera Cruz a wiser man for having matched wits with the First Chief. Wilson suggested as much to Lansing after reading the journalist's last cable. "I have the feeling that our friend is finding out what we already know," the president wrote, "and yet it may be that he has been serviceable in removing some erroneous impressions from Carranza's mind." [74]

Upon his return to the United States, Lawrence again conferred with Arredondo. The *Carrancista* agent told the American that the First Chief had recently indicated a willingness to discuss "international questions" with "several governments" but would not come to the peace conference proposed by the Pan-American diplomats.[75] Lawrence had other inconsequential meetings with Carranza's agent in late September, but neither Lansing nor Wilson gave any indication of taking notice of his advice.[76] With these meetings, Lawrence ended a rather unsuccessful stint as the president's special agent. He remained an ardent champion of Wilson and, in 1924, published his sympathetic recollections of the great man in a book entitled *The True Story of Woodrow Wilson.*[77]

Not until his forces had captured Torreón did Carranza deign to reply to the Pan-American note. The administration

74. Canada (for Laguirre) to State Department, CONFIDENTIAL, for the secretary only, September 1, 1915, in NA 812.00/16187½; Wilson to Lansing, September 7, 1915, *ibid.*/16188½.
75. Lawrence to Wilson, September 11, 1915, *ibid.*/16189½.
76. Lawrence to Lansing, September 27, 29, 30, October 1, 1915, *ibid.*/16345½, 16346½, 16347½, 16348½.
77. Lawrence became one of the giants of American journalism. One of the first Washington correspondents to write a syndicated column, he became, in 1933, president and editor of the news magazine, *U.S. News.* An influential critic of the Roosevelt and Truman administrations, he was founder and editor of the *World Report,* which began publication in 1946. Two years later he amalgamated the two journals with the publication of *U.S. News and World Report.* See *Current Biography, 1943,* 428–30; *Who's Who in America, 1968–1969,* Vol. XXXV, 1286.

already knew how he would respond. No one was surprised, therefore, when he notified Silliman on September 10 that he refused the mediation offer because it would be an encroachment upon Mexican sovereignty and set a precedent for future interference. Since all his subordinates, instead of replying themselves, had deferred to Carranza, he also pointed to the impressive unity of the Constitutionalists. He revealed explicitly what Arredondo had implied to Lawrence. Because the Constitutionalists were unified and virtually dominant in Mexico, Carranza suggested that the would-be mediators join him at one of the towns on the Texas-Mexico border to discuss diplomatic recognition of his regime.[78]

Wilson and Lansing were not distressed by the reply. In conveying the text of the message to the president, Lansing noted: "The position taken by Carranza is not unreasonable." [79] Having previously discussed the matter with the secretary, on September 13 Wilson directed Lansing to call another meeting of the Pan-American diplomats "to discuss the advisability of recognizing him [Carranza] as the *de facto* head of the Republic; having it clearly understood that we think the acceptance of the Revolution absolutely necessary." [80] Not only was Wilson willing to accept the revolution on Carranza's terms, but he was now willing to accept Carranza.

Conditions in Chihuahua accentuated the wisdom of Wilson's decision. In addition to the military defeats, wholesale defections to the *Carrancistas* depleted Villa's ranks.[81] As his empire crumbled, Villa became suspicious of everyone. The more depraved of Villa's followers, Carothers reported, had

78. Silliman to State Department (conveying reply of General Carranza to the Pan-American note), September 10, 1915, in *Foreign Relations, 1915*, 746–48; List of replies to the Pan-American diplomats' message of August 11, 1915, *ibid.*, 753.
79. Lansing to Wilson, September 12, 1915, in *Lansing Papers*, II, 550–51.
80. Wilson to Lansing, September 13, 1915, *ibid.*, 552.
81. Quirk, *Mexican Revolution*, 287.

convinced their chief that the "better element" was guilty of treachery in cooperating with the United States. Among those suspected were Díaz Lombardo and Angeles. Carothers himself was advised that, for his own safety, he should stay out of Mexico.[82] As conditions grew more and more menacing, the State Department sent wires to all its consuls in northern Mexico, directing them to urge all Americans and other foreigners to leave Mexico. The consuls, if they felt they were in danger, were also urged to leave.[83]

In September Villa made a last-ditch effort to hold onto his American support. He sent a commission of six, headed by General Roque González Garza (formerly president of the convention) to Washington to confer with the Pan-American diplomats. The mood of González Garza, as he passed through El Paso, was not likely to win allies. He spoke to Carothers in threatening tones. He hinted that if the *Villistas* did not get what they wanted in Washington, they would commence hostilities against the United States. At about the same time, Carothers learned that Villa was massing his armies. The American agent feared an attack on El Paso. General Pershing, the commander at Fort Bliss, echoed Carothers' fears in a dispatch to his superiors.[84]

Carothers was right about Villa massing his troops, but not for an attack on the United States. He planned to reclaim the Sonoran border towns of Naco and Agua Prieta, which General Plutarco Calles had occupied and fortified in July in violation of the Naco Agreement of the previous January. In preparing for this campaign, Villa came to Juárez. On

82. Carothers to State Department, September 1, 8, 1915, in NA 812.00/15997, 16083. The War Department offered Angeles asylum in the United States. See War Department to Commanding General, Southern Department, September 8, 1915, *ibid.*/16090.

83. State Department to certain American consuls, September 11, 1915, in *Foreign Relations, 1915*, 837.

84. Carothers to State Department, September 17, 1915, in NA 812.00/16219; Pershing to Bliss, September 24, 1915, in Pershing Papers, Box 372.

October 9 Carothers met with his old friend for the first time in over a month. Villa expressed confidence that Carranza would not be recognized; but, if he was, the ex-bandit pledged that he "would fight until killed." In the course of their conversation Carothers bluntly asked Villa if the rumors were true that it would be unsafe for him to rejoin the *Villista* camp. Villa replied: "No matter where I am or what happens, or what you may hear to the contrary, I will always be glad to see you." Villa, however, ended the interview on a warning note. He told Carothers that he felt quite certain that, as soon as he attacked Calles at Agua Prieta, officials in Washington were going to protest his violation of the Naco agreement. The protest will be ignored, he said, and "only God Almighty will stop me from attacking Agua Prieta."[85] This was Carothers' last meeting with Villa.

In Washington, Wilson and Lansing started the final acts of their charade. At a September 18 meeting, Lansing tried to maneuver the six Latin American diplomats into agreeing to recognize Carranza. But they would agree only to study the matter further and be prepared to report at the next meeting, scheduled for October 9, what recommendations they would make to their own governments.[86] The president and the secretary of state were disappointed that the conferees had not agreed to immediate recognition, but they had committed themselves to Pan-American action and were willing to see it through.

While they waited, anti-Carranza sentiment in the United States intensified as United States Army and Texas Ranger units clashed with Mexican bands along the border in the lower Rio Grande valley. Most of the Mexicans who raided American soil were bandits, but American witnesses claimed

85. Carothers to State Department, October 8, 9, 1915, in NA 812.00/16427, 16441; El Paso *Morning Times*, October 11, 1915.
86. Stenographic report of the conference on Mexican affairs, September 18, 1915, in *Foreign Relations, 1915*, 754–62; Text of the agreement of the conference of diplomatic representatives, in *Lansing Papers*, II, 554.

that often the raiders joined with Constitutionalist army units after crossing the Rio Grande to the Mexican side.[87] Under orders from Washington, Silliman protested; but Foreign Minister Jesús Acuña, while expressing regrets over the incidents, denied that the bandits came from the revolutionary army. In Washington, Arredondo charged irately that the American press was inventing falsehoods to embarrass Carranza and that the Texas Rangers, who were notorious for baiting Mexicans, were largely responsible for the border troubles.[88]

Even while negotiating with the *Carrancistas* over the border troubles, Silliman suddenly departed for Washington on about September 30, evidently at the request of the First Chief. Arriving on October 7, Silliman presented a strong case in favor of Carranza. The New York *Times* reported that the agent brought data to prove that the Constitutionalists were completely dedicated to the First Chief and that they would be able to establish a stable government.[89] Lansing, of course, had already made up his mind to push for the recognition of Carranza at the next Pan-American conference. Since he had been charged by the conferees to present them with additional information on both the Carranza and Villa factions, Silliman's appeal, having been given full publicity in the newspapers, gave the secretary of state additional bargaining material.

On October 9 Lansing presented his case to the Pan-Ameri-

87. New York *Times*, September 4, 1915, p. 1; *ibid.*, September 7, 1915, p. 12; *ibid.*, September 8, 1915, p. 14; *ibid.*, September 18, 1915, p. 5; *ibid.*, September 29, 1915, p. 6; *ibid.*, October 6, 1915, p. 11; Allen Gerlach, "Conditions Along the Border, 1915: Plan of San Diego," *New Mexico Historical Review*, XLIII (July, 1968), 199–205. Gerlach suggests that the border troubles may have been fomented by the Germans.

88. State Department to Silliman, August 28, 1915, in NA 812.00/15956; Silliman to State Department, September 1, 1915, *ibid.*/16000; Arredondo to State Department, September 6, 21, 1915, *ibid.*/16041, 16252.

89. *Mexican Herald*, October 1, 1915; *El Demócrata*, October 19, 1915; New York *Times*, October 8, 1915, p. 4.

The Final Accounting 363

can conferees. The weight of his arguments convinced the Latin American diplomats that the Constitutionalist regime deserved *de facto* recognition. After the conference, Lansing told reporters that the conferees had unanimously agreed to recommend to their governments that Carranza be recognized as head of the *de facto* government of Mexico. On October 18 the Latin American diplomats again met with Lansing and, since their respective governments accepted their recommendations, they agreed to take the final step on the following day.[90]

The announcement of recognition found Carranza at Monterrey, in the midst of a triumphal tour of the northeastern states. He received the news with quiet dignity from John W. Belt in a simple ceremony at the Hotel Salvador. With no show of emotion, Carranza expressed gratitude and pledged his government to assume full protection of the lives and interests of foreigners.[91] The same day that recognition was extended to Carranza, the administration went the full measure by cutting off all support to Villa. Wilson clamped an embargo on munitions to Mexico, exempting the *de facto* government.[92] Lansing ordered the American inspectors withdrawn from the Juárez meatpacking house, which meant Villa's beef could no longer meet required standards.[93]

Wilson's recognition of Carranza marked the end of a two-year struggle between two great leaders, each equally convinced of his own rectitude. In the end, it was Carranza who won. Under his steady hand, Mexico maintained her sovereignty and worked out her revolutionary solution, which culminated in the Constitution of 1917. Ironically, it was the

90. New York *Times*, October 10, 1915, p. 1; *ibid.*, October 19, 1915, p. 1.
91. Belt to State Department, October 19, 1915, in *Foreign Relations, 1915*, 773.
92. A proclamation by the president of the United States, October 19, 1915, *ibid.*, 772–73.
93. State Department to Department of Agriculture, October 19, 1915, in NA 312.114P19/61.

ideas of the *Zapatistas* and the *Villistas*, as expressed at the Convention of Aguascalientes, that emerged in the constitution. Although their ideas became the "warp and woof of the real revolution," Carranza's triumph made their realization possible.[94]

With the recognition of Carranza, the State Department was still represented in Mexico by two special agents, Carothers and Silliman, and by Hall, who acted as if he were a special agent. Hall returned to Mexico City in early April, 1915, where he was finally given the department's letter of January 19, directing him to cease posing as a special agent. He was angered because the note claimed that he had "never had any connection whatever" with the State Department. He asked for funds so that he might come to Washington to vindicate himself. Before Bryan and Cardoso de Oliveira could decide just how much money he would need to pay his passage, Hall again disappeared into Morelos.[95]

Between April and August, 1915, Hall moved back and forth between Mexico City and Cuernavaca. Apparently unable to face the fact that Bryan had disowned him, he continued to send lengthy letters praising the *Zapatistas* and damning the other revolutionaries. His plans for an agricultural colony matured.[96] Available evidence (which is skimpy)

94. Quirk, *Mexican Revolution*, 292–93.

95. Hall to State Department, April 4, 13, 1915, in NA 812.00/20609½; Cardoso de Oliveira to State Department, and State Department to Cardoso de Oliveira, April 14, 1915, *ibid.*/14847; Cardoso de Oliveira (for Hall) to State Department, and State Department to Cardoso de Oliveira (for Hall), April 19, 1915, *ibid.*/14884.

96. Calling his dream "Colonia Cooperativa Ejército Libertador," Hall planned to create several more or less self-sufficient communities of yeoman farmers. Although he intended for a founders association, members of which would subscribe to stock at nine hundred pesos per share, to profit from the sale of land, they would also be required to provide nonprofit services such as a hospital, a system of wagon roads, irrigation works, experiment stations, and even an agricultural school modeled after Tuskegee Institute in Alabama. All the mercantile and industrial establishments were to be cooperatives organized by the colonists. See Hall to Palafox, April 7, 1915, in

indicates that Hall twice came close to realizing his dream.[97] All of his hopes perished in the spring of 1916, when Carranza launched a military offensive into Morelos. As the seige tightened on Cuernavaca, the Mormon, fearing that he would be treated as any other *Zapatista*, felt compelled to flee for his life. After weeks of perilous journey by foot and mule across the wilds of southern Mexico, he arrived in Vera Cruz in late August and appealed to the State Department for funds to pay his passage to Washington. Lansing had no desire to confer with Hall, but did provide sufficient money to pay his fare to his family's home in Utah.[98]

Hall's expectations for the ultimate dominance of the *Zapatistas* never materialized, but his letters could have provided Washington with a fairly accurate and sympathetic picture of Zapata's revolutionary program. Since the good Mormon never functioned as an official agent, the administration ignored his advice. His letters piled up in the files of

---

NA 812.00/20609½; "Plan of Operations for Colonia Cooperativa Ejército Libertador" enclosed in Hall to Davis, April 3, 1915, *ibid.*

97. Claiming the support of Palafox, Otilio Montaño (a coauthor of the Plan of Ayala), Antonio and Ignacio Díaz Soto y Gama, plus ninety others who pledged to form a founders association, Hall sought to promote his colony under the auspices of the convention. He did issue a "Carta Circular," inviting prospective colonists to make inquiries, and a Mexico City newspaper reported on May 25, 1915, that Palafox had granted land to a colony headed by "a foreigner named Hall." Denied this chance when the convention collapsed later that summer, he sought again to promote his scheme under Zapata's own agrarian reform program as outlined in the Agrarian Law of October 26, 1915. In a letter to a friend, dated December 11, 1915, Hall indicated that his proposed colony was taking shape. See flyer signed by Hall and Ignacio Díaz Soto y Gama (secretary of the Founders Association), March [n.d.], 1915, in NA 812.00/20609½; Colonia Cooperativa Ejército Libertador, Carta Circular No. 1, May 5, 1915, *ibid.*; Hall to Davis, May 9, 1915, *ibid.*; Hall to Adalberto Hernández, December 11, 1915, *ibid.*; *Mexican Herald*, May 25, 1915; New York *Times*, May 27, 1915, p. 7. For the nature of Zapata's Agrarian Law, which included provisions for agricultural colonies, see Womack, *Zapata*, 246–47, 405–11; Josefina E. de Fabela (ed.), *Documentos históricos de la Revolución Mexicana* (México, D.F., 1970), XXI, 246–53.

98. Hall to Davis, August 26, September 11, 1916, in NA 812.00/20609½.

Chief Clerk Davis. Important passages in them were not bracketed or underlined by State Department officials, as were such passages in the reports of the official agents. Instead, the administration discounted Zapata, partly because he rivaled neither Carranza nor Villa militarily. Perhaps more important was Wilson's aversion to the *Zapatistas'* brand of radicalism. A middle-class reformer, the president was willing to accept the Mexican revolution on its own terms, but only if they were the more moderate terms of the Constitutionalists.

As soon as Wilson recognized Carranza, Carothers was directed to cease his representations to Villa. Obviously worried about Villa's possible response to the recognition, Lansing directed the agent to maintain his contacts on the border so the department might be apprised of Villa's activities. Carothers dismantled the equipment in his railroad car and did not thereafter return to Mexico.[99] In late October he reported that reliable informants in El Paso hinted that Villa might cross the border before reaching Agua Prieta and attack from the American side. Hastening to Douglas, Arizona, across from Agua Prieta, Carothers met an American newspaperman who had just come from an interview with Villa. The reporter claimed to have given an enraged Villa his first news of the recognition of Carranza.[100]

In the dead of the night, on November 2, Villa launched a massed cavalry attack on Agua Prieta from the Mexican side of the border. He was again soundly defeated, as powerful searchlights were used to illuminate the battlefield. Rumor spread through the ranks of his retreating army that the searchlights had been located on the American side of the

99. State Department to Carothers, October 19, 1915, in NA 111.70C22/16a; Carothers to State Department, October 20, 1915, *ibid./*16.
100. Carothers to State Department, October 21, 24, 25, 27, 29, 1915, in NA 812.00/16541, 16580, 16588, 16606, 16627; Carothers to State Department, October 31, 1915, in *Foreign Relations, 1915,* 775.

border. Added to this rumor was the fact that the State and War Departments had allowed the *Carrancistas* to send reinforcements to Agua Prieta via American railroad from Laredo, Texas. Villa had reason to nurse a monumental grudge against the United States. Carothers felt that after the defeat at Agua Prieta, Villa was as bitter and vengeful an enemy as the United States had in the world.[101]

Carothers now saw Villa as nothing more than a menace. "He is absolutely irresponsible . . ." the agent reported, "and is capable of any extreme. No promises nor assurances of good intentions can be relied upon." [102] Carothers joined Cobb in recommending that all border ports be closed to Villa's commercial agents. Access to supplies would only sustain his opportunities to commit atrocities and resist the *de facto* government.[103]

Although Carothers made no more representations to Villa, he remained in Douglas to keep track of his former friend's whereabouts. He was there when General Obregón arrived on November 6, to organize the pursuit of Villa. Although Obregón greeted Carothers cordially, he told American army officers and representatives of the press that he resented the agent's presence. He charged that Carothers was an active paid agent of Villa and that he was *persona non grata* in Mexico. American military officials, uneasy after weeks of threatening conditions on the border, wanted nothing to hinder peaceful relations with Obregón. They joined Obregón in requesting that Carothers be relieved of his duties in Douglas. Realizing that his presence would only

101. Clarence C. Clendenen, *Blood on the Border: The United States and the Mexican Irregulars* (Toronto and London, 1969), 186–88; Testimony of Carothers, *Senate Documents*, 66th Cong., 2nd Sess., No. 285, p. 1780.
102. Carothers to State Department, November 8, 1915, in NA 812.00/16739.
103. Carothers to State Department, October 27, November 8, 1915, *ibid.*/16627, 16739; Cobb to State Department, November 2, 8, 1915, *ibid.*/16674, 16735.

aggravate matters, the special agent returned to El Paso of his own volition.[104]

Although the State Department answered Obregón's charges against Carothers by claiming that he was no longer attached to Villa but had reverted to his former status as consular agent, officials in Washington realized that Constitutionalist hostility would prevent Carothers from ever again effectively representing the United States in Mexico. Consequently, on December 4 Lansing, evidently assuming that Carothers could take advantage of one of the business opportunities previously offered to him, notified the special agent that his services would be terminated on December 31. It appeared that Carothers, like Villa, had served out his usefulness.[105]

Justifiably distressed, Carothers reported that Constitutionalist hostility prevented him from even returning to his home in Torreón and that business opportunities were not likely to come his way. These regrettable circumstances, he complained, resulted from his service to the department. He requested, therefore, that he be retained in a different capacity. Coming to his former colleague's rescue, Canova called Carothers to Washington for conferences. Canova and Lansing, now fearing that Germany might be fomenting the border troubles, decided that Carothers, with all his contacts, was the man to make a continuing investigation of the border activities. Carothers was retained in this capacity until he resigned in 1918 to pursue a business opportunity in the United States.[106]

104. Carothers to State Department, November 6, 1915, *ibid.*/16733; Carothers to State Department, November 10, 1915, in NA 111.70C22/23, 24; Col. H. J. Slocum to General Funston, November 9, 1915, in Scott Papers, Box 20; Funston to Scott, November 22, 1915, *ibid.*; New York *Times*, November 7, 1915, II, p. 4; *ibid.*, November 12, 1915, p. 10; *El Demócrata*, November 12, 1915.

105. State Department, December 4, 1915, in NA 111.70C22/28a; New York *Times*, November 8, 1915, p. 9.

106. Carothers to State Department, December 13, 1915, in NA 111.79C22/30; Canova to Carothers, December 24, 1915, *ibid.*/28; State

Carothers never again made representations to Pancho Villa, but he kept track of the movements of Villa's band.[107] In fact, he reported to Washington on March 8, 1916, that Villa was directly south of Columbus, New Mexico, just a few miles from the border. He also warned Colonel H. J. Slocum, who commanded the American contingent at Columbus. Replying that his intelligence reports located Villa elsewhere, Slocum refused to accept the special agent's advice. Carothers bought a ticket on the next train to Columbus; Villa arrived there first. At 4:00 A.M. on March 9, Villa crossed the border into Columbus, killing seven Americans and burning several buildings. Arriving at 2:00 P.M., Carothers searched through two portfolios of documents found on the scene and quickly confirmed that Villa had made the attack.[108] The demand in the United States for intervention now became too strong for even Wilson to resist. The result was General John J. Pershing's famous Punitive Expedition, which attempted to bring Villa to justice.[109]

While troops and supplies were being massed in El Paso for the Punitive Expedition, Carothers wrote to his friend, General Scott, that "it looks like hell will be popping soon,

---

Department to Carothers, December 31, 1915, *ibid.*/28a. Documents in the State Department's 812.00 and 111.70C22 files, too numerous to cite individually, describe Carothers' movements and activities until his retirement in 1918.

107. Officials of Carranza's government continued to suspect an official relationship between Carothers and Villa. Consequently, the American's movements along the border were monitored. See Secretario de Relaciones Exteriores a Luis Cabrera, September 26, 1916, AGRE, L–E–729R, Leg. 8; Sixto Spada a C. J. J. Pesqueira, ConsulMex, Los Angeles, December 22, 1916, *ibid.*, L–E–803; Pesqueira a Secretario de Relaciones Exteriores, January 5, 1917, *ibid.*

108. Carothers to State Department, March 8, 10, 1916, in NA 812.00/17637, 17401; Carothers to Scott, March 5, 1916, in Scott Papers, Box 22; Cobb to State Department, March 9, 1916, in *Foreign Relations, 1916*, 480; Testimony of Carothers, *Senate Documents*, 66th Cong., 2nd Sess., No. 285, p. 1781.

109. Arthur S. Link, *Wilson: Confusions and Crises, 1915–1916* (Princeton, N.J., 1964), 205–209.

and I am in thorough accord with what is being done." The documents found at Columbus, he revealed, indicated that Villa had an "obsession to kill Americans." He was inspiring his men by claiming "that they could conquer the United States." *Villista* prisoners that Carothers interrogated claimed that their chief suffered from "delirio de grandesa" (delusions of grandeur). Carothers diagnosed Villa's malady similarly. "This is a different man than we knew," he wrote to Scott. "All the brutality of his nature has come to the front, and he should be killed like a dog." [110] Thus even Carothers made the full cycle. Having helped to elevate Villa to a position of prominence and political power, Carothers, like his superiors, turned his back on the former ward of the United States.

Silliman rejoined Carranza in early November, 1915. He journeyed to Eagle Pass, Texas, in the company of John Lind, who came to the border at the invitation of the First Chief to receive personal thanks for his efforts in behalf of the Constitutionalists.[111] Silliman was given a hero's welcome at Piedras Negras by Carranza and his staff, much as if he had truly influenced the decision in favor of recognition. The special agent's immediate task was to ask the First Chief to do something about the border troubles in the lower Rio Grande valley. Carranza assured Silliman, as he already had Belt, that he had ordered his officers to make every effort to prevent bandits from crossing the border. Fatefully, Carranza also suggested that the United States and Mexico enter into an agreement that would give the nations mutual rights to cross the border in hot pursuit of bandits.[112]

110. Carothers to Scott, March 13, 1916, in Scott Papers, Box 22.
111. W. P. Blocker, American Vice Consul, Piedras Negras, to State Department, October 30, 1915, in NA 812.00/16650; San Antonio *Express*, November 5, 1915; New York *Sun*, November 5, 1915.
112. Silliman to State Department, November 3, 1915, in NA 812.00/16686; Belt to State Department, November 2, 1915, *ibid.*/16660, 16676.

Silliman accompanied Carranza on the remainder of his tour through the northern states of Mexico, during which time the First Chief received the adulation he deserved but seldom received. Silliman continued making representations to the officials of the *de facto* government. For the most part, the responses were more favorable than in the past.[113] Silliman was with Carranza in February, 1916, when he declared Querétaro the provisional capital of Mexico and announced the calling of a revolutionary convention to draft a new constitution for the republic.[114] On March 9, after Villa's raid on Columbus, New Mexico, the agent received orders to tell the First Chief that President Wilson thought the attack created "the most serious situation which has confronted this government during the entire period of Mexican unrest." Silliman was to urge Carranza to immediately deploy as many troops as necessary to "pursue, capture and exterminate" Villa and his band.[115]

Distressed by the tone of the note from Washington, Carranza approached Silliman the following day and renewed his offer to allow authorities to pursue bandits across the Mexican frontier, if the United States would grant reciprocal rights to Mexico. Wilson and Lansing jumped at the opportunity. Moving quickly, Lansing replied to Silliman on March 13 that the United States agreed to the proposal and considered the arrangement to be currently in effect.[116] When Wilson did not request specific permission for Pershing to cross the border, it appeared momentarily that Carranza's troops might block the Punitive Expedition. On the eve of the expedition's scheduled entry into Mexico, Silliman eased

113. Too numerous to cite individually, documents in the State Department's 812.00 and 125.8276 files describe Silliman's tour with Carranza and his representations to the *de facto* government.
114. Silliman to State Department, February 4, 1916, in NA 812.00/17217, 17227.
115. State Department to Silliman, March 9, 1916, *ibid.*/17382.
116. Silliman to State Department, March 10, 1916, in *Foreign Relations, 1916*, 485; State Department to Silliman, March 13, 1916, *ibid.*, 487–88.

372   Emissaries to a Revolution

tensions in Washington when he reported from Querétaro that he had spoken to both Obregón and Foreign Minister Cándido Aguilar and that they had approved and acquiesced to the sending of American troops to capture Villa.[117]

The Punitive Expedition did provoke trouble between the United States and Carranza's *de facto* government, but Silliman played no part in the settlement. Acting under the assumption that Henry P. Fletcher would soon be confirmed by the Senate as ambassador to Mexico, Lansing, in February, 1916, issued orders changing Silliman from his consular post at Saltillo to the more prestigious post at Guadalajara. As it turned out, Fletcher was not confirmed until March, 1917, because of antagonism between the United States and Mexico that grew out of the Punitive Expedition.[118]

Silliman died at his post in Guadalajara on January 17, 1919.[119] Before moving to that city, he wrote an emotion-charged letter to Lansing in June, 1916, reviewing his service near Carranza. Reminiscing on a particular conversation, Silliman recalled that he had told the First Chief that "whatever good there was in the revolution could not be lost. It would remain a permanant benefit of the Mexican people. . . . If the revolution failed to establish an orderly government for Mexico," the agent had warned Carranza, "and if the task should fall, not by choice, but of necessity, upon the United States, it would be solely because, after a fair trial, the men of the revolution had proven themselves unequal to it."[120] In so speaking, Silliman probably summed up Woodrow Wilson's own thinking on the Mexican revolution in the summer of 1916.

117. Silliman to State Department, March 15, 1916, *ibid.*, 491.
118. State Department to all American consuls in Mexico, March 18, 1916, NA 123.R61/158a; *Register of the State Department, 1917*, 137; New York *Times*, February 23, 1916, p. 2; Link, *Confusions and Crises*, 290–91.
119. *Register of the Department of State, 1922* (Washington, D.C., 1922), 179.
120. Silliman to Lansing, June 30, 1916, in NA 125.8276/6.

Bibliography

I. PRIMARY SOURCES

Manuscripts

Papers and Diaries of Chandler P. Anderson, 1914–1915, Division of Manuscripts, Library of Congress.
Eugene C. Barker Collection, University of Texas.
William Jennings Bryan Papers, 1913–1915, Division of Manuscripts, Library of Congress.
William F. Buckley Manuscripts, 1913–1915, Latin American Collection, University of Texas.
Josephus Daniels Papers, 1914, Division of Manuscripts, Library of Congress.
Albert B. Fall Papers (Microfilm copies), 1916, Zimmermann Library, University of New Mexico.
John Lind Papers, Minnesota Historical Society, 1913–1915, St. Paul, Minnesota.
John J. Pershing Papers, 1914–1915, Division of Manuscripts, Library of Congress.
Hugh L. Scott Papers, 1914–1916, Division of Manuscripts, Library of Congress.
Papers of Woodrow Wilson, 1913–1915, Division of Manuscripts, Library of Congress.

Archival Materials

Estados Unidos Mexicanos. Archivo General de la Secretaría de Relaciones Exteriores, Ramo de la Revolución.
National Archives. General Correspondence, 1889–1934, of the Records of the Division of Botany, Bureau of Plant Industry, Soils, and Agricultural Engineering, Department of Agriculture, Record Group 54.
———. General Records of the Department of State, Record Group 59.
———. The Correspondence of Secretary of State Bryan with President Wilson, Record Group 59.

373

————. Papers of Robert Lansing, General Correspondence, Record Group 59.

————. Personal and Confidential Letters from Secretary of State Lansing to President Wilson, 1915–1918, Record Group 59.

————. Records of the Secretary of Agriculture, 1904–1964, Record Group 16.

Public Documents

Congressional Record, 63rd Cong., 1st, 2nd, and 3rd Sess., 1913–1915.

Estados Unidos Mexicanos. *Diario Official*, CXXVII (August 27, 1913).

U.S. Department of State. *Department of State Bulletin*, XLIX (August 5, 1963), 199–203.

————. *Papers Relating to the Foreign Relations of the United States, 1912*. Washington: Government Printing Office, 1919.

————. *Papers Relating to the Foreign Relations of the United States, 1913*. Washington: Government Printing Office, 1920.

————. *Papers Relating to the Foreign Relations of the United States, 1914*. Washington: Government Printing Office, 1922.

————. *Papers Relating to the Foreign Relations of the United States, 1915*. Washington: Government Printing Office, 1924.

————. *Papers Relating to the Foreign Relations of the United States, 1916*. Washington: Government Printing Office, 1925.

————. *Papers Relating to the Foreign Relations of the United States: The Lansing Papers, 1914–1920*. 2 vols. Washington: Government Printing Office, 1940.

————. *Register of the Department of State, 1917*. Washington: Government Printing Office, 1918.

————. *Register of the Department of State, 1922*. Washington: Government Printing Office, 1922.

U.S. Senate. "Investigation of Mexican Affairs," *Senate Documents*, 66th Cong., 2nd Sess., No. 285.

Edited Correspondence and Documents

Fabela, Isidro (ed.). *Documentos históricos de la Revolución Mexicana*. Vol. I: *Revolución y régimen Constitucionalista*. México, D.F.: Fondo de Cultura Económica, 1960.

Fabela, Isidro (ed.). *Documentos históricos de la Revolución Mexicana*. Vol. III: *Carranza, Wilson y el ABC*. México, D.F.: Fondo de Cultura Económica, 1962.

Fabela, Isidro, and Josefina E. de Fabela (eds.). *Documentos históricos de la Revolución Mexicana*. Vol. IX: *Revolución y régimen Maderista*. México, D.F.: Editorial Jus, 1965.

Bibliography

Fabela, Josefina E. de (ed.). *Documentos históricos de la Revolución Mexicana*. Vol. XV: *Revolución y régimen Constitucionalista*. México, D.F.: Editorial Jus, 1969.
Fabela, Josefina E. de (ed.). *Documentos históricos de la Revolución Mexicana*. Vol. XXI: *Emiliano Zapata, el Plan de Ayala y política agraria*. México, D.F.: Editorial Jus, 1970.
González Ramírez, Manuel (ed.). *Fuentes para la historia de la Revolución Mexicana*. Vol. I: *Planes políticos y otros documentos*. México, D.F.: Fondo de Cultura Económica, 1954.
McAdoo, Eleanor Wilson (ed.). *The Priceless Gift: The Love Letters of Woodrow Wilson and Ellen Axson Wilson*. New York: McGraw-Hill Book Co., Inc., 1962.

Memoirs and Reminiscences

Barragán, Juan. "De las memorias de Don Venustiano Carranza," *El Universal, Magazine para todos*, April 30, 1930; March 1, 8, June 22, 1931.
Cronon, E. David (ed.). *The Cabinet Diaries of Josephus Daniels, 1913–1921*. Lincoln: University of Nebraska Press, 1963.
Dehesa y Nuñez, Raúl. "Yo Conocí a Mr. Lind," *Excélsior* (Mexico City), February 20, 1954, p. 6.
Fabela, Isidro. "Carranza," *Excélsior* (Mexico City), December 27, 1957, A-6.
Grayson, Rear Admiral Gary T. *Woodrow Wilson: An Intimate Memoir*. New York: Holt, Rinehart and Winston, 1960.
Guzmán, Martín Luis. *The Memoirs of Pancho Villa*. Trans. Virginia H. Taylor. Austin: University of Texas Press, 1965.
Houston, David F. *Eight Years With Wilson's Cabinet*. 2 vols. Garden City, N.Y.: Doubleday, Page & Co., 1926.
Huerta, Victoriano. *Memorias de Victoriano Huerta*. México, D.F.: Ediciones "Vertice", 1957.
King, Rosa E. *Tempest Over Mexico: A Personal Chronicle*. Boston: Little, Brown and Co., 1935.
Lawrence, David. *The True Story of Woodrow Wilson*. New York: Doran, 1924.
Obregón, Alvaro. *Ocho mil kilómetros en campaña*. México, D.F.: Librería de la Vda. de Ch. Bouret, 1917.
O'Shaughnessy, Edith. *A Diplomat's Wife in Mexico*. New York: Harper and Bros., Pub., 1916.
Phillips, William. *Ventures in Diplomacy*. Boston: Beacon Press, 1952.
Prida, Ramon. *From Despotism to Anarchy*. El Paso: El Paso Publishing Co., 1914.

376 Bibliography

Reed, John. *Insurgent Mexico.* New York: International Publishers, 1969.
Scott, Maj. Gen. Hugh Lenox. *Some Memories of a Soldier.* New York: The Century Co., 1928.
Thord-Gray, I. *Gringo Rebel.* Coral Gables, Fla.: University of Miami Press, 1960.
Viereck, George Sylvester. *Spreading Germs of Hate.* New York: H. Liveright, 1930.
Wilson, Henry Lane. *Diplomatic Episodes in Mexico, Belgium and Chile.* Garden City, N.Y.: Doubleday, Page & Co., 1927.
Wilson, Woodrow. *The New Freedom.* Garden City, N.Y.: Doubleday, Page & Co., 1913.

Newspapers

Austin (Tex.) *American,* May 18, 1949.
Border Vedette (Nogales, Ariz.), June 14, 1913.
Churabusco (Mexico City), May 11, 1914.
Daily Picayune (New Orleans), January 1–5, 1914.
Dallas (Tex.) *News,* May 15, 1949.
El Demócrata (Mexico City), September 8, 1915–November 12, 1915.
El Diario (Mexico City), July 7, 1913–September 26, 1913.
Diario del Hogar (Mexico City), July 9, 1913.
El Paso *Morning Times,* June 10, 1913–October 10, 1915.
El Imparcial (Mexico City), June 18, 1913–April 9, 1914.
El Independiente (Mexico City), August 7, 1913–August 30, 1913.
El Liberal (Mexico City), September 6, 1914–October 18, 1914.
Los Angeles *Examiner,* June 10, 1913–July 31, 1913.
Los Angeles *Times,* June 7, 1913–September 25, 1938.
Mexican Herald, May 18, 1913–October 1, 1915.
El Monitor (Mexico City), December 5, 6, 1914.
New York *Herald,* December 21, 1914.
New York *Sun,* June 28, 1914–November 5, 1915.
New York *Times,* April 25, 1895–November 8, 1915.
New York *World,* March 7, 1913–December 29, 1914.
Nueva Patria (Mexico City), September 26, 1914.
La Opinión (Vera Cruz), September 5–9, 1913.
El País (Mexico City), August 10, 1913–August 1, 1914.
El Pueblo (Mexico City and Vera Cruz), October 18, 1914–June 12, 1915.
San Antonio *Express,* January 18, 1914–November 5, 1915.
El Sol (Mexico City), July 31, 1914–December 14, 1914.
The Times (London), February 24, 1914.
Tucson (Ariz.) *Daily Citizen,* June 10, 1913–November 22, 1913.
Tucson (Ariz.) *Daily Star,* June 10, 1913.

La Verdad (Mexico City), May 5, 1915.
La Voz de Sonora (Hermosillo, Sonora), June 14, 1913.
Washington *Post*, October 9, 1914.
Washington *Times*, August 11, 1913.

Contemporary Articles

"The British Press on Benton's Fate," *Literary Digest*, XLVIII (March 7, 1914), 481.
Carroll, Raymond G. "United States Special Agents Powerful in Mexico," New York *Sun*, August 15, 1915.
Hale, William Bayard. "Our Danger in Central America," *The World's Work*, XXIV (August, 1912), 443–51.
———. "Our Moral Empire in America," *The World's Work*, XXVIII (May, 1914), 52–58.
———. "With the Knox Mission to Central America," *The World's Work*, XXIV (June, July, 1912), 179–93, 323–36.
Jenkinson, Charles. "Vera Cruz, What American Occupation Has Meant to a Mexican Community," *The Survey*, XXXIII (November 7, 1914), 133–34.
"John Lind as a Strong Personality," *American Review of Reviews*, XLVIII (September, 1913), 281.
"Letting The Guns Into Mexico," *Literary Digest*, XLVIII (February 14, 1914), 303–304.
Lind, John. "The Mexican People," *The Bellman*, XVII (December 5, 12, 1914), 716–19, 718–19, 749–50, 752, 754.
Mason, Gregory. "The Mexican Man of the Hour," *Outlook*, CVII (June 6, 1914), 292–306.
"Mediation as a Remedy for Mexico," *Literary Digest*, XLVII (August 9, 1913), 193–95.
"Mexico: What Does Mediation Mean," *Outlook*, CIV (August 16, 1913), 833–34.
Murray, Robert H. "Huerta and the Two Wilsons," *Harper's Weekly*, LXII (March 25–April 29, 1916), 301–303, 341–42, 364–65, 402–404, 434–36, 466–69.
"Our Debt to Villa," *Literary Digest*, XLVIII (May 16, 1914), 1166–67.
"The Week: Mexico," *Independent*, LXXIV (June 5, 1913), 1310.
"The Week: Mexico," *The Nation*, XCVII (August 7, 1913), 112.
Whitaker, Herman. "Villa—Bandit-Patriot," *Independent*, LXXVII (June 8, 1914), 450–52.
Wilkes, Allene Tupper. "The Gentle Zapatistas," *Harper's Weekly*, LX (January 16, 1915), 56–57.

378   Bibliography

II. SECONDARY WORKS

Books

Alamada, Francisco R. *La Revolución en el Estado de Chihuahua.* 2 vols. México, D.F.: Instituto Nacional de Estudios Históricos de la Revolución Mexicana, 1965.

Alessio Robles, Miguel. *Historia política de la Revolución.* 3rd ed. México, D.F.: Ediciones Botas, 1946.

Atkin, Ronald. *Revolution! Mexico, 1910–1920.* New York: The John Day Co., 1970.

Baker, Ray Stannard. *Woodrow Wilson: Life and Letters.* 8 vols. Garden City, N.Y.: Doubleday, Doran & Co., 1931.

Barragán Rodríguez, Juan. *Historia del ejército y de la Revolución Constitucionalista.* 2 vols. México, D.F.: Talleres de la Editorial Stylo, 1946.

Bazánt, Jan. *Historia de la deuda exterior de México, 1823–1946.* México, D.F.: El Colegio de México, 1968.

Blum, John Morton. *Woodrow Wilson and the Politics of Morality.* Boston and Toronto: Little, Brown and Co., 1956.

Braddy, Haldeen. *Cock of the Walk: The Legend of Pancho Villa.* Albuquerque: University of New Mexico Press, 1955.

Brenner, Anita, and George R. Leighton. *The Wind That Swept Mexico.* New York: Harper & Brothers, 1943.

Callahan, James Morton. *American Foreign Policy in Mexican Relations,* New York: The MacMillan Co., 1932.

Callcott, Wilfrid Hardy. *The Caribbean Policy of the United States, 1890–1920.* Baltimore: The Johns Hopkins Press, 1942.

Calvert, Peter. *The Mexican Revolution, 1910–1914: The Diplomacy of Anglo-American Conflict* ("Cambridge Latin American Studies," No. 3) Cambridge: Cambridge University Press, 1968.

Carreño, Alberto M. *La diplomacia extraordinaria entre México y Estados Unidos.* 2 vols. México, D.F.: Editorial Jus, 1951.

Casasola, Gustavo. *Historia gráfica de la Revolución Mexicana, 1910–1960.* 4 vols. México, D.F.: Editorial F. Trillas, S.A., 1960.

Clendenen, Clarence C. *Blood On The Border: The United States and the Mexican Irregulars.* Toronto and London: The Macmillan Co., Collier-Macmillan, Ltd., 1969.

———. *The United States and Pancho Villa.* Ithaca, N.Y.: Published for the American Historical Association, Cornell University Press, 1961.

Cline, Howard F. *The United States and Mexico.* Cambridge, Mass.: Harvard University Press, 1953.

Cockroft, James D. *Intellectual Precursors of the Mexican Revolu-*

tion, 1910–1913. ("Institute of Latin American Studies, The University of Texas: Latin American Monographs," No. 14) Austin: University of Texas Press, 1968.

Coletta, Paolo E. *William Jennings Bryan.* Vol. I: *Political Evangelist, 1860–1908.* Lincoln: University of Nebraska Press, 1964.

———. *William Jennings Bryan.* Vol. II: *Progressive Politician and Moral Statesman, 1909–1915.* Lincoln: University of Nebraska Press, 1969.

Cumberland, Charles Curtis. *The Mexican Revolution: Genesis Under Madero.* Austin: University of Texas Press, 1952.

Curry, Roy Watson. *Woodrow Wilson and Far Eastern Policy, 1913–1921.* New York: Bookman Associates, 1957.

Dillon, Robert P. *Zapata: The Ideology of a Peasant Revolutionary.* New York: International Publishers, 1969.

Dromundo, Baltasar. *Vida de Emiliano Zapata.* México, D.F.: Editorial Guaranía, 1961.

Dulles, John W. F. *Yesterday in Mexico: A Chronicle of the Revolution, 1919–1936.* Austin: University of Texas Press, 1961.

Fabela, Isidro. *Historia diplomática de la Revolución Mexicana.* 2 vols. México, D.F.: Fondo de Cultura Económica, 1958–1959.

González Ramírez, Manuel. *La Revolución Social de México.* Vol. I: *Las Ideas—La Violencia.* México, D.F.: Fondo de Cultura Económica, 1960.

———. *La Revolución Social de México.* Vol. III: *El Problema Agrario.* México, D.F.: Fondo de Cultura Económica, 1966.

Grieb, Kenneth J. *The United States and Huerta.* Lincoln: University of Nebraska Press, 1969.

Gruening, Ernest. *Mexico and its Heritage.* New York and London: The Century Co., 1928.

Guzmán, Martín Luis. *The Eagle and The Serpent.* Translated by Harriet de Onís. Garden City, N.Y.: Doubleday & Co., Inc., 1965.

Hendricks, Burton J. *The Life and Letters of Walter Hines Page.* 3 vols. Garden City, N.Y.: Doubleday, Page, & Co., 1922–25.

Horgan, Paul S. *Great River: The Rio Grande in North American History.* 2 vols. New York: Rinehart & Co., Inc., 1954.

Kemmerer, Walter Edwin. *Inflation and Revolution: Mexico's Experience of 1912–1917.* Princeton: Princeton University Press, 1940.

Lieuwen, Edwin. *Mexican Militarism, 1910–1940: The Rise and Fall of the Revolutionary Army.* Albuquerque: University of New Mexico Press, 1968.

Link, Arthur S. *Wilson: Confusions and Crises, 1912–1915.* Princeton: Princeton University Press, 1964.

———. *Wilson: The New Freedom.* Princeton: Princeton University Press, 1956.

———. *Wilson: The Struggle for Neutrality.* Princeton: Princeton University Press, 1960.

———. *Wilson the Diplomatist.* Baltimore: The Johns Hopkins Press, 1957.

———. *Woodrow Wilson and Progressive Era.* New York: Harper & Row, Publishers, 1954.

Magaña, Gildardo, and Carlos Pérez Guerrero. *Emiliano Zapata y el agrarismo en México.* 5 vols. México, D.F.: Editorial Ruta, 1951–52.

Mancisidor, José. *Historia de la Revolución Mexicana.* México, D.F.: Ediciones el Gusano de Luz, 1958.

McBride, George M. *The Land Systems of Mexico.* New York: American Geographical Society, 1923.

Meyer, Michael C. *Huerta: A Political Portrait.* Lincoln: University of Nebraska Press, 1972.

———. *Mexican Rebel: Pascual Orozco and the Mexican Revolution, 1910–1915.* Lincoln: University of Nebraska Press, 1967.

Notter, Harley. *The Origins of the Foreign Policy of Woodrow Wilson.* Baltimore: The Johns Hopkins Press, 1937.

Nye, Russel B. *Midwestern Progressive Politics.* East Lansing, Mich.: Michigan State University Press, 1959.

Pinchon, Edgcomb. *Zapata The Unconquerable.* New York: Doubleday, Doran & Co., 1941.

Pitt, Leonard. *The Decline of the Californios.* Berkeley and Los Angeles: University of California Press, 1966.

Preston, William, Jr. *Aliens and Dissenters: Federal Suppression of Radicals, 1903–1933.* New York: Harper and Row, 1966.

Quirk, Robert E. *An Affair of Honor.* Louisville: University of Kentucky Press, 1962.

———. *The Mexican Revolution, 1914–1915.* Bloomington: Indiana University Press, 1960.

Ramírez Plancarte, Francisco. *La Ciudad de México durante la Revolución Constitucionalista.* México, D.F.: Ediciones Botas, 1941.

Ross, Stanley R. *Francisco I. Madero.* New York: Columbia University Press, 1955.

Sherman, William L., and Richard E. Greenleaf. *Victoriano Huerta: A Re-appraisal.* México, D.F.: Mexico City College Press, 1960.

Simpson, Lesley Byrd. *Many Mexicos.* 3rd ed., rev. Berkeley: University of California Press, 1964.

Stephenson, George M. *John Lind of Minnesota.* Minneapolis: University of Minnesota Press, 1935.

Stuart, Graham H. *American Diplomatic and Consular Practices.* New York: D. Appleton-Century Co., 1952.

————. *The Department of State: A History of Its Organization, Procedure and Personnel.* New York: The MacMillan Co., 1949.

Teitelbaum, Louis M. *Wilson and the Mexican Revolution, 1913–1916.* New York: Exposition Press, 1967.

Tinker, Edward Larocque. *Corridas and Calaveras.* Austin: University of Texas Press, 1961.

Turlington, Edgar. *Mexico and Her Foreign Creditors.* New York: Columbia University Press, 1930.

Turner, John Kenneth. *Barbarous Mexico.* Austin: University of Texas Press, 1969.

Vera Estañol, Jorge. *La Revolución Mexicana: Orígenes y resultados.* México, D.F.: Editorial Porrúa, S.A., 1957.

Who's Who In America, IX (1916–1917).

Who's Who In America, XII (1922–1923).

Who's Who In America, XXXV (1968–1969).

Womack, John, Jr. *Zapata and the Mexican Revolution.* New York: Alfred A. Knopf, 1969.

Articles

Bemis, Samuel Flagg. "Woodrow Wilson and Latin America," in Edward H. Buehrig (ed.), *Woodrow Wilson's Foreign Policy in Perspective.* Bloomington: Indiana University Press, 1957.

Blaisdell, Lowell L. "Henry Lane Wilson and the Overthrow of Madero," *Southwestern Social Science Quarterly,* XVIII (September, 1962), 126–35.

Brandt, Nancy. "Pancho Villa: The Making of a Modern Legend," *The Americas,* XXI (October, 1964), 146–62.

Challener, Richard. "William Jennings Bryan," in Norman A. Graebner (ed.), *An Uncertain Tradition: American Secretaries of State in the Twentieth Century.* New York: McGraw-Hill Book Co., 1961.

Chrislock, Carl H. "A Cycle of the History of Minnesota Republicanism," *Minnesota History,* XXXIX (Fall, 1964), 93–110.

Coker, William S. "Mediación británica en el conflicto Wilson-Huerta," *Historia Mexicana,* XVIII (October–December, 1968), 244–57.

Coletta, Paolo. "Bryan, Anti-Imperialism and Missionary Diplomacy," *Nebraska History,* XLIV (September, 1968), 167–87.

Curry, Roy Watson. "Woodrow Wilson and Philippine Policy," *Mississippi Valley Historical Review,* XLI (December, 1954), 435–52.

"David Lawrence," *Current Biography, 1943.* New York: The H. W. Wilson Co., 1944.

382 Bibliography

"Documentos secretos del Departamento de Estado de Washington sobre el incidente provacado por el escandalos caso Benton-Villa," *El Universal* (Mexico City) July 24, 25, 27, 30, 1923.

Gerlach, Allen. "Conditions Along the Border—1915: The Plan of San Diego," *New Mexico Historical Review*, XLIII (July, 1968), 195–212.

Grieb, Kenneth J. "El Caso Benton y la diplomacia de la Revolución," *Historia Mexicana*, XVIII (October–December, 1969), 282–301.

———. "The Causes of the Carranza Rebellion: A Re-interpretation," *The Americas*, XXV (July, 1968), 25–32.

———. "Reginald Del Valle: A California Diplomat's Sojourn in Mexico," *California Historical Society Quarterly*, XLVIII (December, 1968), 315–28.

Gunn, Drewey Wayne. "Three Radicals and a Revolution: Reed, London, and Steffens on Mexico," *Southwest Review*, LV (Autumn 1970), 393–410.

Harrison, John P. "Henry Lane Wilson, El Trágico de la Decena," *Historia Mexicana*, VI (January–March, 1957), 374–405.

———. "Un análisis norteamericano de la Revolución Mexicana," *Historia Mexicana*, V (April–June, 1956), 598–618.

Hicks, John D. "The People's Party in Minnesota," *Minnesota History*, V (November, 1924), 531–60.

Hill, Larry D. "The Progressive Politician as a Diplomat: The Case of John Lind in Mexico," *The Americas*, XXVII (April, 1971), 355–72.

Hinckley, Ted C. "Wilson, Huerta and the Twenty-one Gun Salute," *The Historian*, XXII (February, 1960), 197–202.

Jiménez, Alberto Morales. "Alvaro Obregón," *Hombres de la Revolución Mexicana*. México, D.F.: Instituto Nacional de Estudios de la Revolución Mexicana, 1960.

Kahle, Louis G. "Robert Lansing and the Recognition of Venustiano Carranza," *Hispanic American Historical Review*, XXXVIII (August, 1958), 352–72.

Livermore, Seward W. " 'Deserving Democrats': The Foreign Service Under Woodrow Wilson," *South Atlantic Quarterly*, LXIX (Winter, 1970), 144–60.

Meyer, Michael D. "The Arms of the *Ypiranga*," *Hispanic American Historical Review*, L (August, 1970), 543–56.

Niemeyer, Victor. "Frustrated Invasion: The Revolutionary Attempt of General Bernardo Reyes from San Antonio in 1911," *Southwestern Historical Quarterly*, LXVII (October, 1963), 213–25.

Quirk, Robert E. "Cómo se salvó Eduardo Iturbide," *Historia Mexicana*, VI (July–September, 1956), 39–58.

Rausch, George J. "The Early Career of Victoriano Huerta," *The Americas*, XXI (October, 1964), 136–45.

————. "The Exile and Death of Victoriano Huerta," *Hispanic American Historical Review*, XLII (February, 1962), 131–51.

————. "Poison-pen Diplomacy: Mexico, 1913," *The Americas*, XXIV (January, 1968), 272–80.

Scholes, Walter V., and Marie V. Scholes. "Wilson, Grey and Huerta," *Pacific Historical Review*, XXXVII (May, 1968), 151–58.

Smith, Daniel M. "Robert Lansing," in Norman A. Graebner (ed.), *An Uncertain Tradition: American Secretaries of State in the Twentieth Century*. New York: McGraw-Hill Book Co., 1961.

Tinker, Edward L. "Campaigning With Villa," *Southwest Review*, XXX (Winter, 1945), 148–54.

Unpublished Works

Massingill, Eugene F. "The Diplomatic Career of Henry Lane Wilson in Latin America." Unpublished Ph.D. dissertation, Louisiana State University, 1957.

Rausch, George Jay, Jr. "Victoriano Huerta: A Political Biography." Unpublished PhD. dissertation, University of Illinois, 1960.

Index

Pact of the Embassy, 10, 13, 34, 37, 75
Pact of Torreón, 206–207, 208, 229, 259
Page, Walter Hines, 22, 23, 107
Palafox, Manuel, 296, 300, 301
Pan-American conferences on Mexico, 339–40, 350, 351–53, 363
Parker, Charles B., 342
Pass Christian, Mississippi, 138–39
Penrose, Boies, 73, 87
Pérez Romero, M., 96
Pershing, John J.: and Vera Cruz intervention, 177, 179; on Carothers, 188; leads Punitive Expedition, 369; mentioned, 236, 237, 238, 360
Pesquiera, Ignacio L., 17, 48
Pesquiera, Roberto V., 167, 288
Phelps Dodge Company, 33
Phillips, William, 140
Piedras Negras, Coahuila, 16, 46, 47, 51
Pierce, Henry Clay, 26, 102
Pino Suárez, José M., 9, 10–11, 16, 37
Plan of Ayala, 15, 266, 301
Plan of Guadalupe, 15–16, 207, 225, 271, 306
Portillo y Rojas, José López, 171, 172
Progreso, Yucatán, 317–21
Puebla, 277, 301

Querétaro (city), 371

Rabago, Jesús M., 105
Rabb, Frank W., 273
Ramos Martínez, Jacobo: and Zapata, 247–48, 249–50, 252–53; and Hall, 247–48, 252–53; threats of, 249–50; Bryan's suspicions of, 250; exposed by Jenkinson, 251
Rausch, George J., Jr., 36n
Red Cross, 251
Reed, John, 190, 191
Reyes, Bernardo, 6
Rivera, Felipe, 45
Roberts, John W., 295–96
Robles, José I., 289, 294

Roman Catholic church: supports Huerta regime, 74; Lind's antipathy for, 126–27; and Canova, 217–19; Constitutionalist attitude toward, 221; Fuller appeals for just treatment of, 234; American spokesmen for, 331
Roosevelt Corollary to Monroe Doctrine, 152

Saltillo, Coahuila, 132, 191–92, 193, 203, 204, 211, 212, 220, 222
Samalayuca, Chihuahua, 152
San Antonio, Texas, 132, 136, 203, 310, 314
San Luis Potosí (city), 192, 203, 210, 215, 220, 289
Scott, Hugh L.: and Villa, 158–59, 287–88, 289–90, 347–48, 349; attempts to influence Carranza, 166; interviews Canova, 199; attempts negotiation with Obregón, 349; mentioned, 181, 307–308
Senate Committee on Foreign Relations, 60, 73
Serratos, Alfredo, 324
Shanklin, Arnold, 26, 247, 253–54
Sheppard, Morris, 273
Silliman, John R.: background and qualifications of, 212–13; and Carranza, 213–14; lacks fluency in Spanish, 214–15; his role in Carranza-Carbajal negotiations, 219–20, 222–23; and Constitutionalists, 221, 223–24; and Carranza, 241–43, 267–69, 270–71, 308–309, 315–17, 320, 338–39, 342–43, 362, 370; and Zapata, 241–42; his relations with Hall, 251–52; in Washington, 270; assigned to aid Cardoso de Oliveira, 279–80, 281; and escape of Iturbide, 294–95; described by Carothers, 303; and Progreso crisis, 318–21; and Wilson, 338; and Lansing's ultimatum on Aguilar, 340–41; appointed consul at Guadalajara, 372; mentioned, 170, 211, 240, 245, 280, 289, 301, 306, 341, 371